PENGUIN CLASSICS

LETTRES D'UN VOYAGEUR

George Sand was the pseudonym of the French novelist, Amantine-Aurore-Lucie Dupin (1804–76). She was brought up by her aristocratic grandmother at Nohant, the family's country estate in Berry, which she inherited at the age of seventeen. The next year she married Casimir Dudevant, a former army officer, and had two children. The marriage was increasingly unhappy and in 1831 she left for Paris, where she began to earn her living by her pen. Her first romantic novel, *Indiana* (1832), created a furore with its modern views on marriage. George Sand was soon known throughout Europe, not only for the stream of novels which followed (e.g., *Valentine*, *Lélia*, *Mauprat*) but for her Bohemian life, masculine attire and succession of love-affairs – of which the two most discussed have been her passionate liaison with Alfred de Musset and her lengthy tender relationship with Chopin, with its bitter ending. By the 1840s her novels were reflecting her new concern with social and political issues, with workmen and peasant girls as heroes and heroines – as in *Le Compagnon du Tour de France* and *Jeanne*. But the works which were most loved were *Consuelo* (1842–3) – a remarkable re-creation of eighteenth-century musical society – and the gentle, pastoral novels (*La Mare au Diable*, *La Petite Fadette* and *François le Champi* in the late 1840s) in which, as so often in her books, the closely observed, haunting background is that of her beloved Vallée Noire. After her brief involvement in the 1848 revolution, she returned to Nohant where, now respectable as well as famous, she dispensed generous hospitality to devoted friends and distinguished admirers and wrote on indefatigably for almost thirty years more – many plays, many novels and essays and one fine 'autobiography', *Histoire de ma Vie* (1855), which memorably re-created her youth.

Sacha Rabinovitch was born in Egypt and educated in both English and French. She also speaks Italian and has translated numerous works from both French and Italian into English.

Patricia Thomson is an MA of Aberdeen University and a PhD of Cambridge. She was a lecturer in English at Aberdeen until 1964 and then, apart from a year as Visiting Professor at the State University of New York at Buffalo, a Reader at the University of Sussex. She was early in the field of feminist literary research with her book *The Victorian Heroine* (1956) and also broke new ground with *George Sand and the Victorians* (1977) – her study of the influence of George Sand in England. She edited *The Changeling* for the New Mermaid series. She is now Emeritus Reader of the University of Sussex.

**Translated by Sacha Rabinovitch and Patricia Thomson,
with an introduction and notes by Patricia Thomson**

★

George Sand

★

Lettres d'un Voyageur

Penguin Books

Penguin Books Ltd, Harmondsworth, Middlesex, England
Viking Penguin Inc., 40 West 23rd Street, New York, New York 10010, U.S.A.
Penguin Books Australia Ltd, Ringwood, Victoria, Australia
Penguin Books Canada Ltd, 2801 John Street, Markham, Ontario, Canada L3R 1B4
Penguin Books (N.Z.) Ltd, 182–190 Wairau Road, Auckland 10, New Zealand

First published by Bonnaire in 1837
Published in Penguin Classics 1987

Made and printed in Great Britain by
Hazell, Watson & Viney Ltd,
Member of the BPCC Group,
Aylesbury, Bucks

Typeset in Linotron Bodoni by
Rowland Phototypesetting Ltd,
Bury St Edmunds, Suffolk

Contents

★

A Note on the Text

★

There were three French editions of *Lettres d'un Voyageur* in George Sand's lifetime: the original edition, published by Bonnaire in 1837; the second edition, published by Perrotin in 1843; and the third edition, published by Michel Levy in 1857. It is the 1857 text that has been republished twice of late years and has been used for this translation. The relevant French editions came out in 1971. One, in paperback (Garnier-Flammarion), has a Chronology and an interesting Introduction by Henri Bonnet. The other, fully edited, introduced and annotated by Georges Lubin, forms part of the second volume of his edition of George Sand's *Oeuvres autobiographiques* (Gallimard, Pleiade, 1970–71).

Lettres d'un Voyageur comprises twelve articles in letter form which were written by George Sand between 1834 and 1836. They were published at intervals in the *Revue des Deux Mondes*, except for one which appeared in the *Revue de Paris*. Although the Letters are substantially the same as those published in the journals, they were edited by the author in 1837, for publication in two volumes. She omitted several passages and modified the order of the Letters, a point discussed in the Introduction. The original order of publication in the *Revues* was as follows:

Revue des Deux Mondes	*Lettres d'un Voyageur*
15 May 1834	Letter One
15 July 1834	Letter Two
15 September 1834	Letter Three
15 October 1834	Letter Eight
15 January 1835	Letter Five
15 June 1835	Letter Six
1 September 1835	Letter Seven

★ Introduction ★

This is the first English translation of *Lettres d'un Voyageur* since 1847.
That publication was prefaced by the two enthusiastic sonnets which
Elizabeth Barrett had daringly addressed to her 'sister', George Sand,
and a glowing foreword by Mazzini, who had long been an admirer of
the remarkable Frenchwoman. Victorians were already familiar with
many of her novels in the original; the less initiated reader of today may
find even the title of this text misleading. It sounds as if it might be a
guidebook or at least a series of impressions from abroad, of which so
many were published in the eighteenth and early nineteenth centuries,
and, indeed, the matter-of-fact opening, 'I had arrived in Bassano at
nine o'clock on a cold, wet evening,' seems to encourage such expectations. But quite soon uncertainty creeps in as to what sort of a work
this is. If it is any consolation, this bewilderment must have been felt
even in 1834 by readers who came across the first of these Letters in the
Revue des Deux Mondes – for it was printed in close proximity to an
entirely orthodox account of the Far East, entitled '*Lettres de Chine*',
the sort of solid travelogue that the *Revue* tended to feature.

Now, as then, a great many questions arise in the course of the
reading; the first Letter alone provides quite a few. Who, for instance, is
the 'doctor' who is so summarily dispatched back to Venice? Who the
absent '*tu*' whom the author so frequently, eloquently and embarrass-
ingly apostrophizes and who seems to be both a thoroughly bad lot and a
Christ-figure? And why does the Traveller, who would have us believe
that he is an undersized, cigar-smoking young man dressed in a blue
cotton smock and trousers, alternate between such despair and happiness as he tramps along the foothills and through the beautiful countryside of the Brenta valley? Although notes can provide the answer to such
questions as these, I know from experience that a certain amount of
mystification does not detract from the interest. Possibly the best way to
broach George Sand is to take her straight, as the Victorians did. They

certainly read the book unannotated and got a great deal from it without treating it as a *roman à clef*.

But they had an advantage over the modern reader who comes fresh to George Sand with only a vague impression of her as a femme fatale and an iconoclast. Victorians knew something of her scandalous background – it was perhaps as well that they did not know it all – but what they responded to in this startling blend of conversational narrative and introspection, of doubt and agonizing and belief and confession, was the speaking voice, not only of a quite exceptional young woman, but of a contemporary. Her lack of inhibition in baring her soul was an inheritance from Rousseau, but she was not, like him, a voice from a previous age. Her revolt in her youth against an orthodox faith was an experience shared by many honest doubters, but it had left her deep religious and mystical sense unimpaired. The heartfelt earnestness with which she philosophized and moralized appealed to a wide public, and readers as ill-assorted as Charlotte Brontë and Dostoevsky, Matthew Arnold and Samuel Smiles, Turgenev and Jane Carlyle, George Eliot and Mazzini, Emerson and John Stuart Mill, testified to the stimulus and, at times, the comfort they derived from her musings – no matter how protracted they were.

It is inevitable that for readers at a distance of a century and a half there will be stumbling blocks which biographical knowledge or even a well-developed historical sense cannot remove. While there can be a great deal of pleasure in making the journey back into a fully Romantic consciousness and sensibility and in allowing ourselves to come under the spell of the writer whom Henry James called 'the great magician', there are times when the spell does not work and irritation, boredom and even incredulity may take over. It should then be remembered that although *Lettres d'un Voyageur* contains some of George Sand's most brilliant and memorable writing,[1] it has always been acknowledged by author and addicts alike to be a very uneven miscellany. And it is also important to remember that *longueurs* can seem a great deal longer, bathos much more obtrusive, self-pity less dignified in English than in French. In the original, the music of her famous flowing style, so much admired by Proust (as well as his grandmother), so much despised by Baudelaire,[2] carries the reader effortlessly along, as does the grandeur of the rhetoric of her despair, which is much more difficult to take seriously in English.

The different personae which George Sand adopts in the course of the Letters – all male and of different ages – also present difficulties. In both the 1843 Preface and later in *Histoire de ma vie* she explained that, as a young woman, she had felt unprepared to accept the full responsibility of philosophizing about life from a fixed position and had sought escape from accusations of inconsistency behind her chosen masks. How successful or credible these personae are is another matter.

The male role certainly came easily for her. In her childhood she had been a tomboy; as a young girl she had worn men's clothes for riding about the countryside; and on escaping to Paris, in 1831, from her unhappy marriage, she had outfitted herself with overcoat, top hat, trousers and boots in order to get around the cobbled streets and to enjoy the camaraderie of her new, bohemian life. And once she had accepted the suggestion of a male pseudonym her letters were almost always signed George (whether ardent love-letters or brisk, man-to-man notes to her publisher), so that the duality of the rebellious young woman and gamin was one to which she was accustomed. Consequently, when her role is that of the carefree student, or country lad from Berry, or truant schoolboy, it is easier to accept than her other masks. The 'gouty old uncle' to whom she refers in her Preface may well represent the world-weariness of age, but he is certainly no adequate mouthpiece for her sudden outbursts of uncontrollable anguish and despair. And the 'fiery and restless young soldier' scarcely rates equal billing with the others, for he is introduced only in Letter Six, when the Traveller is recruited metaphorically into the army of republicans. For the most part, the reader is conscious only of the unmistakable personality of an eloquent and passionate young woman, so that when a long-forgotten 'character' surprisingly reappears, the effect can be, to say the least, disconcerting.

But George Sand is on sure ground in describing herself as a Traveller. In saying that she was fated to be *'voyageur et artiste'* she is employing a favourite Romantic symbol, that of the solitary wanderer. It could be applied to any exceptional figure, whether poet or outlaw or genius: to the Ancient Mariner or the bust of Newton,

> The marble index of a mind for ever
> Voyaging through strange seas of Thought, alone.

The age-old and infinitely evocative metaphor of life as a voyage or as a pilgrimage had always appealed to her, as her schoolgirl writings[3] show. Throughout the Letters, even when there is no physical travel – and

13

indeed, the only two major excursions are to Italy and Switzerland – the Voyageur motif is effortlessly sustained in dreams and visions. These journeys of the spirit, 'beautiful dreams of travel and solitude', are also journeys of self-discovery which allow her to put into perspective 'other illusions which I have lost . . . other lands where I shall not set foot again'.

It is the moment of departure, the sense of escape from the present situation, which catches her imagination: 'It is not so much a question of travelling as of getting away.' In this respect she was in good company – and remained so. The Romantic legacy lingered and the highways and oceans of literature continued to be filled with travellers faring forward – such as Tennyson's 'Ulysses',

> . . . Come, my friends,
> 'Tis not too late to seek a newer world.

or Baudelaire's Voyageur,

> Mais les vrai voyageurs sont ceux-là seuls qui partent
> Pour partir;

But this does not mean that George Sand ignored the importance of real travel. In fact, she informed Musset that she felt it was a condition of their profession, a duty, however pleasant, for writers 'to travel and *see* a little'. And in the first three Letters of this book at least we can see how she fulfilled that duty.

Letters One to Three

At the end of March 1834, George Sand's passionate affair with Alfred de Musset had officially terminated after three harrowing months together in the mists and cold of Venice. The relationship between the young poet and the novelist had started the previous year in Paris and their trip to Italy, which should have been a romantic idyll, had turned into a sorry tale. Had they both stayed healthy, things would no doubt have been different, but first one, then the other succumbed to illness. Musset's disenchantment with his ailing, and later repressively hard-working, mistress took the form of a humiliating rejection of her and escape into debauchery – a situation of desolate loneliness for George Sand which, she was later to plead, gave her the right to look for love elsewhere. Musset's subsequent, near fatal, illness turned her for long, desperate weeks into his nurse but it also brought to his bedside and into her life a handsome young doctor, Pietro Pagello. The comic aspect of this new triangle was, not surprisingly, lost on the invalid and it was only after many horrifyingly abusive and tempestuous scenes that he became reconciled to the situation and left the couple, with his blessing. The maternal side of George Sand's nature, always strong but intensified by Musset's youth and frail health, now re-emerged and she accompanied him to Mestre, to see him off to Paris – her tenderness miraculously rekindled, as indeed was his for her, by the prospect of loss. The letters exchanged in the weeks that followed were suitably anguished, for the truth was that neither Alfred nor his 'Georgeot' was as yet immune from the other.

This did not mean, however, that George Sand did not get enormous delight and relief from the walking tour in the Veneto that she immediately started upon with Pagello – not, as in the text, on her own. Her descriptions of the countryside with its almond and peach trees in bloom, the scented breezes, the glitter of the snow-covered Alps in the distance, her first breakfast of coffee and aniseed-flavoured bread and mountain butter, eaten out of doors on primrosed grass, convey a reborn zest for living and for simplicity after all the tortuous complexities and recriminations of her long bout with Musset. There is initially, in Letter One, a sense of being off the leash at last. But once she has dismissed the doctor from her narrative his place is immediately taken by her absent poet, with whom she longed to share her thoughts.

She wanted, however, to share them not just in private but in print – for, as so often in the course of her life, it was she who had had to shoulder the financial responsibility for the trip. Throughout all these months she had been trying, most scrupulously, to pay off the editor[4] of the *Revue des Deux Mondes* with the short stories that she had promised him would come out of his two contributors' Italian stay – and a little tour of the foothills of the Alps was obviously marketable material. She had managed already to capitalize on her sufferings with Musset by using him as copy for the schizophrenic and irresistible central character of her Venetian tale, *Leone Leoni*; now she would use him in a different way, both for herself and for the editor, Buloz. And perhaps for Musset himself? . . . Often in reading George Sand's accounts of her motivation Dr Johnson's comment on a very different young letter-writer, Clarissa Harlowe, comes to mind: 'There is always something she prefers to truth.' One is always aware of the supreme ease with

15

which George Sand can present herself in an admirable light. She wrote to Musset:

> I have written you a long letter about my trip to the Alps which I intend to publish in the *Revue* if you don't object . . . I wrote it down as it came to me without a thought of all those who are likely to read it. I have seen it only as a framework for my love for you, a pretext for shutting up those who won't fail to say that you have ruined and deserted me.

There is an element of fantasy in her suggestion of public censure of Musset. While he was certainly a notorious rake, her own reputation was scarcely unsullied – not only as the author of three fearlessly outspoken novels but as a wife and mother who had left home and had, at a conservative estimate, already had more than one lover. But if Musset had not ruined her he had certainly brutally renounced her and, amidst all the fulsome praise and Romantic rhetoric lavished upon him in this first Letter, she does make sure that readers will have no illusions about his pride, split personality, self-destructive excesses and debauchery. I think it highly unlikely that Musset was blind, as has been suggested, to the implications of these passages when, with what Georges Lubin appreciatively calls 'a master-stroke', she sent her manuscript to him for vetting. He had never denied either in his correspondence or, later, in *Confessions d'un enfant du siècle* (where he, in turn, put the experience to good use) the extent of the suffering he had inflicted upon her. At all events, he gave his verdict without hesitation. The Letter was 'sublime' and she had never written anything so beautiful. Buloz, to whom he handed it over, was equally enthusiastic about its 'poetry' and 'vigour' and suggested that she should stay longer in Venice and send home more impressions.

The idea was congenial to her. She not only needed money badly to pay all the debts they had accumulated, but for the first time she had the chance to express her views in the first person, not only about the life going on around her but about her own lot. She had been writing for three years and all her eponymous heroines – Indiana, Valentine, Lélia – had, of course, to a certain extent been her mouthpieces; but the demands of the plot had inhibited the personal tone in a way that letters would not. Letter-writing was always a solace and a pleasure to her – as the twenty volumes of correspondence so far edited by Georges Lubin testify – and she seized the opportunity to write letters in public.

Twenty years later she commented simply: 'I felt I had many things to say and that I wanted to say them to myself and others.'

The brilliant vignettes of Venice which appeared in the next two dispatches were the result. The occasional apostrophe reminds us that Musset is still her imagined correspondent, but Venice had been transformed by the spring and he was remote from the surge of life going on around her. She was enchanted by the wonder and beauty of Venice, which can surely never have been better or more memorably conveyed than in some of the lyrical passages of the second Letter – perhaps most hauntingly in the description of an evening on the lagoon, when the music of her prose corresponds superbly with the harmonies of the oboes, violins and harps, wafted 'like a scent' from a passing gondola. But she was also at home with the scene. It was Prosper Mérimée[5] who unexpectedly and appreciatively noted as 'admirable' George Sand's ability to write, not as a tourist but as 'someone who had associated with the common folk and had studied their idiom'. Life on a shoe-string with Pagello, indeed *en famille* at the Ca' Mezzani with his brother and stepsister and friends and relatives, was at a far remove from the Danieli with Musset and, as usual, all was grist that came to her busy mill.

The lively domestic chatter in the doctor's household, the gossip in the cafés and taverns, the arguments, songs and shouts of the gondoliers, the street cries of the water-carriers and fish-traders and the clashes between the rival bands of Nicoloti and Castellani – these are the sounds of the city that animate the episodes. There is comical authenticity, too, in her sketch of their own octogenarian gondolier, Catullo, quarrelsome, hoarse, obstinate and lame – the last feature entitling him always to claim an affinity with a former Venetian, Lord Byron: 'I saw him, he was lame!' But the looseness of the letter-form allowed George Sand to meditate aloud as well as to observe; not only are there above Venice 'five hundred thousand more stars visible than in our northern clime', but life is far easier here for the poor and, even with rigid class distinctions, seems more democratic, more leisured because of the convenience of the canals. She takes the opportunity to preach religious toleration through the fictional Abbé – both on the quayside to Catullo and, one may feel, at excessive length on the island of San Lazzaro to Brother Hieronymus. While the Abbé supports the 'heretic', Lamennais, she maintains her own pose as the laconic Traveller whose only contribution to the argument is the opinion that 'the world is dying and religion is disappearing'. It is a stance of detachment which is well maintained till the end of the final scene of the third Letter when, alone in the silence and antiquity of Torcello, the Traveller strolls along the fragrant lanes, 'more beautiful, alas, than those of the Vallée Noire', and finds, after this fleeting thought of home, that when he shuts his eyes the beauties of the island have been replaced by a bleaker, less inviting, and yet compelling vision of France. The melodious cadence – and at the same time the lead-in to further Letters, to harsher strains – is handled with an artistry at once professional and moving.

Letters Four and Five

The three Venetian episodes stand apart from all the other Letters. Although they were all published in the *Revue* under the Voyageur title, George Sand herself always referred to them as 'the letters to Alfred' or 'on Italy' and, indeed, suggested to Buloz at one point that they could make a book in themselves, along with a short story she had written in Venice. Her correspondence at the time shows how conscious she was of the four months after Musset's departure as a breathing space – not from hard work but from being a celebrity, eternally Madame Sand, the object of interest and gossip – and also from involvement in a demanding, emotional relationship. She was to return in August of that year to an autumn and winter of mortifying, unfinished business, both in Paris and at Nohant. It is small wonder that her vision of France in Torcello was both haunting and grim.

Before two months had passed, Musset and she were once more in the grip of a passionate and very public affair which, shot through with jealousy and recrimination, ecstasy and grief, was to drag itself painfully to extinction in the following February. Musset had reaffirmed his love for her the moment she returned and, torn between her desire for him and her obligations to Pagello, who had accompanied her, she retreated from them both to Nohant where, in September, the letters were written that later formed the basis of Letter Four. There, in the face of the resentment and hostility of her husband,[6] she turned for consolation to her old Berrichon friends – especially the two most disenchanted and melancholy among them, who would be most in tune with her despair – Néraud, the botanist, and Rollinat, the lawyer.

Letter Four could be described as a protracted suicide note, except that it is difficult to imagine anyone with the volatility of George Sand actually taking her own life. This is not to deny her anguish – in Letter Eleven she recalls this time as 'two of the saddest months of my life' – or indeed, her self-despising, most painful of all for someone who always needed to believe that she acted from the highest motives. Her sudden loss of feeling for Pagello raised again all the unanswerable questions about life which she had so exhaustively explored in *Lélia*, in a mood of disenchantment and spleen which she had thought she had left behind her. Now, once more, she doubted whether any enduring relationship was possible for her and whether survival in a barren world was worth the struggle. In the course of these two Letters, but especially in the first of them, there are many passages which demand to have the courtesy extended to them that we would normally give to a poem which is using recognized conventions. The friendship of her correspondents is real and comforting but they easily become transformed into traditional figures, 'kindred spirits' such as we accept in Gray's *Elegy*, for instance:

> On some fond Breast the parting Soul relies,
> Some pious Drops the closing Eye requires . . .

They, too, will be 'mindful of th'unhonour'd Dead'; Néraud, passing one day by her tomb – if she has one – will pause and drop some tears and will offer up a prayer; Rollinat, whom even now she visualizes as the physician, feeling the pulse of her despair, pillowing her dying head with his arm, will be in attendance at her last hours. Such monstrous self-pity and self-indulgence are indeed hard to take if read too prosaically, and in Letter Five the change of tone comes as a relief, when she is both shrewd and scathing in her analysis of her inability to commit suicide.

The element of surprise in George Sand's writing is, indeed, a characteristic and very welcome feature. Just as an excessively lengthy and didactic digression is becoming unreadable, it can quite miraculously give way to a totally other topic, handled quite differently. George Sand was, as Henry James put it, 'open to everything': her discourse might be 'amatory, religious, political, aesthetic, pictorial, musical, theatrical, historical'. It might also be, as we see in *Lettres d'un Voyageur*, botanical, astronomical, mythological. In fact, about almost anything that seized her interest and imagination she was remarkably knowledgeable.

But, above all, it was her style upon which her effect depended –

and that, alas, is a strength which is very difficult to capture in translation. For Victorian readers, most of whom read her in French, it was what made common ground between friends and enemies. Thackeray, who was shocked by George Sand, wrote of her 'brief, rich and melancholy sentences . . . like the sound of country bells . . . falling sweetly on the ear'. G. H. Lewes, who was devoted to her, commented, 'Poetry flows from her pen as water from a rock; she writes as the birds sing.' Both would have understood Matthew Arnold's nostalgic tribute: 'How the sentences from George Sand's work of that period still linger in our memory and haunt the ear with their cadences.' And it is easy to see what Arnold means in the fine climax to Letter Five which begins, '*L'hiver étend ces voiles gris sur la terre attristée, le froid siffle et pleure autour de nos toits.*' Here, with remarkable sureness of touch, the wintry scene is used as a deeply moving symbol of her hopelessness and despair. Even later, when free of her spell, one can still admire the way in which the sinuous flow of her eloquence is halted and intensified by such 'brief, rich, melancholy sentences' as: '*Tout est silence, regret, tendresse*', '*Voici le froid, la nuit, la mort*', '*Mon âme est veuve.*'

Those, however, who got most from reading George Sand made no distinction between style and content; for them her convictions were as important as her nuances of expression. In 1847, George Eliot (then Marian Evans) copied out and sent to her friend, Sara Hennell, the passage towards the end of Letter Four in which George Sand defends herself for having written *Lélia*. She says that she knows to whom the work will go home: '*Ceux-là seuls qui, souffrant des mêmes angoisses, l'ont écouté comme une plainte entrecoupée, mêlée de fièvre, de sanglots, de rires lugubres et de jurements, l'ont fort bien compris, et ceux-là l'aiment sans l'approuver.*' The plangency of such a sentence overwhelms any sense of the egotism of her private woe and seizes the heart and imagination. But it did more for Marian Evans, immured at the time 'in a doleful prison of stupidity and barrenness'; it appealed to her intellect also, for the case that George Sand was making was for 'the truth of feeling', that substitute for religious faith to which the English writer was to cling all her life. She was asserting that the cry of agony from a fellow-sufferer does far more good than all the moral platitudes which can be uttered (such as Madame de Staël's on the inadvisability of suicide), and which gets short shrift in this Letter. The sense of solidarity with another doubter, another sufferer, another woman, who was not afraid to speak out openly, to 'expose the workings of her *live* heart', brought George Eliot much-needed relief. 'It has a very deep meaning to my apprehension,' she said gravely.

Letters Six to Eight

By spring 1835, the Musset drama was over and George Sand, though deeply depressed, was in her own estimation a convalescent. She was about to enter into the two other major dramas which form the background to the remaining Letters. For years now her incompatible marriage had threatened to fall apart; it was to survive precariously for another six months or so, with quasi-amicable arrangements about property rights drawn up and then regretted and reneged on by her husband as soon as they were signed. Feeling herself a failure both in love and marriage, she sat quietly at Nohant reading the Koran and Plato and wondering what to turn her energies to next, what to do and write which would make life seem worthwhile. The answer was speedily given her by a new acquaintance, the brilliant local lawyer, Michel de Bourges, who was, in both background and fervid republicanism, a total contrast to the aristocratic Musset – and, indeed, to herself.

Michel (or Everard, in the Letters) not only restored her self-respect by falling in love with her but, more important and lasting, he turned her thoughts outwards, away from her own sorrows to the sufferings of humanity. She was later to recall that when she first met him she had the impression, not of a man in his thirties, but of someone small, old and frail, with a bald dome – although as soon as he began to talk she and her companions were dazzled by the fervour, the eloquence, the passionate logic of his revolutionary arguments. This was to be the start of a new phase for her – a phase above all political and humanitarian – and the imprint of his teachings, with those of Lamennais, and of Pierre Leroux later, can be seen not only in most of her writings of the next decade but in her active involvement in the 1848 revolution.

Letter Six was a swift and fascinated response, partly to the excitement of a new relationship which was, before long, to turn into another stormy love-affair, but, even more, to the startling ideas with which he bombarded her from their first meeting – ideas which, however stimulating, she refused to swallow whole. The opening of the Letter is clearly that of a changed mood; things are on the move once more: 'Your friend, the traveller, has arrived home without mishap.'

She has travelled no further than from Nohant to Bourges – some forty-five miles – but a whole new world has been opened up for her. She makes it clear that it is one which, as an artist, she feels she can only peep into. It is alien to her, and yet undeniably admirable. The tone is sceptical, ingratiating, satiric, defensive by turn; she agrees that till now she has been a slave to egoism and passion but still insists that because she is, unlike her mentor, by nature 'poetic, not legislative' she sees things differently. He may be right about many things in the world that are in need of reform, but he has his own shortcomings: he has a thirst for glory and power, he is too solemn and is a Philistine in his destructive egalitarianism about art and artists. She assures him that, come the revolution, artists like everyone else will pitch in but that, when the cause of liberty is won, individuality should be allowed to reassert itself and each should return to his last – Taglioni to her ballet shoes, Liszt to his instruments and she herself to her pen.

This Letter seems more than usually discursive. It is the longest in the book and is a sort of running battle, so familiar in the 1830s, between the man of action and the artist. But an apparent digression – the extended account of her relationship with Néraud (the Malgache) – is not without its point. It can be welcomed as giving flesh and blood to a friend who has till now been used solely in a supporting role, but it is also a means of clarifying the difference between the sort of companionship and shared interests she has been accustomed to and the very different way of life advocated by Everard – to whom, despite everything, she is much attracted. When she escapes from all thought of politics to listen to the throbbing song of the nightingale in the misty garden, to have her senses assailed by the heavy perfumes, to cry aloud 'O God! my God, I am still so young!' this is surely a clear indication to him (by courtesy of the columns of the *Revue*) that she has been stimulated by more than the passion of his republicanism. By the end of the Letter she has not only slipped easily into the relationship of pupil to her '*cher maître*', of John (the 'youngest, most romantic disciple') to Jesus but is even playing up to Everard's idea of her as frivolous and immature. She sees the danger of being dominated by him and, as a dénouement, she makes the Traveller bow himself out of any political involvement and set off on a trip to Bohemia, but the gesture seems rather one of defiant escapism than a serious disavowal. The impact of Everard was not to be so easily ignored, as the next Letter shows.

Letter Seven is addressed to her friend, Liszt, and it is Franz whom she now imagines as having gone to '*la verte Bohème*' accompanied by his fellow-musicians, while she inhabits a deserted house in a town 'on the banks of the Loire'. It is true that throughout July 1835 George Sand did go to ground, inaccessible to everyone but her new lover, Michel de Bourges, whose presence (like that of Pagello in Letter One) is artistically suppressed. The blend of fiction and fact is here particularly interesting. Two months earlier she had promised to go off and '*vieillir*' and it is clear that she feels she has made remarkable headway towards maturity under Everard's guidance. The persona she now adopts is that of the solitary wayfarer, 'alone, totally alone', drawing near to the decline of life.

Liszt and George Sand admired each other. She not only loved music but was highly knowledgeable and Liszt had praised the Letters, especially Letter Five, and had urged her to continue. But more than this, he was a disciple of the Abbé Lamennais, to whom he had introduced her, and he had met Michel de Bourges, so that she knew he would be sympathetic to the committed turn her thoughts had taken. For Plato and the Koran had been abandoned of late in favour of action. She had been caught up in the excitement of a great political trial of strike leaders and republican agitators, for whom Michel de Bourges had acted as one of the leading defence lawyers – so she could no longer be accused by him of 'social atheism'. But now, in this interlude of peace, she had time to draw breath once more and take stock – '*résumer*' was a favourite term of hers. And Liszt, a fellow-artist, who not only shared her republican sympathies but her mystical bent, was the ideal confidant.

The title of the Letter is exact: On Lavater and a Deserted House. The evocation is effortless and haunting of the big, dusty empty rooms, the overgrown garden, the blissful sense of being shut away from the world, the mysterious little noises of a house at night. And in the solitude (whether total or *à deux* scarcely matters, for she was always able, even in company, to retreat into contemplative silence or to the refuge of her writing-desk) it was of her reacquaintance with an old favourite, Lavater, on which she chooses to expatiate. In explaining to Liszt her preoccupation with his volumes on physiognomy she speaks of the importance to her of long, slow reading: 'I am one of those for whom the knowledge of a book can be a truly moral event.'

Anyone who even glances at Lavater's drawings will see their appeal, though I think it is doubtful that many Victorians, then in the grip of the more modern and 'scientific' counter-attraction of phrenology, would have been stimulated by the quotations from his commentaries to investigate his finely drawn, quaintly ingenious Characters. Why George Sand should have felt so strongly at this time his 'immense power' over her is a matter for conjecture. It is likely that he reinforced her sense of her own individuality when she felt she was in danger of being swamped by her doctrinaire lover. She could enjoy fitting her two new 'saints', Everard and Lamennais, into Lavater's theories and could even (for she was of an idealizing disposition) imagine Lavater encouraging her to follow them as guides and masters. But it is evident that all the things she praises in the eighteenth-century figure – his belief in free-will and tolerance, his humour, intuitive wisdom, humility and religious sense – are all qualities which she herself had long cherished but which Everard lacked.

None the less, in matters of social and political reform she is now a total convert to the views of Everard. She may remind Liszt of all the laughter and happiness and poetry they share as artists, but she chooses to end the Letter on a grimmer note, as reverberations from a revolutionary explosion in the outside world break into the peace of her retreat.

Letter Eight, though written earlier, fits in neatly here because of its republican tone. It had, in fact, been written and published in September 1834, soon after George Sand had returned from Italy and had gone on an outing with her liberal-minded Berrichon friends to Talleyrand's château at Valençay. She did this, not from political motives, but in order to escape briefly from Nohant, from her guilt over Pagello and her apprehensions about her future with Musset. This savage attack on Talleyrand, 'the Prince', provides a highly subjective glimpse of the statesman in his old age, and predates by two years her apprenticeship in radicalism with Michel de Bourges. Throughout George Sand's youth the emotional tug-of-war between her aristocratic grandmother and her plebeian mother had meant divided loyalties for her, but she was by nature a rebel, and her instincts were strongly democratic. This diatribe against Talleyrand is much blunter and more bad-mannered than anything else in her writings, and its venom occasionally compares with that of caricatures of royalty and politicians in England, about the same time. It is, however, the impatient and aggressive 'friend' who is made to utter most of the invective in the dialogue; the Traveller, the 'poet', complacently and, at times, sanctimoniously adopts the more moderate stance.

Letter Nine

This deceptively artless and brief Letter was written to her friend and neighbour, Néraud, as from one exile to another. But he, unlike her, is a *voluntary* exile from his home, on a botanizing trip to North Africa, whereas she is shut out from Nohant, her rightful inheritance, by a temporary decree of the court. Her account of the delights of a morning's wandering in early summer through the much-loved countryside near their homes is punctuated with outbursts of anguished questioning of the justice of her lot as an outcast. Hers is the high Romantic view of herself as the artist, the 'poet', always pilloried for telling the truth about the greed, hypocrisy and suffering in society. It is also the more personal vision of herself as the wife whose only sin has been her over-articulacy in her writings about the miseries of marriage.

The background to the Letter is complex. It was very important for her, in the summer of 1836, that she should ensure for herself as much public sympathy as possible and that her image should compare very favourably with that of her husband, Casimir, who had appealed yet once more against the court decision which had been given in her favour in April. As Georges Lubin has sympathetically pointed out, George Sand was playing for very high stakes; she was, in effect, using her pen to enter a plea on behalf of home, income and the custody of her children. Not only was the law heavily weighted against women; her 'adversaries and enemies', as she called her husband and half-brother, had not scrupled to present her extra-marital relationships in the most crudely scandalous and defamatory light. She was sensitive to every public utterance which told against her – whether swingeing abuse by Croker in the *Quarterly Review* or an equally damaging reference to her in the *Revue de Paris* as 'an enemy to marriage'. This last she dealt with promptly (see Letter Twelve). The matter of her notoriety demanded more oblique handling. At the end of April she wrote to the editor of the *Revue des Deux Mondes*:

My dear Buloz,
        Will you please include a little packet of little letters from me in your next number? – I have personal reasons for asking this of you.

This 'little packet' consisted of passages selected from the despairing correspondence she had had two years earlier with her friends, Néraud and Rollinat, and which she had edited; these now constitute Letter Four. To these she added a new Letter to Néraud (now Letter Nine). It was only when the Voyageur Letters were turned into a book that she returned them to their chronological sequence. Her aim, no doubt, was not only to let the world know how wretchedly unhappy her marriage had been and how she had depended for support on loyal and innocent friendships but also how little she had deserved her lot. In some respects, then, these are the most 'arranged' Letters in the book. It is scarcely likely, for instance, that just as she is involved in a lawsuit of desperate importance to her she should come appositely upon her youthful and admirably high-minded discussion of the nature of justice (included in Letter Four under the title, Portrait of a Just Man). On the other hand, it does accord absolutely with the idealism of the sixteen-year-old convent schoolgirl, Aurore Dupin, as it does also with the tone and tenor of the correspondence of the woman now twice her age. Two years before the lawsuit George Sand had, in a letter to Sainte-Beuve, shown herself to be much concerned with that very topic: 'Who will portray the just man,' she asked him, 'as he must be, as he can be, in the state of our society? That is my great preoccupation.'

For she felt passionately that she, who had started out on marriage, young, romantic, innocent and absolute for love, had had no justice dealt her in her emotional life, and now she felt herself threatened by law as well as equity. The sense of outrage in Letter Nine is very different from the unalleviated bitterness and hopelessness of the earlier correspondence with Rollinat and Néraud on which she drew for Letter Four. Her concern now is much more with presenting her case as sympathetically as possible, with stressing her lack of materialism, her love of the simple life. Again the picture, though purposeful, is true. Her generosity was undeniable and she was a countrywoman by upbringing and instinct. The account of her day suits all we know of her habits at Nohant: she goes out at dawn, after a sleepless night, carrying her basket to supply her few needs – paper, ink, cigarettes; she sits sheltered from the wind in a niche, drying her bare feet on a sun-warmed rock, and enjoys her spartan breakfast of a crust, washed down with water from the spring; she is soothed by the cadences and trills of the nightingale and soaring lark's song and watches the villagers in the valley going to mass. But how well-timed is the close of this pastoral scene when the innocent tranquillity is shattered suddenly by her dramatic recollection; 'Ah God! At this hour my enemies are also awakening! They wake up to hate me.'

As she was aware that it would seem very strange to readers of the *Revue* of June 1836 that most of the letters she was using were two years old, she took the bull by the horns and in a special and very interesting preface stated that the 'anachronism' could be justified: it was the recipients of the letters who had suggested to her that they formed a sort of diary of despair and might be of comfort to those '*amis inconnus*' who could be going through similar sorrows. 'It is in order to help those sick souls to recognize their malady, to examine it and to cure themselves that I dare sometimes to publish quite personal sentiments. Without this aim such revelations would be puerile . . . The pages I offer you today will show how far discouragement and doubt can extend. I hope soon to tell you how one recovers strength and hope.' She went on to point out that those who had recovered would, in reading, get pleasure from looking back on past hardships, 'just as the traveller who has crossed the threshold of his home once more, enjoys dreaming of the obstacles and trials of the pilgrimage he has completed. Those who still stray in storm and darkness will at least learn from what perplexities one can emerge, from what bottomless pits one can escape.'

This could be considered a good example of George Sand's ability to 'fib neatly . . . to arrange the facts as they suit her best', as Henry James put it. The truth once again is certainly partial. She was publishing this time neither 'at request of friends' nor out of purely humanitarian reasons. On the other hand, her emotions were genuine enough, as was her belief in the therapy of a shared grief. And there were, indeed, 'unknown friends' out there, waiting to be comforted. One such was Mazzini, whose introduction to her writings must have been this very foreword, as he speaks of first reading her in the *Revue* in 1836, 'at a time of crisis and despair . . . I no longer had faith in myself . . . This sisterly voice, its accent broken by suffering, yet finding strength to throw a word of encouragement and hope to those yet wandering amid storm and darkness, was sweet to me as is the cradle song to the weeping child.' Whatever the proportion of art to nature and of self-interest to altruism in George Sand's arrangement of the facts, such a heartfelt tribute disarms scepticism.

Letter Ten

By the end of August 1836, George Sand was in holiday mood. Her long drawn out lawsuit had been successfully concluded, and clad once more in smock and trousers, instead of the demure dresses she had been wearing for her court appearances, she set off for Switzerland to join Liszt and his aristocratic mistress, Marie d'Agoult. She was accompanied by her two children, Maurice and Solange, which has the effect of making the first person role in this Letter more androgynous than ever, with the proud mother taking over at times from the irresponsible gamin.

The playfulness promised at the outset does not materialize for some time. Instead, the reader may find his patience tried by the pages which follow: of informative musing and myth and moralizing on the blessings and evils of wine – 'the generous blood of the grape' – a democratic digression prompted by an encounter with some drunken gentry at Autun. But when the journey proper gets going and the Traveller is discovered, lying wrapped in his coat on the deck of the little steamer which plies between Châlons and Lyon, thereafter the simplicity of the style and the briskness of the dialogue complement perfectly the *en route*, subjective nature of the impressions. There is none of the brilliance of the Venice descriptions, but the sense of the moment is caught again and again: the surprise of the travellers, as they eat their picnic inside their carriage in driving rain and mist, at finding themselves poised 'with one wheel in the void, glass in our hand'; the eternal melancholy of the ruined monastery, guarded by the farouche forester and his daughter, gigantic as their own fir trees and 'proud as ruined Hidalgos' – until the sight of tourists rouses their mercenary instincts; the clamorous bustle of the arrival at the hotel in Chamonix and the convergence of all these strangely clad bohemians under the disapproving gaze of the other guests.

It is worth observing that in the racy analysis of the national characteristics of tourists, it is the British who come off worst. Englishmen are not only protected from the elements by wearing three pairs of trousers on top of each other, they are psychologically insulated in their 'British fluid', as under a bell jar; Englishwomen are prudish and conventional, with never a hair out of place. No doubt her memories of the rules of propriety imposed on her at her English convent school in Paris gave an extra edge to her defiant pride in her own muddy, rumpled, sunburned state. This is very much an 'in-group' Letter. She is among friends and acutely aware of how different are their preoccupations, as well as their appearance, from those of normal tourists. We are given very revealing glimpses of the sort of idealistic argument and banter and horseplay going on at this time in Sandian circles. The talk is far from literary as this Romantic little caravan of gifted artists theorize their way across the mountain passes from Chamonix to Martigny. Throughout, while Liszt holds forth on the back of his mule upon how to educate the human race and while the more academic Major, wrestling with universals, mutters distractedly, 'The absolute is identical with itself,' George Sand clings doggedly to her distrust of applied systems and to her faith in the common man. Though she did not have the physical companionship of Michel de Bourges on this trip, as she had hoped, at least she had brought his doctrines with her.

This is to be seen even in the last scene at Fribourg, when politics and philosophy seem at last to be giving way to music. After the antics of the cathedral organist on the great Mooser organ are over, Liszt plays the Dies Irae with an austerity which is perfectly matched by the purity and pallor of his Florentine profile. As the thunderous notes roll over George Sand's head they inspire, not fear, but a sudden surge of confidence that the wrath of God will be reserved for the tyrants of the world. She will be swept along, 'forgotten, forgiven perhaps', under the great harrow with the multitudes of the oppressed on the Day of Judgement. Such optimism is new in the Letters and, while it can be attributed largely to her acquired sense of solidarity with suffering humanity, another explanation could be her recent triumph over her 'adversaries and enemies' in a terrestrial court of justice. This comfortable conviction that a just God would be on her side was to stay with her through all the remaining dramas of her life.

Letters Eleven and Twelve

The final Letters, unlike the others, are not addressed to intimate friends and are rather an embarrassment to those critics who want to make out a case for *Lettres d'un Voyageur* as a consistent work of art. But both have something to offer – Letter Twelve, in particular, to feminists.

Letter Eleven, addressed to the composer, Meyerbeer, was

broached in April 1836, when George Sand was having a brief respite from litigation. She took the opportunity in Paris of going twice to his opera, *The Huguenots*, which had had a stunningly successful début but had been reviewed disapprovingly in the *Revue des Deux Mondes*. It was no doubt this that led her to offer an article which would do more justice to the composer, with whom she was on good terms, and to the work. '*J'adore* Les Huguenots,' she wrote to Liszt.

The Letter hung fire for several months while her lawsuit was being fought and then she delayed it further till her trip to Switzerland, where she knew she would be able to discuss her musical criticism with Liszt. In fact, although this Letter is often referred to as being 'on music', it is just as much concerned with contemporary attitudes to religion and with a critic's responsibilities. As always she felt she had 'many things to say', and it is these, rather than the fulsome tributes to Meyerbeer's achievements and character which are of more interest now, when neither *Les Huguenots* nor *Robert le diable* can be said to come high on the opera-goer's list.

It must have been artistically satisfying for her to head the Letter, 'Geneva'. Not only did this fit in perfectly with the Protestant theme of the opera, but she could turn her article into an account of a day in her travels, starting with a visit to the great cathedral where, she tells Meyerbeer, 'I thought of no one but you,' and ending it with a session at the theatre, 'where I spoke of no one but you.' In praising the great reforming ideal of Protestantism she is free to point out 'many things': how far removed from it had been the snuffling materialism of that morning's preacher and how misguided her fashionable contemporaries are when they excuse religious persecution in the name of political expediency. In discussing the opera, she can seize the chance to damn Scribe and, using as a pretext the hapless reviewer who had slated Meyerbeer, she can lecture young and opinionated critics on the necessity for disinterestedness in their profession. This Letter may not be the most exciting in the collection, but it is a very good example of George Sand's versatility and also of her ability to weld the most unlikely material into a reasonably coherent whole.

Letter Twelve was addressed to a total stranger, Désiré Nisard, who, as far as she was concerned, chose just the wrong moment to write an article on her in the *Revue de Paris*. Normally she ignored criticism but in May 1836 her separation case was pending. It was not that M. Nisard did not find much to admire and appreciate in her work. He, too, in his own way, was a Traveller, engaged in writing a series of *Souvenirs de voyage*, and he explained that, at Verviers, he had been forced to take refuge from the rain in an inn with, for reading matter, several volumes of George Sand. He re-read 'with delight the beautiful pages' and was still sitting hunched up over them, trying to analyse their effect upon him, when darkness fell. But amidst all the praise of her seductive and dazzling talents, her transparent style, there is one reiterated belief: she is the sworn enemy of marriage, its most passionate adversary. There had been no more powerful analyst of marriage than George Sand, but on the whole she 'defends false views with just ideas'.

At this moment of crisis in her marital affairs she could not let such a judgement go unchallenged. Buloz was the owner of the *Revue de Paris* as well as the editor of the *Revue des Deux Mondes*. She wrote to him peremptorily, reminding him of his obligations to her; and persuasively, pointing out that a reply from her would be good for business. Anything she wrote in her present circumstances would not fail to interest 'the rabble of subscribers'. A fortnight later her diplomatic and dignified reply to Nisard was published in the *Revue de Paris*.

It was an *apologia* about which she felt strongly enough to write to Buloz later, when the book was being planned: 'You must end *Lettres d'un Voyageur* with the Letter to Nisard.' It opens with a considerable amount of tactful prevarication regarding what she had said and not said about marriage in her novels and how many actual cases of adultery had taken place in them. But gradually she moves into a strong and resolute position, setting out what she felt to be wrong with the relationship between men and women. Her conviction (which never wavered) was that there was nothing wrong with marriage as an institution but a great deal wrong with husbands, their rights, their habits and their assumptions. Probably some of the most influential feminist views expressed by George Sand occur in this very Letter, when she challenges the whole creed of womanly patience and silence: 'Lying is not virtue; cowardice is not abnegation.' More than a decade later, Charlotte Brontë (who had warmed to *Lettres d'un Voyageur* as being 'full of the writer's self . . . whose very faults spring from the excess of her good qualities') makes her own gentle heroine, Caroline Helstone, echo George Sand's sentiments: 'Does virtue lie in abnegation of self? I do not believe it. Undue humility makes tyranny; weak concession creates selfishness . . . every human being has his share of rights.'

31

With Casimir's deficiencies in mind, George Sand pleads her own case skilfully, employing heavy irony in her comment, 'A husband who light-heartedly neglects his responsibilities to indulge in blasphemy, merriment and drink *is sometimes* less excusable than the woman who betrays hers in tears, suffering and propitiation.' At the same time she is trying to put some backbone into her own sex. Here, in her plea for justice, she is not thinking only of the courtroom at Bourges; and in her call to other women for courage, her idealism takes precedence over her self-interest. It is easy to understand why she chose to end her book with this Letter.

Lettres d'un Voyageur

Preface to the Second Edition

★

Never was a work – if indeed this can be called a work – less planned and less contrived than these two volumes* of letters written at longish intervals, almost always in the throes of some emotional crisis which they reflect without actually describing. They were for me no more than a natural and instinctive relief from worries, hardships or despondency that made it impossible for me to start or continue writing a novel. Some were even written at great speed, broken off abruptly to catch the mail and posted without any thought of publication. Later the idea of putting them together and filling in the gaps made me reclaim them from those friends I thought most likely to have preserved my epistles;[1] and these are the ones which are possibly the least unworthy – understandably enough, since we are always more open and at ease when talking about our feelings to one person in private than in the presence of someone unknown. That unknown third party is the reader, the public; and were it not that writing has a definite appeal – often painful, sometimes intoxicating, but ever irresistible – which makes us forget the unknown witness and be carried away by our subject, I don't think we would ever have the courage to write about ourselves – unless we had a great deal of good to say. However, reading these letters no one will fail to agree that such was not my case, and that it required a great deal of daring, or a great deal of thoughtlessness to talk about myself for two whole volumes.

I mention all this so that those of my readers who are addicted to novels and accustomed to see me do nothing worse may forgive me for my misguided decision to come on-stage myself in the place of rather more sedate characters who possess all the required trappings to appear in public. As I have said, it was at those times when my tired brain was devoid of heroes and plots that, like an impresario whose company is late for the performance, I came forward worried,

* The first edition of this work was in two volumes.

35

distraught and not dressed for the part, to speak as best I could the prologue to the awaited play. But I do believe, on the other hand, that certain intimate letters, certain apparently insignificant events in an artist's life, may present, for those who are interested in the secret workings of the human heart, the best introduction to his works and their clearest exposition.

And may the lovers of fiction not judge me too severely either. For it is with them in mind that in many of these letters I dressed up my sad hero, my poor *self*, in an outfit which is quite foreign to him and tried to conceal as far as possible his material being under a truer, more interesting *personality*. Thus it is hard to tell when reading these letters whether the writer is an adult, an old man or a child. What does the reader care about my age and my bearing? It is only at the Opera that youth, beauty and grace engage the eyes and the imagination. In a book of this sort it is the emotion, the musing, the sadness or the rapture or the anxiety which should appeal to the reader. What he can ask of the writer who submits his soul to the indignity and censure of scrutiny is that he disclose the workings of his *live* heart, as it were. Thus by speaking now as a truant schoolboy, now as a gouty old uncle[2] and now as a restless young recruit I did no more than portray my state of mind at a given time – careless and playful at moments, at others morose and weary or yet again fiery and vigorous. Which of us does not contain within himself at every hour of his life these three moral, intellectual and physical ages of being? What old man has not time and again felt himself a child? What child has not felt occasionally the burden of age? Who has not felt young and old simultaneously for most of his emotional life? Have I done anything else than tell the story of each one of us? No, I have done nothing more, and that is all I intended to do. I did not want the reader to seek some strange or remarkable personality behind the mask of this hypothetical traveller. No one who considers how little I have spared myself in thus exposing my bleeding heart to psychological investigation could accuse me of such puerile preoccupations. Indeed, if I submitted myself to this ordeal without shame or dread it is because I knew what anxieties also prey upon my contemporaries and the need that they all have to understand themselves, examine themselves, sound their consciences, throw a light upon themselves by the revelation of their instincts and their wants, their wrongs and their aspirations. My soul has, I am convinced, served as a mirror to most of those who have looked into it. Thus not a few have been horrified by what they saw and, confronted with so much weakness, fearfulness, irresolution, inconsistency, wounded pride and unexploited potential, have decreed that I am a sick man, a lunatic, an exceptional person, a monster of pride and scepticism. But no. I am no different from you, hypocritical reader;[3] I am different only in that I acknowledge my plight and don't try to hide my terror-stricken features under a youthful, carefree mask. You have drunk from the same cup. You have suffered the same torments. Like me you have doubted, like me you have denied and blasphemed, like me you have gone astray in the darkness, cursing God and mankind because you failed to understand either. Fifty years ago Voltaire inscribed these famous lines on Cupid's statue:

> *Quoi que tu sois, voici ton maître,*
> *Il l'est, le fut ou le doit être.*

Today he would set this solemn verdict on the pedestal of another god; it is no longer Love but Doubt which his trembling old hand would immortalize in this couplet. Yes, doubt, scepticism, moderate or doctrinaire, daring or timid, boastful or desolate, criminal or penitent, oppressor or oppressed, tyrant or victim. Man of our times,

> Who e'er you be, *there* is your master,
> He is or was or must be later.

So let us not blush for each other's shortcomings nor be such hypocrites as to conceal the burden of our misery. All of us, no matter who, are going through a grave illness or will fall prey to it if we have not already done so. Only atheists represent doubt as something criminal and shameful, just as it is only sham heroes who claim they have never lacked fortitude and courage. Doubt, like cholera, is the sickness of our age. But, like all the crises through which God guides the human intellect, it is the precursor of moral health and of faith. Doubt is born of questioning. It is the sickly and feverish offspring of a powerful mother, Freedom. But it is not tyrants who will cure it. Tyrants are atheists: tyranny and atheism can only kill. Freedom herself will take her ailing child in her arms; she will hold it up to the heavens, to the light, and it will grow strong and trusting like her. It will be transformed, it will become Hope and it will beget a daughter in its turn, a daughter of divine nature and descent, Knowledge, who will also bear a child, and this last born will be Faith.

As for me, poor convalescent who but yesterday was knocking at the gates of death, I am well aware of the cause and the effects of my disease; I have told you of them and I shall tell you again. My disease is yours, it is questioning coupled with ignorance. A little more knowledge will save us. So let us go on questioning, learning, and arrive at knowledge. When we denied the truth (and I was among the first), we did no more than proclaim our lack of vision, and the generations to come will learn a useful lesson from the blindness of our age. They will say that we did well to complain, to rebel, to fill the world with our cries, to weary the heavens with our questions and to avoid through our anger and impatience the ills that are fatal to those who slumber. As Napoleon's troops were returning from the Russian campaign, spectral figures could be seen running in bewilderment over the snows, trying, amid moans and curses, to find the way that led back to their native land. Others, apparently composed and resigned, lay down in the snow and were frozen to death. Woe betide those who are resigned today! Woe betide those who accept injustice, error, ignorance, sophistry and doubt with serenity! These will die, these are already dead, buried in the snow and ice. But those who are wandering with bleeding feet and crying out with bitter complaints will find the way to the Promised Land, they will see the light of the sun.

Ignorance, did I say? Doubt, sophistry, injustice? Yes, those are the rocks through which we try to steer our way; those are the evils and dangers with which our life is strewn. Re-reading and assessing *Lettres d'un Voyageur* – something I had not dared to do for many years – I was not really surprised to see that I had been ignorant, sceptical, sophistical, inconsistent and unjust all the way through. Yet I have made no changes in this unstructured manuscript, apart from correcting a few inaccuracies and a page or so of dull commonplaces. The second volume[4] is generally not worth much from any point of view. The first, though riddled with still more naïve errors of every kind, has one unquestionable value: that of having been written with a spontaneous carelessness which is full of youth and candour. If it were to fall into the hands of serious-minded people it would make them smile; but if these solemn people happened to be generous and sincere as well, they would find in it matter for pity, for consolation, for the encouragement and the instruction of the dreaming, ardent and blind youth of our day. Having acquired, through my confessions, a better insight into the cause and nature of our suffering, they would become more compassionate and realize that it can be cured neither by bitter ridicule nor by pedantic anathemas, but by true precepts and a deep feeling of human charity.

Letter One[1]

★

I had arrived in Bassano at nine o'clock on a cold, wet evening. I had gone to bed sad and weary after silently shaking hands with my companion. At sunrise I woke up and saw from my window, against the bright blue of the sky, the high, ivy-clad battlements of the ancient fortress that dominates the valley. I hurried out to explore the place and make sure that the day was as fine as it seemed.

I hadn't gone fifty yards before I came upon the doctor sitting on a rock smoking a seven-foot carob-wood pipe he had just bought from a peasant for eight *soldi*. He was so pleased with his acquisition and so lost in billows of tobacco smoke that it was some time before he noticed me. When he had expelled the last puff he could extract from what he called his *pipetta* he suggested we go and have breakfast in a coffee-shop overlooking the castle moat while the driver, who was to take us back to Venice, got everything ready for the trip. I accepted.

If you ever come back to these parts I recommend the Moat Café in Bassano as one of the best things that can befall a sightseer who has had enough of Italy's classical masterpieces. You may remember that when we left France all you wanted, you said, was to feast your eyes on sculptured marble. You called me a barbarian when I said I would give all the palaces in the world to go and see the rough marble flanks of an Apennine or Alpine peak. You may also remember that after some days you had had your fill of statues, frescoes, churches and galleries. The pleasantest memory you preserved was of a chill and limpid fountain in a park in Genoa where you bathed your hot, weary brow. That is because works of art speak to the mind alone, whereas the wonders of nature appeal to all the faculties. They reach us through every pore as well as through all our thoughts. The contemplation of nature adds sensual delight to the purely intellectual feeling of admiration. The chill waters, the scent of flowers, the music of the wind circulate in our blood and in our nerves at the same time as the radiance of colours and the harmony of forms appeal to our imagination. All constitutions – even the coarsest – are susceptible to this sense of delight and well-being – animals experience it to a certain extent. But nobler natures only get a fleeting satisfaction from it, a pleasant break from their more arduous intellectual activities. Great minds need the whole world, God's creations as well as man's. The fountain of clear water attracts and delights you, but you can only rest there briefly. You will have to have exhausted Michelangelo and Titian before stopping again by the roadside, and as soon as you have washed away the dust of the journey in the spring's waters you will set off again saying: 'Let's find out what else the world has to offer.'

Ordinary, lazy natures like mine would be content to sleep away their lives at the side of a ditch, if it were possible to make this hard and barren journey while sleeping and dreaming. But only if the ditch were like the one at Bassano, that is to say, a hundred feet above a pleasant valley, and only if one could breakfast every morning on a green, primrose-studded carpet, off excellent coffee, local butter and aniseed-flavoured bread.

It is to such a breakfast that I invite you when you have the time to relish tranquillity. By then you will have learnt everything; life will have no more secrets for you. Your hair will have begun to turn grey; mine will be white; but the Bassano valley will be just as lovely, the snow on the Alps as immaculate; and our friendship . . . ? I trust in your heart and can answer for mine.

The countryside wasn't yet in its full splendour; the meadows were a listless yellowish-green and the leaves were only just budding on the trees. But here and there the pink and white festoons of flowering almond and peach trees broke up the dark masses of cypress. Through this vast garden the Brenta ran swift and silent on its sandy bed, between these two wide banks of pebbles and stones which it wrenches from the mountain-side and which, in its days of fury, it strews over the plain. A semi-circle of fertile hills, covered with those long branches of knotty vines which hang from every tree in the Veneto, formed an inner frame to the picture; while beyond, the snowy peaks glistening in the sun's first rays made an immense outer border which stood out like silver fretwork from the solid blue of the sky.

'I would have you know,' said the doctor, 'that your coffee is getting cold and that the driver is waiting for us.'

'Doctor,' I retorted, 'do you really believe I intend to go back to Venice now?'

'Why the devil not?' exclaimed the doctor, anxiously.

'What's the matter?' I asked. 'You apparently brought me here to see the Alps. Do you expect me to return to your swampy city when I have barely set foot on them?'

'Fiddlesticks! I've scaled the Alps more than twenty times,' said the doctor.

'It's not quite as enjoyable for me to know you've done so as it is to do it myself,' I answered.

'Why, yes,' he went on without hearing me. 'You must know that, in my time, I was a famous chamois hunter. Look – can you see that gap up there, and that peak over there? Well, one day . . .'

'*Basta*,[2] *basta*, Doctor! You'll tell me all about it some summer's night in Venice as we smoke our outsize pipes under the awnings of the Piazza San Marco with your Turkish friends. They are far too solemn to interrupt a story-teller, however nonsensical the yarn he spins; and there isn't the slightest risk of their showing any sign of impatience or doubt before the end of the tale, were it to last three days and three nights. For the time being, I want to follow your example by climbing that peak up there and coming down through that gap over there . . .'

'You!' said the doctor, casting a scornful glance at my puny person.

Then he stared complacently at one of his own hands that covered half the surface of the table, smiled and swayed superciliously from side to side.

'Battles are won by light as well as by heavy infantry,' I replied defiantly. 'And the smallest goat climbs mountains better than a carthorse.'

'Let me remind you,' said my companion, 'that you are in poor health, and that I undertook to bring you back to Venice dead or alive.'

'I am well aware that in your capacity as doctor you have taken my life into your hands; but such is my whim, Doctor, that I desire my freedom for another five or six days.'

'You are most unreasonable,' he replied. 'On the one hand I promised not to leave you alone; on the other I swore to be in Venice tomorrow morning. Do you want to make me fail in one of my two undertakings?'

'Indeed I do, Doctor.'

He sighed deeply; then, after a moment's reflection:

'I've noticed,' he said, 'that small men are usually gifted with great strength of character, or at any rate with a tremendous dose of obstinacy.'

'And in view of this learned observation you will let me do as I please, then, kindest of doctors?' I cried, jumping from the terrace onto the path below.

'You will force me to compromise with my conscience,' he said, leaning over the balustrade. 'I swore to bring you back to Venice; but I didn't say I would bring you back one day rather than another . . .'

'Certainly, my dear Doctor, I might not return to Venice before next year, and so long as we arrived together at the Giudecca . . .'

'Are you making fun of me?' he snapped.

'Certainly, Doctor,' I replied. And we had a tremendous row that ended in mutual concessions. He agreed to leave me alone and I undertook to be back in Venice before the end of the week.

'You will be in Mestre on Saturday night,' said the doctor. 'I shall be there to meet you with Catullo and the gondola.'

'I shall be there, Doctor, I swear.'

'To make sure that you continue to see reason, swear by our dearest friend, by the man[3] who was here only a few days ago.'

'I swear by him,' I answered. 'And you can hold such a vow sacred. Farewell, Doctor.'

He took my hand in his great red one and nearly reduced it to pulp. Two tears trickled silently down his cheeks. Then he shrugged his shoulders and thrust my hand away, exclaiming: 'Go to the devil!' When he had taken about a dozen steps at a brisk trot he turned round to shout: 'Have the heels of your boots cut down before you venture up into the snow. Never lie down too close to rocks; there are a lot of vipers around here. Don't drink indiscriminately from every spring; make sure that the water is not polluted; some mountain streams are unwholesome. You can trust all the mountain folk who speak the local dialect, but if some loiterer starts begging in a foreign tongue or with a suspicious accent, don't reach for your purse or have any truck with him; go your way but keep an eye on his stick.'

'Is that all, Doctor?'

'You can trust me never to forget anything important,' he replied crossly, 'and to know more than anybody else what should and should not be done on a trip.'

'*Ciao, egregio dottore,*' I said, smiling.

'*Schiavo suo,*'[4] he answered curtly, pulling on his hat.

*   *   *   *   *   *   *   *   *   *

I admit that I am one of those who would gladly break their neck for a wager, and that no schoolboy could be prouder of his pluck and agility than I am. That's because I'm undersized and because all undersized men always want to do everything big men do. None the less, you must believe me when I say that the thought of setting out on what we call an expedition had never been further from my mind. On my good days – those days now few and far between – when I wouldn't mind going out, like Kreissler,[5] with two hats on my head, one on top of the other, I might, like him, *venture a merry caper on the banks of the Acheron*; but on my days of *spleen*[6] I trudge along in the middle of the most level roads and steer clear of cliff-tops. I know only too well that at such times an insect's importunate buzz in my ear, or an impudent hair tickling my cheek, would be enough to fill me with such rage and despair that I would be capable of drowning myself in the bottom of the lakes.

So I walked all through that morning up the Trento road, towards the source of the Brenta. The gorge is dotted with hamlets on either bank of the river, and with isolated cottages on the mountain slopes. All the lower part of the valley is carefully cultivated. Higher up are vast stretches of natural pastureland. Then a scarp of barren rocks rises to the clouds with snow draped like a cloak over their summits.

Since the thaw had not yet set in, the Brenta flowed peacefully in its narrow bed. Its waters, troubled and polluted for the past four years by a rock which had disintegrated, were now clear again.

Flocks of children and lambs cavorted together along its banks in the shade of the flowering cherry trees. This is the ideal season to travel around here. The countryside is an uninterrupted orchard, and though it may not yet be in its full luxuriance and though green is absent from the scenery, yet the snow crowns it with a sparkling halo and it is possible to walk between hedges of hawthorn and wild plum for a whole day without meeting a single Englishman.

I would have liked to go as far as the Alps of the Tyrol. I don't really know why I think they must be so beautiful, but the fact is that they are fixed in my mind as one of the parts of the globe to which I am inexplicably drawn. Should I believe, like you, that fate leads us relentlessly towards those places where we must undergo some moral crisis? I cannot accept the fact that fate has such a significant role in my own life. I think there may be a special Providence for men of exceptional genius or virtue; but why should God bother about me? When we were together I was as fatalistic as a true Moslem. I was convinced that all the good or evil that befell us was due to the singular intentions, the parental affection or the mysterious previsions which this Providence had for you. I felt obliged to use my own will in one way or another, like a kind of lever destined to set you in motion. I was one of the cogs in the mechanism of your life, and at times I felt God's hand upon me, directing me. Now that this hand has separated us, I feel useless and forsaken. Like a piece of rock torn from the mountain, I am impelled by chance and only the unevenness of the road decides my direction. I was a hindrance to the course of destiny: – God's breath has swept this rock away: what does it matter to Him where it lands up?

*　　*　　*　　*　　*　　*　　*　　*　　*　　*

I'm inclined to think that my long-established affection for the Tyrol derives from two insignificant memories: that of a ballad of which I was very fond as a child which began:

> Towards the Alps of the Tyrol in pursuit of the deer,
> Engelwald, the bald hunter, passed over the snow, etc.,

and that of a young lady with whom I travelled one night, ten years ago, during a journey from — to —. Our coach had broken down on a slope. The icy road was dangerously slippery and the moonlight spectacular. I was in a mood at once ecstatic and ridiculous. I should have liked to be alone; but courtesy and kindness required that I offer my fellow traveller my arm. I had thoughts for nothing but the moonlight, the river flowing steeply by the roadside and the meadows bathed in silvery mist. The lady's attire was nondescript. She spoke French imperfectly, with a German accent, and spoke moreover very little, thus I had no clue as to her status or interests. Only some knowledgeable remarks she had made at the inn concerning the almond custard had led me to suppose that this modest and discerning person might be a cook in some well-to-do family. I racked my brains for something pleasant to say to her; finally, after a good fifteen minutes of incredible effort, I produced this: 'Isn't this a truly *enchanting site*, Mademoiselle?' She smiled and shrugged her shoulders ever so slightly. I assumed that, owing to my platitudinous observation, she took me for a travelling salesman, and was somewhat mortified till, after a moment's silence, she mournfully observed: 'Oh, sir, you have obviously never seen the mountains of the Tyrol!'

'Are you from the Tyrol?' I exclaimed. 'Good heavens! Once upon a time I knew a ballad about the Tyrol that filled my head with dreams. So it's really a beautiful country? I don't know why it has stuck in a corner of my mind. Will you be kind enough to describe it for me?'

'I am from the Tyrol,' was her gentle, sad reply. 'But I'm sorry, I cannot talk about it.'

She dabbed her eyes with her handkerchief and didn't say another word for the rest of the journey. As for me, I scrupulously respected her reticence and felt no inclination to be told more. Such devotion to her homeland, expressed in a single phrase, in her reluctance to speak and in two hastily dried tears, seemed more eloquent to me and more profound than a whole volume. I read into this silent stranger's melancholy a complete romance, a whole poem.[7] Hence this Tyrol, so sensitively and tenderly regretted, became for me an enchanted land. When I got back into the coach, I closed my eyes to shut out the landscape I had formerly admired but which henceforth aroused in me nothing but the scorn we feel for reality at the age of twenty. And I saw spread out before me, as in a vast panorama, the lakes, green mountains, pasturelands, Alpine forests, flocks and streams of the Tyrol. I heard those joyous and nostalgic songs that seem to have been expressly made for echoes worthy of them. Since then, carried on the wings of Beethoven's Pastoral Symphony, I have often strolled happily through that land of dreams. How pleasantly have I slumbered in its sweet-smelling meadows! What beautiful flowers I have plucked there! What bands of happy, laughing shepherds I have seen dancing past me! What austere solitudes I have discovered there in which to commune with God! What distances I have travelled across its mountain ranges while the orchestra played two or three chords!

*   *   *   *   *   *   *   *   *   *   *

I was seated on a rock just below the track. Darkness was gradually engulfing the peaks. At the far end of the valley, towards the river's source, I could vaguely distinguish an endless array of mountains. Those faint, distant phantoms, lost in the evening mist, were the Tyrol. Another day's journey and I would have reached the land of my dreams. – From those far peaks, I thought, my golden dreams took flight. They flew to meet me like a flock of homing birds; they visited me when I was still a little peasant boy leading my goats along the hedgerows of the Vallée Noire and singing the ballad of Engelwald. They passed over my head on a pale winter's night when I had just returned from a strange pilgrimage to other illusions which I have lost, to other lands where I shall not set foot again. They became violas and oboes in the hands of Brod and of Urhan,[8] and I recognized them by their sweet voices, even though we were in Paris, even though I had to wear gloves and put up with lamplight at noon to hear them. They sang so well that I had only to shut my eyes for the hall of the Conservatoire to turn into an Alpine valley and for Habeneck,[9] bow in hand at the head of all that harmony, to turn into a mountain huntsman, *Engelwald the Bald*, or some other. Beautiful dreams of travel and solitude, wandering doves that fanned my brow with your wings, you have returned to your enchanted haunts and are waiting for me. I am almost there, I can almost grasp you. But O my untamed friends, will you not take flight like all my other dreams? When I stretch out my hand to stroke you, will you not fly away? Will you not go and perch on some further, unattainable peak, where my longing will pursue you in vain?

*   *   *   *   *   *   *   *   *   *

During the day, in bright sunshine, I had snatched a few hours' sleep in the heather. To avoid the squalor of wayside inns I had contrived to travel at night when it was cold and sleep out of doors in daylight. The night was not as calm as I had hoped. Clouds covered the sky and the wind got up, but the road was so good that it was easy to follow it in the dark. The mountains rose to my left and to my right like black giants; the wind rushed headlong between them and raced along the ridge with a long drawn out deep sigh. Fruit trees, shaken roughly by the wind, showered their sweet-smelling blossoms over me. The world was shrouded and drear but full of scents and wild harmonies. A few ominous raindrops made me seek shelter in an olive grove not far from the road; I waited there for the storm to pass. After an hour, the wind had dropped and the sky was stretched overhead like a long blue ribbon, oddly fretted by the craggy granite walls that confined it. On a vaster scale, it was very similar to the view we used to glimpse in Venice when we strolled after sunset along those dark, narrow, deep alleys, with the night unfurled above the rooftops like a slender azure scarf dotted with silver spangles.

The murmur of the Brenta, a last moan from the wind in the heavy foliage of the olive trees, the raindrops falling from the branches onto the rocks with the gentle sound of a kiss – all these caused an indefinable sense of sadness and tenderness to suffuse the air and sigh through all the vegetation. I thought of Christ's vigil on the Mount of Olives and recalled how once we discussed that chapter of the divine poem the whole night through. It was indeed a sad night, one of those dark vigils in which we drained together the cup of bitterness. For you, too, have endured a ruthless martyrdom; you, too, have been nailed to a cross.[10] Was it to atone for some terrible sin that you were sacrificed on the altar of suffering? What could you have done to deserve such humiliations and punishment? At your age, can one be guilty? Can one tell the difference between good and evil? You were overflowing with youth and you thought that to live and to enjoy life were one and the same thing. You wore yourself out savouring all the pleasures that came your way, in one go and without a thought. You disregarded your greatness and let your life flow with the tide of passions that exhausted and spent it, as if you had the same right to dispose of it as an ordinary mortal. You calmly assumed such a right, but you forgot that you are of those who do not belong to themselves. You wanted to live for your own sake, and your disdain for all that is human led you to sacrifice your glory. You flung indiscriminately into the abyss all the precious stones of the crown God had set on your brow – strength, beauty, genius, and even your youthful innocence you would have trampled underfoot, like an arrogant child!

What then was the self-destructive passion that smouldered in you? And what was your grudge against the heavens that made you scorn all their precious gifts in this way? Did your great destiny terrify you? Did the spirit of God appear to you in too stern a guise? The angel of poetry, who shines on his right hand, bent over your cradle to kiss your brow; but you were no doubt alarmed to see the fiery-winged giant so close to you. Your eyes could not sustain the radiance of his countenance and you fled to escape him. You could barely walk and already you wanted to race through life, ignoring its pitfalls, avidly grasping all it had to offer, seeking in its pleasures shelter and protection against the horror of your sublime and terrible vision. Like Jacob you wrestled with it, and like him you were overcome. In the midst of your passionate revels the mysterious phantom came to reclaim and possess you. You had to be a poet, and you became one despite yourself.

You forswore the worship of virtue in vain; you should have been one of her loveliest young acolytes, serving at her altars, singing the most sublime canticles to the accompaniment of a golden lyre, and the white robes of chastity would have become your fragile form better than Folly's cap and bells. You could never quite forget the divine ecstasies of your first faith. You returned to it from the dens of iniquity and your voice, raised to blaspheme, against your will intoned songs of love and hope. Then those who heard you looked at each other in wonderment: 'Who can this be?' they said, 'and in what language does he celebrate our joyous rites? We had taken him for one of us, but he is a convert from some other faith, an exile from some other world more melancholy yet happier. He seeks us out and sits at our board, but intoxication does not provide the same escape for him as it does for us. Why is it that a cloud sometimes passes over his brow and makes him turn pale? Of what is he dreaming? Of what does he speak? Why are strange words constantly on his lips, like memories from another life? Why do *virgins*, *cupids* and *angels* continually haunt his dreams and his poetry? Does he mock us or himself? Is it his God or ours whom he scorns and betrays?'

And you, you went on singing your sublime and capricious strains, alternately cynical and spirited as an antique ode, or chaste and gentle as a child's prayer. Couched among the roses that are of this earth you dreamt of the roses of Paradise that never fade; and, breathing the ephemeral perfume of your pleasures, you spoke of the eternal incense angels burn before the throne of God. Had you, then, breathed that incense? Had you plucked those immortal roses? Had you preserved the vague and delightful memories of that land of the poets, which made all the wild passions you indulged in this world seem inadequate?

Midway between heaven and earth, drawn to the one, unable to renounce the other, scorning fame, terrified of the void, hesitant, tortured, fickle, you dwelt alone among the throng; you shunned solitude and found it everywhere. You were worn out by your own powers. Your thoughts were too vast, your desires too boundless, your frail shoulders gave way under the burden of your genius. You tried to forget, amid the paltry delights of this world, the unattainable blessings you had glimpsed from afar. But when your body had succumbed to exhaustion, your mind was stirred to greater heights, your thirst grew unquenchable. You fled the embraces of your wanton mistresses to stand sighing before the madonnas of Raphael. 'Who is that youth,' a pious and gentle dreamer asked on seeing you, 'who is so deeply moved by the pallor of marble statues?'

Like the mountain torrent I hear roaring in the darkness, you set out from your source, purer and clearer than crystal, and at first your waters only mirrored the whiteness of virgin snows. But, no doubt startled by the silence of solitude, you rushed on towards the steepest descents, plunged between terrifying reefs and, from the depths of chasms, your voice rose in a roar of harsh, frenzied delight.

From time to time you would be still, lost in some peaceful lake, glad to relax in tranquil waters and reflect the sky's serenity. Enamoured of every star that sought its image in your bosom, you bade to each a sad farewell when it sank beneath the horizon:

Linger an instant more among the lakeside reeds,
Star of love, descend not from the skies![11]

But idleness soon wearied you and you set off again on your breathless course among rocks with which you grappled hand-to-hand; and when you had overthrown them you departed in triumph and never noticed that, in falling, they blocked your way and inflicted deep wounds on your breast.

Then, at last, your proud, lonely heart discovered friendship. You deigned to trust someone other than your own haughty, unhappy self, and you sought peace and confidence in his affection. The mountain torrent lay becalmed under a cloudless sky; but its waters had collected so much rubble torn from its rugged banks that it could not easily grow clear again. Like the Brenta it remained troubled for a long time, and scattered barren sand and jagged rocks over the valley that lent it its blossoms and its shade. And so, for a long time, the new life you were trying to lead was troubled and tormented; and the memory of the vileness you had beheld came to poison with cruel doubts and bitter thoughts the innocent delights of your still apprehensive and suspicious soul.

Thus your body, as tired and enfeebled as your spirits, yielded once more to its former weakness and *like a lovely lily stooped to die*. God, resenting your rebellion and your pride, laid on your brow his angrily burning hand, and all at once your mind was in turmoil and you had lost your reason: the divine order which had once been established in your brain was overturned.[12] Memory, perception, all the lofty functions of the intellect, so acute in you, became disturbed and dispersed like clouds by a gust of wind. You sat up in your bed shouting: 'Where am I, O my friends? Why have you lowered me alive into the grave?'

The one faculty that survived all the others in you was your will; but it was a blind unruly will like an unbridled runaway horse racing across country. You were spurred on by a devouring restlessness; you brushed aside the restraining hand of your friend; you wanted to get away, to run; your strength could not be contained: 'Let me go!' you cried, 'Let me escape; don't you see that I am alive and young?' Where did you want to go? What visions appeared to you in the mists of your delirium? What heavenly spirits urged you to a better life? What secrets beyond human understanding did you perceive in your frenzied ecstasies? Tell me, do you still remember them? You endured the pangs of death; you saw the grave open to receive you; you felt the chill of the tomb and you cried out: 'Take me, Oh, take me out of this dank earth!'

Did you see nothing more? When, like Hamlet, you pursued the tracks of an invisible being, what haven were you seeking? What was the mysterious power you asked for help against the horrors of death? Tell me, Oh tell me, so that I may invoke it in your days of anguish, that I may summon it to be near you in your heartrending despair. It saved you, this unknown power, it snatched from you the shroud that was already about you. Teach me how to worship it and what sacrifices will propitiate it. Is it a gentle providence whom one hallows with hymns and offerings of flowers? Is it a sombre divinity who requires the total sacrifice of those who love you? Tell me in what temple, in what cave is its altar. When your heart aches I shall offer up my heart to it; I shall give it my life when yours is threatened.

*   *   *   *   *   *   *   *   *   *   *

The only power in which I believe is that of a just but paternal God: the power that inflicted suffering on every human soul and which, in return, revealed to mankind the hope of everlasting life. It is a Providence you have often underrated but to which you return in your hour of greatest joy or distress. It has been propitiated, it has granted my prayers, it has restored you to my affection; I can but bless it and be grateful. If you owe it a debt of gratitude for its mercy I shall pay it for you, here, in the silence of the night, in the solitude of these mountains, in the loveliest temple it has made available to man. Merciful and terrible God, hear my voice! It is not true that you have no time for men's prayers; you have enough time to bestow on each blade of grass its share of morning dew! You are infinitely solicitous of all your creatures; how would you forget the soul of man, your most intelligent, your most incomprehensible work? Hear then the voice of one who, in the wilderness, blesses you and, today as every day, offers up his life, yearning for the time when you will deign to accept it. This is no importunate beggar wearying you with his worldly wants but one, resigned and solitary, thanking you for the good as for the evil you have bestowed.

*   *   *   *   *   *   *   *   *

This is what made me turn back to the Veneto and postpone my expedition to the Tyrol till next week. I reached Oliero at about four in the afternoon, having covered sixteen miles on foot in ten hours, which was rather too much for a youth my size. I was still a bit feverish and my head was on fire. I lay down on the grass at the mouth of the cave and went to sleep. But I was soon awakened by the barking of a large black dog which I had some difficulty in placating. The sun had set behind the mountain peaks, the weather was turning mild and pleasant. The sky, ablaze with the most fantastic hues, gave a rosy flush to the snow. My hour's slumber had done me a world of good, my feet were no longer swollen, my mind was clear. I began to explore my surroundings; it was an earthly paradise, where nature's most delicate and most impressive wonders were combined. Let us hope we shall come here together.

When, proud as a conqueror, I had explored this enchanted place, I came back and sat down where I had slept, in order to savour the joy of my discovery. I had been two days wandering in the mountains without finding one of these spots, just suited to my taste, which abound in the Pyrenees but are rare in this part of the Alps. I had grazed my hands and knees trying to reach secluded places which never – though each had its peculiar charm – possessed the qualities I required at that moment. One seemed too wild, another too rustic. In one I felt too miserable, in another too cold, while yet a third bored me. It is hard to find a natural environment perfectly suited to our temperament. Usually the aspect triumphs over our mood and gives us new impressions, but when a mind is sick it resists the influence of time and place: it rebels against all things that are alien to its misery and cannot bear the fact that they are not in harmony with it.

I was worn out on reaching Oliero, and that is perhaps why I let my feelings get the better of me. It is certain that there, at last, I was able to give myself up to that leisurely contemplation which the least departure from our physical well-being can wholly destroy. Imagine a mountain nook covered in flowering thickets, criss-crossed by steep paths and gentle grassy slopes studded with rhododendrons, periwinkles and daisies. The walls of the gorge are hollowed out to form three grottoes, remarkable for the beauty of the colour and formation of the rock. One was used for many years by a band of assassins as a hide-out: another contains a little, gloomy lake which can be crossed by boat, and which is overhung by very fine stalactites. But it is one of those sights which, unfortunately, encourage the useless and intolerable tourist trade. Already I seem to see arriving, in spite of the snow that lies thick on the Alps, those insipid and monotonous faces which each summer brings back to intrude upon even the most sacred and solitary places: they are truly the scourge of our age, bent on altering with their presence the nature of all the countries of the world and ruining with their idle curiosity and idiotic questions the pleasure of contemplative walkers.

I went back to the third cave; it is the least spectacular and the most beautiful. It has no drama attached to it nor mineralogical singularities but a sixty-foot-deep spring under a rocky dome which opens onto the loveliest natural garden on earth, hemmed in by gracefully curved, richly overgrown hillocks.

Opposite the grotto, at the end of a vista of flowers and tender greenery strewn like a huge bouquet which fairy hands might have loosened and shaken over the mountain slope, there rises a magnificent giant, a perpendicular rock which time has fashioned in the shape of a citadel flanked by its towers and bastions. This enchanted castle, veiled in mist, adds a savage grandeur to the tender delicacy of the foreground. Contemplating this awesome peak from the depth of the grotto — seated by the spring between the underground chill of the rock and the warmth of the valley, my feet resting on a carpet of violets — all this was such a pleasure, such a delight that I would gladly have deprived myself of it to send it to you.

In the water some scattered rocks form stepping-stones right up to the centre of the cave. I reached the last and bent over the spring, a mirror as transparent and still as a block of emerald. I saw in its depths a pale face so calm that it frightened me. I tried to smile at it and it returned my smile with such indifference and bitterness that tears welled in my eyes and I stood upright so as not to see it. I remained erect on the rock.

Gradually I was overcome with cold. I felt that I too was turning to stone. Some fragment or other from an unpublished book came to mind: 'You too, old Jacques, you were once pure, solid marble and you came from God's hand as proud and flawless as the statue that emerges in its pristine whiteness from the workshop to step arrogantly onto its pedestal. But now time has eroded you like one of those weathered allegories left standing in abandoned parks. You are a most fitting ornament for the wilderness; why do you seem to weary of your solitude? Do you find the winter hard and the time long? You cannot wait for the moment when you will be dust again and no longer obliged to hold up your once proud head which the wind now buffets, and over which the damp has spread a mourning veil of dark mosses. Your splendour has been tarnished by so many storms that those who chance to pass by cannot tell whether, under your funereal drapes, you are marble or clay. Stay, stay in your nullity and count no more the days. You may yet last many years, wretched stone! You prided yourself once on your hard, indestructible substance; now you envy the lot of the dry reeds that snap in the storm. But frost splits marble. The cold will destroy you, put your faith in that!'[13]

I came out of the cave with a feeling of unspeakable sadness and, wearier than ever, lay down where I had formerly slept. But the sky was so clear, the air so invigorating, the valley so lovely, the luxuriant spring landscape so full of youthful, bursting life that I gradually began to revive. The colours were fading and the sharp outline of the mountains grew gentler in the mist that covered them like a blue gauze. A last ray of sunshine lingered on the cave's dome and fringed its lining of moss and hart's tongue with gold. Above my head, strands of ivy, twenty feet long, swayed in the breeze. A whole nest of robins clung, twittering, to these fragile fronds and let themselves be rocked by the wind. The stream that gushed from the cave kissed the primroses scattered along its edge as it passed them. A swallow flew from the depth of the cave and skimmed across the sky. It is the first I have seen this year. It soared towards the great rock on the horizon; but when it saw the snow it returned, like the dove to the Ark, and dived into its shelter there, to await the spring for another day.

I too began to think of seeking shelter for the night; but before abandoning the Oliero grotto and my trip to the Tyrol, before turning my face towards Venice, I tried to sum up my feelings.

I was no better off for it. I discovered a deplorable weariness in my soul and an even more deplorable energy; not a hope, not a desire – a terrible ennui; the ability to take every good or evil in my stride; too much despondency or idleness to seek or to avoid anything whatsoever; a physique which is as strong as an ox; a spirit, unquiet, sombre and questing, allied to a slothful and taciturn disposition, calm as the waters of this spring, which has not a ripple on its surface but which a grain of sand can set in turmoil.[14]

I don't know why, but any thought of the future upsets me intolerably. So I had to turn and look back at certain aspects of the past, and only then did I recover my calm. I thought of our friendship and was overcome by guilt at having allowed so much bitterness to invade my wretched heart. I recalled the joys and sorrows we had shared. Both are so dear to me that I began to sob like a woman when I remembered them.

Burying my face in my hands, I breathed in the scent of a sage-bush whose leaves I had fingered some hours earlier. That little plant was still blooming there on its mountain-side a few miles away. I hadn't tampered with it; I had carried off nothing but its delicious perfume. Why had it relinquished it? What a precious thing is a scent which, without depriving the plant that exhales it, can cling to the hand of a friend and follow him around on his travels, enchanting him and reminding him for hours to come of the beauty of the flower he loves. – Remembrance is the perfume of the soul. It is the heart's most delicate and sweetest quality which leaves it to cling to another heart and follow it everywhere. The affection of an absent friend is no more than a scent; but how sweet and agreeable it is, what heartening visions and dear hopes it brings to a downcast, wretched soul! Never fear, you who have left on my path this perfumed token, never fear, I shall not allow it to vanish. I shall fold it in my silent heart like a rare essence in a sealed flask. No one will breathe it but me and I shall raise it to my lips in my days of anguish to draw comfort and strength from it, in dreams of the past and oblivion of the present.

* * * * * * * * * *

I remember when I was a child how hunters would bring home, in the autumn, lovely, soft, bloodstained wood-pigeons. Those that were still alive were given to me to tend. I did so with all the love and tenderness a mother has for her children, and I managed to save a few. As they recovered their strength they began to resent their captivity and refused the green beans which they had greedily taken from my hands when they were still ailing. As soon as they were able to spread their wings they fluttered about in their cage, beating against the bars. They would have died of exhaustion and misery if I had not set them free. Besides, selfish as I was, I had learned to sacrifice the pleasure of possession to that of generosity. The day that I brought one of my wood-pigeons to the window was always one of keen emotions, of triumphant joy and invincible regret. I kissed it again and again. I begged it to remember me and come back to eat the tender beans from my garden. No sooner had I opened my hand than I closed it once more around my pet. With a heavy heart and tears in my eyes I kissed it a last time. Finally, with immense reluctance and effort, I set it on the window-sill. It would stay there motionless for some time, surprised and hardly daring to believe its good luck. Then it would take flight with a little cry of joy that pierced my heart. I followed it with my eyes for as long as I could; and when it had disappeared behind the rowans in the garden I cried bitterly and looked so depressed and unwell for the rest of the day that my mother would start to worry.

When we parted I was proud and happy to see you restored to health; I believed that my loving care had contributed somewhat to your recovery. I dreamt of happier days for you, a quieter life; I saw you young, loved and famous again. But when I had set you on the quayside and found myself alone in my gondola, black as a tomb, I felt as if my soul had departed with you. It was only a sickly, stupefied corpse that was left rocking in the wind on the stormy lagoon. A man[15] was waiting for me on the Piazzetta steps. 'Courage!' he said. 'Yes,' I replied, 'that's what you told me one night as he lay dying in my arms, and we thought he had no more than an hour to live. Now he is saved, he is on his way, he is going back to his country, his mother, his friends, his pleasures. That is good. But think of me what you will, I have still some yearnings for that dreadful night when his ashen face was resting on your shoulder and his icy hands were in mine. He was there between us and he is there no longer. You too are crying, though you shrug your shoulders. You see that your tears are no more rational than mine. He has gone, and that's how we wanted it; but he isn't here any more and we are broken-hearted.'

*　　*　　*　　*　　*　　*　　*　　*

Before going to bed I went out to smoke a cigar on the Bassano road. I wasn't more than a quarter of a mile from Oliero and it wasn't yet dark, but the road was already as deserted and silent as at midnight. All at once, to my surprise, I found myself face to face with a gentleman who looked much more respectable than I did. He was wearing a blue tail-coat, hussar boots and a Hungarian cap with a magnificent silk tassel dangling over his shoulder. He barred my path and addressed me in a mixture of broken German and Italian. Thinking he was asking for information about the village I pointed to the church spire, standing white above the dark valley, and simply said: 'Oliero.' But he continued his harangue in a mournful tone; I decided he must be begging. I couldn't possibly give less than a *svansic* to so smart a beggar, but neither was it in my power to be so lavish. At the same time I recalled the doctor's warning and I went my way. But, either because he had taken me for a capitalist in disguise, or because he found my blue cotton to his taste, he persisted in following me for some distance, carrying on his incomprehensible chatter in a dreadful accent that I didn't take to at all. This *monsu* carried a fine holly-wood staff in his hand, while I had nothing but a sprig of honeysuckle. The doctor's precise words were in my mind: 'Keep an eye on his stick!' – though I couldn't see what advantage there was in knowing exactly where the danger lay. I decided to try to think of something else and to whistle, while reciting to myself those profoundly philosophical words you once taught me, advising me to use them in moments of great stress: 'Music in the open is something extremely pleasant; the harp's harmonious strains' etc. I glanced over my shoulder and saw my German turn on his heel. Since I had no desire to cultivate his acquaintance, I went on walking in the direction of Bassano, whistling.

I had been frightened almost out of my wits. I am a coward by nature, though I am also rash; this is what made my tutor say that I was like a blackbird. I only believe in danger when it is upon me and I forget it as soon as it is over. No bird is more easily caught twenty times over in the same snare than I am; I circle round it tempting it with a light-heartedness that might well be taken for courage; but when I'm caught I behave no better than the next one. I have no shame in acknowledging the fact because I feel that someone who is only four foot ten inches tall doesn't have to be as stoical as Milo of Croton,[16] and because I've seen many a huge lout no bolder than me when in danger.

I retraced my steps to Oliero and, groping, found the spray of juniper overhanging the inn door. The first person I saw was my

German friend sitting by the fireside smoking a very fair pipe and waiting, his longing eyes glued to the spit, for the portion of lamb that he had ordered to be ready. On seeing me he got up and invited me to sit down beside him. I was rather embarrassed at the blunder I had made in taking such a well-bred person for a highway robber. We were served dinner at the same table – roast lamb for him, goat's cheese for me; a generous Asolo wine for him, pure spring water for me. After swallowing three mouthfuls – either because he wasn't hungry or because my elegant table-manners appealed to him – he asked me to share his meal, which I accepted without demur. Then, in an almost incomprehensible Venetian dialect, he jokingly reproved me for refusing to let him light his pipe from my cigar when we had met earlier on the road. I excused myself profusely and tried, inwardly, to make light of my scare; but despite his courtesy – maybe even because of it – there was something indefinably rascally about this gentleman that recalled *L'Auberge des Adrets*.[17] The landlord, while hovering round our table, stared suspiciously at each of us in turn. As I climbed up to my attic, convinced that I was about to brave all the dangers of a traditional Italian deathtrap, I overheard him say to the waiter: 'Mind the Tyrolese and the little *forestière*[18] (meaning me). Lock up the plates and put the keys of the linen-press under my pillow; chain the dog to the hen-house door and call me at the slightest noise.' '*Cristo!* Don't worry,' answered the waiter. 'The little fellow can't budge without my hearing him. I'll put the pitchfork under my bed and, *per Dio santo*, he'd better watch out if he thinks he can get away before daybreak!'

I took good note of his words and slept peacefully, well guarded from the Tyrolean rogue by this honest mountain lad who thought he was guarding his master's house from me.

When I woke up the Tyrolese had long since taken off and, despite the landlord, the waiter and the dog, he had left without paying his bill. There was some question of my being his accomplice and having to settle his account. I compromised and, since I had shared his dinner, I paid for half of it; after which I set out across the mountains.

*　　*　　*　　*　　*　　*　　*　　*　　*　　*　　*

That day I travelled through incredibly lonely and gloomy landscapes. I went at random, trying to head roughly for Treviso, but not really caring whether I covered three times more ground than was necessary or whether I spent the night under a juniper bush. I picked the hardest and least trodden paths. Sometimes they led me up to the very edge of the snow-line; at others they sank down into barren passes where no man seemed ever to have set foot. I love those wild, uninhabitable regions that belong to nobody, are hard to reach and even harder to get out of. I stopped in a rocky amphitheatre; no particular rock-formation, flora or fauna gave it its character which was, however, formidable, austere and desolate, not like any country in particular, though more like any other part of the world than Italy. I closed my eyes at the foot of a rock and let my mind wander. In a quarter of an hour I had circled the globe; and when I emerged from this feverish, brief slumber I thought I was in America, lost in one of those eternal wastes man has not yet reclaimed from nature. You can't imagine how real my vision seemed; I almost expected to see a boa-constrictor unwind its coils across the withered brambles, and the sound of the wind was like the cry of panthers roaming around the rocks. I crossed this wilderness, and there was not a thing on my way that did not fit into my dream; but, round a bend, I came upon a little sanctuary cut into the rock, with its madonna and its votive lamp which is carefully tended and relit every night by pious mountain people, even in the most remote solitudes. At the foot of the rustic altar there was a bunch of freshly cut cultivated flowers. This lamp still alight, the lowland flowers still fresh, many miles up in the arid, uninhabited mountains, were the offerings of a more touching and innocent faith than any I had ever known. Such sanctuaries or simple crosses generally mark the spot in these wildernesses where a violent death has occurred, either an accident or a murder. Close by this little madonna there was a steep precipice which had to be skirted in order to get out of the gorge. The lamp – if not the protection of the Virgin – must be a great help to nocturnal travellers.

. . . Some crazy idea, a passing illusion, a vision that flits through one's mind can totally change a mood, sweep a whole day's happiness or misery away. My journey in America had, in the space of a few minutes, unfurled a vast future before my eyes and when I came to, on the top of the Alps, I felt that I could take off from the earth and soar into infinity. The lovely plains of the Veneto, the Adriatic floating like a veil of mist on the horizon, were outworn conquests, something already behind me. It seemed that I only had to wish it and I would be on the summit of the Andes tomorrow. All the days of my past life faded away and merged into one. Thirty years of hardship were perfectly contained in the one word *yesterday*; that terrible word *today* which, in the Oliero cave, had seemed to betoken the frightful stillness of the grave, was erased from the book of my life. That loathsome energy, that stubborn ability to endure which had so depressed me stirred in me, active and violent, painful still, but as proud as despair. I trembled for joy and eagerness at the thought of being alone forever, as once I trembled at the thought of love, and I felt my will rise up to welcome a new stage in my life. – 'So this is where you have got to, is it?' asked an inner voice. 'Well then, get going, advance, learn.'

* * * * * * * * * *

At sunset I found myself on the crest of a ridge of rocks; it was here that the Alps ended. The Veneto was spread out beneath me, vast, breathtakingly bright and wide. I had emerged from the mountains, but at what point of the compass? Between the plain and the peak from which I overlooked it lay a charming little oval valley, nestling on one side against the foot of the Alps, on the other rising in terraces above the plain, and sheltered from the sea winds by a rampart of fertile hills. Just below me, a village was scattered in picturesque disorder down the mountain slope. The humble hamlet is surmounted by a large and beautiful marble temple,[19] quite new, dazzlingly white and set proudly on the brow of a hill. This monument seemed strangely human to me – it was as though it gazed down over Italy unfurled before it like a map, and dominated it.

A workman cutting marble straight out of the mountain-side informed me that the church, built on a pagan model, was the work of Canova, and that the village of Possagno below it was the birthplace of this great sculptor of modern times. 'Canova,' he added, 'was the son of a stone-cutter; he was a poor workman like myself.'

How many times the young labourer who was to become Canova would have sat on the very rock where now a temple to his memory is erected, his eyes wandering over a country that would award him so many garlands, over a world where his genius would reign peacefully supreme beside that other turbulent reign of Napoleon! Did he wish, did he hope for fame? Was it even in his thoughts? When his hand had cleanly cut a section of rock, did he know that from this same hand made for rough toil would emerge all the gods of Olympus, all the kings of the earth? Could he foresee the new breed of rulers that would ask for immortality from his chisel? When he looked with a young man's –

perhaps even a young lover's – eyes at the handsome, sturdy girls from his own village, could he ever have dreamt that the Princess Borghese[20] would pose for him naked?

The valley of Possagno is shaped like a cradle; it is made to the measure of the man who emerged from it. It might well have produced more than one genius, for in this beautiful countryside under so clear a sky it seems that there is nothing to restrict the mind's development. The crystal clarity of streams, the richness of the soil, the luxuriant vegetation, the beauty of the people in this part of the Alps and the superb perspectives the little valley commands from all sides seem expressly designed to nourish the highest faculties of the mind and excite the noblest aspirations. This kind of earthly paradise, where a budding intelligence can thrive in all its youthful vigour, this vast horizon which seems to invite deeds and projects for the future – are not these the two basic conditions for the unfolding of a great destiny?

Canova's life was fertile and generous, like the soil of his native land. Simple and sincere as a true mountain-dweller, he never ceased to be fondly attached to the village and the humble cottage where he was born. He had the latter unostentatiously improved and, every autumn, would come here to recover from his year's toil. He would then enjoy sketching the Herculean forms of the peasants and the truly Greek heads of the girls. The inhabitants of Possagno proudly assert that the main models for Canova's varied collection of sculptures came from this valley. Indeed, one has only to pass through it to find at every step the type of frigid beauty that characterizes Empire statuary. Yet the one feature marble cannot reproduce and which constitutes the main charm of these highland girls is their fresh complexions and transparent skin. To them, the well-worn metaphor of lilies and roses could apply without the slightest exaggeration. Their extremely clear eyes are of that indeterminate shade, between green and blue, which is peculiar to the stone called aquamarine. Canova loved the *morbidezza*[21] of their fair, abundant and heavy locks. He would do up their hair himself before sketching them, arranging their tresses according to the various styles of Greek statuary.

These girls usually have a sweet, innocent expression which, transferred to finer features and more delicate forms, must have inspired Canova's adorable head of Psyche.[22] The men have great heads with protruding brows, thick fair hair like the women, large, lively, bold eyes and short, square faces. There is nothing profound or refined about them, but they possess a directness and spirit reminiscent of classical huntsmen. Canova's temple is an exact replica of the Pantheon at Rome. It is built of fine white marble, veined with pink and russet, but fragile and already pitted by frost. Canova had the church erected with the philanthropic idea of attracting a large number of tourists and foreigners to Possagno, and thus providing for the poor mountain-dwellers a little money and trade. He meant it to be a sort of museum of his works. The church was to have housed the sacred products of his chisel and the upper galleries, the profane. He died before realizing his project, but left a considerable sum for this purpose. Despite the fact that it was his own brother, Bishop Canova, who was in charge of the work, the sculptor's last wishes have been carried out with remarkable stinginess or arrant dishonesty. The fabric, the marble shell of the church, was too far advanced for economies to be made, but they have responded most shabbily to the need to furnish the interior. Instead of the twelve colossal marble statues that were to have occupied the twelve niches in the cupola, there are twelve grotesque giants which an otherwise skilful painter is supposed to have botched in order to get his own back on the contractors for their sordid chicanery. Very little of Canova's sculpture decorates the interior of the monument. Some bas-reliefs, small but pure and elegant in design, are inserted round the side chapels; you saw them at the Academy of Fine Arts in Venice and you particularly admired one of them. There you also saw the group representing Christ's entombment, which is certainly Canova's least inspired conception. The bronze of this group is in the Possagno temple, as well as the tomb containing the sculptor's remains – a very simple and very beautiful Greek sarcophagus, executed according to his own design.

There is also an oil painting of Christ in winding sheets which decorates the high altar. Canova, who was the most modest of sculptors, prided himself on being a painter. He spent some years retouching this (mercifully) single product of his later years which his heirs would be better advised – out of affection for him and consideration for his reputation – to keep safely at home, hidden from public view.

*   *   *   *   *   *   *   *   *

I followed the Asolo road along a ridge of hills overgrown with fig trees. I feasted my eyes on this sumptuous perspective of the Veneto for some miles without ever feeling weary of its vastness, thanks to the varied foreground which descends in gradients of hillocks and ravines right down to the level of the plains. Crystalline streams meander and tumble amid gorges whose contours are bold without being harsh and whose profile changes at every turn in the road. The soil here produces the most delicious fruit in the whole of Italy and the climate is the healthiest. At Asolo, a village situated, like Possagno, on an Alpine slope at the mouth of a no less beautiful valley, I found a peasant, proudly perched on a cart drawn by four asses, who was about to leave for Treviso. I asked him if, for a modest fee, he would make room for me among the kids he was taking to market, and I reached Treviso the next morning, after sleeping in the friendly company of innocent beasts who would shortly succumb to the butcher's knife. This thought made me feel such an insuperable horror of their owner that I did not exchange a single word with him throughout the whole journey.

I snatched a couple of hours' sleep in Treviso, with a slight cold and fever; at noon I found a carrier who was setting off for Mestre and let me ride beside him. Catullo's gondola was waiting for me at the entrance to the canal. The doctor, sitting in the stern, was cracking Venetian jokes with this jewel among gondoliers. There was an unusual beam on the face of our friend. 'What's happened?' I enquired. 'Have you come into money? Has your rich uncle made you his doctor?'[23]

With a mysterious air he gestured to me to sit down beside him. Then he took out of his pocket a letter with a Geneva postmark. I turned aside after reading it to hide my tears. But when I looked again at the doctor I found him busy reading it himself. 'Don't mind me!' I said. He took no notice and simply went on; then he raised it to his lips with a passion and ardour which was totally Italian, and handed it back to me with no further excuse than, 'I've read it.'

We clasped hands, weeping. Then I asked if he had received any money for me. He answered with a nod. 'And when is your friend Zuzuf leaving?' 'On the fifteenth of next month.' 'Reserve a passage for me on his ship for Constantinople,[24] Doctor.' 'Yes?' 'Yes.' 'And will you come back?' he asked. 'Yes, I shall come back.' 'And he too?' 'He too, I hope.' 'God is great!' said the doctor, raising his eyes to heaven with an innocent yet emphatic expression. 'This evening we'll see Zuzuf at the café,' he added. 'In the meantime, where do you want to stay?' 'No matter where, my friend, since the day after tomorrow I shall be leaving for the Tyrol . . .'

Letter Two

I have told you many a time of a dream I often have; it always leaves me with a feeling of mingled joy and sadness when I wake up. At the beginning of this dream I see myself seated on a lonely shore, and a boat carrying a band of sweetly singing friends comes towards me on the fast flowing waters. These young people hail me, stretching out their arms, and I leap into the boat beside them. They say: 'We are going to . . .' (the land they name is unfamiliar), 'let's make haste to get there.' They abandon their musical instruments, they stop singing; and each one seizes an oar. We land . . . on what enchanted shore? I am incapable of describing it, yet I have been there twenty times over, I know it; it must exist somewhere on earth or on one of those planets whose pale light you are so fond of contemplating in the woods when the moon has set . . . We jump from the boat and scatter, running and singing, through the sweet-smelling thickets. Then everything vanishes and I wake up. This beautiful dream recurs again and again, but I have never been able to take it any further.

The strange thing about it is that, in real life, I have never set eyes on these friends who allure and captivate me. On awakening, my imagination can no longer conjure them up. I forget their features, their names, their ages and their number. Somehow I know that they are all young and beautiful; men and women alike are wreathed with flowers and their long hair floats about their shoulders. The boat is large and they fill it. They are not paired off in couples and seem all equally and indiscriminately bound to each other by some kind of divine love. Their songs and their voices are not of this world. Every time I have this dream I immediately recover the memory of the previous dreams in which I saw them; but only at that moment is it distinct, and on waking it blurs and disappears.

When the boat first appears on the waters I think nothing of it. I am not expecting it; I am unhappy and, very often, I am just sitting, dabbling my feet in the shallows. But this occupation is always pointless. As soon as I step on to the strand, my feet sink into the mire again and this fills me with childish despair. Then the boat appears in the distance; I hear the sound of far-off voices singing. Gradually they draw near and I know that they are the voices I love so much. Sometimes on waking I can still recall snatches of their songs but these bizarre phrases make no sense to my awakened consciousness. It would perhaps be possible, if I were to annotate them, to write the most fantastic poem of the century. But I would never do such a thing; I would be too afraid that by drawing inspiration from my dream I might transform or add anything to the faint memory I preserve. I long to know if dreams have a prophetic significance, if they foretell in some way what is to come in this world or in the next. Yet I prefer not to know, for it might detract from the pleasure of wondering.

Who are these unknown friends who come to summon me in my sleep and lead me joyously into the land of fantasy? Why can I never explore the enchanted landscape I glimpse from the shore? How is it that my memory retains every detail of my places of departure and arrival and is yet incapable of recapturing the features and names of those who accompany me? Why can I not draw aside in the daytime the magic veil that conceals them? Are they the souls of dead people? Are they the spirits of those I have ceased to love? Are they the vague shapes which will turn into new objects of worship? Or are they merely the colours blended on a palette by my imagination that cannot give up its activity even during its nightly repose?

I have often told you, on waking, when I have just returned from my unknown island and am still pale with emotion and longing, that I can find nothing in this world to compare with the deep affection these mysterious beings awaken in me or the joy I experience in finding them again. It is so keen that I am still physically aware of it when I wake up and cannot think of it for the rest of the day without a quickening of the pulse. They give me the impression of being so kind, so handsome, so innocent! I dwell, not on their features, but on their expressions, their smiles and the sound of their voices. They are so happy and invite me so tenderly to share their happiness! But what is it, this happiness of theirs?

I remember their words: 'Come,' they say, 'what are you doing on this lonely shore? Come, sing with us; come and drink from our cup. See, here are flowers, here are harps,' and they give me a strangely shaped instrument such as I have never seen before. But my fingers seem to have been long familiar with its workings, for I draw divine strains from it And they listen spellbound. 'Oh my friends, my loved ones,' I say to them, 'where have you been and why have you forsaken me for so long?' 'It is you,' they answer, 'who are always forsaking us. What have you done and where have you been since last we saw you? How old and tired you look, how muddy your feet are! Come and rest with us and recover your lost youth. Come to — where the moss lies like a velvet carpet on which we walk barefoot.' (No, that is not what they say. What they say is infinitely sweeter and so blurred in my memory I cannot recapture it.) And I am amazed that I have been able to live without them, and it is my real life that seems to me then like a half-forgotten dream. I go on asking them where they have been all this time. 'How have I been able,' I say, 'to live with other people, to have had other friends? What remote land did you withdraw into? And how could the memory of our friendship have been obliterated? Why did you not follow me into this world where I have been miserable? Why did I not think of searching for you there?' 'Because we were not there. Because we never go there,' they answer, smiling. 'Come this way, come this way with us.' 'Oh yes, yes! For ever!' I exclaim. 'Do not abandon me, my dear friends! Do not let me be carried off by the surge that always sweeps me away from you. Do not let me set foot ever again on this quicksand, into which I sink until I lose sight of you and I find myself in a different world with different friends who cannot be compared to you.' 'Shame on you!' they say, gently bantering. 'Shame on you for your folly and ingratitude! You are always longing to go there and when you come back you don't even recognize us any more.' 'Oh yes, I recognize you! Just now it seems I have never left you. You are there, young as ever, happy as ever,' and I name them one by one and they kiss me, calling me by a name I can't recall and which is not the name I answer to in the world of the living.[1]

This vision of a band of friends whose boat carries me off to happy shores has been with me since my earliest years. I can clearly remember seeing, as I fell asleep in my cot at the age of five or six, a group of beautiful children wearing garlands of flowers, who hailed me and invited me to join them in a giant seashell of mother-of-pearl floating on the water which carried me off to a marvellous garden. This garden was different from the imaginary shores of my island – as different as my childhood friends were from the friends of my dreams today. Instead of the tall trees, vast prairies, rushing torrents, wild flowers and plants of my present dreams, I saw then a symmetrical garden, with carefully tended lawns, diminutive flowering shrubs, perfumed fountains falling into silver basins, and blue roses in Chinese vases (I don't know why these blue roses seemed to me, at the time, to be the most desirable and amazing flowers). In fact, my childhood dream was like the fairy-tales with which my head was already crammed, though I usually embroidered my memories of them a little. Now my dream is drawn from the vast, virgin lands I thirst after, and peopled with the most ideal friendships and unattainable happiness.

At all events, the other evening I really did find myself in a rather similar situation to that of my dream – though it ended differently.

I was in the park towards sunset. As usual there were very few people about. Venetian ladies dread the heat and would not think of going out during the day; but they also dread the cold and do not venture out at night. There are about three or four days in the year that suit them to perfection, when they have the awning of their gondola raised; but they rarely take a step abroad. They are a species unto themselves, so delicate and fragile that a ray of sunshine mars their beauty, a breath of air puts their lives at risk. Civilized males on the other hand prefer to frequent places where there is a chance of meeting the fair sex – such as the theatre, the *conversazioni*, the cafés or the sheltered enclosure of the Piazzetta at seven in the evening; so that the only people one meets in the parks are a handful of grumbling old men, some senseless smokers or some bilious melancholics. (You can put me in which category you please.)

Gradually the place emptied and I was alone; and the smart café that juts out over the lagoon extinguished all its candles, set in holders of Murano crystal, in the shape of irises or seaweed. The last time you saw this park it was very damp and very dreary. As for me, I had not come here in search of happy thoughts and I had no hope of getting rid of my depression here. But the spring! As you say, who could resist the attractions of April? This, my friend, is doubly true in Venice. Even the stones grow green again; the great, polluted swamps our gondola shunned two months ago have become water-meadows, covered in cress, algae, rushes, gladioli and every kind of marine moss whose peculiar scent is quite irresistible to those who love the sea, where thousands of gulls, divers and bustards nest. Giant petrels skim incessantly over these floating meadows where the waters of the

Adriatic, renewed at each tide, deposit countless insects, madrepore and shellfish.

Instead of the icy alleys from which we fled together the day before you left and which I had not had the courage to revisit, I found warm sands, carpets of daisies, and sycamore and sumac copses burgeoning in the warm breeze that blows from Greece. The little promontory with its English garden is so pretty, so leafy, so full of flowers, scents and perspectives that I began to wonder if it was not the magic landscape of my dreams. But no! The promised land is devoid of suffering and this was already drenched with my tears.

The sun had already set behind the hills of Vicenza. Great purple clouds were passing over the Venetian sky. The tower of San Marco, the dome of Santa Maria and the nursery-garden of spires and steeples rising from every corner of the city stood out as black needles against the sparkling horizon. The sky turned by subtle gradations from cherry red to cobalt blue while the water, smooth and clear as a mirror, faithfully reproduced its infinite iridescence; it lay like a vast sheet of copper below the city. Never have I seen Venice more beautiful and enchanted. Its black silhouette, cast between the sky and the glowing waters as on to a sea of fire, seemed to be one of those sublime architectural aberrations the poet of the Apocalypse must have seen floating on the shores of Patmos as he dreamt of the New Jerusalem and likened it in its beauty to a newly wed bride.

Gradually the colours faded, the outlines became denser, the depths more mysterious. Venice began to look like a gigantic fleet, then like a wood of tall cypress trees into which the canals forced their way like high roads of silvery sand. At such moments I love to gaze into the distance. When outlines merge, when objects seem to tremble in the mist, when my imagination soars up into a limitless region of surmise and fancy, when I can, by half-shutting my eyes, turn a city upside-down and topsy-turvy, change it into a forest, a camp or a graveyard; when I can make gently flowing rivers out of dusty highroads and rushing torrents out of sandy paths that wind down dark green hills — then it is that I really enjoy Nature, I arrange it as I please, I reign over it, I take it in at a glance, I people it with my dreams.[2]

When I was a youth, still tending my flocks in the most peaceful and rural place in the world, I had grand visions of Versailles, Saint-Cloud, the Trianon and all the palaces my grandmother was always talking about as the most beautiful sights in the universe. I wandered down the country lanes at nightfall or in the first light of dawn and I conjured up, in large outline, the Trianon, Versailles and Saint-Cloud in the mists floating over our fields. A hedge of ancient pollarded trees bordering a ditch became a line of marble tritons and nymphs with seashells on their intertwined arms. The coppices and vineyards of our hillsides were parterres of yew and box; the walnut trees in our meadows cast the sumptuous shade of a royal park, and the smoke rising thinly from the roof of a cottage hidden among the trees, which traced a quivering bluish thread on the greenery, became in my eyes one of those grand fountains which the humblest citizen of Paris was able to see playing on festive days, and which was then, for me, one of the wonders of a fantastic world.

That is how, using my imagination to some purpose, I created on a vast scale exaggerated models of the trivial objects I was to see later. It is because of this tendency to use my brain as a magnifying glass that I have always, at first, found reality small and lacking in grandeur. It has taken time to accept it without contempt and, finally, to find in it specific beauties and things to admire other than those I sought. Yet I still love to adorn reality, however beautiful it may be. Such a tendency denotes neither the artist nor the poet, I know; it denotes the madman. You have often mocked me for it, you who admire purity of outline, boldly drawn contours and the rich splendour of light. You like to face beauty squarely, to feel and see what is there, to find out why and how nature is worthy of your admiration and devotion. I was explaining that to our friend the other evening as we passed together in a gondola under the sombre arch of the Bridge of Sighs. Do you remember the little light that glimmers at the far end of the canal and is reflected and multiplied in the shining weather-worn marble of Bianca Cappello's house?[3] There is not a more mysterious and melancholy canaletto in all of Venice. That single light shining on all things and lighting none, dancing on the water and seeming to play in the wake of a passing boat like a will-o'-the-wisp bent on pursuing it, reminded me of that long row of street-lamps quivering in the Seine and tracing fiery zigzags upon its waters. I told Pietro how one night I had wanted you to enjoy this aquatic fireworks, and how, after making fun of me, you greatly perplexed me by asking: 'What is beautiful about it?' 'Indeed,' said our friend, 'and why did you find it beautiful?' 'In the reflection of those lights,' I replied, 'I fancied I saw fiery pillars and cascades of sparks plunging out of sight into a crystal cave. The bank seemed to rest on and be supported by these shining columns, and I felt like jumping into the river to see what strange sarabands the spirits of the water were dancing with the spirits of fire in this enchanted castle.' The doctor shrugged his shoulders, and I realized that he had nothing but the profoundest scorn for such nonsense. 'I have no sympathy with fanciful notions,' he remarked. 'We have imported them from Germany; they have nothing to do with the true beauty the art and artists of ancient Italy pursued. In those days we had colour, we had form. Fantasy has passed a sponge soaked in northern mists over us. As for me,' he added, 'I am like your friend, I like to observe. Enjoy your dreams, if that's what pleases you.'

Once and for all I must beg your indulgence for my digressions, and I return to my evening in the park.

I was absorbed in my usual fantasies when I noticed on the canal San Giorgio, among the black specks with which it was dotted, one black speck that was swifter than the rest and had soon outstripped them all. It was young Catullo's brand-new gondola. As it drew near I recognized that flower among gondoliers wearing a nankeen jacket. This jacket had been the subject of a heated discussion that morning *a casa*.[4] The doctor wanted to get rid of it under the pretext that he had put on a little weight, and had intended it for his brother Giulio; but Catullo, arriving on the scene, begged for the doublet with irresistible grace. Cattina, my housekeeper, who found that the scapular[5] admirably became the gondolier's white, thick-set neck, declared that Signor Giulio had grown exceedingly in the last year and that the jacket would be too short for him. Thus Catullo, who is four times as big and fat as the two brothers put together, undertook to squeeze into a jacket that was too short for the one and too tight for the other. I cannot imagine how this Minotaur managed to do so without splitting it; but one thing is certain, and that is that I saw him appear on the lagoon in the doctor's summer garb. This sumptuous garment did, indeed, hinder the flow of his movements a little, and he lacked some of the usual elegance with which he balances himself on the prow. But before dipping his oar into the water's untroubled mirror he would cast from time to time a satisfied glance at his dazzling image, and, fascinated by his appearance, filled with gratitude for his patron's generosity, he would urge on the gondola with a vigorous stroke that made it skim over the surface like a wild duck.

Giulio was at the opposite end of the gondola and assisted with the ease of a true child of the Adriatic. Our friend Pietro was stretched lazily on the carpet and the lovely Beppa, seated on the black leather cushions, let the breeze play with the ebony locks she wears parted over her noble brow and falling in soft, careless ringlets to her breasts. Our mothers used, I believe, to call these two long curls, *repentirs*. This rather pretentious term came to my mind when I saw them framing Beppa's sad, passionate face. The boat slowed while one of the oarsmen got his second wind; and when it was close by the shady bank, it glided gently with the tide that lapped against the white steps of the park. Then Pietro asked Beppa to sing. Giulio took his guitar and Beppa's voice rose into the night like the amorous call of a siren. She sang a verse from a song Pietro had written for some woman or other – perhaps Beppa:

> *Con lei sull'onda placida*
> *Errai dalla laguna*
> *Ella gli sguardi immobili*
> *In te fissava, o luna!*
> *E a che pensava allor?*
> *Era un morrente palpito?*
> *Era un nascente amor?*[6]

'Why, there you are, Zorzi!' she cried on seeing me, above the steps. 'What are you doing, you wretch, all alone and miserable? Come and have coffee with us at the Lido.' 'And have a smoke of a good carob-wood pipe,' added the doctor. 'And take my place at the oar,' said Giulio. 'Giulio,' I replied, 'thanks for the offer! As to the doctor, all his pipes are not worth one of my cigarettes. But what excuse can I make to you, sweet Beppa?' 'Then come,' she said. 'No,' I answered. 'I'd rather confess to being unsociable and stay where I am.' 'Shame on you for being such a bore!' she said, throwing her wilting posy in my face. 'Will you never get any more civil? And why don't you want to come with us?' 'How can I tell?' I replied. 'I have no wish to do so, and yet I am as happy as can be to have met you.'

Catullo, who like all domestic animals of his ilk, tends to butt into every conversation and give his advice, shrugged his shoulders and said to Giulio with a knowing look: '*Foresto!*'[7] 'Precisely!' answered Giulio. 'Did you hear, Zorzi? Catullo here is treating you like an eccentric invalid.' 'Never mind,' I said. 'I shan't join you. You are too lovely this evening, Beppa; the doctor is too tedious; I cannot bear the sight of Catullo's jerkin and Giulio is worn out. After a quarter of an hour's bliss Beppa's eyes would drive me mad and I might compose for her a poem as bad as the doctor's; then the doctor would be jealous. Catullo can't fail to die of apoplexy before reaching the Lido, and Giulio would force me to row. So good night, my friends; you are lovely as the moon and swift as the wind; your boat has come to me like a sweet vision; go away quickly before I discover that you are not immortal!'

'What's he eaten today?' Beppa enquired of her companions. '*Erba*,'[8] the doctor replied solemnly. 'You have guessed right, O my great Aesculapius!' I said. 'Green peas, salad and fennel. I had what you call a Pythagorean meal.' 'A very healthy diet,' he answered, 'though not substantial enough. Come and have some rice and oysters with me and we'll drink a bottle of Samos at the Quintavalle.' 'Go to the devil, you poisoner!' I said. 'You would like to stupefy me with indigestible food and take the sting out of my temper with sweet wine, till you see me stretched out on the carpet like an old spaniel back from the hunt, and you won't need to blush for your own excesses and slothfulness, you Venetian.' 'And what do you expect to do in Venice if not *farniente*?'[9] asked Beppa. 'How right you are, *benedetta*,'[10] I answered, 'but you can't guess how enjoyable my *farniente* is here where I am, looking at you! You can't imagine the pleasure I have in seeing this gondola glide by without any effort on my part. I feel as if I were sleeping and having a dream which is very dear to me, my Beppa, in which mysterious beings appear to me in a boat and pass on their way singing, like you.' 'Who are these mysterious beings?' she asked. 'I don't know,' was my reply. 'They are not human, for they are too beautiful and too good; and yet they are not angels, Beppa, since you are not among them.' 'Come and tell me about them,' she said, 'I dote on dreams.' 'Tomorrow,' I said. 'Today give me back the illusion of my dream. Sing, Beppa, sing with that lovely throaty voice of yours that can also be as clear and pure as the ring of crystal; sing in that indolent tone that can become so passionate and reminds me of a lazy odalisque gradually pushing aside her veil and finally throwing it off to plunge, white and naked, into a scented bath; or perhaps a sylph, slumbering in the fragrant twilight mists, who slowly spreads her wings to soar with the sun into the flaming sky. Sing, Beppa, sing, and go your way. Tell your friends to move their oars like the wings of some sea bird, and to carry you off in your gondola like a white Leda on the tawny back of a wild swan . . . Go, romantic girl, pass on and sing; but know that the breeze lifts the folds of your black lace Mantilla, and that the rose your lover's hand has stealthily concealed in your hair will shed its petals one by one if you are not careful. Thus love too forsakes us, Beppa, when we believe it is safely guarded in the heart of the one we love.' 'Farewell, I leave you to your melancholy,' she retorted. 'That should cheer you! But to punish you I'll sing in dialect and you won't understand a word.' I smiled at Beppa's claim to make her dialect unintelligible to a pair of French ears. I listened to the barcarole that was indeed written in the sweetest words of that gentle Venetian speech which seems to be made for the lips of children:

Coi pensieri malinconici
No te star a tormentar.
Vien con mi, montemo in gondola
Andremo in mezo al mar.

Pasaremo i porti e l'isole
Che contorna la città:
El sol more senza nuvole
E la luna nascarà.

. . . .

Co, spandendo el lume palido
Sora l'aqua inarzentada,
La se specia e la se cocola
Como dona inamorada.

Sta baveta che te zogola
Sui caveli inbovalai,
No xe torbia de la polvere
Dele rode e dei cavai.

Sto remeto che ne dondola
Insordirne no se sente
Come i sciochi de la scuria,
Come i urli de la zente.

. . . .

Te xe bella, ti xe zovene
Ti xe fresca come un fior;
Vien per tuti le so lagreme,
Ridi adeso e fa l'amor.

. . . .

In conchiglia i greci, Venere,
Se sognava un altro di;
Forse, visto i aveva in gondola
Una bela come ti.[11]

The night was so calm and the water so resonant, that I was able to hear the last verse distinctly, although it was wafted to my ears like the mysterious farewell of a soul lost in space. When I could no longer hear anything I began to feel sorry I was not with them. But I found some comfort in the thought that, had I gone, I would by now be repenting.

There are days when it isn't possible to live with one's kind, when everything inclines one to spleen, everything turns one's thoughts to suicide; and there is nothing sadder in the world, and nothing more ridiculous, than a poor devil procrastinating with his last hour, parleying with it for weeks and years like the man in Shakespeare[12] with his revenge. People make fun of him. They gather round him to watch him and shout out, like the spectators around a clumsy clown who doesn't dare burst the balloon: 'He'll do it! He won't!' . . . And they are right to laugh at someone who can neither put up with them nor do without them, who doesn't want to give up life and doesn't want to accept it as it is. They take their revenge on him for the ennui he has the impertinence to feel and to show. But theirs is a hard justice. They do not know how much suffering and misfortune has been required to bring even a moderately proud and steadfast nature to such an unseemly predicament.

My advice to anyone who might find himself either chronically or accidentally in such a state is to eat frugally so as to avoid the irritation of the brain caused by a difficult digestion, and to stroll by himself at the water's edge, his hands in his pockets and a cigar in his mouth, for a period of time that will vary according to the power and tenacity of his indisposition.

I came home at midnight to find Pietro and Beppa singing in the *galeria*. It is Giulio who has dignified the ante-chamber with this pretentious title by hanging on its walls four oil paintings[13] in which the sky is green, the water russet, the trees blue and the earth rose-coloured. The doctor hopes he can make a fortune by selling them to some imbecile Englishman, and Giulio hopes to have the name of our *palazzo* included in the new edition of the *Traveller's Guide to Venice*. In order, no doubt, to get inspiration from the sight of woods and mountains, the doctor has had the little piano on which he has the habit of improvising installed under the landscape most begrimed with smoke. The hours in which the doctor improvises are the most blissful of the day for every one of us. Beppa sits at the piano and languidly picks out with one hand a little tune that serves as a theme for the doctor's extempore lyrics. Thus in a single morning thousands of stanzas take wing while I fall into a profound slumber in the hammock; Giulio rests astride the balustrade of the balcony at the risk of falling into a passing boat and waking up in Chioggia or Palestrina; Beppa, for her part, lets her long black lashes droop onto her pale cheeks and her hand goes on playing automatically while her mind sinks through clouds of sleep into dreams of love, and the cat, rolled into a ball on a pile of scores, emits from time to time a bored and plaintive miaou.

On this particular night Beppa was alone with Pietro and Vespasiano (as the cat is called). 'What a miracle!' I exclaimed as I came in. 'How have you managed to stay up so late?' 'We were worried,' the doctor said reproachfully as the last rhyme expired *amorosa*[14] on his lips. 'You know very well that we cannot sleep till you have come home.' 'Well, of all things!' I replied. 'Your concern bothers me, my friends. Now I am obliged to feel guilty for your insomnia when I thought I was only taking an innocent stroll!' 'My dear,' said Beppa, seizing my hand, 'we have a request to make of you.' 'Who could deny you anything, Beppa? Speak!' 'Give me your word of honour that you will not go out after dark any more!' 'There you go again with your exaggerated solicitude, Beppa. You treat me like a four-year-old child when I am older than your grandfather.' 'You are surrounded by danger,' she said, with that little touch of declamatory sentimentality that so becomes her. 'The woman[15] who pursues you is capable of anything. If you value your life just a little for our sakes, Zorzi, stay indoors or leave this country for some time.'

'Doctor,' I said, 'be good enough to take our Beppa's pulse. She is certainly feverish and a bit delirious.'

'Beppa over-estimates the danger,' he admitted. 'Besides, whatever it might be, it could not force a man to do something as ridiculous as to flee from a woman's anger. However, there are certain threats of revenge in this country which you shouldn't take too lightly, and it would be wiser to avoid walking alone late at night through the more deserted and dangerous quarters of Venice.'

'Dangerous!' I replied shrugging my shoulders. 'How you exaggerate! My poor friends, you are working yourselves into a frenzy to preserve your national reputation; but try as you will, you are no longer anything, not even assassins! There is not a woman amongst you capable of touching a dagger without swooning away, just like any fine Parisian lady, and you would have to search for a long time before you could find a hired assassin prepared to carry out a murder plan, even if you were ready to reward him with all the treasures of San Marco.'

The doctor made that imperceptible gesture with one finger which in Venice serves to express so much and which awoke my curiosity. 'Come,' I said, 'what have you to say to that?' 'I say,' he replied, 'that I can find you in less than twelve hours, and for the modest sum of fifty francs at most, an excellent hired assassin capable of administering to whomsoever you wish as good a *coltellata*[16] as was ever struck in the Middle Ages.'

'Many thanks, Maestro,' I said. 'Yet a *coltellata* seems to me to be so romantic and so well suited to the latest fashions that I would gladly receive one, even if it kept me in bed for three days.'

'You French make fun of everything,' he grumbled, 'and you are no better than the rest when faced with danger. As to us, though our skill in the art of wielding a knife has happily deteriorated, there are still amateurs who cultivate it, and there is no danger of it disappearing completely like the other arts.'

'Would you have me believe that it constitutes part of a dandy's education?'

'It is part of nobody's,' he replied with a touch of complacency. 'However, the Venetian hand has a certain natural dexterity that enables it to become expert in a very short time. Come, let us have a try.' He went and took from his desk an ugly little old dagger; then, opening the door to my room, he took up a position about ten yards away from the target, which was a wafer stuck to the furthest wall and lit by strategically placed candles. He was handling the dagger carelessly, as though it were the least of his preoccupations. 'You see,' he said, 'this is how it is done: one hand in your pocket, a glance at the weather and whistling a snatch of an opera, you pass at a distance from your man without anybody being the wiser; hardly moving your arm, you cast your dart. Look! Did you see?'

'I see, Doctor,' I said, 'that your wig has fallen on to Beppa's lap and that the cat has fled in terror. When you decide to play your dagger game seriously you had better make sure that such comical incidents don't give you away.' 'But the dagger,' he said, quite unperturbed and without attempting to retrieve his wig, 'where, I ask you, is the dagger?' I looked at the target: the dagger was indisputably stuck into the wafer.

'Good Heavens!' I exclaimed. 'Is that how you bleed your patients, my dear doctor?'

'It is true I lost my wig,' he said triumphantly; 'but then I was dealing with a solid oak door which is undoubtedly harder to penetrate than the breastbone, abdomen or heart of a man. As regards women,' he added, 'beware of those who are fair-skinned, small and blonde. There is a certain type of woman that has not changed. When you come across one whose iris is deep blue and the colour in her cheeks comes and goes, either see to it that she has nothing against you or else refrain from serenading her under her balcony.'

*　　*　　*　　*　　*　　*　　*　　*　　*　　*

You can't imagine what Venice is like at present, my friend. When you saw those ancient pillars of Greek marble whose colour and shape reminded you of bleached bones, she hadn't yet discarded the mourning drapes she puts on in the winter. Now the spring has blown an emerald dust over all that. The base of the *palazzi*, where oysters used to cling to stagnant moss, are covered in mosses of tender green, and the gondolas glide between two carpets of velvety, beautiful verdure, while the sound of the waves languidly dies away in the foam of their wake. All the balconies are covered with vases of flowers, and the flowers of Venice, planted in a warm soil and blossoming in a humid atmosphere, have a freshness, rich texture and languid air which makes them resemble the women of this clime, whose beauty is as dazzling and as shortlived. Brambles twine around each pillar and hang their garlands of tiny pink and white rosettes from the black wrought-iron balconies. Irises smelling of vanilla, tulips from Persia so delicately striped in red and white that they might be made of the very stuff used for the costumes of Venetians of old, roses from Greece and pyramids of gigantic campanula cluster in pots all along the balustrades; sometimes an arbour of honeysuckle with garnet-red flowers crowns the whole balcony from end to end, and in two or three green cages hidden among the leaves, nightingales sing night and day as in open country. The vast population of caged nightingales is a luxury peculiar to Venice. The women are remarkably skilled and successful in the difficult training of these poor captive songsters, and know how to ease the boredom of their confinement with all sorts of delicacies and refinements. At night one hears these birds calling and answering each other from side to side of the canals. When a serenade floats by they all keep quiet and listen, but as soon as it has passed they start singing again, and seem bent on surpassing the harmonies they have heard.

At every street corner a Madonna shelters her mysterious little light under a canopy of jasmine; and from the *traghetti*[17] shaded by great trellises, the sweetest of all natural perfumes, that of the flowering vine, is wafted over the Grand Canal.

These *traghetti* are the stations for the public gondolas. The *facchini*[18] congregate in those on the banks of the Canalazzo where they chat and smoke with the gondoliers. These gentlemen are often grouped there with a certain theatrical effect. While one lies on his gondola yawning and smiling up at the stars another stands on the bank, dishevelled, defiant, his hat set rakishly on a mop of long curls, casting his huge shadow on the wall. This particular gondolier is the daredevil of the *traghetto*. He frequently makes expeditions at night to the neighbourhood of Canareggio in a boat in which no passenger would dare to venture, and sometimes when he comes back in the morning his head is slashed by an oar-stroke he says he has received in a tavern. His family sets great store by him and his chest is decorated with holy images, relics and rosaries that his wife, his mother and his sisters have had blessed to protect him from the dangers of his nocturnal trade. Despite his exploits he is neither a braggart nor insolent. No Venetian ever lacks prudence. The boldest smuggler will never say a word too many even in front of his best friend; and when he chances on the very guard who fired at him the previous night, he will discuss the night's events with him so coolly and collectedly he might have known of them only through hearsay. At his side is a surly old man who knows more than all the rest put together, and whose voice has grown hoarse from shouting across the canals those words from an unknown tongue, derived perhaps from Turkish or Armenian, which gondoliers call out to each other to avoid colliding in the dark or round a bend in the canal. Stretched on the pavement like a resentful hound, he has, in his time, witnessed the glories of the Republic; he used to row the last Doge's gondola and was one of the crew on the Bucentaur.[19] He will reminisce about great fairy-tale festivities whenever he gets a hearing, but if he suspects that he will not be listened to with due respect, he retires into

78

a profound disdain for present-day matters and studies the holes in his jacket philosophically, thinking of the days when he wore the many-coloured silk jerkin, floating scarf and feathered biretta of the ducal uniform. Three or four others stand close together before the Madonna; they seem to be discussing some weighty problem; one might almost take them for a group of bandits planning a murder on the *Terracina*. In fact they are about to indulge in one of their more innocent pastimes, that of singing in chorus. The *tenore*, who is usually a fat, jolly fellow with a full, high-pitched voice, opens with a falsetto from the top of his head and the back of his nose. It is he who, according to their pithy expression, 'gloves' the note and sings the first verse on his own. One by one the others join in, and the bass, huskier than a bull with a cold in its head, attacks the three or four notes that constitute his part, but which he pitches to perfection and which are undoubtedly most effective. As a rule the bass is a tall, lean, bronzed youth with solemn and supercilious features – one of the four or five physical types of which, in Venice as everywhere else, the population is composed. His is perhaps the least common, the handsomest and the most untypical. The pure insular blood of the lagoons produces the type Gozzi describes as *bianco, biondo e grassotto*.[20] Robert[21] will probably select for the picture he is now painting in Venice the best examples of all the different types, and give us a simultaneously poetic and true idea of this distinguished race.* His colours, ground in the hot sunshine of southern Italy, will doubtless undergo a change in Venice and their harsh, blinding warmth will be toned down. Happy the man who can turn his impressions and memories into lasting moments!

The songs that echo at night through the public places of the city are taken from every possible Italian opera, ancient or modern; but they have been so distorted and restructured to suit the vocal range of those who borrow them that they are now local products and most composers would be ashamed to acknowledge them. Our medley-

---

* In his beautiful painting of *Venetian Fishermen*, Robert has not portrayed a single individual from the pure native race. He went to Chioggia, got Chioggians to sit for him, and has depicted some examples of an extremely handsome race, sturdy, wiry, dark and serious but in no way Venetian. The Chioggia peninsula, close by Venice, is inhabited by a colony which is probably of Greek or Asiatic extraction. They intermarry but rarely mix their blood with that of the Venetian population.

makers will stop at nothing! A cavatina by Bellini is instantly transformed into a four-part chorus. A Rossini chorus is adapted for two
voices in the middle of a duet by Mercadante; and the refrain of an old
barcarole by an unknown composer, adapted to the solemn tempo of a
church anthem, becomes the quiet finale of an abridged canticle by
Marcello. But the musical instinct of these people can make the most of
any monstrosity and link mutilated fragments with such skill that the
seams are often hard to detect. Their method consists in simplifying
every piece of music and divesting it of ornament – which doesn't make
it any the worse. These ardent dilettanti, untutored in musical nota-
tion, store in their memories all the snatches of tunes they can get hold
of outside a theatre or under the balcony of a great *palazzo*. They stitch
them together, with other scattered bits they have got elsewhere, and
the more experienced, those who preserve the traditions of contrapun-
tal singing, control the tempo of the whole. This tempo is a relentless
adagio to which even Rossini's most brilliant fantasies have to submit;
and it would indeed almost make me believe those who assert that music
has no character of its own but can be made to express every possible
situation and mood, according to the measure the players choose to
impart to it. It is the widest and freest sphere available to the imagination, and the composer is much more liable than the painter to create
for others effects that may be very different from those he intended for
himself. The first time I heard Beethoven's Pastoral Symphony I was
unaware of its true subject-matter and to this enchanting harmony I
made up in my head a poem in the manner of Milton. At the very point at
which the composer makes the quail and the nightingale sing, I had set
the fall of the rebellious angel and his last cry to heaven. When I learnt
of my mistake I revised my poem at the second hearing, and it turned
out to be in the manner of Gessner, my response being readily attuned
to the impression Beethoven had meant to create.

The absence of carriages and horses and the sonority of the canals
make Venice the perfect city for unending songs and *aubades*. It may be
something of an overstatement to say, as I have heard certain enthusi-
asts assert, that the choruses of *facchini* and gondoliers are superior to
those of the Paris Opera House, but there is little doubt that one such
chorus, wafted from afar to the ears of a stroller under the arches of a
moon-blanched Moorish palace, gives more pleasure than better music
performed against the stage set of a painted colonnade. These rude
amateurs bellow in tune and measure; cold marble echoes prolong their

grave, rough harmonies across the waters like a sea breeze. Such enchanting acoustical effects, combined with the need to fill the silence of our magical nights with some kind of harmony, make for indulgent, almost grateful, listening to the humblest little song that makes its way to us, passes and is lost in the distance.

When we arrive in Venice and a well-groomed gondolier in his cloth jerkin and round cap comes to wait for us at the door of the inn, it is hard to see a trace in him of that elegance which they had in Venice's splendid past. Nor would it be apparent under the rags of those gondoliers who assume a more picturesque disarray. But the sharp, penetrating, subtle wit of this famous caste has not entirely vanished. As a rule their features have a kind of bland delicacy that might, at first sight, be taken for kindly cheerfulness but which masks a mordant sarcasm and a deep-rooted craftiness. The main characteristic of these men – as of the whole Venetian race – is still what it has always been: prudence. In no other place are there more words and fewer deeds, more quarrels and fewer blows. These *barcaroles*[22] are masters in the art of slinging insults; but it is not often that they come to fisticuffs. Two gondolas meet and knock into each other round a bend because one of the oarsmen is clumsy and the other inattentive. They both wait in silence for the crash which can no longer be avoided; their first care is for the boats: when they have both made sure that neither has been damaged, they begin to measure each other up while the boats float apart. Then the discussion starts. 'Why didn't you shout *siastali*?'* 'I did!' 'No!' 'Yes, I did!' 'I bet you didn't, *corpo di Bacco!*' 'I swear I did, *sangue de Diana!*'[23] 'Do you call that a voice!' 'What have you got ears for?' 'Where do you do your boozing to get such a voice?' 'What kind of a donkey was your mother dreaming about when she was expecting you?' '*Your* mother was a cow and should have taught you how to bellow!' '*Your* mother was a donkey and should have given you the right kind of ears!' 'What's that you say, you son of a bitch!' 'What's that you say, you son of a trollop!' Gradually tempers rise and continue to do so as the two antagonists drift further and further apart. When they have set a couple of bridges between them the threats begin: 'Just come a bit closer and I'll show you what my oars are made of!' 'Just you wait, you

---

* The gondoliers' *stali*, which I believe to be a relic of the lingua franca spoken by the Turkish gondoliers, once fashionable in Venice, means 'to the right'; *siastali* means 'to the left'.

ugly oaf, and I'll sink your nut-shell by spitting on it!' 'If I sneezed near your eggshell it would be blown away!' 'Your gondola could do with a bath at the bottom of the sea to wash off the worms that are eating it!' 'Yours must be full of cobwebs since you pinched your woman's petticoat to line it with!' 'Curse the Madonna of your *traghetto* for not sending the plague to get rid of the likes of you!' 'If the Madonna of your *traghetto* weren't the Devil's whore you'd have drowned long ago!' And so from metaphor to metaphor they indulge in the most hair-raising curses; but luckily their voices are lost in the distance by the time they are ready to cut each other's throats and their insults continue for a long time after the two opponents have ceased to hear each other.

Nowadays the gondoliers of private establishments wear rounded cotton jackets printed in various colours. A jacket with a grey-green pattern on a white ground, white trousers, a red or blue sash and a black velvet cap with a tassel hanging over one ear, Chioggia-style, is a typical example of an elegant gondolier's uniform. Some fashionable youths still wear it when they amuse themselves in taking out their little boats on the canals. Once upon a time such an exercise was the equivalent of horse-riding for young Parisians. They preferred to navigate the narrower canals, where they could be closely overlooked and admired by the young girls at their windows. And even today they can occasionally be seen. Every evening two such dandies ply the waters of our own canaletto with remarkable speed and power. I do believe that they are rather attracted by the charms of Beppa on the balcony, and that one of them hopes she may find him to her taste. He stands perched at the prow – the most dangerous and honourable position – and the boat scarcely moves out of her field of vision. I must admit that there are not many professional gondoliers who could teach these two performers anything worth learning. They propel their skiff like an arrow and I doubt if a well-mounted rider could keep up with them alongside on the bank. The major feat – and one which our amateurs perform very adequately – consists in launching the boat at full speed towards the side of the bridge and stopping it dead just as the bow is about to touch. It is a skilful, daring game and one whose disappearance I would regret more than that of all the wealth and luxury of Venice. As long as vigour of body and mind is not lost, there is no cause for despair. Besides, it is not too bad a way of attracting a woman's attention. I would not be surprised if Beppa looked with a favourable eye upon this tall, fair, brightly clad youth who, poised on the tip of his slender *barchetta*, seems at every minute about to be dashed to pieces with it and, twenty times in a quarter of an hour, overcomes a danger he risks for the sole purpose of obtaining a single glance from her. Beppa claims that she doesn't even know the colour of his eyes. Hmm! Beppa!

All amateurs are not as lucky as these. Woe betide those who fail in front of the ladies stationed at their windows and the gondoliers congregated on the bridges to cast their verdict! The other day two gallant citizens, boasting half a century each and given over for at least ten years to the pleasant occupation of cultivating their obesity, decided to challenge each other in a regatta for some unknown reason. Presumably each had taken it into his head to boast of youthful exploits, and vanity then played its part. At any rate these two honest bachelors had invited their friends to place their bets. At the appointed time gondolas gathered on the battlefield. The backers, together with a crowd of dilettanti and idlers, flocked to the banks and onto the neighbouring bridges. The two rival boats advance, and the two champions rise slowly and majestically to their feet, each in the prow of his boat. Ser Ortensio proudly steps forward and seizes his oar with vigour. But before Ser Demetrio has time to do likewise, either by spite or misadventure, one of the spectators' boats happened to nudge his ever so slightly, and the worthy, losing his balance, fell heavily into the water like a willow uprooted by the storm. Luckily the canal was not deep. Ser Demetrio found himself up to his neck in lukewarm water and up to his knees in mud. You can imagine the laughter and boos of the spectators, amongst whom were a good number of sharp-tongued gondoliers. Ser Demetrio's friends hastily pulled him out; he was bathed and tucked up in a warm bed and his housekeeper spent the rest of the day plying him with cordials. In the meantime his opponent, unanimously acknowledged the winner, went to Santa Margherita to eat a splendid meal paid for with the prize money and donations from the backers of both parties.

As for the freelance gondolier, he owns nothing but a pair of trousers, a shirt, a pipe and sometimes a little black poodle who swims beside the gondola as nimbly and tirelessly as a fish. The gondolier has the Madonna of his *traghetto* tattooed with a red-hot needle and some gunpowder on his chest, and on each arm one of his patron saints – the male on one arm and the female on the other. Unlike our cab drivers, he is not for hire by all and sundry at any hour of the day and night. He only takes orders from the chief of his *traghetto*, a simple gondolier like himself elected by vote and approved by the police, who decides the days he will be on call. For the remainder of his time each gondolier earns his living as he likes and, when a couple of fares in the morning have taken care of his meals and his pipe for that day, he goes to sleep in the warm sunshine, oblivious to those who pass (were the Emperor himself among them) and deaf to any proposal which requires effort. True, his duties are more strenuous than those of driving two peaceful horses from a seat on the top of a cab. But he is also more carefree by nature and more independent. Pliant, fawning and mercenary when his stomach is empty, he has as little time for the customer who haggles over his fare as for the one who overpays him. He can be drunken, free-and-easy and rascally – that is to say that he would not dream of touching your scarf, umbrella, wrapped parcels or unopened bottles; but if you leave him alone with an uncorked bottle or a pipe, you will come back to find him savouring your wine and smoking your tobacco as calmly as if he were doing no more than what was expected of him.

* * * * * * * * * *

No one has ever done justice to Venice's incomparable skies and exquisite nights. The lagoon is so still on a fine evening that the stars stare up from it unblinking. When one is in its midst it is so blue, so even, that the eye cannot distinguish the horizon, and water and sky merge in a single azure veil where reverie is lost in slumber. The air is so transparent and pure that five hundred thousand more stars are visible than in our northern climes. Here I have seen starlit nights when the silver-white of the stars took up more space in the dome of the heavens than the ethereal blue. It was a seed-bed of diamonds diffusing almost as much light as the moon in Paris. Not that I wish to speak ill of our moon; she is a pale beauty whose wistfulness has perhaps a greater appeal for the intellect than this. The misty nights of our temperate provinces have charms which no one has appreciated more than I have nor is less ready to deny. Here nature, with its more vigorous impact, tends to impose perhaps too much silence on the mind. It inhibits thought, perturbs the heart and dominates the senses. No one but a genius should think of writing during those voluptuous nights: they are for love or sleep.

As for sleeping, I know a delightful place: the white marble steps that lead from the Viceroy's gardens to the canal. When the golden gates on the garden side are closed, a gondola will take you to these flagstones that are still warm from the setting sun, where no importunate stroller will disturb you, unless the faith that Saint Peter lacked moves him to follow in your footsteps. I have spent many a solitary hour there, thinking of nothing at all, while Catullo and his gondola slept, a whistle-call away, in the midst of the waters. When the midnight breeze skims over the lime trees and scatters their blossoms on the waves, when the scent of geraniums and gillyflowers wafts upwards as though the earth breathed out perfumed sighs under the moon's gaze; when the domes of Santa Maria lift their alabaster hemispheres and turban-crowned spires to the skies, when all is white – water, sky and marble, the three elements of Venice – and when from Saint Mark's tower a great bronze voice soars above my head, I start to live through my pores alone, and woe betide any one who would try to appeal to my mind! I vegetate; I relax; I forget. And who would not do the same, in my place? How can you expect me to bother about whether Monsieur So-and-So has reviewed my books, or Monsieur Such-and-Such has condemned my principles as dangerous, my cigar as immoral? . . . All I can say is that it is extremely kind of these gentlemen to take any notice of me and that, if I had no debts, I would never leave the Viceroy's steps to expose myself to their censure at my desk. *Ma la fama*, says proud Alfieri. *Ma la fame*, is Gozzi's cheerful reply.[24]

How can anyone stop me from sleeping peacefully when I see Venice, so decayed, so oppressed and so impoverished, refusing to allow time or mankind to mar her beauty and serenity? She is there around me, admiring her reflection in the lagoon like a sultana; and this tribe of fishermen who sleep on the pavement at the other end of the shore summer and winter alike, with no other mattress than a tattered coat, no other pillow than a granite step, are they not admirably philosophical too? When these people can't afford to buy a pound of rice they sing a chorus to forget their hunger; that is how they defy their masters and their poverty, accustomed as they are to braving the cold, the heat, the sudden tempest. It would take many years of slavery to brutalize entirely this happy-go-lucky, frivolous disposition, which for so long has been nurtured on fêtes and entertainments. Life is still so simple in Venice! Nature is so rich and easy to exploit! The sea and the lagoons overflow with fish and game; you can catch enough shellfish from the very streets to feed the whole population. The yield of the gardens is excellent; there is not a corner of this fertile clay which does not produce generously more fruit, flowers and vegetables than a whole field on the mainland. From the thousands of islets dotted over the lagoon, boats arrive laden with fruit, flowers and vegetables whose scents are carried on the morning mists. The duty-free harbour provides cheap foreign provisions; the most exquisite wines from the archipelago cost less in Venice than the humblest table wine in Paris. Oranges arrive from Palermo in such profusion that, on the day the Sicilian boat comes in, you can buy ten of the best for four or five French sous. So day-to-day sustenance is the least of one's expenses in Venice, and the ease with which goods are delivered encourages the inhabitants' natural indolence. The provisions arrive by water on the very doorstep; the shopkeepers go to and fro along the streets and bridges. Supplies are exchanged for money by means of a basket at the end of a string. Thus a whole family can survive in luxury without anybody, not even the servant, setting foot outside. What a difference between this comfortable existence and the infinite pains an average family has to take in Paris every day in order to eat worse than the least of Venice's workmen! What a difference too between the serious, preoccupied expressions on the faces of a shoving, pushing and bespattered crowd elbowing its way through the crush of Paris, and the nonchalant gait of the Venetians, who saunter around singing and stretch out on the warm, smooth stones of the quays whenever they please! All these tradesmen who bring their goods to Venice each day in a basket are gifted with a very ready wit and exchange their banter with their goods. The fishmonger, worn out by a morning's work and hoarse from shouting his wares, sits down at a crossroads or on the quay wall. There, to get rid of what's left, he bombards those passing by or smoking at their windows with the most ingenious offers! 'See!' he exclaims. 'Here is the choicest fish of the lot! I have kept it till now because I know that, these days, the best people eat late. See these lovely sardines, four for two centimes! Pretty chambermaid, take a look at this magnificent fish – and spare another look for the poor *pescaor!*' The water-carrier jests as he cries his wares: '*Aqua fresca e tenera!*'[25] The gondolier stationed at the *traghetto* tempts his passengers with fabulous suggestions: 'Shall we go to Trieste this evening, milord? Here is a beautiful gondola that can weather any storm at sea and a gondolier who is capable of rowing non-stop to Constantinople.'

The true pleasures of this world are always unexpected. Yesterday I wanted to go and see the moon rise on the Adriatic; I had never been able to get Catullo senior to row me to the shore of the Lido. He claimed, as they all do when they have no inclination to obey, that the wind and the tide were against him. I heartily consigned the doctor to the devil for having sent me this asthmatic fellow who expires at each stroke of his oar and is more garrulous than a starling when he is tipsy. I was in the worst of tempers when, just opposite the *Salute*, we met a boat sailing slowly towards the Grand Canal and wafting behind it like a scent the strains of an enchanting serenade. 'Turn the boat round,' I said to Catullo. 'You will, I trust, have the strength at least to follow that gondola.'

Another boat that was loitering nearby followed my example, then a second, then yet another, then, finally, all those who were enjoying the cool of the evening on the canalazzo, and even some empty boats whose gondoliers set about steering towards us, crying: '*Musica! Musica!*' like hungry Israelites crying for manna in the wilderness. In the space of ten minutes a little fleet had gathered around the performers; every oar was still and the boats glided with the tide. The melody flowed gently with the breeze and the oboe sighed so quietly that we all held our breath for fear of interrupting its plaints of love. The violin began to sob with a voice so sad and with so appealing a tremor that I let my pipe drop and pulled my cap down over my eyes. Then from the harp came two or three scales of harmonious notes that seemed to have come down from the heavens as a promise to sufferers on earth of angelic caresses and consolation. And then, as from the depth of the woods, the horn joined in and each of us thought he saw his first love emerge from on high, from the forests of Friuli, and approach to the joyous accompaniment of a fanfare. The oboe murmured to it in tones more passionate than those of a dove pursuing its mate through the air. The violin sobbed out its convulsive joy; the harp's rough strings vibrated generously like the beat of an ardent heart, and the voices of the four instruments mingled like blessed souls greeting each other before setting off together for Paradise. I stored up their strains and they echoed in my imagination long after they had fallen silent. They left in their wake a magical warmth, as though the air had been stirred by the wings of love.

There followed a few minutes of silence which nobody dared to break. The melodious bark took flight as if it wanted to be rid of us, but we shot forth in its wake. We might have been a flock of petrels vying to catch a dory. We pressed hard upon it with our prows, their great steel scythes glittering in the moonlight like the flaming fangs of Ariosto's dragons. The fugitive got away, as Orpheus did: a few chords on the harp reduced us all to order and silence. At the sound of those gentle arpeggios three gondolas lined up on either side of the one with the music and strictly followed the slow pace of the adagio. The others stayed in the rear like a cortège – and this was not the worst place from which to listen. That row of silent gondolas gliding slowly along the wide, majestic canal was a sight beyond the most beauteous dreams. As I listened to the most melodious tunes from *Oberon* or *William Tell*[26] it seemed that every undulation of the waters, each slight ripple of the oars responded sympathetically to the mood of each musical phrase. The gondoliers, erect on the stern in their bold stance, were outlined against the azure background like thin black spectres behind the groups of friends and lovers they were transporting. The moon was slowly rising and her enquiring face was beginning to peep over the rooftops; she too seemed to listen and to love the music. On one bank of the canal the *palazzi*, still shrouded in darkness, defined against the sky their great, fretted Moorish outlines, blacker than the gates of hell. The other bank received the light of the full moon, by then as large and white as a silver shield, upon its silent and severe façades. This endless row of fairy-like buildings, lit by no other light than that from the heavens, had an aspect of solitude, peace and stillness that was truly sublime. The slender statues rising by their hundreds into the sky seemed like a flight of mysterious spirits charged with protecting the repose of that silent city, sunk in the slumber of the Sleeping Beauty, and condemned like her to sleep for a hundred years and more.

Thus we sailed for about an hour. The gondoliers' spirits had been stirred. Even old Catullo rowed allegro to keep up with the swift little fleet. Then his oar would sink down again *amorosa* to andante and he accompanied this graceful movement with a grunt of ecstasy. The band stopped under the portico of the White Lion. I leant forward to see Milord get out of his gondola. He was a splenetic youth of eighteen or twenty, smoking a long Turkish pipe he was certainly incapable of finishing without becoming consumptive to the last degree. He seemed utterly bored; but he had paid for a serenade I had enjoyed much more than he had, and for that I was extremely grateful to him.

I sailed up the canal again and, as we stopped at the Piazzetta where I had arranged to meet my friends to go and have a sorbet together, I met a boatload of gondoliers in a merry mood, who shouted: 'Monsiou, get your gondolier to sing us some Tasso!' This was a joke at the expense of old Catullo, who suffers from a chronic infection of the trachea and has lost his voice once and for all. 'These people appear to know you, *vechio*,' I said. '*Ah, lustrissimo!*' he replied, '*E gnente, semo Nicoloti!*'[27] 'You? a Nicoloto? Got up as you are?' I exclaimed. 'A Nicoloto,' he repeated, 'and of the best.' 'Noble perhaps?' 'Just as you say, Signore.' 'Is there by chance a Doge in your family?' '*Lustrissimo*, there is something better: three porkers, that is to say, three regatta champions, three portraits at home with the banner of honour; and the last was my father, a very big man, you know, Master, twice as big and stout as my son. I am a miserable spider, crippled by an accident; but *mio fio*[28] is proof enough that we come from a good stock. If the Emperor were good enough to let us have a regatta, they would soon see whether the Catullo blood is watered down!' 'Well, well!' I said. 'Would you be so good, *lustrissimo* Catullo, as to let me disembark and not to steal my tobacco during the hour I shall ask you to wait for me?' 'You have nothing to fear, Master,' he replied. 'Tobacco gives me a sore throat.'

'Are there any Nicoloti or Castellani left?' I asked my friends who were waiting for me at the foot of the Lion's column. 'Too many, alas!' said Pietro. 'There is a rumour circulating in town just now, and causing some anxiety to the police, that the gondoliers are about to revive their old feuds.' 'I would have thought,' said Beppa, 'that they could be left to sort things out between themselves; they are a peaceful lot and their quarrels will do no harm to anybody; it will all end up as a farce.' 'I wouldn't be too sure,' said the doctor. 'The last attempt they made to restore the party spirit isn't so far away, and their attempts were not unsuccessful.' 'That was in 1817, I believe,' said Beppa. 'And you must know, Zorzi, you who despise so much the little knives of Venice, that in four or five days there were so many goodly *coltellate* exchanged between the two camps that more than a hundred people were seriously wounded, some of whom never recovered.' 'Indeed?' I replied. 'Then, could you tell me, most erudite doctor, you who even know how Doge Orsolo wore his beard, what was the source of these dissensions?' 'The source is lost in the mists of time,' was his reply. 'It is as old as Venice. What I can tell you is that this dissension split the nobles as well as the plebeians. The Castellani inhabited the Island of Castello, that is to say, the eastern extremity of Venice as far as the Rialto bridge. The Nicoloti occupied the eastern verge of the Island of San Nicolo, where St Mark's square, the Riva dei Schiavoni, etc., are situated. The Grand Canal was the border-line between the two camps. The richer, more distinguished Castellani represented the aristocratic faction. Their noblemen held the highest posts in the Republic and the Castellani commoners had jobs in the naval dockyard. They provided pilots for the warships and oarsmen for the Doge on the Bucentaur. The Nicoloti constituted the democratic party. Their gentry were sent as governors to the little towns on the mainland or held subordinate positions in the army. The people were poor but brave and independent. Fishing was their main activity and they had their own Doge, who was a commoner and under the orders of the other Doges, but was none the less invested with splendid prerogatives, among others, that of sitting on the right hand of the Great Doge at assemblies and solemn feasts. As a rule this Doge was an experienced old mariner who bore the title of Gastaldo dei Nicoloti; his function was to preside over the fishing rights and to ensure peace among those who were under his jurisdiction and who saw him both as their superior and as their equal. Thus a Nicoloti could taunt his rivals with the words: "You row for the Doge, but I row with the Doge." *"Ti, ti voghi el dose, et mi vogo col dose."* The Republic upheld such rivalry and scrupulously protected the Nicoloti's rights, ostensibly to maintain the population's physical and moral vigour, but more positively, to counterbalance, by a clever equilibrium, the patrician power.

'The government,' continued the doctor, 'never missed a chance to flatter the pride of these good plebeians and gave them fêtes where they were called on to show off their strong muscles and nautical skills. The Nicoloti's exploits are still the occasion of endless boasting and pride among the descendants of this Herculean race, and you may have noticed, in the hovels we sometimes visit together to take care of the injured, crude oil paintings depicting such sporting feats as the human pyramid and the portraits of regatta champions, with their banners embroidered and fringed with gold, ornamented in the middle by a large pig in needlework. The award of a live pig accompanied this prize which, though only ranked third, was nonetheless much envied. The Nicoloti practised wrestling; and their wives had their regattas where they rowed competitively and with undeniable strength and skill. You can imagine what this population would have been like in a fit of passion if the government had not kept it happy and contented by shrewdly pandering to its vanity and by a scrupulously fair administration!' 'Foreign rulers use other means; they put people in prison and punish the slightest manifestation of courage and strength,' I said. 'It must be admitted,' he replied, 'that the repression of the 1817 disorders was not altogether wrong; but they ought to have found a means of preventing the recurrence of such outbreaks as well.' 'Do you think they are now a thing of the past? Judging by the way Catullo has just been talking about his plebeian nobility, I rather believe that the Castellani are still none too dear to the Nicoloti.' 'So much so,' answered the doctor, 'that a Nicoloti conspiracy has just come to light and the arrest of forty or fifty of them is being seriously considered.'

When we had finished our sorbets we rejoined Catullo, and found him so sound asleep the doctor had no other recourse than to sprinkle a handful of sea-water gently over the grey beard ('*le oneste piume*',[29] as Dante would have said) of the octogenarian gondolier. He took the joke in good part and bravely set to work. On the way the doctor asked him: 'Weren't you at last week's famous dinner party at Saint-Samuel's?' 'Who, me, *paron*?' replied the old hypocrite. 'Why do you ask?' 'I am asking whether you were there or if you were not,' said the doctor. '*Mi son Nicoloti, paron.*'[30] 'That's not what I'm talking about,' said the doctor angrily. 'Just see if he is capable of giving a straight answer! Do you take me for an informer, you old crook?' 'Of course not, *illustrissimo*, but what do you want to get out of a poor half-blind, half-witted old man like me?' 'Answer him, you half-drunkard, half-rogue,' I intervened. 'There's not a chance,' said the doctor, 'that these rascals will answer without knowing why they are being questioned. Well, since you don't want to talk then I shall; I warn you, my old fox, that you are going to go to prison!' '*In preson! Mi! Perche, lustrissimo?*'[31] 'Because you had dinner at Saint-Samuel's,' said the doctor. 'And what's wrong with dining at Saint-Samuel's, *paron*?' 'Because you conspired against the safety of the state,' I said. '*Mi Christo!* What harm can a poor man like me do to the state?' 'Aren't you a Nicoloto?' asked the doctor. '*Mi, si!* I am a Nicoloto by birth.' 'Well then! All the Nicoloti are accused of conspiracy,' I said, 'and you with the rest!' '*Santo Dio!* I never conspired in my life.' 'Don't you know a certain Gambierazi?' asked the doctor. 'Gambierazi?' said the cautious old man, with an air of surprise. 'Which Gambierazi?' 'Good God! Gambierazi, your comrade. One would think you'd never set eyes on him!' '*Lustrissimo*, I didn't quite catch the name you said, Gamba . . . Gambierazi? There are quite a lot of Gambierazi.' 'Well, you'll answer a bit more explicitly tomorrow when the police question you,' said the doctor. 'Look at that wretch, whose neck I have saved twenty times over and who ought to trust me as he trusts God; there he is trying to outwit me and as wary of me as if I were an agent of the police! Let him go to the devil! I'd sooner be hanged myself than help him out of this scrape!'

This morning as we were having coffee on the balcony we saw Catullus *pater* and Catullus *filius* go past in a gondola with two *sbirri*.[32] 'Just look at that!' exclaimed the doctor. 'I never thought my predictions were so accurate! But what does the old windbag want with his croaking frog's voice and conspiratorial gestures?' Catullus *pater* was indeed making a tremendous effort to attract our attention; but as his chronic hoarseness made it impossible for us to hear him, he had a conciliatory chat with one of the guards who consented to stop the gondola and conduct the prisoner up to us. 'Ah ha!' said the doctor. 'What are you here for? Don't you know it was I who denounced you?' 'Oh, I know very well that is not so, *lustrissimo*! I have come to recommend myself to *su protezion!*'[33] 'But what have you done, you miserable wretch?' asked the doctor ferociously. 'Didn't I tell you, you had meddled in some infamous conspiracy?' The unhappy prisoner hung his head so piteously and the *sbirro*, standing at the door in a tragic posture, assumed such an imposing look, that Beppa and I burst into sympathetic laughter. 'But after all, what crime have you committed, you old sinner?' asked Giulio. '*Gnente, paron!*' 'It's always the same,' said Pietro. 'How the devil do you expect me to help you if I don't know what you are accused of?' '*Gnente, lustrissimo, altro che gavemo fato un Nicoloto.*'[34] 'What does that mean?' I enquired. 'Indeed, I don't know,' replied Giulio. 'What do you mean by that, *vechio birbo*?'[35] 'We made a Nicoloto,' Catullo repeated. 'And how do you set about making a Nicoloto?' asked the doctor frowning. 'With Christ, with four candles and a sepia broth.' 'Well, well, that's all too mysterious for me,' said the doctor. 'Explain your witchcraft, you reprobate! I'm a Christian and know nothing of Devil cults!' '*E nù ancà! semo cristiani!*'[36] exclaimed the old man disconsolately. 'But there is no harm in it, *paron*. It's an old, old custom. Our fathers observed it and we have preserved it without adding anything wrong. We elected our chief and baptised him.' 'Oh, now I understand. You wanted to install a Doge?' '*Sior, si!*' 'And you baptised him with sepia ink because black is the Nicoloti colour?' '*Sior, si!*' 'And you made him swear by Christ that he would defend the rights and privileges of the Nicoloti?' '*Sior, si!*' 'And that he would cut the throats of twenty Castellani every day?' '*Sior, no!*' 'And this Doge is the famous gondolier Gambierazi?' '*Sior, si, mi compare Gambierazi.*'[37] 'The one you didn't know last night?' '*Sior, si!*' 'And your son took part in this sacrilegious farce too?' '*Ancà mio fio!*'[38] 'And what do you expect me to do for you when you acknowledge such accusations? Do you realize that you are compromising me and that I might be suspected of having suborned you to incite your companions to rebellion?' The word suborn coming from Pietro's lips made Beppa laugh so heartily the doctor lost his gravity and the *sbirro* – who looked the nicest *sbirro* imaginable – was overcome by hilarity without knowing why, but fearing no doubt that this might have somewhat impaired his dignity, he immediately made a frightful grimace and, showing Catullo the door, said, 'Come on! That's enough!' Catullo left after kissing the doctor's hands and begging him to go and see the police superintendent. 'Quick! Out of my sight, you confounded cur!' said the doctor who, as usual, became twice as surly when he felt himself beginning to soften, 'I'll be damned if I'll do anything for you.' – And as soon as the criminal was out of the room he seized his hat and hurried off to the commissioner. There he learned that the affair was more comic than serious, that about forty Nicoloti had been arrested and, amongst them all, the gondoliers of the traghetto della Madonetta to which Catullus, father and son, were affiliated; but that after keeping them under lock and key for three or four days so as to give them a scare, they would let them go about their business as usual.

Venice, July 1834

During the last few days we have been roaming over the Venetian archipelago in search of a breath of life-giving air in the outskirts of this marble city, which has become a burning mirror; this month particularly the nights are stifling. Those who dwell inside the town sleep all day, some on their large sofas that are so well suited to this indolent climate, others on the floors of their boats. At night they take the air on their balconies or linger under the awnings of cafés which, luckily, never close. But their customary laughter and songs can no longer be heard. The nightingales and the gondoliers have lost their voices. Thousands of tiny phosphorescent shellfish glitter at the foot of every wall, and sparkling seaweed floats through the black waters around the sleeping gondolas. Only the shrill squeak of a fieldmouse, frolicking on the steps of a porch, breaks the silence of these nights. Long dark clouds float down from the Alps and spread great silent sheets of lightning across the Venetian sky; but they drift on to break beyond the Adriatic, and the air smoulders with the electricity they have left in their wake.

The urchins and the poodles of Venice are, together with the fish in the sea, the only beings that do not suffer from the drought. They only come out of the water to eat or sleep and the rest of the time they swim about helter-skelter. Those of us who are unlucky enough to have shirts and who cannot spend our lives putting them off and on, seek the sea breeze which, thank goodness, is always delightful and which, even at noon, skims generously over the lagoons. The only wayfarers we come across are the poor famished little butterflies who venture from islet to islet in the hope of finding the odd flower that the sun has spared, but who generally die of exhaustion and are swallowed up by a wave before achieving the long and perilous crossing.

Yesterday we passed by the island of San Servilio, where the insane and the crippled dwell. Behind a barred window giving onto the sea we saw a pale, emaciated old man sitting with his elbows on the sill. He was clasping his forehead in one hand, his sunken eyes fixed on the horizon. For a second he withdrew his hand, wiped his narrow, balding brow, then lapsed once again into his former immobility. His very stillness was somehow so terrible that my eyes were involuntarily riveted to him. When we had turned the corner of the façade I noticed that Beppa's gaze had followed mine and was now turned on me. 'Was that a madman?' she asked. 'A raving madman,' I replied.

A man, still young, rather stout and ruddy, whose pleasant face was overshadowed by fine, sweat-damp black curls, emerged from the bushes bordering the garden and advanced onto the beach. He had a rake in his hand and there was nothing abnormal about him; but when he spoke to us in a friendly tone, the incoherence of his words betrayed his deranged mind. The Abbé was sitting in the prow and, with that lively, compelling expression no one who has seen him can ever be indifferent to, he looked affectionately at the madman. '*Addio, caro!*'[1] shouted the amateur gardener when he realized that we were not going to land at the hospice. His voice was filled with tender, gentle regret; then waving goodbye to us he resumed his occupation with childish zeal. 'There must be kind thoughts in that poor head,' said the Abbé, 'for his face has an air of serenity and his voice is melodious. Who knows what makes men go mad? One only need be born better or worse than most to lose either one's reason or one's happiness. Good madman,' he added, cheerfully calling out a blessing to the horticulturist, 'may God preserve you from being cured!'

We reached the island of San Lazzaro where we had a visit to pay to the Armenian monks. Brother Hieronymus came to meet us; above his long, white beard he had a black moustache and a face that seemed at first sight to be handsome and gentle. With the inexhaustible complaisance of monastic self-esteem he took us from the printing press to the library and from the laboratory to the gardens. He showed us his mummies, his Arabic manuscripts, the book printed in twenty-four languages under his supervision, his Egyptian papyri and his Chinese prints. He spoke Spanish with Beppa, Italian with the doctor, German and English with the Abbé and French with me: and whenever we complimented him on his vast erudition his look seemed to say – with that mixture of hypocrisy and ingenuousness peculiar to oriental features – 'Had I not taken the vow of humility I could show you that I know a great deal more.'

'You are French,' he said to me. 'Do you know the Abbé de Lamennais?[22] I long to meet someone who knows him.' 'Of course, I know him very well,' I answered boldly, in the hope of finding out what the Armenians thought of the Abbé de Lamennais. 'Well, when you next see him,' said the monk, 'tell him that his book . . .' He stopped short, looked suspiciously at the Abbé and, continuing apparently otherwise than he had intended, added, 'Tell him that his last book grieved us sorely.' 'Ah!' cried the Abbé – who, though only a Venetian, has all the shrewdness of a Greek – 'Don't you know, Brother, that M. de Lamennais is an exceedingly proud man who believes that the whole of Europe is concerned with his opinions? Don't you know that he probably sees your convent as a very negligible fraction of his vast audience?'

'He's a Carlist, a Carlist!'[3] said Father Hieronymus, shaking his head. 'Good Lord! I'm amazed to hear such things talked about in this place and this country,' I whispered to the Abbé while the Armenian's attention was distracted by Beppa, who was fingering his great manuscript Bible and impudently gliding her little fingers over the brightly coloured Byzantine illuminations that decorated the margins. 'You can be sure he will criticize Lamennais if he doesn't trust us,' said the Abbé. 'Try stirring him up a bit.' 'Don't you find, Father,' I asked the monk, 'that M. de Lamennais is an important religious poet?' 'A poet! A poet!' he repeated, in alarm. 'Don't you know the opinion of ' is Holiness?'[4] 'No,' I replied. 'Well, my son, listen to it: this new bo   ﹍ abomination and every Christian is forbidden to read it.' 'Unfortunately, I was not aware of this,' I answered, 'and have read it in all innocence.' 'A similar misfortune must have befallen many another,' said the Abbé, smiling. 'The genius of M. de Lamennais is a very dangerous one! He can be read to the end without one's realizing the danger.' 'Exactly,' said the monk, 'it is only after we have read him and when we think over what we have read, that we perceive the serpent hidden among the seductive flowers.' 'That's what happened to you after reading him, isn't it, Brother?' asked the Abbé. 'I never said that I'd read him,' retorted the monk. 'I might well have done so without being really at fault; for this is what happened: the Abbé de Lamennais came here after his audience with the Pope; he spoke to me. In fact he was in the very place where you are now. Were I to live a hundred years I should never forget his face, nor his voice, nor his words. He made a great impression on me, I admit, and I realized at once that he was one of those men who can, when they choose, be of immense service to religion. I believed he had, in good faith, returned to the bosom of the Church, that he would henceforth be one of its staunchest champions. Can you wonder? He spoke so eloquently. He spoke as he writes . . . That is, *people say he writes well*,' added the Armenian, who was still wary of the Abbé's sardonic smile. 'I was so won over,' he went on, 'that I sincerely begged him to send me the next book he published.' 'And he sent it?' asked the Abbé. 'I didn't say he had sent it,' the monk said hastily. 'Had he done so it would be no fault of mine. Who could foresee that so pious and virtuous a man would produce so abominable a book?' 'But are you sure it is so abominable?' I said. 'And how could I not be sure?' 'If you haven't read it?' 'But what about the Pope's encyclical?' 'Oh yes, I forgot,' I said. 'At the time that the encyclical reached us,' said the monk, 'I, like you, was mistaken as to the true nature of M. de Lamennais. I said to my brothers: see what ineffable blessings God has bestowed on this saintly man! See how his momentary doubts and distress have given way before a live, all-consuming faith! This is the outcome of his audience with the Pope!' 'You went on saying that after reading the book?' asked the Abbé, continuing to tease him. 'I didn't say that I said it then,' replied the monk. 'But what if I had? I hadn't yet received the encyclical!' 'I am very unhappy about that encyclical,' I said. 'You see, I was enthralled by the book and by its author. While reading it I felt a livelier faith dawn in me; the love of God, the hope of seeing his kingdom come on earth had transported me to the foot of the eternal throne. Never had I prayed so fervently. I felt somehow athirst for martyrdom – a thing unheard of in our day and age. Didn't it have the same effect on you, Father?' 'Had I not received the Pope's encyclical . . .' said the monk, obviously moved and troubled. 'But what can be done? When the Pope decrees that this book is prejudicial to religion, the Church, customs and the State of . . . of . . .' – he clasped his brow, unable to recall the name of Louis Philippe I. This was the one and only time he was at all Armenian and monkish. 'The French,' he continued, 'are very set in their political views. M. de Lamennais is a Carlist.' 'Do you know exactly what it is to be a Carlist?' I asked him. 'It appears,' he replied, 'that it is to be in strong disagreement with the views of the Pope.' 'Well, well! I am totally confused!' I murmured to the Abbé. 'Either this Armenian's head is in a terrible muddle or the Pope is as afraid of the happy medium as Armenian monks are afraid of the Pope.' 'I beg your pardon,' said Brother Hieronymus, approaching us with an enquiring air. 'I hope I haven't offended your personal views by saying such things?' Since I showed no sign of replying the Abbé nudged me, saying: 'Didn't you hear Father Hieronymus ask for your own views on the subject?' 'The truth is,' I replied, 'that I have none, apart from this: the world is dying and religion is disappearing.' 'Alas! How right you are. Religion will indeed disappear if we don't take care,' said the Armenian. 'New doctrines are gradually infiltrating the ancient truth as water infiltrates marble, and those who could be the torch-bearers of religion use their light to lead the flock astray. As for me,' he went on confidentially, 'there is one thing I dearly wish to do, and have half-decided to do; and that is to ask permission to go and see the Abbé de Lamennais wherever he may be and to implore him, in the name of religion, in the name of his reputation and in the name of the friendship I felt for him when I first met him, to re-enter the fold of the Holy Roman Church and to mend his ways. There is so much I would like to say to him,' he added guilelessly. 'I am convinced that in the end I could succeed in persuading him.' The Abbé turned away to conceal a sarcastic smile; then he walked round the closet, followed intently by the eyes of the monk – those beautiful, bright, oriental eyes that have something of the eagle and something of the cat about them. After the Abbé had made a show of observing all the items of natural history, he went outside and Beppa asked the Armenian to read aloud a few words from the multi-lingual oriental manuscripts littering the table, so that she might hear and compare the different harmonies of these tongues with which her ear was totally unacquainted. I left the doctor with her just as, having apparently found Syriac very much to their taste, they were about to sample Chaldean, and joined the Abbé who was strolling dreamily in the cloister, along arcades that opened onto a yard full of sunshine and dazzling flowers. 'That's what comes of measuring your wits against your equals,' I said laughing. 'You wanted to have your little joke and you were taken for a spy, Abbé. Serves you right!'

He didn't answer and seemed to be engaged in a lively dialogue with an invisible partner. 'You wouldn't go!' he exclaimed – adding a Venetian expression that means something like our 'not on your life!' 'You talk about it but you'd never do it! You wouldn't give up all this!' – He was looking at the convent gardens and cloisters and gestured towards them as he spoke. Turning, he caught sight of me and burst out laughing. 'I can't get over the idea of that monk wanting to go and convert M. de Lamennais,' he said. 'What do you make of it?' 'But how much would you bet,' I replied, 'that if the Pope were to entrust you with such a mission you wouldn't be too loath to carry it out?' 'Most certainly I wouldn't,' he said. 'Do you think that a poor priest like me could afford to turn down the chance of seeing such a man and of talking to him?' 'And what would you say to him?' 'That I admire him, that I have read him and that I am unhappy.' 'That's no excuse for destroying those shrubs which have never done you any harm, nor for tormenting this good monk who was in awe of your bands and felt obliged to deplore the errors of one he probably venerates as much as you do!' 'This monk? He pretended to take an interest in matters that don't interest him in the least. They are learned and polite, but first and foremost they are monks, and quite indifferent to anything that takes place beyond these walls. So long as they are left in peace to enjoy their wealth they will always kowtow to the power that protects them. They don't care whether it is secular or religious. And don't forget that there is someone they venerate above the Pope; that is the Emperor Francis[5] who gave them this convent and this fertile little island where Lord Byron[6] came to study oriental languages and which M. de Marcellus[7] has visited lately, as four elegant lines he has inscribed in the visitor's book testify.'

'I know an equally beautiful quatrain of his,' I retorted; 'the one he improvised and wrote with his own hand under the statue of Victory in Brescia. Here it is:

> *Elle marche, elle vole, et dispense la gloire;*
> *On est tenté de l'adorer.*
> *Et même en contemplant cette noble Victoire,*
> *Après avoir vu Rome, il nous faut l'admirer.*[8]

'I'm sure that M. de Marcellus can't stand the Abbé de Lamennais,' said the Abbé, 'and that he victoriously refutes him.' 'What's that to you, you unregenerate priest?' I said. 'Let M. de Marcellus improvise his quatrains up and down Italy; let these poor monks enjoy the peace and quiet they bought at the price of violence and fanatical persecutions endured at the hand of the Turk in their own land. The care with which they educate Armenian youths and preserve in print the monuments of their language, which possesses admirable historians and poets – isn't that a noble and useful occupation?' 'But they sell their books and their tuition at a high price, despite the fact that they are enormously rich. One of their pupils made a fortune in America and died there a few years ago, leaving them four millions!' 'Well, all the better,' I replied. 'They needed luxury and they've got it. Tell me, Abbé, can you imagine a convent without rare plants, without porphyry columns, without mosaic pavements, without a library and without paintings? Monks who haven't got all these things are vile creatures we would certainly never come to visit. As for me, I am very sorry that the wonderful convents of old, those veritable museums of artistic and scientific treasures, were plundered for the benefit of a few generals and contractors to the French army who are nothing but murderers and robbers. I deplore the loss of that breed of monks who grew grey over their books and exhausted human learning, till there was nothing left for them on which to exercise their intellectual powers but dreams of alchemy and astrology. That laboratory with its scientific apparatus took me back to all the poetry of a bygone monastic existence. Curse that talkative monk with his misplaced diplomacy and M. de Marcellus with his sublime quatrains for bringing me so abruptly back to the present!' 'You're a flippant creature to make light of all that,' said the Abbé, frowning. 'And you are right to do so; for our age rates nothing but irony and pity. Woe betide the man who still believes in something! Burn yourself out within the circle of your iron cage, useless torch of the intellect! Ardours of faith, dreams of divine grandeur, you consume in vain the heart and mind of the believer. Men smile and pass on, unmoved. Ah! How laughable it all is!' He turned his back on me abruptly and, with a look of vexation, plunged down a vine-covered alley. I wanted to follow him; his grief distressed me. But I caught sight of a sea-bream in the water, pursuing a cuttle-fish, and leaned over the bank, curious to see what defences the poor clumsy creature would put up against the nimble swimmer. Thus I was able to observe the *calamajo*, or 'ink-pot' as the locals call that species of fish, squirt its ink in the face of the enemy who, with a grimace of profound disgust, swam off disappointed. The *calamajo* performed, in its own way, some nice little capers in the sand; but, alas, not for long. The sea-bream came stealthily back, seized it from behind and carried it off to the bottom of the sea before it had had time to put its ingenious tactics to use. This conflict made me forget the one between the Pope and M. de Lamennais, and I basked for a quarter of an hour in the sunshine in stupefied contemplation of a few tufts of seaweed amongst which two or three thousand shellfish dwelt peacefully together. It was, to all appearance, a flourishing colony until, under my very eyes, a gull came and upset it, practically annihilating it with a single beat of its wing. Can nothing survive, I asked myself and thought of the Abbé's disheartened observations. I went in search of him and, to my great surprise, found him laughing outright and stroking his beard, as he read over with obvious satisfaction some lines he had just written with a piece of slate on the sundial in the garden. I leant over his shoulder and read some Venetian verses he had composed on the spot and which I have tried to translate as best I could.

The Enemy of the Pope

Rest in peace, my brothers, and let the Pope settle his own quarrels. Rome's thunderbolts are spent and the fire of wrath has no power to consume the hearts of men of God. The anathema of Rome is no more than a sound for the wind to play with, as it sports with the foam of the raging waves. The arch-heretic is no longer forced to take refuge in the mountains and to wear out the soles of his feet fleeing the reprisals of the Church. Faith has become what Jesus wanted it to be: a hope offered to free souls and not a yoke imposed by the powerful and the rich of the earth. Rest in peace, my brothers, God does not espouse the Pope's quarrels.

You are foolhardy who wish to reconcile them, you do not know the harm you would do the Church if you stifled that rebellious voice! You do not realize that the Pope is well pleased and quite proud to have an opponent: what would he not give to have more, to have a second Luther draw the crowd in his wake! But the world of today is indifferent to theological disputes; it reads the heretic's speeches because they are fine; it does not read the Pope's decrees, because they are Catholic and nothing else. Read them, my brothers, since the Pope has told you to do so; but pray in your hearts for the Pope's enemy.

You have laboured enough, suffered enough on this earth, you scattered remnant of the world's most ancient people! Your hoary beards are still stained with the blood of your brothers, and the snows of Mount Ararat are red with it to the summit on which the holy Ark once rested. The Turkish scimitar has shaved your heads to the bone and the infidel has waded ankle-deep in the tears of Japhet's last descendants.[9] The distrust which sometimes furrows your peaceful brows is the stamp left there by persecution. But comfort yourselves, my brothers, and know that the power of a Roman Pope is as nothing compared to that of the humblest Turkish Cadi[10] of an

Armenian village. Rest in peace. You can be sure that the Pope prays for his enemy, dreading lest God might remove him.

The floods of blood are stemmed, your ark has landed on these fertile shores; do not leave your happy isle. Cultivate your flowers and pluck your fruits. See! Your grapes are already ripening and vine branches laden with fruit hang over the waters as if, in a moment of weariness, they wanted to slake their thirst. Here all is rose-coloured – oleanders, marble, sea and sky. Each morning you greet the sun as it emerges from behind the mountains of your homeland and breathe in, with its rays, the dews from your native heights. Why should you trouble your tranquil souls? Teach the orphans of your kinsmen to speak the language which the first men spoke and make sure you tell them the story of your servitude so that they may preserve the liberty you have bought so dearly. But do not talk to them about the enemy of the Pope; alas, it would be to no avail! By the time they are grown up the Church will be appeased and Capellari's[11] successor will not have an enemy under the sun.

Therefore rest in peace, my brothers, for God has set his bow in the clouds once again. From that unknown world beyond your island a messenger came to you. You took him for a dove, so gentle was his voice, so open his countenance. But the Pope tells you that the dove is a raven. Say as he says, O sons of prudent Noah! But should the Pope's enemy return to you one day, driven by some storm, and seek shelter under your fig trees, creep up behind the foliage, good fathers, and bend down towards him a branch of the beautiful fruit, with their split coats.* The swallows of the Adriatic will not tell of it in Rome. Should he enter your chapel let him bow down his broad forehead to the Virgin. It was a Turk who painted her, yet she is very beautiful and very Christian. She will hear, perhaps, the arch-heretic's prayer. But should she convert him to the Roman faith take care not to boast of the miracle accomplished under your roof, Brother Hieronymus. For then, at the risk of being excommunicated, you would have to declare yourself the enemy of the Pope.

'And you, Abbé,' I asked, 'would you not be tempted, I wonder, to become the Pope's enemy? Doesn't this unusual role lure your vanity with some dangerous promise? But remember that it is harder, nowadays, to fill such a serious role than to write such a satire as this: it

* *El figo col tabaro strapazza* is an expression used by the Venetians.

requires more than priestly eloquence. Only a man of great character can raise the standard of rebellion in the Council. Honour in silence the habit you wear, unless you feel that you too bear the fatal mark of singular destiny.' The Abbé, obviously unaware of the presumptuousness of his reply, and naïvely yielding to his painful obsession, said, shaking his head: 'It would have been a hundred times better to have been strumming a guitar in the boudoir of a Cydalise,[12] to have spent a lifetime amusing myself and tossing off verses, than to be weighed down with the considerations which afflict my poor brain. Oh, Lamennais! Where are you? Oh, Capellari! What are you doing? From out of these black cassocks, shrouds of your past glory, will not one man emerge? Must all those who are wrapped in them go down to the grave unhonoured and forgotten?'

'My dear Abbé,' I cried, grasping his hand. 'Beware of what is happening within you! Beware of the demon of pride! Rub out your lines, here comes Hieronymus; let that monk preserve his quiet prudence and happy obscurity. Don't arouse the serpent hidden in his heart; who knows if he hasn't also dreamed many a time of becoming a man? Let the queen of the new world, the intellect, have her sway. She draws near with giant strides and I know well what she will make of us, without your help or mine.'

*   *   *   *   *   *   *   *   *   *

When we passed in front of the isle of madmen for the second time, Beppa complained of having to go that way twice over. 'I hate their cries,' she said. 'They upset me, and my distress doesn't alleviate theirs.' 'They don't always call out,' I said, pointing to the old man we had seen two hours earlier. He was still in the same position and the same place. His face was as pale and drear as ever and he was still staring at the waters. 'It's worse than if he did cry out,' said Beppa. 'My God! What a terrifying face! What calm despair! What is he thinking of and what is he looking at? What's going on in that bald head that doesn't feel the rays of the sun? They are as heavy as lead and he has been enduring them for two hours!' 'And maybe he puts up with them in the same way every day,' said the doctor. 'I once knew a madman who believed he was an eagle and persisted for so long in staring at the sun that he went blind. The loss of his sight only confirmed him in his fantasy. He was still convinced he was staring at the luminous disc and that in the very midst of the darkness of night he could perceive the room flooded in dazzling light.' 'Would to God,' said Beppa, 'that this one might have some foolish delusion of the sort! He would not suffer then. But I fear he may not be mad at the moment, only aware of his captivity. How he stares at the horizon! Poor man; you will never even reach that first wave of the Adriatic, and there is perhaps a volcano in your brain that would hurl you to the ends of the earth!' 'Perhaps,' said the doctor, 'he only missed by a hair's breadth being a genius and spreading his fame throughout the world. Perhaps there are moments when he is aware of this and realizes he must die in a lunatic asylum!' 'Sail on, sail on,' said Beppa. 'The Abbé is beginning to look worried.'

*   *   *   *   *   *   *   *   *   *

The moon was rising in the sky when, after a leisurely meal and a leisurely chat in a café, we arrived at the Piazzetta. 'That cross between a dog and a cow won't budge an inch!' grumbled Catullo who, that night, was misanthropic in his cups. 'To whom is that genealogical apostrophe addressed?' enquired the doctor. On turning round he saw a Turk who, having taken off his slippers and some of his clothes, was kneeling on the last step of the *traghetto*, so near the water that his beard and his turban were immersed at each of his numerous invocations to the moon. 'Ho ho!' said the doctor. 'This gentleman has chosen an odd prie-dieu; time must have overtaken him as he was hailing a gondola; he must have been forced to bow down to the ground when he heard the hour of his prayers ringing.' 'That's not what it is,' said the Abbé. 'He settled there so that no one should pass in front of him and cross his prayer; his religion compels him to start again every time someone comes between him and the moon.'

As he spoke he stretched out his walking stick to stop Catullo from leaping savagely out of the boat and pushing the Turk aside to enable us to land. 'Let him alone,' said the Abbé. 'He too is a believer.' 'And how are you going to manage,' said the gondolier, 'if that unbaptised animal won't get out of the way?'

Indeed, since the *traghetto* was surrounded by two little wooden balustrades, we couldn't land without encroaching on the Mohamme- dan's prayer. 'All right,' said the Abbé. 'We'll wait till he's finished; sit down and don't say a word!' Catullo went and sat in the bow, shaking his head; it was easy to see that he didn't approve in any way of the Abbé's principles. 'What does it matter,' said the latter, 'whether the

Virgin is called Mary or Phingari? The virgin mother of the Deity always represents the same allegorical idea: it is faith, which gives rise to every cult and every virtue.' 'You are somewhat heretical this evening, Monsieur l'Abbé,' said Beppa. 'I for my part don't like the Turks, not because they worship the moon, but because they keep their women in servitude.' 'To say nothing of cutting their slaves' heads off,' said Catullo indignantly. 'My uncle,' said the doctor, 'once witnessed an event of which this Turk's prayer reminds me. One day about fifty years ago, the hour for prayer came just like this, unexpectedly, upon a Moslem as he was strolling along the Riva dei Schiavoni. He stopped right in the middle of the quays and, after taking off his slippers, began his customary devotions. A band of urchins, obviously witnessing such a spectacle for the first time, began laughing and, gathering round inquisitively, ironically mimicked his genuflexions and the movements of his lips. The Turk continued his prayers without seeming to notice their mockery. The rascals, encouraged, redoubled their antics and, little by little, made bold to pick up some pebbles and throw them in his face. The devout man remained impassive; his face betrayed not the slightest alteration and he didn't omit a single word of his prayer. But when he had finished he got up, seized by the neck the first unfortunate little wretch he could lay hands on and stuck his cutlass in his throat as calmly as if he had been a chicken; then he departed without a word, leaving the bleeding corpse on the spot where his prayer had been profaned. The Senate deliberated over this murder and it was deemed that the Turk had taken a legitimate vengeance. There were no further proceedings against him.'

This tale, which Catullo listened to, crestfallen, hanging his head, seemed to inspire him with the utmost respect for the idolater; for when the latter had finished his prayer, he not only waited for him to put on his dolman but even handed him his slippers. The Turk showed no sign of gratitude, nor did he acknowledge our courtesy, but went to join his comrades who were smoking by the column of San Theodoro – 'Those are silly fellows,' the Abbé remarked as we passed them. 'They didn't say their prayers. They are tradesmen who have settled in Venice and have been corrupted by the atmosphere of our civilization. They drink wine, deny the Prophet, don't frequent the mosque and don't take off their sandals to worship Phingari; but they are no better for it, since they believe in nothing and have lost all the poetic innocence of their idolatry without opening their hearts to the austere truth of the Gospel.

However, they are none the less honest, because they are Turks, and a Turk cannot be a rogue.'

After separating to take a couple of hours' rest we met again at the festival, or *sagra*,[13] of the Redeemer. In Venice each parish rivals its neighbours in the magnificence with which they celebrate their patron saint's day; the whole town attends the services and the festivities that take place on this occasion. The island of the Giudecca, where the Church of the Redeemer is situated, is one of the wealthiest parishes, and provides one of the most spectacular fêtes. The portal is decorated with a gigantic garland of flowers and fruit; a pontoon of boats is erected on the Giudecca canal which, at this point, has almost become a sound; all the quay is covered with the booths of pastry-cooks, tents for coffee and those bivouac kitchens called *frittole*,[14] where the cooks bustle about like grotesque demons among the flames and billows of smoke from the boiling fat, whose pungency is enough to stifle sailors rounding the coast at a distance of three nautical miles. The Austrian government has banned open-air dancing; and anywhere else in the world this would sadly impair the success of the festival; but luckily the Venetians have an unlimited store of natural good humour; their deadly sin is gluttony; but it is a lively loquacious sort of greed which has nothing in common with the stolid English or German variety, and Muscatel wine from Istria at six sous the bottle brings about an open-hearted and jocular kind of drunkenness.

All the food stalls are decorated with foliage, streamers and coloured paper balloons that serve as lanterns; all the boats are adorned with them and those owned by the well-to-do are got up with remarkable good taste. These paper lanterns can be any shape under the sun: here there are acorns falling in luminous festoons round a multi-coloured silk canopy; there it is classical alabaster vases, ranged round a dais of white muslin, whose transparent curtains envelop the guests. For grand suppers are served on these boats and, through the gauze, one can see gleaming silver and candles, along with flowers and crystal. Some youths, dressed as women, peep through the curtains, and make saucy remarks to the passers-by. High on the prow is a huge lantern which can take the form of a tripod, a dragon or an Etruscan vase, into which a bizarrely clad gondolier keeps throwing a powder that flares up in crimson flames and blue sparks.

All these boats, all these lights, reflected in the waters, hurrying and scurrying in all directions along the brightly lit banks, create a magical effect. The humblest gondola, on which a fisherman's family is having a noisy supper, looks enchanting, with its four lamps swaying over the tipsy heads, while its lantern on the prow, hanging from a crossbar above the others, bobs about in the breeze like a golden fruit carried by the waves. The young men row and eat by turns; the father speaks Latin with the dessert – gondolier Latin, which is an assortment of puns and bogus slang translations, sometimes droll, always grotesque; the children sleep, the dogs bark and stir each other up as they pass.

What is still very fine and truly republican about the way of life in Venice is the lack of formality and the *bonhomie* of the aristocracy. Probably in no other place are the distinctions between social classes so marked and in no other place are they abandoned in better faith. You can tell a nobleman ensconced in the depths of his gondola simply by the way he raises and lowers the window. The upstart Jew, however scrupulously he copies the dandy's attitudes, will never achieve the elegance of the most plainly dressed scion of one of these ancient families; and the hired gondolier will never, however hard he tries, row with the majestic grace of those who are known as Palace Gondoliers. But there is not a popular festival which will not unite all ranks of society, without distinction, privilege or antagonism. The common people, who make fun of anything, make fun of the decline of the aristocracy; and, at carnival time, they like nothing better than to masquerade in an outsize wig and a ridiculous costume, and to strut about the streets, a sword at their side, with greasy stockings and down-at-heel shoes, generously volunteering to all and sundry their protection, their wealth and their palaces. This get-up is called the *Illustrissimo*. It has become a classic like Punchinello, Brighella, Giacometto and Pantaloon.[15] But despite their cruel mockery, the people are still very fond of their old aristocracy, those survivors from the last days of the Republic who were so rich, so prodigal and so credulous, so magnificent and so vain, so limited and so kind; those men who chose Manin as their last Doge, Manin,[16] who cried like a child when he was told that Napoleon was approaching, and then sent the keys of the city to the conqueror just as he was about to retreat, having decided that Venice was impregnable.

The aristocracy has always been friendly and paternal towards the people, and never shuns their coarse high-spirits – because, in Venice, unlike other places, they are not really repulsive, and are witty, even in their coarseness. The people respond to this trust and never has any nobleman been molested in a tavern or in the confusion of a regatta. They are all mixed up together. Some laugh at the solemnity of others and in turn are laughed at for their own extravagances. The old nobleman's covered gondola, the banker's or the merchant's resplendent one, and the unadorned gondola of the greengrocer are supping and sailing side by side along the canal, bumping and pushing each other; and tunes from the rich man's band mingle with the poor man's raucous chorus. At times the rich man silences his musicians so as to relish the ribald ditties from the next boat; sometimes the boat falls silent and follows the gondola, listening to the rich man's music.

This good understanding is to be met with everywhere. The absence of horses and carriages on the roads and the necessity for everyone to travel by water contribute largely to the general egalitarianism. No one bespatters or runs over a fellow creature. There, no one knows the humiliation of trudging on foot alongside a private carriage; no one is forced to put himself out for another and they are all willing to give way. In the cafés everyone sits in the open air. The climate makes this necessary and it is not the grand people but those who feel the cold who sit indoors. A fisherman from Chioggia rests his tattered elbows on the same table as the nobleman. Of course the dandies, the artists and the aristocrats have plenty of their own favourite cafés; everyone likes to meet his own circle there every evening; but on occasions (which are made frequent by the heat) they will go to the first tavern they come across; and no one raises an eyebrow if a well-bred lady sits down at a café table to drink a *semata*[17] or eat a freshly caught fish – indeed nobody even notices.

Venetian women are coquettish and love dress. The richness of their attire contrasts strongly with the informality of their ways. Is it because of this aristocratic simplicity that the common people stare at them so brazenly? To the lady who gets into his cab the Parisian coachman is not really a man. Here a gondolier eyes the legs of all the ladies who step out of his gondola. La Bruyère's words: 'A gardener is a man only in the eyes of a nun,' would not make sense in Venice. Beppa is certainly not provocative or flighty in her ways; yet the other day as we were passing a boatful of peasants one of them, who was reciting – or rather slaughtering – a stanza from Tasso, broke off to point her out to his comrades: 'Here comes the lovely Erminia!'[18]

The old aristocracy's ostentatiousness still survives among the people; the practice of the *sagra* is a typical example: every year the parish church and its Chapter sit to elect an organizer for the celebrations of the patron saint's day, somewhat as an alms-collector is chosen in a Parisian parish. This organizer's function consists in allocating the annual product of alms and gifts for the decoration of the church, the lighting and the choir music; as a rule he is chosen for his wealth and generosity. Devout or not, his aim is always to outshine his predecessor in sumptuousness; and should the parish's yield be insufficient, he will make up the deficit from his own pocket. As a result the people have a grand time, and the clergy are satisfied and lavish free absolutions and indulgences on the organizer, his family and his dependants. A few days ago a single, private individual paid no less than fifteen thousand francs for a mass.

At two o'clock, having brought no provisions (because, it must be admitted, there is not a more uncomfortable way of eating in the world than in a gondola), we returned to the town and went to dinner at the restaurant of Santa Margherita, which also had its paper lanterns hung in the arbour. We found a place at the bottom of the garden and the Abbé ordered soles cooked with raisins from Corinth, pine kernels and candied lemon-peel. Giulio and Beppa were so aglow with Braganza wine and clove macaroons that they would not hear of going home; we had to go and see the sunrise on the island of Torcello. Since Catullo was half-drunk and incapable of rowing even a quarter of that distance on his own he suggested calling in his cronies, Cesare and Gambierazzi – the one having been elected a Nicoloto the previous month, having sworn on the cross eternal hatred to the Castellani; the other having performed, with Catullo, the part of High Priest by pouring sepia ink over the neophyte's head and dictating the formula for his vow. To atone for such pagan and republican rites all three had been sent to prison together with twenty or so onlookers; I think I mentioned all this in one of my letters. I was longing to see these famous gondoliers. But alas, famous men too often disappoint the idea one has of them! Cesare, the neophyte, is a hunchback and Gambierazzi, the pontiff, has legs like corkscrews. The handsomest of the three is still Catullo who is only lame in one leg and never omits to say, when mentioning Lord Byron: 'I saw him, he was lame!' Alas! Alas! The sublime poet Catullus was a Venetian; who knows if the crippled drunkard who rows our gondola is not his direct descendant?

These three monsters, wind and sail assisting, brought us very speedily to Torcello, and the sun was rising as we plunged gaily into the green lanes of that beautiful island.

Of all the little islands of the lagoon in which the neighbouring population took refuge at the time of the barbarian invasion of Italy, Torcello is the one that shows most evidence of those years of emigration and terror. The church and a ruined factory are all that is left of the town erected by the refugees. The church, with its irregular structure and its mixture of ancient opulence and coarse building-materials is a reminder of the haste with which it was built. It is made from the remains of a temple to Aquilea, salvaged from the rubble of this capital of the Venetian province. The nave has preserved the circular form of a pagan temple, while costly African marble columns wrought in Greece support the brick roof, now covered with brambles that hang down in festoons and break through the cracks in the cornice. The dome and the inner part of the portal are covered in mosaics which are the work of Greek artists. These eleventh-century mosaics are, like all those of that decadent period, hideous in design[19] but remarkably intact. It is from Venice that the art of the mosaic spread throughout Italy, and the golden background that gives such extraordinary relief to the figures and remains unimpaired and glowing despite the dust of ages, is made out of minute golden glass squares produced in the neighbouring island of Murano. Little by little the art of design, which had been lost in Greece and was reborn in Italy, applied itself to the improvement of mosaic work; in fact, the last of those made for St Mark's Cathedral were the work of the brothers Zuccati[20] after a design by Titian.

The Abbé tried to persuade us that these eleventh-century mosaic virgins possessed an austerity and grandeur that expressed, better than the poetic grace of a more sophisticated art, the true faith. We had to admit that in these great Byzantine figures with their almond eyes and Greek profiles there is something of the steadfastness and solemnity we associate with the teachings of the new faith. The Abbé reverted to his somewhat pagan theory of the Virgin as a religious allegory. He tried to find evidence of this in the different interpretations of the venerated image by various great artists, and to discover, in the characteristics which each one chose to stress, a reflection of their souls. According to him Titian had expressed his strong, tranquil faith in the great figure of Mary, rising up to heaven with so much forcefulness and so radiant a face, while the golden clouds divide and Jehovah advances to meet her.

Raphael and Correggio, both lovers and poets, had given to their Virgins a more melancholy gentleness and a more human love for the Deity; it is not only the heavens that they contemplate but Jesus, the God of love and forgiveness, whom they reverently caress.

Finally Giambellino and Vivarini, Beppa's favourite painters, had imparted their innocent youthfulness of heart to their smiling *madonettes*. 'Oh, Giambellino!' exclaimed Beppa. 'How I should have loved you! How your endearing childishness would have appealed to me! How well I would have cared for your beloved goldfinch! How the viols and mandolins of your little angels, veiled by their long wings, lissom, melodious and dainty as titmice, would have haunted my dreams! With what delight I should have breathed in the fragrance of the flowers, ravished by your hands from Eden and brought into bloom by the tears of Eve and of Mary. How I would have trembled as I kissed the airy garlands floating on the golden curls of your pale cherubim! How timidly I would have contemplated your young Virgins, so pure and holy that human eyes are afraid of profaning them! I would have tried to preserve the serenity of my soul so that I might resemble them!' 'You do resemble them, Beppa,' said the Abbé, flashing a rapid glance at her. But his eyes returned immediately to the contemplation of the great sombre Byzantine Virgin, emblem of suffering and strength, who rose above our heads. 'Oh, sad and sublime faith!' he said, stifling a sigh. The face of this sincere young man expressed the satisfaction of a painful victory, and the bitter smile which a generous indignation frequently brings to his lips was absent for the rest of the day. Many a time I have heard him say: 'It is right that I should have to do penance, to be ordered to overcome and mortify my rebellious imagination, to thrust the seven arrows that pierced Mary's breast into my heart, to be made to suffer. But being inactive is what kills; the feeling that one's whole life is of no use, that all one's energy is wasted, that there is nothing to fight for, nothing to sacrifice!' I should not be surprised if the Abbé occasionally indulged in dangerous thoughts or melancholy feelings for the joy of overcoming them.

The doctor went off to snooze among the nettles on the stone curule chair which is supposed to have been used by the Roman Praetors entrusted with the levying of taxes from the fishermen of the lagoon.

Popular tradition bestows on this chair the name of Attila's throne, despite the fact that the barbarian conqueror, having vainly attempted to invade these islands, and having seen his fleet stranded by the receding tide in the marshes whose navigable channels were unknown to him, had retreated, disdaining even the paltry conquest of the Chioggia peninsula. Giulio hung around inspecting the church's unusual shutters which are made, as in eastern temples, from large flat slabs of stone hinged on to pivots. The Abbé went to call on his Torcello colleague whose white Priory, hidden among the thickly wooded gardens, the romantic Beppa found very much to her taste. I wandered about on my own, dreaming and picking flowers for her in the Torcello lanes which are more beautiful, alas, than those of the Vallée Noire.[21] A profusion of brilliant convolvulus clung to the hedges, stretching here and there above the path to form a more graceful and sumptuous arbour than the hand of man could have achieved. Eight or ten dwellings, twenty at most, scattered among the orchards, house the entire population of the islands. All their occupants had already gone fishing. An inconceivable silence reigned over a countryside so prodigal that it barely needs cultivating and yields freely that which, in our part of the world, is only produced by the sweat of the brow. Butterflies skimmed over the carpet of flowers stretched out under my feet and, obviously unaccustomed to being pestered by children and entomologists, alighted on the posy I was holding in my hand. Torcello is a reclaimed wilderness. Through copses of water-willow and hibiscus bushes run salt-water streams where petrel and teal delight to stalk. Here and there a marble capital, a fragment of Lower Empire sculpture or a lovely, shattered Greek cross emerges from the long grass. Nature's eternal youth smiles in the midst of these ruins. The air was balmy and only the song of the cicadas disturbed the religious hush of the morning. Overhead was the loveliest sky in the world and close at hand were the best of friends. I closed my eyes, as I often do to take stock of the various sensations I have gleaned during a stroll, and to get an overall picture of the landscape through which I have been wandering. I don't know why, but instead of the creepers, copses and marbles of Torcello, I saw level plains, wilting trees, dusty thickets, an overcast sky, a meagre vegetation relentlessly tortured by the plough and the pickaxe, hideous hovels, absurd palaces – France, in a word. 'Oh!' I said to myself. 'So you are calling me!' I felt a strange feeling of desire and revulsion. O Fatherland! Mysterious word which I have never thought about and

112

whose meaning I still find unfathomable! Do I find the memory of past sufferings evoked by you sweeter than my present happiness? Could I forget you if I wanted? And how is it that I do not want to?

Letter Four

★

To Jules Néraud[1]

Nohant, September 1834

How deeply I must thank you, my old friend, for coming to see me at once! I was not expecting this pleasure, and I realize that since your circumstances have not changed,[2] it is a great proof of your friendship which you have given me. I have spent a happy day with you, my good Malgache, amongst my children and my friends. I have laughed very heartily at our past follies; I have renewed our playful quarrels; I have relished your jokes. After an absence of two years (which to me seemed like two centuries) I have picked up the threads of all that past existence with a childish delight, with an old man's enjoyment. Well, my poor friend, for one whole day my worn-out, desolate heart has been filled with all these things; they made it leap for joy, but could neither cure nor rejuvenate it; like a corpse briefly galvanized into life it sinks back more dead than before. Spleen and despair have seized my soul, Malgache. I have told myself everything that I could and should tell myself, I have tried to become once more attached to all around me; I cannot live, I cannot do it. I have come to say farewell to my country, to my friends. The world will not know what I have suffered nor what efforts I made before reaching this stage. It would be useless to try and make you understand my soul and my life; do not talk to me of that; accept my adieu and say nothing to me; it would be of no avail. Come and see me sometimes during my stay here and talk about the past with me. I shall have some favours to ask of you: and you will accept the charge as a sign of my trust in you. Think of me – and, if – somewhere – one day – you pass by my grave, will you pause and shed a few tears there for me? Oh! pray for perhaps the only one who has truly understood and truly valued your heart.

Thank you, Malgache, my good old friend, thank you for your letter; no potion could be more effective than those friendly words, and that tender compassion which could not possibly wound my pride. You know only a tiny fraction of the sufferings I have endured. If fate ever brings us together for a few hours I shall tell you about them; but the main thing is not that you should know them but that your affection should make them easier to bear. Believe me, persuasion, protests, reproaches only embitter the hearts of those who grieve, while a cordial handshake is the most eloquent of consolations. It may well be that my heart has been made weary and my mind deluded by a venturesome life and false ideas: but in that case they are the malady from which I am dying and there is nothing left for my friends to do but lead me gently to my grave. Remove the last thorns from my path, or at least sow a few flowers round my grave and whisper in my ear tender words of regret and pity. No, I am not ashamed of your pity, my friends, and especially not of yours, old castaway, who have weathered the storms of life and have suffered its gnawing cares and overwhelming hardships. I am a patient who should be pitied not contradicted. If you cannot cure me you will at least have made my sufferings more bearable and death less repulsive. Heaven forbid that I should scorn your friendship, disregard its value! But do you know the ills which counterbalance those blessings? Do you know how exacting some joys have made my heart, how mistrustful and discouraged some sufferings have left me? Moreover, you are strong, all of you. I have only energy and not strength. You say that *instinct* will keep me here with my children; you may be right; it is the truest word I have heard. This instinct is so deeply rooted in me that I have cursed it as an indestructible bond; sometimes, too, I have blessed it, hugging to my heart those two little beings who know nothing of all my distress. Write to me often, my friend; be considerate and astute in telling me things that can help me, and try not to give me too harsh a lesson. Alas! I am harsher with myself than you can ever be, and it is stark clearsightedness that drives me to despair. May your heart, that is kind and generous – whatever anyone may say or think – teach you the means of curing me. I have come to seek here what has eluded me elsewhere. Mentors abound everywhere, friendship is rare and discreet; it finds it easier to get out of a difficult situation with a reproach or a jest than with tears and kisses. Oh, may your friendship be full of warmth and tenderness! Tell me again and again that your

affection has followed me everywhere and that, in my hours of discouragement when I thought I was alone in the world, there was one
heart praying for me that sent his guardian angel to restore me.

Wednesday night

Let us, I beg you, write to each other every day. I feel that only
friendship can save me.

It is still hard for me to hope that I shall be able to survive. For the
moment my only wish is to die at peace and not be compelled to
blaspheme with my last breath, like that innocent fellow who was
guillotined in our town four or five years ago and who cried out on the
scaffold: '*Ah, there is no God!*' You, Malgache, are a believer; I, too,
believe. But I don't know whether I should hope for something better
than the hardships and sufferings of this world. What do you think
about the next? That is what gives me pause. It has been successfully
driven home to me that I shall achieve nothing in this world and that
there is no hope for me on earth. But shall I find rest after these thirty
years of travail? Will the new life I enter be a peaceful, bearable one?
Oh! If God is good he will allow my soul at least a year's rest. Who knows
what repose really is and what renewal it might bring about in the mind!
Alas! If I could only rest beside you, among my friends, in my
homeland, under the roof where I was brought up, where I spent so
many untroubled days! But man's life begins where it should end. In his
first years he is granted a happiness and calm he cannot appreciate until
later, in retrospect; for until he has suffered and struggled, until he has
lived through the years of his maturity, he cannot tell what those
childhood days were worth. According to you, my friend, those who are
wise and strong will eventually achieve such repose through meditation
and will-power. Oh, be sincere, I beg of you, and forget the role of
comforter which your friendship constrains you to adopt with me.
Don't mislead me in the hope of curing me; or all the deceptive
expectations you cause to blossom in my path will only increase the rage
and the pain I shall experience on losing them. Tell me the truth, are
you happy? – No, that's a stupid question and *happiness* is a ridiculous
word that stands for a notion as nebulous as a dream. But do you put up
with life willingly? Would you be sorry if tomorrow God were to deliver
you from it? Is there anything you would miss apart from your children?
For that *instinctive* affection, as you say so well, is the only one that
despair can't undermine. – Tell me, Oh tell me, what has been

116

happening to me for the last ten years and more: this disgust with everything, this all-consuming boredom that follows on the heels of my keenest pleasures and overwhelms and crushes me more and more, is it a disorder of my brain or a consequence of my fate? Am I terribly right to detest life? Am I criminally wrong not to accept it? Social considerations apart and even supposing that we had no children and had both been afflicted by an equal dose of suffering and hardship – do you believe that, in view of our different constitutions, we would find ourselves such as we are, you reconciled to life, me more weary and desperate than ever? Do you all have a faculty which I lack? Am I less well provided for than most and has God denied me that natural love of life which he has given to all creatures for the preservation of the species? Think of my mother: she has suffered materially more than I have, the story of her life is one of the most stormy and melancholy that I know; her natural strength has saved her from everything; her carefree good spirits have survived all her shipwrecks. At sixty she is still attractive and youthful, and every night before going to sleep she prays that God will preserve her life. Ah! my God, my God! Can living really be a pleasure? Why am I not like that? My social position could be excellent; I am independent, the material difficulties of my life have ended; I can travel, indulge all my whims; why are there none left to satisfy?

Don't answer these questions, it's too soon. You don't know the events which have brought me to this state of mind and you might get the wrong idea from an insufficient knowledge and appreciation of the facts. But write about what concerns you. – You have suffered, you have loved, you are highly intelligent, you have seen a great deal, read a great deal; you have travelled, observed, meditated, considered life from many different angles. – You, who could have had a brilliant career, have landed up here, in a little corner of the country, where you have consoled yourself for everything by planting trees and watering flowers. You admit that, at first, you were not happy, that you had a struggle with yourself, that you had to force yourself to do manual labour. Tell me all about these early days and then tell me what has been the outcome of all these struggles and all that courage. Are you at peace? Can you put up with the daily vexations of domestic life without bitterness or despair? Do you fall asleep as soon as your head touches the pillow? Or does a demon in angel's guise not haunt your bedside and shout: 'Love, love! Happiness, life, youth!' while your desolate heart replies: 'It is too late! That might have been, and it has not been.' – O my friend! Do you pass whole nights in weeping for your dreams and saying to yourself 'I have not been happy'?

Oh, I know it, I feel it, that does happen to you sometimes; and maybe I ought not to revive memories of a grief which time and your courage have allayed; but telling me what you did and describing what you have achieved will give you the chance to exercise some of the strength you have stored up. Alas! If only I could, like you, become enthralled by an insect![3] Yet I am interested in such things and I have as much potential as anyone to enjoy life. Like you, I can examine a butterfly's wing with infinite pleasure, for hours on end. Like you, I am enraptured by the scent of a flower. I too would like to build myself an *ajoupa*[4] and take my books there; but I would be incapable of staying there long, and flowers and insects cannot relieve my sufferings. The contemplation of Mont Blanc's unchanging summits for three or four days last month, the sight of that eternal snow, immaculate, sublime in its whiteness and calm, was enough to restore to my soul a serenity it had not known for a long time. But no sooner had I crossed the border into France than that exquisite peace collapsed like an avalanche, when I thought of my troubles and became irritated by my surroundings. The dusty roads, the stench of the stage-coach and hideous nakedness of the landscape were sufficient to make me say: 'Life is unbearable and man is wretched,' and my inner sufferings, true, deep and incurable, were revived.

I console myself with the thought that I shall die reconciled, at least, with the past. There is something strangely powerful about the feel of the countryside, the silence of autumn, the magic of memories and especially the affection of my friends. I walk a great deal and, either because I am tired out or from peace of mind, I sleep better than I have done for over a year. My children are still a source of great sorrow despite the joy they give to me; they are my masters, the sacred ties that bind me to life, to an odious life! I would like to snap these terrible ties but fear of remorse restrains me. And yet there would be much to excuse me if I could tell the story of my heart. But it would be too long, too painful! – Good-night, remember our leavetakings long ago under the great tree, '*the parting's tree*'.[5] We had read *Les Natchez*[6] and each night we repeated: 'I wish you a blue sky and hope.' – Hope in what? . . .

My days flow by drear as death and my strength is fast running out. The day before yesterday I was pretty well, I felt myself sinking into a kind of apathy that was not unpleasant. My heart and my body were so very weary that I was almost incapable of feeling anything. I have accepted the ups and downs of the day without saying, as usual: 'Will I be able to endure another?' I had cast myself back to the past and I enjoyed this absurd illusion to the extent of believing I had been transported into bygone days. I came back from the river with Rollinat and the children. It was hot and it was hard going. I felt a kind of satisfaction at crossing a ploughed field with Solange on my back. Maurice was walking ahead with a little friend; and the house dog, although he normally looks ugly and dejected, followed us so confidently, so assured of having a roof over his head, so faithfully attached to our every step that he seemed to be one of the family. Rollinat,[7] merry in his own way, was joking with my mother, and I brought up the rear with my burden, dividing my attention between the obstacles on my path and thoughts of the advice you had given me. Here, I said to myself, are the simple, honest pleasures my friend praises and prescribes for me. And, for some unknown reason, my weariness, the children's happy voices and my mother's gaiety – though they clashed with the sadness that consumes and overwhelms me – exerted none the less an indefinable charm. I recalled our races to the huge tree, our mushroom picking in the meadows and the time when my son too was small enough to be carried home on my back. I almost forgot the terrible years of experience, activity and passion dividing me from all that.

But this feeling of well-being – which I can only ascribe to exterior circumstances, to the fresh air, the delightful stillness of the country-side, the light-heartedness of my companions – soon wore off and I was plunged again into my habitual gloom on reaching home.

Rollinat is one of the most perfect and affectionate beings on earth, gentle, simple, even-tempered, quiet, sad and compassionate. I don't know of anyone whose intimate daily company can be more salutary; I don't know whether I love him more or less than you; my heart hasn't the strength to question and understand itself any longer; I know that the friendship I feel for Alphonse, for Laure, for each of you, does not detract from anyone in particular. But I can't talk about my sufferings to these youngsters for fear of disturbing their happiness, and can only talk about them to you and Rollinat. He gives me neither advice, encouragement nor comfort; we exchange few words during the day; we walk side by side along the lanes in the valley or up and down the paths in my garden, bent like two old men, wrapped up in a silent grief and understanding each other intuitively. At night we walk in the garden again till midnight; I need to be worn out physically in order to get some sleep, and so does he, for his nerves are always painfully frayed. At such times we recount the details and vexations of our lives. Occasionally we relapse into a profound silence; he stares up at the stars, where he dreams of finding a retreat for me, and I peer blindly into the dark shadows through which we wander. Sometimes their mysterious silence fills me with dread and I have the impression that it is my ghost and not myself who walks in these desolate, tomb-like regions. Then I take his arm, as if to reassure myself that I am still in the world of the living, and he says in that monotonous, hollow voice of his: 'You are ill, very ill!' Despite the little encouragement he gives me (for his disposition is too similar to mine) his friendship means a great deal to me and his company is almost indispensable. It seems to me that so long as I have a true, faithful friend at my side I cannot die hopeless; I made him promise, this evening, to be with me at my last hours and have the courage not to hold me back. There is, in the voices, the eyes, the whole being of those we love, a magnetic fluid, a kind of invisible aura, sensitive to the touch of the soul, as it were, which has a powerful impact on our inmost feelings. Rollinat's presence silently instils sad resignation and a mournful, mute serenity into my being. His silence has perhaps more effect on me than his words. When, at one o'clock in the morning, he is seated at the farthest end of the big drawing room and, in the dim light of a single candle which had been left burning on the table, I glance from time to time at his serious, dreamy face, his sunken eyes, his tightly closed lips, his forehead furrowed by ceaseless meditation, then it seems that I have before me unassuming courage and sad patience personified. O friendship, so sparing in demonstration, so rich in devotion, who can repay you for the dark hours and melancholy thoughts endured at the side of a dying soul? Sitting there like a hopeless physician by the deathbed of a friend, it is as though Rollinat counted the pulse of my despair and calculated the number of painful days I have still to endure. Longing in his conscience to hear the hour of my deliverance ring out, yet heartbroken in his affection at having so soon to abandon this corpse on which he continues to lavish his useless and generous care, he sees my misery; he neither prays nor weeps; he contrives with his arm a last pillow for my head and says nothing of what he will feel when my eyes have closed forever. O just God! Give him a friend who will live for him and not forsake him in death!

I am frequently overcome by shame at my cowardice which stops me from putting an end to all this straight away. Can I not make up my mind about anything? Can I neither live nor die? There are times when I think work, love or suffering must surely have worn me out and that I am no longer good for anything at all; yet it takes very little to make me aware that this is not so and that I am going to die in full possession of all my bodily strength and intellectual faculties. Oh, no! It isn't the strength to go on living and hoping that I lack; it is the faith and the will. Whenever an external event rouses me from my depression, when chance obliges and compels me to behave according to my nature, I act with more presence of mind, more calmly than I ever did. – I am still myself despite the humiliations and the wounds inflicted on me, despite the mud and the stones that have been thrown at me in the vain hope of blocking the live and plentiful flow of the qualities God has bestowed on me. Alas! That stream has been sadly troubled and no longer reflects the sky's splendour. But when any sufferer draws near, it still flows for him and he can drink freely without being denied its salutary waters. Moreover, this good that I do without enthusiasm and even without pleasure, the duties I fulfil without any trivial satisfaction or without any hope of finding some comfort in doing so are stern sacrifices but perhaps more valuable in God's eyes than the eager offerings of a happier, younger heart. It is now that I feel deeply that I am still sound at the core since, unawares, the love of goodness flowers in me among the most dismal ruins. O my God – if only there could fall upon me from your paternal hand a single firm belief, a purpose or even just a desire! But I search my empty soul in vain. Virtue for me is no more than a habit, strong enough to have become a need but providing no pleasure; faith is no more than a far-off glimmer, lovely still in its sorrowful pallor, but silent, indifferent to my life and to my death, a voice lost in heaven's vastness that does not command me to believe but only to hope. My will is no more than a humble, silent attendant upon this remnant of virtue and religion. It restricts its activity to what is required of it and has perhaps, a third master, more powerful than faith or virtue, which is pride.

Yes, pride – wounded but still haughty and erect under the afflictions and defamation with which they have tried to overwhelm it.

No one has been more insulted and slandered than I have and no one has clung more painfully and stubbornly to faith in a heavenly justice and to the belief in one's own innocence. Oh! How could pride be absent when one has to fight such an unjust war? Why has God let me be made so unhappy? And why does he allow the effrontery of cowards to sully and destroy the lives of honest men? Must then the innocent rise up in his grief and, in wiping away the tears of rage and shame, cleanse himself of the mud that has been cast at him? Lord! Lord! What is your purpose when you send a guardian angel to the infant at its mother's breast, and when your providence cares for the tiniest blade of grass in the meadows, but yet allows the weak to be bruised and insulted, and when honour, the brightest flower that grows on our path, is crushed and trampled underfoot by the first schoolboy who passes? Is then the man whose brow is furrowed by thought and suffering less important to you than the passive, untried soul of a mother's nursling? Is our sad human glory more despicable in your sight than the nettle that thrives in the churchyard? O God in Heaven! Look down, hear me, and make justice prevail.[8]

To Rollinat

Friday night

How are you, my friend? You were dejected and ailing when you left. Reassure me at least as to your health. Your soul is naturally disposed to sadness and you weren't happy even before you knew me. But I feel guilty none the less; for I must have cruelly encouraged your tendency to suffering and the perpetual anxiety that consumes you. My sombre, incurable grief must have contaminated you and the dismal resolutions I have been talking about all these last days while you were here must have overshadowed and tried your friendship, so loyal and so precious as it is. Forgive me, my poor friend; I wanted to lean on you, to rest for a moment on your arm; I wanted to tell you of my anguish so as to accustom myself to the calm of despair, so as to carry it with me to the grave, eased and tempered by the tears of friendship. You have had the courage to hear me in silence and to refrain from any vain consolations; you simply told me of your affection, the one thing of which I could think without bitterness and suspicion. Oh! I thank you! I have obtained from you the difficult and sacred promise that you would come and, as it were, commune with me at my last hour. Malgache would not have that strength; it demands an older, more resigned heart to say: 'Go!' rather than 'Come back to us!' – I can come back to nothing and to no one.

Do not let yourself be moved or shaken by this desperate state in which you see me; do not let compassion turn into suffering; do not let melancholy destroy what is pleasant and what is important in your life. Why should it? You are useful, you are needed, you are good, and yet you would find existence hard to endure! Oh, no! Do not cast off the burden of life which you bear with such a nobility that it will always ensure for you instant communion with noble souls. You will have other friendships, greater, less barren, less unhappy than mine. You will find, at the heart of your humble and painful destiny, a glorious old age. O, my friend, if only I had a labour such as yours to accomplish, if the handle of that plough with which you cut such a vigorous furrow in the world were put into my hands, then I would not only recover from my despair but would put to good use all the strength I have in me, which the world has scorned as a source of error and crime.

But you, at least, you know me. You know whether or not there are in this lacerated heart any base passions, any trace of cowardice, of treacherous duplicity, the slightest inclination towards a single vice. You know that if there is anything that distinguishes me from all the despicably second-rate beings that encumber the earth, it is neither the vainglory of a name nor the frivolous talent of writing a few pages. You know that it is the strong passion for truth, fierce love of justice. You know that I am devoured by pride, but that this pride is neither mean nor culpable, that it has never induced me to commit a shameful deed, and might even have led me to an heroic fate had I not been born in fetters! Well, my friend, what shall I do with such a disposition? What good will come of a strength of character that has always made me scorn public opinion and conventions – not insofar as they are worthy and necessary but insofar as they are odious and degrading? To what use can I put it? Who will listen to me, who will believe me? Who will live by my ideas? Who will rise up at my word to tread the straight and splendid path I long to see mankind follow? No one. – Oh, if I could at least bring up my children with such opinions, flatter myself with the hope that these beings who are of my blood will not become like cattle under the yoke or puppets controlled by the strings of prejudice and convention, but really intelligent, warm-hearted beings, indomitable in their pride, faithful unto martyrdom in their affections! If I could make of them a man and woman in God's image! But that can never be. My children, condemned to walk in the mire of beaten tracks, surrounded by warring influences, warned at every step by those who oppose me to be wary of me and of what they call dreams; my children, themselves spectators of my sufferings in the midst of this ceaseless struggle, conscious of my embittered heart, of my knees broken at each step as I stumble against the obstacles of everyday life; my poor children, my flesh and my soul, will they not perhaps turn on me and say: 'You are leading us astray; you would ruin us with you! Aren't you unhappy, rebuffed and slandered? What have you to show for your unequal struggle, for your bragging duels against convention and belief? Let us do as others do; let us glean the rewards of this easy permissive world; let us indulge in the thousand and one little meannesses that procure peace and happiness among men. Don't speak to us of those stern, unknown virtues which others call madness and which only bring isolation and suicide in their wake.'

That is what they will say to me. Or if, out of affection and their natural disposition, they listen to me and believe me, where shall I lead them? Into what abyss shall we hurl ourselves then, all three? For we shall be three on this earth, and no one with us! What shall I tell them if they come and say to me: 'You are right, life is unbearable in such a world; let us die together! Show us the road to Bernica, or the lake of Stenio, or the glaciers of Jacques!'[9]

It is not that in my pride I want to suggest that I am isolated by my opinions in this world only because of my exceptional greatness or intelligence. No! I am a creature riddled with faults and weaknesses, and the thickest veils of ignorance shroud my mind's brightest insights. I am alone as a result of disenchantment and lost illusions. Those illusions were palpable; but who has not been taken in by them? They were shattered; who has not also seen his own turn to dust? But there was one I had in particular, vast and beautiful, such as my soul was in those early years when I had just emerged from adolescence. That one proved to be a seal of everlasting calamity, a death sentence. But all this would require a great deal more space and a kind of history of my youth. I shall give it to you, some day.[10]

When you are dropping off to sleep think of me; think of that midnight when the stars were so white, the air so mildly humid, the paths so dark; think of that sanded walk bordered with thyme and flowering shrubs which we walked up and down a hundred times in half

124

an hour and where we exchanged such dismal confidences and such sacred vows! Then sleep in peace, once you have sent me a blessing and a good-night. I shall be writing to you at that time so that I shall not have missed one of these midnight talks of which you deprive me, kind, weary heart, but which you will grant me for a few more days, before I leave you for ever!

Saturday

Yes, in those days I had a strange illusion, as naïve as my youth, as boyish as my turn of mind and habits. It would take too long to tell you of all the future it encompassed, but it can be summed up in these few words: to find justice in this world and the next we only have to be truly just, ourselves.

This was not so much a theory as a conviction. I was well aware that there were some honest, pure hearts that were misunderstood by men and seemed to have been forsaken by providence. Even in the restricted circle I inhabited I could name quite a few; but I had created a complete moral universe from the words *a just man*, and I had an image of him in my mind – which, in those days, was crammed full of the Bible, history, poetry and philosophy – perfectly suited to my dreams. I came across this portrait of the just man[11] among the scribblings I used to hide under my pillow when I was sixteen. Here it is, a rough diamond:

The just being has no moral sex; he is man or woman according to God's will; but his law is always the same, whether for an army general or the mother of a family.

The just man has no status. He is a beggar, an explorer or one of the princes of the earth according to God's will. His aim, his profession is to be just.

The just man is strong, calm and chaste. He is brave, active, deliberate. He watches over all his first impulses until all his first impulses are good. He despises life and, if someone better than himself has the least need of his place in this world, he yields it with a good will and offers himself to God saying: 'Lord, if I hinder my brother, take my life. I shall ride this charger, I shall leap over this hedge, I shall cross this swamp, I shall or shall not survive the danger according to your good pleasure, O my God!' – The just man is always prepared to stand forth in front of God.

The just man has no fortune, no home, no slaves. His servants are his friends if they are worthy of being so. His roof belongs to the wayfarer, his purse and his clothing to all the needy, his time and his judgement to all who require them.

The just man loathes the wicked and despises cowards. He gives them bread if they are hungry and advice if they seek it. If they mend their ways he commends them and forgives them; if they persist in their evil he ignores them but does not fear them; and if a murderer attacks him he valiantly kills him and considers he has served as an instrument of God's justice.

The just man is never idle. He works as hard as he can with his hands or his brain according to his needs and the needs of others. When he is weary he rests and thinks about God; when he is ill he resigns himself and dreams of Heaven.

The just man opens his heart to friendship. What he loves best after God is his friend; and he is never afraid to love him too much because he can only love those who are worthy of him.

The just man is proud but not vain. He doesn't care whether he is young, handsome, rich or admired, but he cares about being just; and although he forgives those who misjudge him, he keeps them at a distance. He knows that those who fail to understand him do not resemble him and that, were he to love them, he would cease to be just.

The just man is, above all else, sincere, and that is what requires a sublime strength, because the world is nothing but lies, imposture or vanity, betrayal or prejudice.

The just man scorns public opinion; he champions the weak and the oppressed and only raises his voice among men to defend those whom they unjustly accuse. He trusts nobody's verdict but his own. He only believes in evil when it is irrefutable and, unconcerned with the censure and mockery of others, goes to listen to Job's lamentations even on his dung-heap.

The just man sins seven times a day, but his sins are the sins of the just. There are sins he never commits and whose existence he doesn't even suspect.

The just man is often abused and slandered; but he always obtains justice because he loves it, because he wants it, because he is strong and knows how to enforce it. He has enemies, and there are many others who are indifferent to him; sometimes the mob itself is against him; but he has for his friends a handful of just men like himself who seek each other out and are to be found together in this world and will inherit the kingdom of God in the next.

This curious proclamation of what, schoolboy that I was, I called my *Rights of Man*; this artless mixture of heresy and religious common-place, contains none the less, don't you think, a definite ordering of ideas, a plan of life, a choice of resolutions and evidence of a scrupulously chosen and faithfully pursued ideal? It illustrates more or less accurately my adolescent illusions and, mingled with notions fresh from the Gospels, a kind of rebellious strictness dictated by a budding pride, innate stubbornness, hazy dreams of human grandeur mingled with deeper Christian aspirations.

Presumptuous or foolish, I had this hope of achieving the status of a *just man* – that is, of exercising mercy, frankness and austerity with calm and joy; of bearing contradiction and blame with indifference and steadfastness, and of leaving behind a name that would be honoured by the chosen few of the men encountered in this life. That desire for a humble but worthy reputation, for a long hard task, a struggle against society finally crowned with success (or, at least, with the respect of that little band of good people I hoped to rejoin on the unknown seas of the future), that faith in divine and human justice was the dream, the illusion of my happiest years. What has come of it? A terrible regret, the source of world-weariness and disgust for which the only cure is death.

That was the source of my good qualities and my defects; or perhaps it was my good qualities and defects that suggested these false ideas to me. To them I owe plenty of useless virtues, much pointless courage, many pieces of foolhardy heroism, many acts of noble imbecility and sublime self-denial, whose purpose and outcome were unspeakably ridiculous. I wanted to play the strong man and I was as powerless as a child. Shall I rue it, now that I am about to appear before my God? No! For if divine justice is a dream like human justice, at least there is the peace of nothingness which must be welcome after the tribulations of a life such as mine.

And those just men, I really have met them and have shaken them by the hand; and their respect, especially yours, O my friend, has been a soothing balm to my wounds. I have practised that justice – not always as steadfastly as I had planned in those days of youthful puritanism – because emotion, exhaustion, suffering or love frequently numbed or turned aside this arm that was to have been always at the service of the weak and the needy. If that harsh and prudent severity towards evil has sometimes been led astray by a judgement too prone to err, by a heart too readily beguiled, yet I never committed any act, indulged in any vice or accepted any principle that made me depart from the path of justice; I have trodden it slowly, stopping more than once and wasting a lot of time and trouble in the pursuit of mirages. But the impulse, the need to be true to myself always kept my steps on the ivory track,[12] and if I am not yet the just man I wanted to be, there is nothing in my past to prevent me from becoming so in the future; it is in the present that there lies an obstacle huge as a fallen mountain: that obstacle is despair.

And why has this ghostly phantom spread its oppressive, icy limbs over me? Why has the bitterness penetrated my heart so deeply that every blessing, every consolation which my reason acknowledges, my instinct rejects? Why did I say to you the other night in the garden, my heart filled with dark foreboding: 'Some voice calls out to me from nature everywhere – from the grass and the leaves, the echo and the horizon, from the sky and the earth, the stars and the flowers, and from the sun, the darkness, the moon and the dawn, and even from the eyes of my friends: *"Go away, you have nothing more to do here!"*'

Perhaps it is because my ambitions centred on the intellect and the heart; because I took my notion of the just man's character too much from antiquity and was unable to keep my mind free from the paltry vexations of the present day. I said: 'I shall do this and I shall be at peace'; I did it and I was still troubled. Then I said: 'I shall confront those dangers and I shall not shrink'; I confronted them and emerged wan with fear. Finally I said: 'I shall obtain these good things and ask for nothing else'; I obtained them and they do not satisfy me. I have done my duty tolerably well; but I have found the task harder and the satisfaction less pleasurable than I had imagined. Why does reality, instead of showing itself as it really is – huge, gaunt, naked and terrible – pretend to be smiling, beautiful and blossoming, when it appears to children in their dreams?

To the Malgache

I have been reading voraciously for the last few days. I say 'voraciously' because it is well over three years since I last read the equivalent of an octavo volume, and now I have devoured and digested three whole books in a fortnight: *The Eucharist* by the Abbé Gerbet, *Reflections on Suicide* by Madame de Staël and the *Life of Alfieri* by Victor Alfieri.[13] I read the first by chance; the second out of curiosity to see what that male-female made of life; the third out of sympathy, because someone commended it as a book that would strongly appeal to me.

A sermon, a dissertation and an autobiography. Alfieri's life is like a novel; it is interesting, exciting and moving. The Abbé's Catholicism has the narrow solemnity and the inevitable uselessness of ascetic writings. Only Madame de Staël's dissertation is really what it sets out to be, an accurate, logical piece of writing, commonplace in its ideas, beautiful in its style and skilful in its structure. I found no other solace in this book than the pleasure of learning that Madame de Staël loved life, had a thousand motives for holding on to it, that she had an incomparably happier fate and an incomparably stronger and more intelligent mind than mine. I think, moreover, that her book has increased the attractions of suicide for me. When I happen to meet a village pedagogue he bores me, but I put up with him because he is doing his job. But if I come across an eminent professor and, in the hope that he will be able to help me, consult him in order to clarify my doubts and calm my anxiety, I would be much more shocked and far more upset than before if he were to impart, in elegant phrases and well-chosen words, the same platitudes as the village schoolmaster had just delivered in Dog Latin. He had the merit, at least, of sometimes making me smile at his barbarisms and his pomposity could be comical; the academic coldness of the other is only dreary – like an oak tree we cling to for safety that snaps like a reed and lets us down more harshly than ever.

The Eucharist is undoubtedly a distinguished work despite its shortcomings. I am very glad to have read it; not that it has helped me in any way – it is too Catholic for my taste, and specialist books do good only to a few people – but because it took me back to the days of my first youth, so devout, tender and credulous.

Alfieri is a man after my own heart. I like his pride and am interested in these terrible struggles between his pride and his weakness. What I admire is his energy, his patience and the tremendous pains he took to become a poet. Alas! Yet another of those who have suffered, loathed life, wept and (as he puts it) *roared* in suicidal anguish; and he, like the rest, was comforted by a bauble! He was acquainted with love, with dreadful disappointments and with remorse mingled with shame and contempt, and the boredom of solitude, and the chill of scorn, and a sad insight into all things . . . except the last bauble that saved him: fame!

This *Life of Alfieri*, considered as a *book*, is one of the best I know. True, I know very few, especially from that period, about which my memory is quite blank; this one is written with great simplicity, and a detachment which none the less involves the reader; with conciseness and rapidity, marked by order and moderation. I think that all those who decide to write their lives should take as model the form, dimensions and manner of this work. That is what I resolved while reading it, and that is precisely what I am sure I shall never do.

To sum up, I want to tell you that reading does me much more harm than good. I want to wean myself of it as soon as possible. It increases my uncertainty of any truth, my despair of any future. All those who write the story of human afflictions or of their own preach from the height of their serenity or their forgetfulness. Tamely seated on the peaceful hobby-horse that extricated them from danger, they talk to me about the method, the faith or the vanity that comforts them. One is devout, the other wise, the great Alfieri writes tragedies. Through the mists of their present contentment they see their past afflictions as insignificant specks of dust, and treat mine as the same; they don't realize that mine are in fact mountains as their own once were. They have surmounted them while I, like Prometheus, remain at the foot with only my breast exposed for a vulture to feed on. They smile calmly, the cruel creatures! One pronounces upon my agony with this verdict of religious scorn: *vanitas!* The next calls my anguish *weakness*, and the third, *ignorance*. 'When I lacked faith,' says one, 'I too lay under that rock: have faith and arise!' 'Are you at death's door?' asks Madame de Staël. 'Think about the great heroes of antiquity and make up a few fine phrases about them. Nothing is more consoling than rhetoric.'[14] 'You are bored?' says Alfieri. 'Ah! How tedious I, too, found life! But *Cleopatra*[15] got me over that!' Well, yes, I know it, you are all happy, good and famous. You all cry: 'Get up, do as I do, write, sing, love, pray.' Even you, my good Malgache, who tell me to build an *ajoupa* and read the classifications of Linnaeus[16] in it! My masters and my friends, have you nothing better to say to me? Can none of you put his hand on this rock and remove it from my bleeding and exhausted body? Oh, well! If I must die without help, at least recite for me the lamentations of Jeremiah or of Job. They were not pedants; they said simply: *Rottenness is in my bones and the worms of the sepulchre have entered my flesh.*

To Rollinat

I am extremely vexed at having written that bad book known as *Lélia*. It is not that I regret it: that book is the most daring and genuine thing I have ever done – even if it is the most foolish and the most calculated to make me disgusted with the world, because of its results. But there are many things that one fumes about while knowing they don't matter; many wasps that sting and irritate without infuriating; many vexations that make life dreary but not totally insupportable. The satisfaction of having done these things soon makes one forget the hostility caused.

If I am vexed at having written *Lélia* it is because now I can't write it any more. The frame of mind I'm in is so similar to the one I described and experienced while writing the book that it would have been a great relief to be able to start it again today. Unfortunately one cannot write two books on the same theme without making many changes. The frame of mind in which I wrote *Jacques* (which has not yet come out) allowed me to modify the personality of *Lélia* considerably, to dress it up differently and make it more acceptable to the public. At present I have finished *Jacques* and instead of finding a third frame of mind I relapse into the first. What! Will I never reach the point when my mind is made up? O, my friends! If ever I do, you'll see what profound philosophers, aged stoics and grey-bearded hermits will stalk the pages of my books! What weighty dissertations, magnificent orations, lofty reproofs and pious sermons will flow from my pen! How I shall beg forgiveness for having been young and unhappy, how I shall extol to you the saintly wisdom of old age and the peaceful joys of egotism! Let no one dare to be miserable when that time comes; for I'll set to work, on the spot, covering three quires of paper to prove that he is a fool and a coward and that, for my part, I am perfectly happy. I'll be as insincere, as turgid, as frigid and as useless as Trenmor,[17] a type I scoffed at more than anyone else did, and before anyone else; but no one was aware of this. They didn't realize that having embodied different passions and opinions in human form, I was logically constrained to personify human reason also, which I had gone to a prison to find. And after having set it up like a gibbet in the midst of the other chatterers, I made it end up as a great white staff that goes wandering off towards the pastures of the future, led on by will-o'-the-wisps.

I can hear you asking me if the book you took so seriously is a comedy, you who are a veritable Trenmor of strength and virtue, capable of thinking all the things my Trenmor says, of doing all the things he merely suggests. My answer is yes and no according to the time of day. There were nights of self-communion, of austere suffering, of enthusiastic resignation, when I wrote some very fine passages in good faith. There were morning hours of weariness, sleeplessness and rage when I derided the work of the previous night and believed all the blasphemies I wrote. There were afternoons of ironic, playful humour when, escaping like today from the pedantry of comforters, I enjoyed creating Trenmor the philosopher, more hollow than a gourd, and more improbable than happiness. This book that is so bad and so good, so true and so false, so serious and so mocking is certainly the most deeply, the most painfully and the most bitterly felt work that a demented mind has ever produced. That is why it is deceptive, mysterious and incapable of being a success. Those who thought they were reading a novel were justified in saying it was odious. Those who took for reality all the sadness of purity that the allegory concealed had every reason to be shocked. Those who hoped to see a treatise on morals or philosophy emerge from these fancies were right in finding the conclusion absurd and tiresome. Only those who, suffering the same anguish, have listened to it as to a broken lament mingled with feverish sobs, baleful laughter and oaths – only they have completely understood it and they care for it without approving of it. They think of it exactly as I do: that it is a hideous, very well dissected crocodile, a naked, bleeding heart[18] – an object of horror and of pity.

Where are the days when no one dared publish a book without furnishing it – not only with the King's licence – but with a good moral: substantial, bourgeois, well-worn and quite useless. People of heart and intellect never failed to prove the polar opposite of what they had set out to prove. The Abbé Prévost,[19] while clearly stating through the lips of Tiberge that it is most unfortunate and extremely debasing to fall in love with a prostitute, proved by the example of des Grieux that love elevates everything and that nothing a generous heart feels deeply can ever be vile. To crown the blunder, Tiberge is futile, Manon is adorable and the whole book is a sublime monument to love and truth.

Whatever Jean-Jacques does, the reader can only take Julie to his heart again when she is about to die and writes to Saint-Preux[20] that she has never ceased to love him. It is Madame de Staël, that logical, argumentative, practical woman, who points this out. Madame de Staël also observes that the letter in defence of suicide is very superior to the letter that condemns it. Alas! Why in your writings do you go against your nature, Jean-Jacques? If it is true, as many believe, that you killed yourself, why should that have been hidden from us? Why so much sublime nonsense to conceal an overwhelming despair? Unhappy martyr, who tried to be a classical philosopher like anybody else, why didn't you cry out at the top of your voice? It would have consoled you and we should partake of your blood with more fervour; we should pray to you, as to Christ, dropping holy tears.

Is it fine, or is it childish, this affectation of a benevolent purpose? Is it the freedom of the press, or the example of Goethe followed by that of Byron, or is it the century's rationality that has set us free from it? Is it a crime to reveal all our griefs, all our disenchantment? Is it a virtue to conceal it? To be silent – perhaps, yes; but to lie! . . . to have the courage to write volumes in order to conceal from others and from ourself the depths of our soul!

All right, yes, I do think it is fine! These men were struggling to cure themselves and to use their recovery to help other sufferers. In trying to persuade others they persuaded themselves. Their pride, wounded by the world, was restored by declaring to the world that they had been able to heal their wounds on their own. Guileless saviours of your guileless contemporaries, you didn't notice the ills you were sowing under the cover of the sacred flowers of your eloquence! You hadn't dreamed of a generation such as this one, whom nothing can deceive, who examine and dissect every emotion and who, beneath the haloes of your Christian glory, perceive your pale brows, furrowed by the storm! You hadn't foreseen that your precepts would become outmoded, and that only your sufferings would survive – for us and for our descendants.

To François Rollinat[1]

January 1835

Why the devil didn't you come yesterday? We waited dinner for you till seven o'clock – something which is beyond a joke for appetites stimulated by the brisk country air. Did some long-winded client detain you? You are not ill, I trust? Now, we are not expecting you till Saturday. In the meantime let me know how you are – mind you do so, Pylades[2] – we shall be anxious. The way you have looked these three months has done nothing to put our minds at rest. Poor little yellow old man, what is wrong with you? I know what your usual reply to such a question is: 'What about you? What is wrong with you? Are you so wealthy, young, hale and hearty that you can afford to worry about my state of health?' Alas! We both cut a poor figure, and these parchment envelopes of ours contain sadly weary and blighted souls, my fellow sufferer!

Nonsense! What am I talking about? We were livelier than ever last night; though we missed you sorely, we drank your health and after many toasts to you were all of us rather merry. Certainly, Pylades, the good things Fate keeps in reserve for us cannot be denied. Just as we think that all is lost, the kind Goddess who smiles at our despair is there, behind our backs, wrapping a pretty little rattle in tinsel and putting it into our hands so sweetly we never suspect her intentions; for if we imagined for a moment that she was making fun of us and didn't take our wrath seriously we would be capable of killing ourselves to make her believe us. But we hope that she is not unimpressed by our threats and that she will treat us better in future; little by little we condescend to look at the plaything she has given us, then begin to shake its bells muttering: 'Bells of folly, you can tinkle for all you are worth, we are not amused.' But we shake it again and listen so willingly that we soon become rattles ourselves and laughter and joyous songs come from our empty, desolate hearts. We have now all sorts of good reasons for accepting life, quite as good as those that had made us reject it the previous week. What a bad joke the human heart is! What is this heart we talk about so much and so well? What makes it so whimsical, so inconsistent, so reluctant to suffer, so willing to rejoice? Is there a good and a bad angel who take it in turns to breathe upon this miserable life-giving organ? Can this diaphragm, which expands in response to a cup of coffee and a kind word, be a spirit, a spark of Divinity? But if it is nothing but a blood-soaked sponge where do these sudden aspirations, these tremors come from? How can anguish suddenly burst from it in harrowing cries when certain syllables reach our ears, or when a lamp, playing on the fringe of a curtain or an angle in the wainscot, throws on the wall some fantastic silhouettes, some profiles sketched by chance, stamped with uncanny resemblances? What is it that makes some of us, in the middle of our dinner parties – where, thank God, there is no lack of noise and merriment – begin to sob without knowing why? 'He is drunk,' the others say. But why should wine, that makes others merry, make some cry? O, human merriment, how akin you are to grief! And what is this power that a certain sound, an object or a stray thought has over us all? When we are a score of madmen together, shouting in all the wrong keys and running the gamut of drunken incoherence in our songs, if one of us says with a solemn gesture: 'Hark!' we all fall silent and listen. Then in the stillness of those vast rooms a distant, plaintive voice is raised. It comes from the furthest reaches of the valley, it rises in a harmonious spiral, circles the fir trees in the garden, then reaches the corner of the house; it glides through a window, floats along the corridors and expires against the door of the salon with heartrending sobs. Then all our faces fall, our lips blanch; we all remain glued to our places in the posture in which the sound surprised us. At last someone cries: 'Why, it's only the wind, it doesn't matter!' And indeed it is the wind, only the wind and the night; but it does matter, there is not one who finds it easy to overcome the sadness such things inspire. But why is it sad? Do the fox or the partridge feel melancholy when the wind sobs in the heather? Is the doe moved by the rising moon? What sort of creature is this then, who claims to be the lord of creation and whose dreams are full of nothing but tears and dread?

Yet why should we be sad unless we have lost our senses? Our wives are charming and our friends – could they be better? Are there many mortals who have had the good luck in life to muster under the same

135

roof, nearly every day for a month, twelve or fifteen noble, true companions, all bound together by the sacred ties of friendship?[3] O, my friends, my dear friends! Do you know what you mean in the life of an unhappy man? You are not sufficiently aware of it, not sufficiently proud of the good you do; it is something to save a soul from despair.

Alas! Alas! What is this mixture of bitterness and joy, what this feeling of detachment and affection that brings me back here each year in the season which is no longer autumn and is not yet winter, this month of melancholy self-communing and tender misanthropy? For there is something of all this in my poor, weary head, oppressed by the paternal roof in all its solemnity. O my household gods! You are here just as I left you. I bow to you with a veneration which is made more profound by each passing year. Dusty idols, who looked down on the cradles of my forebears and on my own and those of my children; who saw the coffins of the former and will see those of the others carried out, greetings, O protectors, before whom my childhood tremblingly worshipped; friendly gods, whom I tearfully invoked, from distant, alien shores, in the midst of stormy passions. What I experience on seeing you once more is very sweet and very terrible. Why did I leave you, you who always favour simple hearts, who watch over little children while their mothers sleep, who let dreams of innocent love hover over the beds of young girls, who give restoring slumber to the aged? Do you recognize me, peaceful Penates? This pilgrim who comes on foot along the dusty ways in the evening mist, do you not take him for a stranger? His faded cheeks, his ravaged brow, his eyes sunk with weeping, as the ravine is hollowed out by the torrent, his infirmities, his sadness and his scars, does not all this prevent you from recognizing the brave heart clothed in a sturdy body that set out from here one morning astride a gallant mare? This steady and untiring mount had been raised on the heath, and it seemed as if horse and rider were off to tour the world. Here is that man; the children have nicknamed him Toby[4] and support him to enable him to walk. The mare is over there, grazing peacefully among the nettles by the graveyard walls; she is Colette who, though now blind, still finds her way back by instinct and memory to the litter where she will soon die.

Well, my Colette! Your happy days are over; but it was a kind deed to keep a corner for you and a bundle of hay in the stables. Who ensured that you had the good fortune not to be sold to the knacker like other old horses? It is the most sacred right, old age. What has been is worthy of respect; what is must always be subjected to doubt and questioning. Why then is your old master treated with affection here? Nobody knows him any more, he has been absent for a long time, he has travelled afar; he looks different; his tastes, his habits, his character are all unfamiliar, for so many things have happened to him since the days when he was still strong and proud. But one simple, tender phrase links him to those who might be suspicious of him. That phrase is 'Once upon a time.' – He was here, they say, we did things together, he was one of us, we knew him; he went hunting over there, he picked mushrooms in that meadow there, don't you remember so-and-so's wedding, so-and-so's funeral . . .? When once we get to the stage of 'Don't you remember?' what precious links of gold and diamonds unite hearts that have gone cold! How faces glow as sudden waves of youthfulness revive forgotten pleasures and neglected friendships! And at such moments one often imagines that the links were stronger than they really were, and certainly past pleasures, like promised pleasures, seem keener than those within reach.

Ah, but what an unalloyed pleasure it is to embrace one's friends after a long absence, crying, 'So there you are, old fellow! And is that you, my child? – and you, my niece, and you, my sister!'

Therefore, my friend, don't tell me that I am plucky and that my cheerfulness is a façade I put on out of friendship for you and for them. Don't believe such a thing! I am in fact happy, happy through you, unhappy through others. And once I am here, what does anyone but you matter? Do you think I worry about the others? – True, I think of them in spite of myself; but why talk about it, why should you be told? Oh no! Let nobody be told, apart from the one or two old friends who can't misinterpret the lines on my brow. But let the others know only how much pleasure they give me. Those poor youngsters would scarcely believe it if they could see the depth of the abyss they cover with flowers. They would shrink from it in terror, saying, 'Nothing can grow on this barren soil!' For incurables have no friends and when men are of no more use to each other those who can save themselves flee and the one for whom there is no hope dies alone. Could those young minds fathom what goes on in the minds of those who have experienced life? Do they know that in their hearts are all the elements of joy and sorrow, but that they are not able to make use of any of them? At their age all suffering either kills or must be killed; at their age there are only mortal griefs, fatal diseases, unflinching resolutions, dark and silent despair. But after these irrevocable stages, youth comes into its own; their hearts are revived and tempered, their energy returns with redoubled intensity to make up for lost time; and they have ten or twenty stormy years of terrible grief and indescribable joy. But once we have been battered by experience, and our passions, not deadened but repressed, flare up again and immediately subside, terrified by the shades of the past, then the human heart, once so ready to promise and to undertake, no longer recognizes itself. It knows what it was but not what it will become; for the heart has struggled for so long that it can't count on its strength any more. And besides, the taste for suffering which is so natural to the young has been lost. The old have suffered enough. Their grief has no poetry left; grief only embellishes what is beautiful.

Pallor lends a touch of the divine to female beauty and ennobles the youth of men. But when grief brings about irreparable havoc, when it traces furrows on faded brows, it becomes disagreeable and threatening. We hide it like a vice, conceal it from view lest the fear of contagion keep those who are happy at a distance. That is when we are really worthy of pity; for we don't complain and dread being pitied. It is at this time of life that contemporaries understand each other with a glance and a word is enough for them to communicate a whole life story.

How is it that when we meet again after some months you are able so easily to read in my face the tale of my woes? How is it that you say without hesitation, as you grasp my hand: 'Well, well! So this is what has happened to you; this is what you have done; I know what is in your heart.' Oh, how you then spell out all the details of my misfortune! Poor creatures that we are! These sorrows we describe so emphatically, whose burden we bear so proudly, are common to all! Everyone has experienced them; it is like the toothache – everyone says to you: 'I pity you, it hurts terribly' – and all is said.

How sad it is! Oh, how sad! But what is fine and generous about friendship is that it worries and cares about our sufferings as if they were unique of their kind. O sweet compassion, motherly indulgence for a child who cries and wants to be pitied! How pleasant to find it in the sober, mature heart of an old friend. He knows everything, he is accustomed to tending your wounds; yet he is not hardened to your sufferings and his pity is constantly renewed. Friendship! Friendship! Balm to the hearts of those whom love has ill-treated and forsaken; generous sister whom we neglect and who always forgives! Oh, I beg you, I implore you, my Pylades, do not see me as a tragic figure, do not tell me that it requires an appalling effort from me to sustain this cheerfulness. No, no! This is not a part I am playing, it is not a duty, it is not even calculated: it is an instinct and a need. Human nature rejects what is bad for it; the soul does not want to suffer any more than the body wants to die, and it is when they are confronted with the greatest suffering and the gravest illness that the soul and body set about denying and fleeing from the hateful presence of destruction. There are extreme cases when suicide becomes a necessity, a mania; part of the brain has been affected and is physically atrophied. But if the crisis passes, then nature, that hardy nature God created to last out its time, stretches out a desperate hand and clutches at the merest blade of grass to stop itself from rolling into the grave. When Providence made men's lives so miserable, it was well aware that it would have to make them dread death. And that is the grandest, most inexplicable of the miracles which conspire towards the duration of the human species; for anyone who could see clearly just how things are would kill himself. These moments of fatal lucidity do occur, but we do not always give in to them, and the miracle that enables flowers to blossom again after the snow and the ice works within the heart of man. And besides, don't all those things we call human reason and wisdom, all those books, all those philosophies, all those social and religious obligations – don't they all bind us to life? Were they not invented to help us to encourage that natural tendency, like all the basic principles such as property, despotism and the rest? Those laws are full of wisdom and made to last; but there might be more noble ones, and Jesus, by suffering martyrdom, set a grand precedent for suicide. As for me, I assure you that if I don't kill myself, it is entirely due to the fact that I am a coward.

And what makes me cowardly? Not fear of suffering a little pain from the knife or the gun; but the dread of ceasing to exist, the grief of leaving my family, my children, my friends; the horror of the tomb; for although my soul hopes for an after-life, it is so intimately bound to this poor body and has become, through living in it, so tenderly indulgent towards it, that it shudders at the idea of leaving it to rot and to be eaten by worms. It is well aware that neither the one nor the other will then know anything about it; but so long as they are united, the soul respects and takes care of the body and can't conceive an existence independent of it.

So I put up with life because I love it; and although the sum of my pains is infinitely greater than that of my pleasures, although I have lost those things without which I thought I could not live, I still love that sad fate which is left to me, and every time I make my peace with it I discover that it has attractions I had forgotten or scornfully denied when I was happy and vainglorious. Oh, man can be so insolent when his passions are satisfied! When he loves and is loved how he despises everything that is not love! How little he values his life! How ready he is to get rid of it as soon as his star begins to fade! And when he loses what he loves, what agony, what convulsions, what loathing for the succour of friendship, for the mercy of God! But God created him as weak as he is boastful; and soon, cut down to size, shamefaced, sobbing like a child and groping his timid way back, he eagerly grasps the hands that are stretched out to guide him. Absurd, childish and unfortunate creature who will not accept his fate and cannot extract himself from it.

But let us not deride this miserable state; it is common to all of us, and we all know that its pettiness, lack of nobility and strength only make it more unhappy and worthy of pity. So long as we believe in our strength we are proud, and pride is a great comforter. We stride about frowning with calm and terrible majesty; we have decided to die that evening or the next morning, and we are so proud of our great resolve (which, in fact, a barber or a prostitute is just as capable of carrying out as Cato of Utica), we are so glad not to be submitting to the decree of fate but to be defying it that we are already half consoled. We experience an enormous lucidity of mind and marvel at it; we make our will, we see to everything, burning some letters, entrusting others to friends, writing solemn farewells; we respect, admire and love ourselves. Yes, that's the worst of it: we become reconciled to ourselves, recover our self-respect; and self-love comes with commendable kindness, and stands between the heroic self and the sacrificial self. The expiator – that is, our pride – is gradually induced to spare the victim – that is, our weakness. The one relents, the other weeps; Pride asks Weakness if he was entirely sincere just now; if he was really willing to offer his throat to the knife. Weakness answers yes; and Pride is quite ready to believe him and decides that intention is as good as the deed, that shame has been washed away, honour satisfied, hope reinstated. Then along comes a friend who hasn't taken our resolution seriously but who, if he has the least tact and kindness, will pretend to be horrified and to wrest the murderous weapon from our hands – which it must be confessed he has no difficulty in doing. Alas! Alas! Let us not laugh at all this. The upshot is that we do not kill ourselves, we go on living; and in the end we cease to believe in our strength, our pride is deflated and our suffering abates; but there remains in the depth of our souls and for ever after a dumb grief, a profound dejection that is willing to be distracted but that no distraction alters; for what we believe is what we want to believe; and what we know, we put up with. And is there so much to choose between the scaffold and a lifetime in the galleys?

But good-night, old friend; it is getting late, in an hour it will be broad daylight; I shall have to get up with the cocks sounding their morning fanfare, and the dogs beginning to howl for the courtyard gates to be opened, and your brother Charles singing like a lark at sunrise. You are coming on Saturday, aren't you? I hope the weather will be as we like it: with no moon and the eastern sky frosty, the stars will shine and the air will be clear and ringing; your brother will sing his Stabat, and we shall go to hear him from afar, under the great fir tree. It does us good to give way to melancholy when we are together; but when we are alone, it is something we should avoid in our state of mind. That is why I am writing to you, in order not to go to bed till I am so sleepy that I will be incapable of thinking of serious things. O Heavens! What a picture we make! – these convivial friends, these amiable old chaps: just imagine them getting ready for bed and being seized with terror at the prospect of the thoughts that await them! That's why we should never go to bed before dawn. That is the time that nightmares take flight from the bed-curtains and have no more power over men. Adieu, give my blessings to your twelve children.[5]

Sunday

Since you can't come today, I've come to cloister myself with you and chat with your ennui through the medium of pen and ink, for you are suffering from ennui, that and nothing more. Don't get it into your head that you have anything worse. Ennui is a pretty serious affliction, but it is a very distinguished disease after all and one from which may emerge all that is best in human nature. It's simply a matter of describing one's ennui adequately and channelling its promptings towards poetic ends. But there's the rub – you are no poet! You define everything, you can't bear to remain uncertain about anything whatsoever. If you only knew what ennui really is and what can be got out of it! I shall try and explain it to you as I understand it.

Ennui is a listlessness of the spirit, an intellectual debility we feel after experiencing strong emotions and strong desires. It is a weariness, a discomfort, a disinclination such as the stomach has when it feels the need to eat but not the desire. Like the stomach, the mind vainly seeks what might stimulate it and finds no nourishment to its taste. Neither work nor play can distract it; what it requires is joy or suffering, and ennui is precisely what precedes or follows either of these. It isn't a virulent condition but a sad one, easily cured and easily aggravated. But once it has been poeticized it becomes touching, melancholy and most becoming both to one's looks and one's speech. To attain this state one has only to give oneself up to it completely. The recipe is simple: dress suitably for the time of year; have a pair of very comfortable slippers, an excellent fire in winter; a light hammock in the summer; a good horse in the spring; in the autumn, a sandy plot in the garden, planted with ranunculus. Apart from that, have a book in your hand, a cigar in your mouth; read about a line an hour, which you will ponder for not more than eight to ten minutes so as not to become set in your ideas. For the remainder of the time day-dream, but taking care to change your place or pipe or the position of your head or the direction of your gaze. – Thus, by not trying to shake off your discomfort you will gradually find that it becomes comfortable. You will start by achieving a remarkable sharpness of observation and peace of mind with which to register images – whether of ideas or objects – in those compartments of the brain which are like the pages of an album. A mild contemplation of yourself and of others will ensue, and what had formerly appeared to you as inconvenient or uninteresting will soon appear pleasant, picturesque and beautiful. The slightest thing that passes before your eyes will have its own particular appeal, the slightest sound will seem like a melody, the slightest visit will be a happy event.

It often happens, I can assure you, that I wake up in a terrible state of spleen. Spleen is a grave form of ennui and really quite disagreeable. I don't quite know what Pascal meant by those *pensées de derrière* which he reserved for himself when parrying polemical attacks or when secretly refuting what he made a show of accepting. It was no doubt the Jesuitry of a mind compelled to bow to duty but rebelling in spite of itself against the absurdity of the decree. For my part I find the phrase a terrible one. It was found not only in his collected thoughts but even scribbled on a scrap of paper, in these terms: *Et moi aussi, j'aurai mes pensées de derrière la tête.*[6] Oh, mournful words, issuing from an afflicted heart! Alas, there are times when the human brain is like a double mirror, with one surface sending back to the other the reverse image of those objects it has received from the front. It is then that everything and everyone and every sentence has its inevitable wrong side, and when there isn't a pleasure, a caress or an idea perceived directly that has not its contrast, which acts like a trigger on the brain. This is a dangerous and unhealthy power, you may be sure of that! Human reason may well consist in seeing everything from every angle, but more benign human nature is none too willing to submit itself to such scrutiny; it is not too clear-sighted, and as Pascal says elsewhere: 'the will that prefers one thing to another forbids the mind to consider the advantages of the one it doesn't like, and thus the will becomes one of the main organs of belief.' – And all this is dreadfully sad; life is only bearable in so far as we forget such grim truths, and the only friendships that are possible are those into which *pensées de derrière* never poke their noses.

Therefore, whenever I feel myself in this distressing frame of mind I'll do anything to extricate myself from it or to alleviate it a little. At such times I smother my thoughts in vast clouds of pipe smoke. In the summer I rock in my hammock till I'm dizzy; in the winter I expose my old shins to the fire with such stoicism that the result is a somewhat severe roasting – a sort of counter-irritant that diverts inflammation from the brain. Then a beautiful verse read in passing–for, thank God, the walls are as crammed with books as a mosque with maxims – or a sunbeam breaking through the frost, a certain dazzling of my sight and thought, make my surroundings seem prismatic once more; nature resumes its customary beauty and, in the big drawing-room, I see our friends grouped in a way I hadn't noticed, which now strikes me so vividly I might be Rembrandt – or even just Gérard Dow. Then I experience an inward thrill, my heart seems to leap, I have an unrealizable longing to fix these tableaux; I rejoice at having glimpsed them and warm towards those who are forming them. Haven't you often had such thoughts when, twisting a lock of your hair persistently, you lapse into one of those silent meditations we know so well? Many a time this year, among our dearest comrades and during our merriest parties, I have been overcome by an unconquerable sadness. And many a time, coming back into the drawing-room after striding down long bare avenues towards the rising moon, I have been suddenly fascinated and delighted by the innocent beauty of these Flemish interiors. Hasn't Dutheil[7] one of the ruddiest, most glowing faces ever painted by Teniers, as he sits wrapped in his ridiculous overcoat (which Hoffmann would have described as being somewhat F-flat in shade) with his plum-coloured cap, and raising the stoneware pitcher full of the humble nectar from our neighbouring hillside? Silence! His eye glitters, his beard bristles, he lowers his brow like a buffalo on the defensive. He is about to sing! Listen, it is a profoundly philosophical and religious song:

> Joy and grief course
> From the same source –
> In that, they don't vary;
> Joy makes us glad,
> Grief makes us sad –
> In that, they're contrary.

This beautiful ode is by Monsieur de Bièvre.[8] I've never heard anything which is more mournfully silly; and while our comrades are all roaring with laughter at this honest country platitude, I always feel sad when I hear it. Do you realize that all is said, both before God and man, when an unhappy soul questions the justice of his fate and gets such an answer? What more is there to say? Nothing. The eternal and inevitable order that metes out good and evil is epitomized here: it is like the toothache to which I compared our moral sufferings the other day. Is any lament that rises up from this earth worthy of more attention than that irony, both bitter and sweet, of hearing another poor wretch, mellow with wine, verify your unhappiness as an observable fact?

When Dutheil's terrible voice has stopped making the window-panes rattle, my brother tries out a few steps, as graceful as any bear ever attempted on the brink of a precipice. Alphonse, stretched out on the floor, plays the violin on the tongs with the shovel; his great Dantean profile is silhouetted against the wall, his laughter makes lugubrious crevices in its austere outline. Charles hovers round them like a perverse, waggish gnome, always ready to empty a glass down someone's sleeve or trip up an unsteady dancer. Oh! these are indeed my old friends of former days, those who know that one can be very merry and very sad at the same time but who are made easily happy by other people's good fortune and who begin life anew after each set-back.

And what should they complain about, these spoilt darlings of destiny? Look at that charming group strewn like a posy round the piano. These are their wives and their sisters: Agasta and Félicie, the two sisters so happily united, so kind, so gentle and so deliciously naïve!

Laure and her mother, both so beautiful, so noble, so saintly! Brigitte with her black eyes and sparkling gaiety; our lovely Rozane and our pretty Flemish Eugénie. Do you know of anything fresher and sweeter than those provincial flowers, blooming in real sunshine, far from the hothouses where our city women fade at birth? How ethereal Laure is with her pallor and her great black eyes and slow, mystical gaze! How adorable Agasta is with cheeks like the Bengal rose blossoming on snow, her mischievous, carefree expression, her trace of local dialect that is so pleasant and her little white nun-like bonnet! Félicie's languor has something sadder about it; hers is a melancholy smile. Love and grief have left their mark here, resignation and self-denial have set their seal on that peaceful brow which has so often bent to shed tears of Christian devotion. For what are you weeping, noble Roman? Have you not preserved, throughout all your sufferings, the precious gift of generosity so easily discarded by unhappy women? My friend, how good it is to live among such unpretentious people, among women as lovely in heart as in face, among strong, hardworking men, who are sincere and devoted friends! Come here often: you will be cured.

Now, if you ask me why, being so happy, I always leave at the approach of winter, I'll tell you; but keep it to yourself. – It is quite impossible for me to be happy anywhere, from now on. Friendship is God's most unmixed blessing but it is one that has not remained long with me and I shall die without achieving my life's dream. It is very easy, pleasant and agreeable to divide one's heart into ten or twelve portions. It is delightful to be the '*bon oncle*' of a happy nestful of children; it is touching to grow old surrounded by an adopted family in the house where one has grown up; but my happiness, compared with that of those around me, bears a significant resemblance to the beggar's wealth, made up from the rich man's charity. These men and women here, who are always smiling, are united by love or by the exclusive companionship of marriage. And I, old friend, am, like you, nobody's other half. Growing old doesn't matter to me; what would matter to me a great deal would be not to have to grow old alone. But I have never met the person with whom I would have liked to live and die, or if I have, I didn't know how to keep her. Listen to this tale and weep:

There was once a good artist whose name was Watelet and who was a better engraver than any other man in his day. He loved Marguerite le Conte and taught her to etch as well as he could. She left her husband, her belongings and her home to go and live with Watelet. The world condemned them; then, being poor and humble, they were forgotten. Forty years later an old man and an old woman were discovered living near Paris in a cottage called the *Moulin-Joli*; an old man who was engraving, as was the old woman (whom he called the miller's wife) beside him, at the same table. The first idler to discover this marvel told it to others and soon fashionable society came flocking to *Moulin-Joli* to admire the phenomenon: a forty-year-old idyll, a labour assiduously pursued and always loved; a matching pair of exceptional talents; a Philemon and Baucis living in the days of Mesdames de Pompadour and Dubarry. It caused quite a stir and the miraculous couple had their sycophants, their friends, their poets, their admirers. Luckily, they both died of old age soon after, for the world would have spoiled everything. Their last etching was of *Moulin-Joli*, Marguerite's home, with the superscription: *Cur valle permutem Sabina divitas operosiores?*[9]

It hangs on my bedroom wall above a portrait,[10] the original of which no one here has ever seen. For a year the person who left me that portrait sat beside me every night at a small table and we worked together to earn our living: at daybreak we discussed our work together and ate at the same little table while talking about art, love and the future. The future failed to keep its promise to us. Pray for me, Marguerite le Conte!

In fact, my friend, the more I think about it the more I see that it is too late to dare to be unhappy. We can't take life seriously any more, at least not the life that lies ahead; for the one that is behind we have believed in, therefore it was real. Have you considered the rough, laborious journey that led us from our swaddling-clothes to our crutches? I know that the road differs according to the wayfarer, that you can't find two identical leaves in a forest; but a general pattern can be drawn from our common destiny and it will accommodate the thousand and one details which go to make diversity. If we see man simply as an organic structure, we can say that all men are the same; that just as their bodies are never composed of anything but one head, two arms, a torso and so on, the structure of their understanding is always composed of the same emotions: pride, anger, lust, good and evil intentions – all in varying degrees, but always part and parcel of his being, permeating his substance and constituting his moral existence. Thus I feel entitled to sum up the history of all, by summing up my own:

Initially: strength, passion, ignorance.

Mid-way: strength put to some use, ambitions achieved, knowledge of life.

Declining years: disenchantment, distaste for action, weariness – doubt, apathy; – and then the grave, as welcome as a bed to the pilgrim, tired by his long day. O Providence!

Youth is the part of human life that varies least from one individual to another; maturity that which varies most. Old age is its outcome and varies accordingly; but the impairment of our faculties blurs the differences, as distance reduces the brightness of hues and veils them in pallor.

It is practically impossible to tell what a man will become, hard to tell what he is and easy to tell what he has been.

We should neither mistrust nor overestimate the young; but we should be very wary of those who have reached maturity, while also refraining from blaming them; they have every possibility, they are the molten metal poured into the cast – God knows how the sculpture will turn out! As to the old, they should be pitied whatever they're like.

For my part, I've seen how miserable and how terrible at the same time the vigour of youth can be; we have no control over it, it carries us off where we don't want to go and lets us down when we have most need of it; and I should be astonished that I was once so proud of possessing it if I didn't know that we are disposed to find reasons for pride in everything, from good looks – which are an unearned gift – to wisdom – which is the outcome of experience. To take pride in one's strength is as sensible as to take pride in having slept well and in being equipped with legs which will set out on a long walk; but watch out for the stones on the way!

Oh! What splendid walkers we think we are when we are about to start off, wearing a pair of sturdy, new-made shoes. I remember how impatient I felt to launch myself into life with my stout footgear. Who can stop me? I said. What thorns, what mud can there be that I won't trample on without fear of getting scratched or dirty? Where are the obstacles, where the mountains, where the oceans that I shall not cross? I hadn't bargained for the pitfalls.

And when I first tried my strength, only good came of it for a while; I was well equipped and my pockets were stuffed with the best books in the world. I condescended to read of Plutarch's great men and join hands with them in a holy vision, lit by the magical sunshine of my own pride.

And by dint of self-confidence and vanity I was convinced that I could not fail, and loudly proclaimed as much to my friends and acquaintances. Thus it was rumoured in these circles that I was a stoic from the past who, as a favour, was wearing a frock-coat and boots.

However, since I walked fast and didn't worry too much about watching my step, it so happened that I tripped over a stone and fell down; this mishap bruised my toes and somewhat mortified my soul. But promptly picking myself up and thinking that nobody had noticed, I carried on, saying to myself: 'It was an accident, a stroke of fate'; and I began to believe in fate, whose existence, till then, I had totally denied.

But I tripped again and fell frequently. One day I realized that I was bruised and bleeding all over and that my turn-out was filthy and ragged so that passers-by laughed at me; especially since I still wore it with an air of grandeur that only made me more ridiculous. Then I had to sit down on a stone by the wayside and woefully inspect my rags and my wounds.

But my pride, ailing and downcast at first, soon recovered and decreed that, though utterly exhausted, I was none the less a good walker and a stalwart stone-breaker. I found an excuse for each of my falls, arguing that they were inevitable, that fate was stronger than I was, that Satan had a hand in all this, and a thousand other things all of them fabricated in order to avoid admitting my own weakness to myself and to others – or the contempt which all honest men must sometimes feel for themselves.

I set off again, limping and stumbling, and telling myself that I was walking all right, that my tumbles were not tumbles, the stones were not stones; and although many people quite understandably jeered at me, others took me at my word because I had what artists call poetry and soldiers call the gift of the gab.

In those days Lord Byron was a shining example of what human presumptuousness can achieve by clothing paltry vanities in purple and setting them in gold like diamonds; that cripple walked on stilts above the heads of those who had two legs of equal length; he was successful because his stilts were sturdy and splendid and he knew how to use them.

As to us, apes that we are, we learnt to use stilts tolerably well and even to walk the tightrope, exciting the admiration of quite a few idlers

148

standing by who knew nothing about it. And we – or above all, I, unhappy man! – I ignored all the pure and humble pleasures, was unable to recognize true feelings, despised simple unobtrusive virtues. I mocked the devout, cultivated insolent vainglory and, swollen with pride, was intolerant of the merest fault in others – I, who harboured many vices of my own. And I refused to make any sacrifices; for nothing on earth seemed more valuable than my peace of mind, my pleasure and my acclaim.

Now, do you know, François, how it was that after all this I became a tolerable old man, gentle, reasonably modest in speech and expectations? Do you know what distinguishes a corrupt man from a man who has gone astray? Doubtless, both have behaved stupidly and wrongly; but the one ceases to do so, while the other carries on: the one grows old – in sabots, alone in his retreat, or in a dressing-gown, with a few friends in his garret; while the corrupt old man each night bedecks and perfumes a mummy that still pretends to a semblance of life till, one morning, there is nothing left of him but a little heap of dust in the alembic. The man who realizes too late that he has taken the wrong turning and has no longer the strength to retrace his steps can at least stop and cry out mournfully to those who approach: 'Do not pass by here. It was here that I lost my way.' The wicked man takes delight in it, he goes on to the end of his days and dies of boredom when he has exhausted all the evil of which man is capable. He gets enjoyment from leading as many poor devils astray as he can: he laughs to see them wallow in the mire in their turn and amuses himself in persuading them that the mud is a precious essence with which only men of high intellect and taste are entitled to anoint and embalm themselves.

And in all that, François, I find no great consolation for us; for we have little merit in not being like them. Didn't we attend their parties and drink there the poison of vanity and lies? If fresh air brought us to our senses it was because chance or Providence made us emerge from the fatal atmosphere and obliged us to live in the country rather than in a palace. My friend, what we call virtue undoubtedly exists, but it exists only in exceptional beings; in the rest of us, what we like to call honesty is a sense of what is good, an aversion to what is evil. And why, I ask you, is this poor wind-battered seedling not blown right away when we expose it so rashly in the storm? Considering the ease with which it is uprooted, can we find much cause for self-congratulation in the fact that we have miraculously avoided danger? What remains to our credit is a very sickly flower indeed. Who is the angel who has protected it with his wings? What ray of sunshine has revived it? However good the soil on which the good seed falls, if the birds of heaven swoop down upon it, they eat it. Whose then is the hand that wards them off? O God! My soul that has been granted your mercy shudders in terror when it looks back!

But you, my friend, you have been able to make amends. It wasn't too late for you when you stopped; you have come back to where you started from, and there you have found a hard task, a noble duty, and have assumed it readily. Oh, François! You have had to fight against the past and its disastrous ways, to endure the present and its consuming cares; you have stood your ground against these dragons; your loins are as strong as the Archangel Michael's, for you have gained the ascendancy. I, who am old and have no mother to console, nor twelve children to keep by my labour, I weep, I pray, and sometimes I cry out: 'Come to me, come down from heaven, alight on my dejected brow, dove of the Holy Ghost, divine poetry! Sense of eternal beauty, love of nature, forever young and forever fruitful; fusion of the great *whole* with the human spirit which breaks free from the body and yields itself up; sad and mysterious joy that God bestows on his desperate children, a tremor that seems to summon them to the unknown and the sublime, a desire for death, a desire for life; lightning that flashes before their eyes in the darkness, a gleam that breaks through the clouds and clothes the sky in unexpected splendour; agonizing convulsions in which a future life is revealed, an ultimate strength that belongs to despair alone — come to me! I have lost everything upon this earth!'

Winter stretches out its grey veil over the sorrowing earth, the cold whistles and moans around our roof-tops. But sometimes towards noon, a glimmer of purple light still pierces the mist and brightens the dark drapes of my room. Then my bluefinch flutters restlessly in his cage, on catching sight of a group of silent sparrows, puffed up into balls and communing in melancholy bliss on the leafless lilac tree in the garden. The black outlines of the branches stand out against the frosty white of the sky. The broom, covered with its brown pods, still thrusts aloft a last cluster of buds which are trying to blossom. The earth now soft and moist no longer resounds under the tread of children. All is silence, regret and tenderness. The sun comes to bid the earth farewell, the frost melts and tears fall everywhere; the vegetation seems to be making a final effort to come to life again; but the last kiss of its consort is so light that, before the Bengal roses have had time to blush and bloom, their petals fall from their drooping heads . . . Cold, night and death are come.

This last glimpse of the sun through my window-pane is my last glimmer of hope. To love such things, to mourn the departing autumn, to greet the spring on its return, to count the last or the first blossoms on the trees, to entice the sparrows to my window-sill is all that is left to me of a life once full and passionate. The winter of my soul has come, an eternal winter! There was a time when I looked at neither the sky nor the flowers, when I was not worried by the absence of the sun and did not pity the sparrows shivering on their boughs. Kneeling before the altar on which burned the sacred flame, I poured on it all the incense of my heart. All the vigour and youthfulness, ambition and rapture God has given to man, I consumed and rekindled at the flame that another passion fanned. Now the altar has been overturned, the sacred fire is spent, a pale thread of smoke still rises and tries to reach the flame that no longer burns; it is the breath of my love trying to recapture the soul that once set it on fire. But that soul has flown far off towards the sky while mine languishes and dies on earth.

Now that my soul is widowed all it can do is to see and listen to God in the outside world; for God is no longer in me, and if I have any cause to rejoice it is in what happens around me. So I shall speak of your mercy to others. O God, who have forsaken me! I shall no longer live, I shall see and explain; from the depths of my grief I shall lift up my voice, loudly, so that my words will carry to the ears of those who pass by: 'Keep away from this spot, for here there is a chasm and I, who came too close, have fallen into it.' I shall further say: 'You have gone astray because you are deaf and blind; it is because I was like you that I also lost my way; I have recovered my hearing and my sight; but then I discovered that I was at the bottom of the precipice and could no longer get back amongst you. I was old.'

Many have, like me, fallen into the abyss of despair. It is a vast world, it is like a world of the dead moving and stirring beneath the world of the living. Something black, a phantom clothed and bearing a name, a listless, broken body, a pale, lacklustre face, is still at large in human society and still shows some signs of life. But our souls are down below in the bitter waters of Erebus,[11] and those who are young have no more idea of what happens there than a child in the cradle has of what death means. But this pit, which has no outlet, has various levels, and different kinds of men go up and down the steps. Weeping and laughter rise from the bowels of this Inferno. At the very bottom are those who have fallen lowest, the most brutish, who wallow in the filth of unspeakable pleasures: a little higher are the madmen who howl and curse God whom they have disowned and who has struck them down; elsewhere are the cynics who deny the existence of virtue and happiness and who try to drag others down to their level. But there are some who raise themselves above the poisonous miasmas of their Tartarus and, seating themselves on the first steps of the fatal stairway, say: 'Lord, since I cannot re-cross the threshold, I shall die here and descend no further.' They weep and wail; for they are still close enough to God to understand what might have been and what they should have done. And they have hopes of another life, because they still have the sense of eternal beauty and of the means of possessing it. Those repent and toil, not to repossess this mortal life, but in expiation; they speak the truth to others without fear of wounding them, because those who are not of this world have nothing to be cautious about and nothing to fear; neither good nor ill can be inflicted on them; they can no longer be made to fall: they have hurled themselves down. If only they could appease, like Curtius, the celestial rage and close the chasm behind them!

But it seems, François, that I am becoming grandiloquent; luckily I can see my old Malgache approaching; it is fifteen months since I last saw him; he is out of breath, quite panting with happiness. There he is under my window; but what the devil! – he's stopping; he has just caught sight of a malformed violet, he's picking it and it is making him ponder. So there I am, obliterated from his memory; if I don't go out and meet him he will go back home with his monster of a violet without having seen me. I must hurry. Farewell, Pylades.

To Everard[1]

Your friend, the traveller, has arrived home without mishap; he is glad and proud of the memory you have preserved of him. He had been none too hopeful in this respect; he thought that a mind as active and voracious as yours would be keenly susceptible to the least impression but that it would promptly forget it to make room for others. That is what duty and necessity require of you; you don't belong to a select few; you belong to everybody, or rather everybody belongs to you. Poor man of genius! It must be very tiring. What a mission is yours! It's a job for a swineherd – Apollo at the court of Admetus![2]

What's worst for you is that, in the midst of your flocks or in the depths of your sties, you remember your divinity; and when you see the merest bird flit by, you envy its freedom and you long for the skies. If only I could bear you away with me on the wing of the changing winds, make you breathe the pure air of open spaces and teach you the secrets of poets and Bohemians! But it is not God's will. He cast you down like Satan, like Vulcan, like all those who stand for the greatness and misfortunes of genius on earth. There you are, employed in base tasks, nailed to your cross, shackled in the wretched prison of human ambitions. Carry on, then, and may whoever has given you strength and suffering for your lot surround with a long-lasting halo of glory the crown of thorns you will earn at the price of freedom, happiness and life.

For I'm very sorry but I don't believe in that philanthropy which you, the reformers, are humble enough to boast of. Philanthropy produces Sisters of Charity. The thirst for glory is something else and brings about quite different destinies. High-minded hypocrite, don't talk to me about such things; you delude yourself when you think that it is a sense of duty and not your instinct for power that leads you up the steep and fatal ascent. As for me I know you are not one of those who submit to duties; you are the kind who impose them. You don't love men, you are not their brother, because you are not their equal. You are an exception among men, you were born a king.

Ah! – I am making you angry! But in your heart of hearts you know it's true; there can be a royalty which is divinely appointed. God would have given all men an equal share of intelligence and virtue had he wished to establish amongst them what you see as the principle of equality; but he makes great men to govern lesser men, as he makes a cedar to shelter the hyssop. The active, almost despotic influence you exercise in this part of France, where everyone who can feel or think bows down to your superiority (so that even I, the most undisciplined truant who ever idled away his life, am obliged to come each year and pay homage to you), is that anything but royalty, I ask you? Your Majesty cannot deny it. Sire, the scarf you wear round your head by way of a toupet is the crown of Aquitaine, until it becomes something greater still. Your bench in the open-air is a throne; Fleury the Gaul is the captain of your guards; Planet,[3] your court jester; and I, if you will allow me, shall be your historiographer; but, by God, behave yourself, Sire! For the higher the hopes your humble bard entertains for you, the more he will demand of you when you reach your goal, and you know that he will not be more easily silenced than the barber of King Midas.[4] And here I ask your pardon for giving the title of King to the late Midas. It is well-known that he bore no relation to you; he was a king of the Establishment, one of that splendid breed of legitimate rulers whose ears tend to lengthen quite naturally under their hereditary crowns.

Do you think then that I challenge your rights? Oh no! Not really: we shan't disagree on that head. Some kings are born to be sycophants; you on the other hand were born a prince of this earth. For my part, poor maker of metaphors that I am, I don't feel your kingly umbrella provides me with much shelter; yet I don't fancy holding it myself. I should do it badly and all the thrones in the world don't seem to me worth so much as a little flower on the banks of some Alpine lake. It would be interesting to know whether Providence has more love and more respect for this skeleton of ours than for the scented petals of the jasmine. It seems to me that it has taken as much trouble over the violet's beauty as over those of women, that the lilies of the field are better clad than Solomon in all his glory, and I reserve all my love and veneration for them. Go, you and your like, and wage your wars, lay down your laws. You accuse me of never coming to any conclusion; much I care about conclusions! I'll go and write your name and mine on the sands of the Hellespont in three months' time; there will be no more trace of them the following day than there will be of my books after my death or, alas, of your deeds, perhaps, O Marius,[5] after the gust of wind which will change the luck of the Sullas and the Napoleons on the battlefield.

Not that I am deserting your cause for a moment. Of all the causes I don't care about, beardless youth that I am, this is the best and the noblest. I can't even conceive how a poet could have another; for if all words are meaningless, at least those of fatherland and freedom are harmonious, while the words legality and obedience are coarse and discordant and fit for the ears of the constabulary. To humour a nation of brave people is fine but to fawn upon a crowned blockhead[6] is beneath human dignity. As for me I flee from human chatter and go and listen to the voice of torrents. Rest assured that I shall beg the spirit of lakes and glaciers to visit you sometimes and to bring you on the breeze a scent of the open spaces, a dream of freedom, and an affectionate sincere remembrance of your friend, the traveller. I'm no more than a bird of passage in human existence; I build no nests and hatch no loves on earth; I'll come and tap on your window-pane with my beak from time to time, and bring you news of the creation through the bars of your prison; then I'll resume my unpredictable course in the aerial fields, feeding on gnats, while you exchange chains and crowns with your equals! O men of destiny, your ambitions are lofty and magnificent! Of all the toys humanity plays with, you have chosen the least childish: glory! Indeed, glory is great! Achilles selected a spear from among the womanish jewels he was offered; you and the likes of you have chosen the martyrdom of lofty ambitions rather than riches, titles and all the petty vanities that attract ordinary people. Generous madmen that you are, do a good job of governing these wretched fools for me and don't spare the whip. I'll be serenading the sun on my branch in the meanwhile. You'll listen to me when you have nothing better to do; you'll come and sit under my tree when you need rest and amusement. Good-night, my brother Everard, brother and king, not by virtue of birthright but by right of virtue. I love you with all my heart and am, Sire, your Majesty's most humble and most faithful subject.

You ask me a number of questions I'd like to be able to answer, were it only to prove that I heed every word your pen traces. To proceed in the manner of my dear Franklin,[7] here they are in the order in which you asked them: 1) Why am I so sad? 2) If you weren't so different from me would I be so fond of you? 3) Do you ever mention me in your conversations? 4) When will you make up your mind about anything? 5) When shall I be able to sit . . .? etc.

I answered the first question yesterday: it is because the quest for glory is both the emperor's role and the convict's slavery; because you are imprisoned in your will as in a fortress, and because the meanest insect grazing the window-pane of your dungeon with its wing makes you start and revives the painful consciousness of your captivity. Take courage, Prometheus! You are greater, chained to your rock with a vulture's talons in your heart, than the fawns of the wood in their liberty . . . They are free, but they are of no consequence, and you could never be happy in their way. This is where the answer to your fifth question comes in: *When shall I be able to sit with you in the long grass by the riverside?* – Never, unless there were an army on the other bank, Everard, and you were waiting there for the call to battle. Can you imagine yourself forgetting about wars and finding repose among the rushes? I should like to know what Marius dreamt about in the marshes of Minturnus;[8] he was certainly not dallying with peaceful naiads. Men of clamour and tumult, do not come and dip your bloodstained, dusty feet in the clear waters that murmur to us; it is to us, to harmless dreamers, that the mountain streams belong; it is to us that they talk of oblivion and repose – all those things our humble happiness requires, but which you despise. Leave that to us, we leave all the rest to you, the laurels, the altars, the toil and the triumph. If some day, wounded in battle or prisoner on parole, you come and sit down beside your friend, the bohemian, we will look up at the sky together and I'll talk to you about the planets that preside over the fate of mortal men. That, I know, is all that could interest you, all that you would wish to see in the limpid waters; you will seek the indistinct, quivering reflection of your own star, and you will promptly look up to the heavenly dome to make sure it is still shining there in all its glory. No, no, you would not like those silent valleys where the eagle is king and not man, those lakes where the cry of the smallest teal would raise more echoes than your words. Waste lands that you can subdue neither with the plough nor the sword, those steep mountains, that rebellious soil, those impenetrable forests where the artist goes piously to invoke the savage gods entrenched there against the assaults of human industry – all this is not a country which would suit you. What you need are towns, fields, soldiers, workmen, commerce, labour, all the trappings of power that the needs of man can offer up to regale the pride of the gods. The gods dominate and protect: when you say that you hold these poor human pygmies lovingly in your heart, what you mean, Hercules, is that you hold them in your lion's skin; but you could not fall asleep in the shade of the woods without their for :ing you to wake up. They would plague you in your dreams, and the storms raging in your soul would disrupt the serenity of the skies right up to the peak of Mont Blanc. My poor brother, I prefer my pilgrim's staff to your sceptre. But since the fiery crown of intellectual sovereignty encircles your brow, since the passion for greatness entered your blood at birth, since you cannot abdicate and since repose would kill you more quickly than exhaustion – in view of this, far from considering your fate with that cold philosophy which might give me a sense of my own helplessness, I must always pity and admire you, victim of your own sublimity! But as I'm good for nothing but conversing with echoes, watching the moon rise and making up melancholy or mocking rhymes for student poets and amorous school-boys, I have, as I told you yesterday, taken to playing truant and making a holiday of my life: I chase butterflies along the hedgerows, fall headlong into thorn bushes to pluck a flower that sheds its petals before I've had the chance to smell it, sing with the thrush and sleep under the first willow I come across, with no thought for the hour or the moralists. I think the best thing I can do will be to plant a laurel to you in my garden. Every time I hear of one of your successes I'll send you a leaf and you'll think for an instant of one who laughs at all the notions upheld by mere pedants but who bows down reverently before a noble heart in which justice dwells.

Second question: *If you weren't so different from me in every respect would I be so fond of you?* Here is my answer: No, indeed you wouldn't love me as you do; you appreciate me for having a certain amount of strength, despite my puny frame and humble circumstances: you think all the more of me because you feel surprise at my having achieved even a little acclaim in these social circumstances, where everything tends to undermine those who give in to them. You probably believe I'm a better person today than I could have been before, and you are not wrong. When I think back, there isn't much to be proud of; but whatever good there is left in my soul makes up a little for the past and qualifies me still for valuable friendships now and in days to come.

That's all I want from now on. I have no ambition of any kind and the very small reputation I enjoy as an artist doesn't make me envious of those who have deserved to do better. Passions and fancies have made me extremely unhappy at certain times: I have completely recovered from my passions, thanks to age and reflection. In every other respect, I've always been and shall always be perfectly happy, and therefore always equitable and good-tempered in all things except in love, when I'm the very devil because then I become ill and *splenetic and rash*.

Do you ever mention me in your conversations? I talk of nothing else. Limbs cannot forget the heart from which their blood flows. Before meeting you I was so eager to do so that this year I decided that I, too, would come and see you so that on my return I would be entitled, like everybody else, to say *Everard thinks . . . Everard wants . . . Everard told me . . .* etc. I hope so much adulation won't spoil you!

When will you arrive at any conclusion? What if you were to die before doing so? Really! Little George can die when God pleases, the world won't be any the worse for not knowing what he thinks. What do you want me to say? I would have to tell you more about myself and nothing is less interesting than an individual who hasn't yet found the answer to his fate. I have no inclination to express any kind of opinion. Some people who read my books make the mistake of believing that my behaviour is a profession of faith and that the subjects I choose for my stories are a kind of indictment of certain laws. Far from it – I acknowledge that my life is full of faults and I would consider it morally wrong to cudgel my brains in order to find a philosophy that would justify them. On the other hand, since I am incapable of considering certain realities of life with any enthusiasm, I cannot take such faults seriously enough for them to require redress or atonement. It would be doing them too much honour and I don't believe my faults have ever prevented those who complain most about them from getting on very nicely. People who have known me for a long time are sufficiently fond of me to be indulgent and to forgive me for the harm I have done myself. My writings, which have always been inconclusive, have done neither good nor ill. I should be glad to give them a conclusion if I could find one; but such is not as yet the case, and I'm not far enough advanced in some respects to risk having my say. I can't stand pedantic moralizing. It may be of some use in the world; but I'm too much in earnest to try to appease, by a hypocritical gesture, the disapproval that my uncertainty has brought upon me – though a brave and honest uncertainty, I would claim. I shall put up with the strictures, however hard I may find them, so long as I have not achieved the certainty I await. Do you blame me? Although my world is a very small one, if seen through a magnifying glass it isn't unlike the one in which you dwell. Would you pretend to have the opinions that are foisted on you in order to increase your popularity or your fame, and put forward as an article of faith something that was still only embryonic in your mind? Your good opinion means too much to me to refrain from making my situation clear; it has taken some space; forgive me for having talked so seriously about the serious side of my life; it isn't my habit. Farewell; I'm sending you a little bundle of published pages which I've selected for you from my, alas, far too voluminous collection!

18 April

My friend, you take me severely to task for my social atheism; you say that anything that exists outside the doctrines of utility can never be either truly great or truly good. You say that my indifference is blameworthy, is a bad example, and that I must put an end to it or commit moral suicide, cut off my right hand and cease to communicate with mankind. You are very harsh, but it is how I like you, it is fine and admirable in you. You say, besides, that non-intervention of any kind is only an excuse for cowardice or egotism, because there is not anything which is human that is not either advantageous or harmful to humanity. Whatever my ambition, you say, whether I want to be admired or whether I want to be loved, I must be charitable – discreetly, thoughtfully and wisely charitable – that is to say, philanthropic. I usually reply to those who speak in such terms with a sophistry or a jest, but in this case it's different; I acknowledge your right to utter that lofty word, 'virtue', which I hardly dare repeat after you. I've always been unruly, and that's the fault of those who saw fit to baptise me with impure hands. To wash away the stains of sin from the humblest convert, as from Christ Himself, John the Baptist is needed, and Magdalene's tresses should never wipe feet that tread in the paths of error.

O you who question me, have you abandoned the perilous paths into which youth rushes headlong? Withdrawn into the sanctuary of your will, have you, during these sober years of meditation, practised those ancient virtues which you prize so highly: temperance, charity, diligence, steadfastness and disinterestedness? – Yes, you have done so, I know; well then, speak: my pride rebels against those who are no

159

better than I am and who want me to bow down to them. You who have a strong heart as well as the power of understanding, say what you will; I shall reply as to a rightful judge and obey you by talking about myself as much as you wish; for I admit that I was guilty more of laziness than true humility in not doing so.

O my brother! This is a grave undertaking, a grave epoch in my sorry life! I did not come here in a mood of keen self-abnegation but with a serious desire to see in you only what might be truly noble. I had steeled myself against those magnetic effects which we should ever be wary of, on coming into contact with superior men. And I can honestly say that I was not dazzled by the spell that you exert on others; the Roman outlines of your brow, the vigour of your discourse, the brilliance and fluency of your thoughts have never engrossed me; what has moved and convinced me were the simplest things I heard you say or saw you do, a gentle, unsophisticated word in the midst of the most exalted enthusiasm, a rough, straightforward gesture of friendship, an exquisite purity in all your expressions and all your feelings. No more foolish slander could be invented than that you are covetous. I'd like your political opponents to tell me what attraction money can have for a man who has no vices, no whims, and possesses neither mistresses nor collections of paintings nor medals; neither English horses, nor luxury, nor self-indulgence of any kind.[9] It means a great deal, Everard: your lack of vices is, in my view, of the utmost importance now. That is the one thing that is beyond question, whereas virtues can assume so many names that don't belong to them! But who can doubt the unobtrusive sobriety with which a strong man enjoys the pleasures of life? Have domestic virtues ever needed equivocation and hypocrisy?

You were talking to me about the way that vices and virtues were positively moulded into Mirabeau's prodigious nature. I'm not sufficiently fond of motley to find a statue made of diamonds and clay more beautiful and impressive than one of pure gold. My friend Heinrich Heine said, in speaking of Spinoza: 'His private life was blameless; it was ever pure and unblemished like that of his divine kinsman, Jesus Christ.' These simple words make me love Spinoza. No doubt it was only in this way that my feeble brain could appreciate his greatness. In you too, my dear brother, there is a side I can't appreciate because my idle or ineffectual mind has never gone deeply into any branch of knowledge. I understand what you are but not what you do. I observe the mechanisms of this splendid thought-machine; but the value and use of its products are unknown and indifferent to me. I see that the word virtue is central to it and I know that this word's meaning is always the same, always sublime no matter to what it is applied: ceaseless abnegation, the sacrifice of every base indulgence of the mind or senses to a supreme and divine satisfaction; the consecration of a human life to the worship of a vast and intelligent will which is at its centre. It is virtue, it is strength, it is the soul's tendency to reach the highest possible point, to take in at a glance more than the common herd and so spread more widely the benefits of its power. It is unselfish ambition, it is faith, it is learning, it is art, it is all the forms Divinity takes to manifest itself in humankind. That is why to reign, even by virtue of the most barbarous and iniquitous rights, even at the price of peace and of life, has always been man's most ardent desire; nor should this surprise us. To reign for better or for worse is to practise a semblance of virtue and moral strength. If words signify anything in the great book of nature, these two expressions are exact synonyms and already in our language they are often used as such. I have just written: 'To reign by *virtue* of an *iniquitous* right', which is, I believe, quite correct and, as far as I know, by no means a contradiction in terms.

All that is hard to accomplish excites man's wonder and the degree of his admiration is commensurate with what he himself can get out of the effort involved; and since nothing in God's creation is more important and valuable to man than his own existence, it is obvious that what he calls a sense of natural equity is a considered awareness of what is useful to him. Since it does not require a great deal of consideration to realize that man can't live in isolation, he has been obliged, on emerging from the most primitive state imaginable, to resort to social structures and gather together in tribes under a system of laws dictated by the ablest or strongest among them. Those who were able to establish such laws to their own personal advantage were the originators of eternal conflict between rebels and oppressors; when the rebels were victorious they, in their turn, became oppressors by right of force. Where in all this is justice?

Stand up, you, the elect, the holy men who have invented virtue! You have devised a less gross felicity than that of the sensual man, more arrogant than that of the valiant. You discovered that the love and admiration of your fellows was a source of greater happiness than all the possessions they fought over. So you renounced the pleasures that make all men alike: in your wisdom you branded with the name of vice everything that made them happy and, in consequence, grasping, envious, violent and unsociable. You gave up your share of worldly wealth and pleasure and, having thus put yourselves beyond jealousy or suspicion, you set yourselves up in their midst as benevolent gods to enlighten them as to what was good for them and to give them useful laws. You told them that it was better to give than to receive, and that where you ruled justice reigned; what sophistries could dispute your excellence, O sublime and vainglorious men? There is nothing in the world greater than you are, nothing more valuable, nothing more necessary.

Go and preach virtue. The day will come when the sensualists, who now mock you in your battle against the greed and vindictiveness of those whose sensual appetites are never satisfied, will realize that there is a more enviable, more sheltered lot than their own; they will see that the shadow of popular rule is hanging over the land, that it has violated their privacy and can in its turn assume the right of enjoyment and consign the vanquished to the plough, to the thatched cottage and to the crucifix, the only consolation of the poor. Then they will be only too happy to find interposed between them and the conqueror's hatred a virtuous man, ready to mete out the riches of the world to the wealthy and the needy and to explain to both of them what justice really is.

I don't know if the day will ever come when man will decide infallibly and definitively what is useful for mankind. I don't have to examine in detail the system you have embraced; I made fun of it the other day but since you compel me to talk sense (which, I confess, is no small victory of your strength over mine) I'm prepared to admit that the great law of equality – impracticable as it may now seem to those who dread it, and doubtful as its reign on earth seems to me who observe such things from the seclusion of my cell – is the first and only consistent law of equity and morality that I've ever come across. All the learned details which go to the formulation of a theory are totally foreign to me, and as for the means by which the theory can be made to govern the world, these unfortunately strike me as depending so largely on the doubts, refutations, scruples and aversions of those who undertake to implement it that I feel petrified by my scepticism as soon as I so much as glance at these to see what they consist of. All that isn't my concern. I am of a poetic, not a legislative, nature, a fighter if need be, but never a parliamentarian. I can be made to do any job, by persuasion first and then by command; but I'm no good at discovering or deciding anything.

I'll always accept whatever is right. So, ask me for my belongings and my life, O Roman! But leave my poor mind to the sylphs and nymphs of poetry. What does it matter to you? You'll always find brains enough – ready and more than ready – to go in for cogitation. Won't you allow minstrels to sing their ballads to the ladies while you lay down your laws for the men?

That's what I was leading up to, Everard: to telling you that we don't all need virtue, only some of us; what we all need is honesty. You be virtuous, I shall try to be honest. Honesty is that instinctive wisdom, that natural moderation I was talking about earlier, that absence of vice, that is to say, of fiery passions which are harmful to society in that they tend to monopolize the sources of enjoyment which a providential Nature intended to be equally distributed among men. Those who are governed have to be honest, temperate, upright, in a word, *moral*, so that those who govern may be able to raise a lasting structure on their strong and willing shoulders. I am still far from possessing what are known as *republican virtues*, which I shall call, less pompously, the qualities of the governable individual or the citizen. I have not lived wisely, I have made poor use of the goods that have fallen to my lot, I have neglected works of charity; I have spent my days in indolence, ennui, useless tears, mad love affairs and frivolous pastimes. I have prostrated myself before idols of flesh and blood and let their heady breath erase the austere maxims inscribed on my brow in my youth by the wisdom of books; I've let their innocent despotism consume my days in puerile amusements, in which for a long time the memory and the love of goodness was extinguished – for I was once good, you know that, don't you, Everard? The people from round here will vouch for it; it's common knowledge in these parts; but there's small merit in that. I was young and there were, as yet, none of the fatal passions smouldering in my breast which have stifled many of its good qualities. I know, however, that some have survived totally unscathed through the worst mishaps of my life, and that none of the others is irredeemably lost. To the question you asked me the other day – Is it out of weakness or indifference that you put off being virtuous? – I reply: neither the one nor the other. It is because I have been side-tracked, made captive by a passion about which I had no misgivings and believed to be noble and sacred. And it may be so; but I have allowed it to have too much or too little sway over me. Even though I resisted it with all my strength, it was to no purpose, and a terrible conflict has consumed the best years of my

163

life; I have been all this time in a land that was foreign to my soul, in a land of exile and servitude from which I have finally escaped, bruised and degraded by slavery and still trailing fragments of the chains I broke and which, even now, cut into my flesh every time I turn to look back at the far-off, forsaken shore. Yes, I have been a slave; pity me, you who are free, and don't be surprised if today I can only dream of travel, open spaces, vast forests and solitude. Yes, I have been a slave, and slavery, I can assure you from experience, makes man vile and debased. It leads to insanity and perversity; it makes him cruel, deceitful, vindictive, bitter and more detestable by far than the master who oppresses him; that is what befell me and, in my self-loathing, I passionately longed for death all the days of my abjection.

None the less I am here, and here with a broken arrow in my heart; my own hand broke it and my own hand will extract it; for each day I twist this sacred dart, and each day as the wound bleeds and widens in my heart, I proudly feel that the iron is beginning to leave my soul. And so you have not before you an incurable but an escaped and wounded prisoner who may recover and be a good soldier yet. Can't you see that I've brought back from the land of Egypt[10] no vices and that I'm sober and strong enough yet for the crossing of the great desert? Just observe what sort of a person you are now talking to: it is neither to a weakling nor to one of those young Athenians with scented locks whom Aristophanes rebuked, by introducing them into the midst of his comedies and exposing them to public censure, by name and with the finger of scorn. You are talking to a ploughboy of sorts with a straw hat, a waggoner's smock, blue stockings and hob-nailed boots. This rustic penitent is still capable, like you, of moderation, charity, hard work, perseverance, unselfishness and simplicity; he will, besides, be chaste and sincere since he has renounced his great folly, love!

Republic! Dawn of justice and equality, divine utopia, luminary of a possibly chimerical future, all hail! Shine in our firmament, star that the earth yearns for! Should you descend upon us before your appointed time you will find me ready to receive you and already clothed according to your sumptuary laws. My friends, my masters, my brothers, greetings! My blood and my bread are yours henceforth, until the time when the republic claims them. And you, O majestic Switzerland; beautiful mountains, eloquent waters, wild eagles, Alpine goats, crystal lakes, silvery snows, sombre fir trees, hidden tracks, fearful rocks! There can be no harm in my throwing myself at your feet, alone and weeping in your midst. Virtue and the Republic can hardly forbid a poor, downcast, weary artist from making his way to you in order to imprint on his brain your sublime outlines and rich prismatic hues. And you, echoes of the solitude, you will surely suffer him to tell you his troubles; soft flower-studded grass, you will surely furnish him with a bed and a table; clear streams, you will not draw back when he approaches; and you, Botany, my sainted botany! O my bluebells, peacefully blossoming beneath the cataract's thunder! O my cyclamens, my *panporcini*[11] of Oliero which I found slumbering at the bottom of the cave, folded up in your calices and which, after an hour, awoke as though to gaze at me with your fresh, vermilion faces! O my little sage-bush of the Tyrol![12] O my solitary hours, the only hours of my life I remember with delight!

But you, idol of my youth, love, whose temple I am abandoning for ever, farewell! In spite of myself my knees tremble and my voice falters as I pronounce this irrevocable word. A last look, a last offering of a garland of rosebuds, the first roses of spring, and I bid farewell! Enough of offerings, enough of worship! Insatiable God, take younger, happier acolytes than I am, count me no longer among those who come to invoke you. – Yet, alas, I cannot bring myself to curse you as I leave all your torments and raptures! I cannot even reproach you; I shall set a funeral urn at your feet, emblem of my eternal bereavement. Your young acolytes will overturn it as they dance around your statue, they will shatter it and will continue to love. Reign, love, reign! Until virtue and the Republic clip your wings.

20 April

What is the matter with you? Why is there sometimes so much sadness in your heart? Why do you say the Lord has forsaken you? Why do you beg the weakest and unruliest of your children to come to your aid and give you courage? Master, what did you dream last night, and why do your disciples, who are used to receive from you the manna of hope, find you downcast and trembling?

Alas! You are finding that a great destiny takes a very long time to achieve! Time drags, your hair grows thin, your soul wears out and the human race doesn't advance. Your high ambitions batter against these brazen walls of indifference and corruption. You find yourself alone, poor worthy man, in a world of usurers and ruffians. You can hear from afar the last heroic cries of your scattered, persecuted brethren stifled in the hideous grasp of avarice and lewdness. Before long, perhaps, *sad innocence* will be extinguished by vice at which men no longer blush. That is what I find most deadly. When the spirit of enthusiasm awakes in my breast, contact with human beings who are hostile or indifferent to my ideals chills me and suppresses my youthful impulses. Then, conscious that my lack of power makes my indignation ridiculous, and seeing the bravado of those gross brutes of men as they cast a contemptuous look at my puny arms and, if equality is mentioned, claim the rights of the strongest, then it is that I say to my companions: 'Let us clothe ourselves in gold and purple; let us drink nectar and madeira, let us extinguish in our heart the last germ of virtue; since virtue must perish anyhow, let us die singing on the ruins of its temple!'

But you, my brother, you are not a prey to such fits of cowardice for long. You soon emerge from your languor; soon your energy, numbed by a passing chill, reawakens, and the old lion shakes his mane. What if the whole world were to crumble to dust around you? You would turn to marble then, and, like Atlas, you would bear the earth on your unyielding shoulders. Thus the clouds which pass over your noble brow don't worry those whom you have gathered around you. They are of the same mettle as you. What do they care if you are sad, so long as on the day of action you don't get up later than usual? I alone, perhaps, pity you as you deserve to be pitied for I have plumbed the depth of your suffering and I know that doubt can give a bitter taste to the greatest victories. I know those night hours when one walks up and down in the silence under the cold gaze of the moon and the stars which seem to say: 'You are but vanity, grains of sand; tomorrow you will be no more and we shall not even notice it.'

When this happens you must flee from yourself, Master, and join us. It is vain to struggle against the decrees of the universe; the eternal stars will always be in the right and a man, however great he may be among men, will always be filled with terror when he wishes to question what is above him. Oh, dreadful silence, the eloquent and terrible response of Eternity!

Come back to us, sit down on the grass of our Cape Sunium[13] among your brothers. When you stand up you are too far above them and you are alone. Come down, come down and be comforted. There is something besides greatness and power, and that is kindness, the sweetest and purest bond between men. A tear can sometimes do more good on earth than all the victories of Spartacus.[14] You possess it, the gift of kindness, you who are overladen with riches! Share it with us; at those times when you are not obliged to put on your buckler and your sword, forget for a while the past and the future. Give up the present to friendship. It's the one thing in which I still trust. If you only know what friends the heavens have sent me! But you do know, you have met them, they are your brothers; and yet you can't guess the extent of their kindness to me. You can't imagine from what depths of despair they have rescued me time and again, with their inexhaustible patience, their splendid compassion, even though I, angry and suspicious, thrust their help aside and spat my ingratitude and scepticism in their faces.

God bless them all! They made me believe in something; they provided an anchor of salvation in my shipwreck. Alas, you may never know the full splendour of friendship for you will not require it. What you inspire is admiration and not pity. Fate provides such compensations for the weak, just as it sends a salutary evening breeze to the blades of grass, drooping and flattened by the heat of the day.

But love my friends for the sake of all that I owe them, and when you are overthrown by Jacob's angel[15] come here to find forgetfulness and serenity in their midst. They are more lighthearted than you; they haven't put on the hair shirt of virtue. They are good and honest, prepared to do anything for their cause; but the hour of martyrdom may perhaps never sound for them. If it does, their trials will be neither long nor hard to bear – no longer than it takes to embrace each other and to die. What's that you say? For you, your agony began the day you were born and the seal of suffering was on your brow when you were in your mother's womb? Come, we'll respect your grief and do our best to make its burden lighter.

22 April

You ask for a biography of my friend Néraud, and here it is. The Malgache (I christened him that because of the endless tales and fantastic descriptions of the island of Madagascar with which he entertained me in the past on returning from his long journeys) enlisted early in the republican ranks. You've seen him; he's a spare, bronzed little man, rather worse dressed than a peasant; a first-rate walker, droll, rather caustic, coolly daring. As a student he was always ready to join in riots and received some nasty sabre cuts on his head without ceasing to taunt the police in the Rabelaisian style to which he is particularly prone. Torn between two passions – science and politics – instead of attending to his law studies while he was in Paris, he went from 'Carbonaro'[16] meetings to the school of comparative anatomy, sometimes dreaming of the reform of contemporary society, at other times of a palaeotherian skeleton whose fossilized leg Cuvier[17] had just discovered. One morning as he was passing a flowerbed in the Jardin des Plantes, he noticed an exotic fern which seemed to him so beautiful in its foliage and so altogether graceful that something occurred to him which has often happened to me: he fell in love with a plant and could dream of nothing else. Law, his meetings and the palaeothere were all neglected and sacred botany became his dominating passion. One fine day he set off for Africa and after exploring the mountainous South Sea Islands he came back, lean, sunburnt, in tatters, having put up with the severest hardships and drudgery, but possessing a treasure after his own heart, a complete herbarium of the Madagascan flora, a strange and magnificent garland stolen from the breast of a black goddess. It might have been worth a fortune; at the very least it could have given him some capital. But the devotee of science laid this trophy at the feet of Monsieur de Jussieu[18] and considered he had been rewarded beyond all his expectations when Flora's high priest bestowed the name of *Neraudia melastomefolia* on a fine fern from the island of Mauritius, till then unknown to our botanists. It was at this time that, seeing the funeral procession of Lallemand[19] go by, he abandoned botany for his country, as he had previously abandoned his country for botany, and after a dragoon's sword had made a gaping wound in his skull, he came back to his family, a maimed bird,

> Trailing his wing and dragging his foot,
> Half-dead and half crippled.

His father, to keep him at home, decided to give him a plot of land on a charming hillside where I hope to take you the first time you come to visit us. Our Malgache planted it with exotic trees, got Madagascan flowers to grow on our Berrichon soil and built, in the midst of its groves, a pretty Indian *ajoupa* which he filled with his books and his specimens. One morning as I was galloping through the valleys at sunrise I reined in my horse to gaze admiringly at some dazzling flowers that rose majestically above the hedge. These were the first dahlias ever seen in our part of the world and ever seen by me in my life. I was sixteen. Oh, how we love flowers at that age! I dismounted, stole one and rode off at a gallop. Shortly after, the Malgache – either because, concealed in his *ajoupa*, he had witnessed the theft or because an indiscreet friend had revealed my crime – sent me some dahlia bulbs which I planted in my garden, and our acquaintance dates from that incident, but not our friendship; it was not till some years later that we had a chance to meet. In the meantime he had married, become a father and added to his property a fine nursery-garden through which he has diverted the waters of a stream.

It was then, as we were both settled in the neighbourhood and as our acquaintance had started so auspiciously, that we became close friends. A free-and-easy trip which we took to the mountains of the Marche as far as the magnificent ruins of Crozant allowed us to get to know each other properly. Although I was born in the opposite camp, I have always been a republican at heart – and all the more so then for being younger and having more illusions. He liked me for being one of those stubborn people who are unaffected by the prejudices of their upbringing and declared that all I lacked to gain his entire confidence and respect was a little knowledge of botany. I promised to study it and with his help I did so until I got to the point of knowing nothing, but of understanding all the mysteries of plant life and of being able to listen to him for as long as he wanted. I've never known a man as agreeable, knowledgeable, poetic, lucid, picturesque and absorbing in his teaching. My tutor had made nature into an unbearable pedant; the Malgache turned her into an adorable mistress. He ruthlessly stripped off her motley robes of Greek and Latin through which I had always feared to look at her. He showed her to me, naked as Rhea,[20] and in her own beauty. He told me too all about the stars, the seas, the mineral kingdom, and every living substance, but mainly about insects, which were already beginning to interest him as much as plants. We spent our time chasing the lovely butterflies that flit over the meadows in the morning when their mottled wings are still heavy with dew. At noon we would seek out emerald and sapphire beetles slumbering in the warm calices of the roses. At evening, when the ruby-eyed hawk-moth buzzes around the oenotheras[21] and becomes intoxicated with their vanilla scent, we would lie in wait to seize on the wing this nimble but dizzy ambrosia drinker. Nothing suggests more the idea of a disguised sylph out to make a conquest than a great hawk-moth with its long waist, bird wings, intelligent face, soft antennae and fantastic eyes. Its upper wings that fold over its back are sombrely and mysteriously coloured and bear magic, incomprehensible letterings. There is an extraordinary similarity between the hawk-moth's or owlet-moth's robes and the plumage of night birds. The basic tint is always a mixture of tawny, brown, grey and pale yellow, under the black and white cabalistic characters which are scattered – along, aslant, across, in triangles, crescents and arrows – on all the seams. But, just as the brown owl and the osprey conceal under their breasts a brilliant down, so, when the hawk-moth spreads its velvet cloak, the under-wings are seen to form a tunic, which is sometimes bright red, sometimes a tender green and sometimes a pure rose colour ornamented with azure rings. I'll wager, you renegade, poor wretch that you are, that you haven't ever seen an ocellated hawk-moth; yet they are hatched in our vineyards, these wonders of creation that have always seemed to me too lovely not to be embodiments of the spirits of the night. Oh! It's because all these things are unknown to you, unhappy men, that your gaze is always riveted to the human race! That's not how it was for my Malgache. He would often leave his evening paper to moulder in its blue wrapping till the following morning, so impatient was he to arrange the flowers in his herbarium and the insects on their stands of elder-pith. What lovely expeditions we used to make along the banks of the Indre, in the damp meadows of the Vallée Noire! I remember an autumn entirely dedicated to the study of mushrooms, and another that was not long enough for us to learn about mosses and lichens. Our baggage consisted of a magnifying glass, a book, a tin box to contain plants and to keep them fresh – and we had my son into the bargain, a fine boy of four who wouldn't be separated from us and who acquired then a lasting passion for natural history. Since he couldn't walk very far we took it in turns to carry him or the tin box. In this way we covered several miles across country, with this quite grotesque turn-out, as conscientiously engrossed as you can be, buried in your study at this late hour, while I am telling you about the happiest years of my youth . . .

The nightingale sent forth such a lovely burst of melody just then that I have abandoned the Malgache and you to go and listen to it in the garden. It is a singularly melancholy night; a grey sky, the stars dim and veiled, not a breath among the plants, an impenetrable darkness over the whole earth. The tall firs raise their vague, black masses on high, into the gloom. Nature is not beautiful like this but it is solemn and speaks only to one of our senses, the sense to which the nightingale sings so eloquently when it has a responsive audience. All is silence, mystery, darkness; not a frog in the ditch, not an insect in the grass, not a dog barking in the distance, even the murmur of the river does not reach us; the wind is blowing from the south and carries it away across the valley. It seems that everything is hushed, intent on listening to the nightingale and absorbing those sounds, fraught with desire and throbbing with joy, which it is pouring forth. *O chorister of blissful nights*, as Obermann[22] calls him . . . Blissful nights for those who love and possess each other; dangerous nights for those who have not yet loved; nights of profound sadness for those who no longer love! Go back to your books, you who only want to live through ideas; this is no place for you. The scent of budding flowers, the smell of sap are too heady and all-pervasive; an atmosphere of forgetfulness and feverishness seems to hover oppressively overhead; the life of feeling emanates from every pore of creation. Let us flee! The spirit of fatal passions wanders among the shadows and in these intoxicating mists. O God! It is not long since I was still in love and a night such as this would have been delectable. Every sigh of the nightingale sends an electric shock through my breast. O God! my God, I am still young!

Forgive me, forgive me, my friend, my brother! At this hour you are looking at the pale stars, you are breathing the warm night air and you are thinking of me with the serenity of a sacred friendship; and I – I have not been thinking of you, Everard! I felt the tears on my cheeks and it was neither the impact of your powerful words nor emotions awakened by your tragic and glorious tales that made me weep! – but a faint light gliding across the horizon, a vague phantom passing, over there on the heath. It's all over: the spirit of the meteor has no longer any power over me; its fugitive gleam can still make me start like a traveller insufficiently armed against the terrors of the night; but I hear your stern voice from the stars on high that serve as our messengers, calling and rebuking me. Sublime fanatic, I obey; the snares and spells the enemy has in store for us in the darkness need present no danger to me. I have for patron the heavenly warrior who tramples dragons under his horses' hoofs. O Saint George! It is God who guides your arm, it is valour and divine pride that make your feet invulnerable. Dear friend, my patron is a mighty fighter, a fearless knight; I hope he will help me to subdue my passions, the deadly dragons who still try to dig their talons into my heart and deprive it of eternal salvation.

I am with you once more, my friend. Don't be upset by these fits of a passion you no longer know. For me, too, a day will come, perhaps soon, when nothing will disturb my serenity, when nature will be an ever-august temple where I shall prostrate myself at all hours of the day to praise and bless it. Anyway, here comes a gentle breeze which has just risen up to dispel the mists. And here is a star revealing its radiant countenance, like a diamond set on the brow of the tallest tree in the garden; I am saved. That star is lovelier than all my memories and that part of my soul which is ethereal soars up towards it, away from the earth and from me. Everard, is that your star or mine? Are you talking to it now? I take up again the story of my Malgache; that is . . . I'll return to it tomorrow; I am tired and shall go and enjoy that good peaceful childish sleep which, since returning to the fold, I've found again, like having a guardian angel at my bedside. I send you a flower from my garden. Good-night, may the peace of the angels be with you, God's confessor and champion of truth!

23 April

I return to the story of my Malgache . . . But in fact it's really finished; for I can't include among the achievements of his life a slight love affair that almost made him most unhappy but which, thank God, amounted to little more than a sentimental and platonic episode. However, here is the episode.

A lady of our neighbourhood[23] to whom he occasionally sent a posy, a butterfly or a shell inspired in him a sincere friendship, which she frankly returned. But his deplorable habit of playing with words made him describe as love what was no more than brotherly affection. The lady, who was our mutual friend, was neither annoyed nor flattered by the hyperbole. She was then of a calm and affectionate disposition, slightly in love with someone else, and making no mystery of it. She continued to discuss philosophy with him and to accept his butterflies, his flowers and his billets in which he always included, here and there, a complimentary little verse. The discovery of one of these missives provoked some violent scenes between the Malgache and another person who had legal rights over him, during which the fancy took him to leave the country and become a Moravian friar. So off he sets on the road once more, on foot, with his tin box, his pipe, his magnifying glass, a little in love, not very happy about the sufferings he had caused, but taking refuge in jocularity, scattering puns like a shower of blossoms over the barren tracks of his life and giving the benefit of them to the road menders, mules and stones on the way for want of a more

172

intelligent audience. He came to a halt at the rocks of the Vaucluse, determined to live and die beside the fountain where Petrarch went to conjure up Laura's image in the waters.

I was not over-concerned at this fatal decision; I knew my Malgache too well ever to believe his grief would be incurable. So long as there are flowers and insects on earth, the arrows Cupid shoots at him will always be wasted. Precisely as the month of March was carpeting the banks of the stream and the rock-faces of the Vaucluse with its greenest mosses and its freshest watercress, the Malgache discarded the role of Cardenio,[24] set about collecting aquatic mosses and, towards the end of April, wrote to me: 'It's all very well; but if my cruel fair imagines I'm going to stay here till she sees fit to reward my constancy, she is mistaken. Tell her to stop mourning my demise, I'm still in my right mind and hearty. My herbarium is full, my boots at their last gasp, and in the meantime my nursery-garden is budding without me. I've no intention of letting some nobody do my grafting for me. Forbid anybody to meddle with it; I need only the time it takes to have my pruning-knife sharpened and I'll be there.'

The sufferer returned and resigned himself to being worshipped by his household, chastely loved by his Dulcinea and cherished by me, his brother and pupil. He built himself a pretty summer-house on the hill overlooking his garden, his meadow, his nursery and his stream. Shortly after he became a father for the second time. His son had been called Olivier. Wishing to give a botanical name to his daughter as well, and knowing of nothing nicer and more appreciated than the febrifugous plant with the rose-coloured petals that grows in our meadows, he decided to call her *Petite Centaurée* (*Centaureum erythrea*).[25] His family had great trouble in dissuading him from giving her such a strange name.

He felt rather uncomfortable when he paid his first visit to the lady of his heart after the Vaucluse escapade; he was afraid she might be offended at his prompt recovery and return. However, she ran to meet him and merrily kissed him on both cheeks. On entering her room he noticed that she had carefully preserved the dried flowers and the butterflies he had once given her. She had, besides, put under glass a piece of Madagascan crystal, a fragment of basalt from Mount Pouce (where Paul went every evening to scan the horizon for the sail which he hoped would bring his Virginie[26] back the following morning) and a wasps' nest, shaped like a nose, that was beginning to crumble into dust.

A big tear rolled down the Malgache's tanned cheek. Love was drowned in it, but friendship survived, calm and purified.

Nowadays the Malgache, completely mummified outwardly, but more brisk and active than ever, leads a spotless life in the depths of his nursery-garden. He held the post of Justice of the Peace for some time but soon wearied, so he says, of all the honours and all the worries that they entail. He resigned and now refuses to open any mail, that isn't addressed to M. — *Nurseryman*. Since he has studied a great deal in his retreat he has learned a great deal and is now one of the most well-informed men in France – though nobody, not even he himself, suspects it. A little melancholy does occasionally cloud his sparkling gaiety, especially when there is frost in April while the apricot trees are in blossom. And moreover the Malgache has one great quality and one great drawback – he's what is known here as a hothead; in other words he's a republican at heart, believes that society is neither just nor generous, and grieves at not being able to provide fresh air, sunshine and food for all those who are in need of them. He finds comfort in the company of a few like-minded persons who grieve and pray with him; but once returned to his seclusion, he becomes deeply depressed and writes to me: 'O my God! Are we only utopians after all and will we have to die leaving the world as it is, without any hope that after us it will improve? Never mind, let's carry on, let's talk and act as if we had some hope, don't you agree, old friend?'

Then he seizes his smock and his hoe to dispel despondency, and after a hard day's work he is calm and humbly philosophical by evening. He then writes to me in the ink of *joy and contentment*. That's what he calls the juice of American grapes which he presses into a shell and which produces a fine red dye, rather prone, unfortunately, to fade like all available joys. Here is his last note:

'I've learnt from personal experience that the best cure for moral diseases is physical exercise. Oh, the worries I've wheeled away in my barrow. My terraces are thick with them. I've no intention of turning you into a navvy, but simply of fitting your occupations to your strength. – I've just finished building my new study; it's another sort of *ajoupa* which I have made of tree trunks covered with broom. A six-foot sheet of zinc enables me to weather storms there. This charming building is situated on a little island to which I've transported my flowerbeds and vegetable plots. The whole is encircled by the trenches of my nursery-garden whose trees today are sturdy and ravishingly beautiful. Apart from the odd fit of misanthropy it's here that I spend many relatively peaceful hours. I don't regret the past much; I made poor use of it; but I also believe that I couldn't have done better; such was my nature. I am not at all sorry to grow old; every age has its pleasures: now I want only peaceful ones. Your friendship above all. Good-night.'

Apart from the tastes that unite us – of which the most important is that love of nature, at once all-embracing and minute, which makes us both tedious and unbearable (except to each other) – we have an infirmity of character in common, which means that we often find ourselves tête-à-tête in the midst of friends. I don't know what to call it; it's sort of natural shyness,[27] peculiar to a certain kind of exuberance, a sort of false modesty that makes us afraid to say out loud what we feel most strongly; it's a total incapacity to express ourselves when we most want and ought to do so.

In fact it's the exact opposite of the quality you pre-eminently possess, which accounts for the sway you have over people, the eloquence of conviction. He, who is a scintillating wit in every other respect, and I, who (as you have noticed) have a reasonably glib tongue when moved by resentment and indignation, are both as stupid as they make them when we should be rising to the occasion. Our friends assume that we are worn out; he by too much joking, I by too much doubting. As far as he is concerned, I can assure you that his heart is still as fervent, youthful and gallant as it was at twenty. Though he is the man who has worked hardest to obtain a modest competence according to his needs, he's the one who attaches the least importance to life. He was saying only the other day: '*I would be ready to go – and I shall go!*'[28] I'm not pampered, what do I care if I have to lie on a mat, on a paving-stone or three planks?'

As for me – perhaps . . . I don't know. You thought you had discovered a great secret in me the other day when you were reading out the account of the death of your comrades. I was ill at ease all through dinner because my silence and unresponsiveness, compared to the Gaulois' enthusiasm, made me blush before you. – But that tear you espied which you thought so indicative of inner warmth, you can take it from me that it was nothing but a profound and bitter jealousy which I had every reason to conceal and which, at that moment, made me violently loathe my lot, my inaction, my helplessness and my life spent in doing nothing. It is all right for you, Everard, to love and weep tenderly over those men, because you are one of them; I am a poet, that is to say, a very woman. When there is a revolution your aim will be the freedom of the human race; I shall have no other than to let myself be killed so as to have done with myself and to have been, for the first and only time in my life, of some use, were it only by heightening a barricade by the addition of one more corpse.

What nonsense! What am I talking about? Don't imagine I'm sad or that I care a straw for glory. You know what I have told you: I've lived too long; I've done nothing worthwhile. Would anybody care to dispose of my present and future life? So long as it's made to serve an idea and not a passion, to serve the truth and not an individual, I'm prepared to accept orders. But, I warn you that I'm only fit, alas, to carry out commands, well and faithfully. I can act but not decide, for I know nothing and am sure of nothing. I can only obey by shutting my eyes and stopping up my ears so as to see and hear nothing that might dissuade me; I can march with my friends like a dog who sees his master sail off in a ship and plunges into the water to swim after him till he dies of exhaustion. The sea is vast and, my friends, I am weak. I'm good for nothing but to be a soldier and I'm not five feet high.

Never mind! This pygmy is yours! I'm yours because I love and respect you. Truth is not in man's dominion; the kingdom of God is not of this world. But in so far as man can rob the Deity of the ray of light which illuminates the world, you have robbed it, sons of Prometheus, lovers of cruel Truth and inflexible Justice! Let us go forward! Who cares what is the shade of the banner you carry so long as your hosts are always on the march towards a republican future! Whether in the name of Jesus, who has only one true apostle[29] left on earth; or in the name of Washington and Franklin, who were not able to do enough and have left us a task to complete; or in the name of Saint-Simon,[30] whose followers are going straight at the heart of the great and terrible problem (God protect them!); what matters is that right prevails and that those who believe in it vouch for it . . . I'm only a raw recruit in the regiment, take me with you!

26 April

Will you tell me who you are getting at with all your diatribes against artists? Say what you will about them, but have some respect for art, you Philistine! I very much like the idea of this rabid sectarian who would clothe Taglioni[31] in homespun and clogs and use Lizst's hands to turn the winepress millstone, but who none the less lies weeping on the ground when the merest Bengali finch warbles and who creates an uproar in the theatre trying to stop Othello from killing Malibran! This austere citizen would like to suppress artists for being social super-fluities and parasites, but the same gentleman is fond of vocal music and would spare all singers. I trust that painters will find another of your right-minded friends who is partial to them and will not tolerate the bricking up of all studio windows. As for the poets, they are akin to you and you don't spurn the structure of their language or the tech-nique of their expression when you wish to impress an audience of half-wits. You are quite ready to turn to them to borrow a few metaphors and learn how best to use them. Besides the poetic talent is such an elastic, pliable substance! It's like a sheet of blank paper from which any clown can make by turns a cap, a cock, a boat, a ruff, a fan, a shaving bowl and twenty-one other different things, to the audience's immense satis-faction. No conqueror has ever lacked bards. Eulogy is a profession like any other and when poets are ready to say what you want, you will let them say what they want: for what they want is to sing and to be heard.

And yet, time-honoured Dante, your muse with its resounding tone is not one which could have been persuaded to perjure itself!

But tell me why you have such a grudge against artists? The other day you held them responsible for every social ill, you called them *disintegrators*, you accused them of adulterating courage, of corrupt-ing morals, of totally weakening the will-power. Your harangue re-mained unfinished and your indictment very vague because I was unable to resist the foolish impulse to argue with you. I would have done better to listen to you: you might perhaps have given me some more substantial reason, since this is the only theory advanced by you which hasn't provided me with food for thought afterwards, however much I disliked it.

Is it *art* itself you want to indict? It couldn't care less for you, or for the likes of you, or for all the theories in the world! Just try to extinguish a ray of sunshine! But that is not the question. Were I to answer you I wouldn't be saying anything newer than if I were to tell you that flowers smell nice; the weather is warm in summer; birds have feathers; donkeys have longer ears than horses, etc., etc.

If it isn't art you want to do away with neither can it be artists. So long as there are people on earth who believe in Jesus there will be

177

priests, and no mortal power will be able to stop a man from making vows of humility, chastity and mercy in his heart. Similarly, so long as there are ready hands, the sacred lyre of art will resound. It would seem that we are dealing with an accidental and particular grudge that the children of the new Rome have against those of ancient Babylon.[32] What has happened? I know nothing about it. The other day one of your friends – that is to say one of ours, a republican – announced half-seriously that I deserved the death penalty. The devil take me if I know what he means by that! Nevertheless it has filled me with delight and pride, as well it should; and I never fail since that day to tell all my friends, in confidence, that I am a very important literary and political personality whose great social and intellectual superiority offends members of his own party. I can see they are somewhat taken aback at this, but they are so kind that they are ready to share my joy. The Malgache begged for my patronage so that he might be hanged on my right and Planet on my left. We cannot fail, in these circumstances, to exchange the most delightful banter and most charming jests. But in the meantime I won't have anybody make a joke of it, and I expect my friends to say of me, 'That fellow there is too clever by half, he won't survive long.'

But come, let's examine the case of my fellow-artists because, for my part, I've no intention of defending myself; I'd be too afraid of being acquitted as the most innocent of men and thus foregoing the honour of being a martyr for my ideas! – Just a minute! I'd be obliged if you would formulate some of the aforesaid ideas after my demise because, strictly in confidence, so far there hasn't been the glimmer of a theory in my head or in my books. Your duty as a friend is to tell anybody who chances to read these books of mine what they prove and what they don't prove. It mightn't, moreover, be a bad thing to tell me too, so that my judges may see by my answers how much depth and perversity there is in my mind and how urgent it is that such a dangerous comet, capable of setting the world on fire, should be extinguished.

This said (and you had better not contradict me or try to plead my cause; God bless the well-intentioned! I'm much obliged to them for their goodwill and beg them to let me be hanged in peace) let us talk about the others. What harm have they done, poor devils? Are they capable of killing a fly? You must know that only Byron and I . . .

But I'm boring you with my incorrigible, heavy-handed facetiousness. Give me a thump and I'll be serious again.

178

I'm prepared to admit that we are all great sophists. Sophistry has taken over everywhere, it has infiltrated the ranks of the Opera and Berlioz has turned it into a 'fantastic symphony'.[33] Unfortunately for the cause of ancient wisdom, when you hear the funeral march of Berlioz you will feel a kind of nervous shock in your lion heart, and you may well start to roar as you did at Desdemona's death which will be most embarrassing for me, your companion, for I pride myself on showing off a beautiful tie and a grave, composed demeanour at the Conservatoire. At the very least you will have to confess that you find the music there rather better than it was in Sparta when we served under Lycurgus,[34] and you will think that Apollo, annoyed at seeing us make our sacrifices exclusively to Pallas, has played a low trick on us by giving a few lessons to this *Babylonian*, so that he may totally bewilder us by exercising a magnetic and baleful influence on us.

You may ask if this is what I call speaking seriously . . . I am being serious. Berlioz is a great composer, a man of genius, a true artist; and since the occasion presents itself I don't mind telling you what a true artist is, because you have obviously no idea of it. The other day you named some so-called artists on whom you vented your rage – a currier, a rabbit-skin dealer, a peer of the realm, an apothecary. You named a few more, celebrities you said, of whom I have never heard. I see that you believe the moon is made of green cheese, that grocers are artists and our garrets are satrapies.

Berlioz is an artist; he is very poor, very brave and very proud. He may well be wicked enough to believe in secret that all the people in the world are not worth a chromatic scale rightly placed, just as I have the effrontery to prefer a white hyacinth to the crown of France. But believe me, it's quite possible to entertain such wild ideas without being an enemy of the human race. You are for sumptuary laws, Berlioz for demi-semi-quavers, and I am for all kinds of lilies; there's no accounting for tastes. When the time comes to build the New Jerusalem of the intellect you can be sure that each of us will contribute according to his strength: Berlioz with a pickaxe, I, myself, with a toothpick and the rest with their arms and their good will. Yet our young city will have, I presume, its peaceful, happy days when some will be allowed to go back to their pianos, others to digging their flowerbeds, and all to the innocent pleasures they are suited to and enjoy. Tell me, what are you doing when you contemplate the great constellations of the firmament at midnight while rambling on to us about the unknown and infinity? If I

179

were to interrupt you when you are uttering these grand words, to ask such brutal questions as: 'What is the use of this? Why rack someone's brains in conjectures of this kind? Does it provide men with bread and boots?' you would answer: 'It provides sacred emotions and mystical ecstasy to those who toil for mankind with the sweat of their brow; it teaches them to hope, to dream of God, to take courage and to rise above the baseness and misery of the human condition by the thought of a future that may be a chimera but is fortifying and sublime.' What has made you as you are, Everard? Surely your nightly dreams and visions. What has given you the courage to live till this day in toil and grief? Nothing but enthusiasm. And it's you, the most candid and delightfully rustic of all men of genius, who want to make war on the levites of your own God? Like Saul, you would kill David because he plays too sweetly on his harp and you go mad when you hear him!

On your knees, Sicambre![35] On your knees! We shall set you right! Alas! I say *we*! although when I remember my lawsuit I feel that I may have already been judged and condemned as an artist! But those who are truly dedicated artists will put you in your place. If only you knew what they are like, these men, when they practise their gospel and conform to the sanctity of their calling! It is true that there are not many such and I am not among them, I confess to my shame! Embarked upon an ill-fated course, neither greedy nor extravagant by nature but exposed to unexpected reverses, and responsible for dear and precious lives whose one support I was, I have failed to be an artist though I have experienced all the weariness, the fervour, the zeal and the sufferings which that sacred profession entails. My efforts were not crowned with real glory because I could seldom wait for inspiration. Always hurried, obliged to earn money, I forced my imagination to create without waiting for my reason to cooperate. I violated my muse when she would not yield; she took her revenge by responding with cold embraces and sombre revelations. Instead of coming to me smiling and garlanded, she arrived pale, bitter, indignant. The pages she dictated were all gloomy and fretful, and she took pleasure in paralysing every spontaneous impulse of my soul with doubt and despair. It is the lack of money that has got me in this plight; the misery of having to commit intellectual suicide that has made me caustic and sceptical. When I was with you one evening I told you about a fine play on the poet Chatterton,[36] performed recently at the Théâtre-Français. Wealthy, well-established people were, for the most part, shocked at the idea that a poet should take his profession so seriously and should complain so bitterly at being obliged to betray it through poverty. For my part, I shed many tears at the sight of this struggle of an independent mind against ruthless necessity, which recalled so many of my own torments and sacrifices. Pride is as touchy and sensitive as genius. Even doing my very best I might never have achieved anything tolerable; but when an artist sits down at his desk to work he must have faith in himself or he would not be there, and whether he is great, mediocre or worthless, he tries and he hopes. But if his time is measured, if a creditor waits at the door and he is reminded of his poverty and of tomorrow's deadline by his child having gone hungry to bed, then, I can assure you, however small his talent, he has an enormous sacrifice to make and a great self-humiliation to bear. He sees others taking their time, working thoughtfully, lovingly; he sees them going over their pages with care, correcting, polishing, minutely studding them as an afterthought with a thousand jewels, removing the least speck of dust, and finally holding onto them in order to revise them once more and excel perfection itself. As for himself, poor wretch that he is, he has made, with great jabs of spade and trowel, a rough, shapeless job, sometimes powerful but always incomplete, hurried and feverish; the ink isn't dry on the paper before the manuscript must be delivered without reading it, without correcting a single mistake!

*   *   *   *   *   *   *   *   *   *

Such sorrows make you smile; they seem childish to you. Yet if you acknowledge that even in the most serious matters man is always motivated by self-love, you will also acknowledge that in the most trifling matters man suffers through the sacrifice of that love. Besides there is something truly noble and sacred in an artist's dedication to his art, which consists in *doing it well* at the cost of his fortunes, his fame and his life. A firm belief is a virtue in itself, *fortitudo* (your favourite expression, I believe). The artisan dispatches his task to increase his production; the artist wastes away for ten years in the seclusion of his garret on a work that might have made his fortune, but which he will not hand over as long as he hasn't completed it according to his own standards. What does it matter to M. Ingres whether he's rich and famous? There is only one opinion for which he cares in the world and it's that of Raphael, whose shade is always at his elbow. O, admirable man! And Urhan, who plays Beethoven with tears in his eyes; and Baillot, who is willing to concede all the glitter of popularity to Paganini rather than add, on his own initiative, a tiny grace-note to the old, sacred themes of Sebastian Bach; and Delacroix, that melancholy, conscientious disciple of Rubens! – And what about you, men of renown and power, when have you been seen to acknowledge someone abler and more ambitious than yourselves for the sake of holy truth? Some of you, I know, have loved humanity and justice as *artists*. That's the greatest compliment you can be paid.

I could name other living artists who are worthy of every intelligent man's respect; but that would be to point out by omission those who are otherwise and who, blind Babylonians, pursue fame and money at all costs. Then you would accuse me of favouritism or envy, and it would be in vain that I would assure you that hardly any of those I have named and none of those I have omitted to name are my personal acquaintances. I have always lived alone amongst people, a lover, a wayfarer or a slave to literature; I've seen from a distance these pure luminaries and I've bowed down before them. I have never had the time either to profit by them or to be jealous of them, for I have not had the time to consider my profession as anything better than a trade. Yet I wasn't born to poverty; I'm not a sybarite by nature, and I might have lived and worked in peace. Those to whom I have devoted my life, dedicated my nightly vigils, sacrificed my youth and perhaps my whole future, will they be grateful to me? Probably not, and it doesn't matter.

29 April

You say that I'm a fool; so be it. Your letters – it's time I confessed as much – have a magical effect on me. They make me serious. What miracle is this? However hard I try I can't speak of you lightly as I do of all my friends, and they've found a way of silencing me when my jokes offend them: they talk about you, they repeat what they have heard you say to me, they tell me (as if I had forgotten it) of that last night we spent alternately accompanying each other home nine times over; of our halt by the church when we discussed death, and of our sudden silence at the top of the palace steps under that dim street-lamp, above the hushed, deserted square where you had just conjured up such a fantastic scene. Looking at you then, I was sorry that I was incapable of being afraid of a human being; otherwise you would have made me feel the sort of keen terrors we sometimes experience in dreams and which are not without pleasure. I shan't easily forget your words as we came down the gothic stairway in the moonlight: you said to me: 'I love you as Jesus loved

John, his youngest, most romantic disciple; yet if ever it were my duty to kill you, I would tear you from my heart and strangle you with my own hands.' Upon my word, my dear master! I wish I were more worthwhile killing than a poor mayfly to see if you would really have such courage and such virtue. But not likely! You wouldn't go to that length, humbug that you are! – Yet, who knows? You who never joke! It's possible. It would be a fine thing, and I'd really give you my head for the pleasure of having seen one true Roman in my life.

I do assure you, there are moments when I believe that virtue has sought refuge and concealed herself within you as in the days when mankind forced her to go and fortify herself in abandoned caves, among impregnable rocks. But what if after all, you were no more than a fanatic! – What of it? It's always something: not everyone can be a fanatic, especially nowadays, and I'd be that much prouder of myself than I have reason to be if only I had a touch of your madness. Those of us who mock incessantly are sometimes very like those madmen who laugh to see people in their senses behaving normally. The other day a peasant comrade of mine (I hope I am speaking in the correct republican style) came into my study and, seeing me busy writing, shrugged his shoulders pityingly. He leant over me and observed what I was doing, almost as if he had paid to see performing apes at the fair. Then he picked up a book from my desk – it was, God forgive me, a volume by the divine Plato – opened it the wrong way up, turning over the pages attentively; then he put it back on the table, saying disparagingly: 'So it's at this nonsense you spend your time, Feast Days and Sundays alike? There are certainly some odd folks living in this world!' And he shook his head, shaking with laughter, so that it required all my democratic philosophy to stop me from taking him by the shoulders and showing him the door.

But I calmed down, thinking that I was in the same situation as this peasant with you and yours a hundred times a day, and I have marvelled at the patience with which you tolerate the impudent, stupid mockery of drones like us, who are good for nothing but criticizing what we don't understand and don't know how to accomplish. But I shall say with Planet: 'Why don't you send me packing!' What business have I in your midst, you early Christians! God knows you must be angels! for nothing discourages or shocks you. You welcome us tenderly, and here you are calling me your younger brother, your son, I who deserve to be sent home to my pipe and my novels? – Sheer proselytism! Let those who want to make nice distinctions do so: I don't care what name people give you as long as I see in you a source of lessons in virtue and acts of charity.

Yet I must tell you what is worrying me, O my poor misunderstood prophet! They are trying to set your followers against you. Party spirit knows no bounds. We are told that you are vainglorious, ambitious, bungling; in short, that you should be shut up in the Petites-Maisons[37] and that all those who love you should join you there.

All this would only be ludicrous if men of good feeling and abilities were not involved; they have taken the word of others and show at the least, by their silence in your presence, that they suspect both us and you. This doesn't disturb those stout fighters who have weathered many a storm; but I, who have just returned from Babylon where I have slept for five years in a drunken stupor, and have landed up rubbing my eyes right in the midst of our new Zion, am saddened and downcast to see the iron ramparts with which the indifference and dislike of the gentiles have encircled us. Shall we ever come out from there, Master? I know that from time to time we venture a brave and forceful sally; but the best of our brothers are cut down, and when we have retreated to our tents the shouts, maledictions and jeers of the victorious army disturb our prayers. – As for me, what most upset me are the jeers. I know them well, these damned gentiles, from having been their captive. I know how cunning they are and what sharp arrows their irony lets fly at us. Bear in mind that I myself am not a well-tried campaigner; I can already hear their jibes at the strange figure I cut as a soldier of the republic. I therefore beg you, my dear master, let me go off to Istanbul. I've some business over there. I must pass through Geneva, buy a donkey to cross the mountains with my baggage, go up through the Black Forest to find a plant which the Malgache wants me to bring back. In Corfu there's a Mohammedan friend who has invited me to come and drink a sorbet in his garden; Dutheil has asked me to buy him a pipe in Alexandria and his wife would like me to go as far as Aleppo in order to bring her a shawl and a fan. You see that I cannot delay, that I have really demanding engagements and obligations. – But listen: if you proclaim the republic during my absence, take everything there is in my house, don't hesitate! I have land; give it to those who haven't. I have a garden; let your horses graze there. I have a house; turn it into a hospital for your wounded. I have wine; drink it. I have tobacco; smoke it. I have my published works; use them for wadding for your guns. There are only two things in all my patrimony whose loss I would mourn: the portrait of my old grandmother and a six-foot plot of grass planted with cypresses and rose bushes. That's where she rests together with my father. I entrust this grave and the picture to the care of the republic and shall require, on my return, compensation for certain losses I shall have incurred, namely a pipe, a pen and ink, by means of which I shall earn my living happily and spend the remainder of my days writing about how well you have done.

If I don't come back, here is my will: I leave my son to my friends, my daughter to their wives and sisters; the grave and the portrait, my children's heritage, to you, head of our republic of Aquitaine, as provisional guardian; my books, minerals, herbarium, butterflies to the Malgache; all my pipes to Rollinat; my debts, should there be any, to Fleury so as to keep him busy; my blessing and my last joke to those who made me suffer so that they may be comforted and forget me.

I name you my executor; so, farewell; I am off.

Farewell, O my children! Up till now I've been more childish than you; I'm going far away, alone, on a pilgrimage, to try and grow old quickly and make up for lost time. Talk sometimes round the hearth about one who owes you the best days and the sweetest memories of his life; and to you, my master, farewell! I bless you for having forced me to look a great enthusiast in the face without laughing, and to bend my knee to him on departing.

O, evergreen Bohemia! Land of fantasy, of souls without ambitions and without bounds. Shall I indeed see you again! I have often strayed among your mountains and hovered above the tops of your fir trees; it is all so clear in my memory, although it was before I came into the world amongst men, and it has been my sorrow throughout my life here not to be able to forget you.

Letter Seven

To Franz Liszt[1]

On Lavater and on a Deserted House

Not knowing your present whereabouts, my dear Franz, and no less ignorant of where I shall go, I am making use of your obliging friend Monsieur —[2] to convey this missive to you. I am confident he will be able to track you down in your lair sooner than I who am cloistered in my own retreat for a few days more.

I need hardly tell you how sorry I am not to be able to come and join you. I hear that your mother is setting off, and Puzzi[3] with his family. I presume that you are going to establish an artists' colony in beautiful Switzerland or in verdant Bohemia. Happy friends! How noble and pleasant a vocation is the art you have chosen and how arid and tedious mine seems in comparison! I must work in silence and solitude whereas a musician thrives on a good understanding and sympathy with his pupils and performers. Music teaches, reveals, diffuses, communicates itself. Doesn't the harmony of the sounds demand it of the will and the emotions? What a superb republic is achieved by a hundred instrumentalists united in a similar spirit of order and love to perform a great master's symphony! When Beethoven's spirit hovers over such a blessed choir what a fervent prayer rises towards God!

Yes! Music is prayer, it is faith, it is friendship, it is the epitome of cooperation. 'Where two or three of you are gathered together in my name,' said Christ to his disciples on leaving them, 'there am I also, amongst you.' The disciples, forced to travel, to toil and to suffer, were soon dispersed. But whenever, between imprisonment and martyrdom, between the chains of Caiaphas and the stones of the synagogue, they happened to meet, they knelt together at the side of the road, in an olive grove or an upper room on the outskirts of some city and they talked of their master and friend Jesus, of the Brother and the God to whose worship they had dedicated their lives. And when each in turn had spoken, the need to invoke the spirit of the beloved in unison probably suggested the idea of singing; probably too, the Holy Ghost, who descended upon them in tongues of fire and revealed to them hidden things, had bestowed upon them the gift of that sacred language which is the prerogative of the elect. Oh surely, if there were beings who were great enough before God to deserve the sudden acquisition of new faculties, if their minds were opened, if their tongues were loosened, divine songs must have flowed from their lips and men must have listened in rapture to the first concerted harmony.

That withdrawal of the Twelve for forty days, that fervent union and that unimpaired purity of twelve believing and devoted souls which stood the test for so long a time is a unique fact in the history of mankind, and one before which I have to prostrate myself whenever I think of it. Even if I had any doubts concerning the miracles that ensued I would not like to say so; and neither, I believe, would you – isn't that so? If it were shown me that these men were for their time exceptionally skilful sorcerers and alchemists, I'd say that this in no way detracted from the reality of a divine man nor from the existence of a race of saints powerful enough to walk on the waters and resurrect the dead. What I find indisputable is the miraculous power of faith in man. So that if it were proved that the disciples did have to resort to the wonders of what was then called magic, I'd think that they had their days of doubt and affliction when heavenly power was withheld from them. Let there be found, I would reply, twelve men from amongst us who surpass the disciples in steadfastness of faith and in the holiness of their lives, twelve men who are capable of spending forty days under the same roof without finding fault with each other and vying for precedence; twelve men solely intent on praying, on begging God for the knowledge of truth and the power of good, neither half-hearted nor proud, never yielding either to spiritual exhaustion or to the dictates of the flesh; and you can be sure, O my friends, that we will see miracles, new knowledge, unheard of powers, and a universal faith. Man *re-deified* will emerge from this congregation one fine spring morning, the sacred fire upon his brow, the secret of life and death in his hands, with the ability to make rocks weep tears of pity, with the knowledge of tongues spoken by nations as yet unheard of, but above all with the gift of the divine language made perfect – that is to say, of music carried to its highest degree of eloquence and persuasiveness.

187

For when the miracle of the descent of the Holy Spirit amongst the disciples of Jesus occurred, the Heavens opened above their heads and they must have heard and preserved a vague memory of the hymns of the fiery Seraphim and of the golden harps played by those crowned elders who appeared again later in their splendour to Saint John of the Apocalypse, and whose divine harmonies he was able to hear mingling with the winds during some stormy night on the deserted shores of his island.

O you, who in the silence of the night are at one with the holy mysteries, you, my dear Franz, whose ears the Divine spirit has opened so that you may listen from afar to the heavenly measures and transmit them to us, the infirm and forsaken, how fortunate you are to be able to pray during the day with those who understand you! Your work doesn't condemn you to solitude like mine; your fervour is rekindled at the hearth to which all who love you bring their offering of sympathy. Go then, pray in the tongue of angels, and praise God upon your instruments, which vibrate to a single heavenly breath!

For me, the solitary traveller, things are very different. I go by deserted ways and seek my lodging within silent walls. I had set out to meet you last month; but the wind of fancy, or of fate, blew me off my course and I stopped to avoid the heat of the day in one of the towns of our medieval France, on the banks of the Loire. While I was slumbering the steamer weighed anchor and when I awoke I saw its black streamer of smoke rapidly disappearing along the silver ribbon which the river was tracing on the horizon. I decided to go back to sleep till the next day; and the next day as I came out of my room to enquire about a horse or a boat, a friend of mine whom I didn't in the least expect to see there (having lost sight of him during the years of my vagabond existence) appeared before me in the courtyard. He told me over lunch that he was married and had settled in the town but spent most of his time in a country house nearby, to which he was just going. He had come to the inn to hire a horse, since his own were either sick or in use and he wanted to drive me over in a buggy to meet his new family. The invitation didn't greatly appeal to me; the day was even more dusty and hot than the previous one; I still felt a bit feverish; the springing of the buggy was, to put it mildly, rustic; I don't much fancy making new acquaintances when I'm travelling and I'm unwilling to be excessively polite when I'm excessively tired. I refused point blank and told him I wanted to stay at the inn until I'd got over my indisposition. This admirable friend didn't force a ruthless hospitality upon me. He consented to leave me there; but just as he was climbing into his buggy it occurred to him to say: 'I've a house in the town, small, very modest and not very well kept, I'm afraid; but you might perhaps sleep more peacefully there than here. If, despite the neglected state it has got into because of my having been in the country all through the spring, you could make use of it . . . I daren't insist, it's such a mess! However, you're a poet and a lover of solitude unless you've changed. It might appeal to you. Anyhow, here are the keys; should you go before I come back to see you, leave them with the innkeeper's wife, who knows me.' Having said this he embraced me and drove away.

I found this invitation most agreeable. I was obviously too unwell to continue my journey for two or three days. I asked to be shown the way to my friend's house. It wasn't easy to reach; we had to go up and down narrow, steep, scorching, badly paved streets that grew ever more deserted and dilapidated as we penetrated further into the suburbs. Finally we arrived by a series of worn steps at a kind of broken-down terrace supporting a block of very old houses, each with its courtyard or garden surrounded by high, dark walls festooned with climbing plants. I had only to open the door of the one assigned to me to be overcome with joy at its appearance and, reluctant to forgo the sacred pleasure of entering it alone, I took my suitcase from my guide's hand, thrust his wages on him, and hurried inside, shutting the door in his face, which must have made him take me for a madman, a conspirator or worse.

It would seem that nature was not made exclusively for man, or that, before his extensive domination of the earth, rural deities really did hold sway; that this superhuman race has not completely retired to the heavens, and that its scattered remnants still haunt the sites man has deserted. If not how can we account for the religious awe that overcomes us when our steps tread on ground on which no human foot has yet trampled? Why are we so fond of solitude and at the same time so frightened of it? Why do we welcome ruins, unexplored shores, untrodden snows? Why does the sound of our footsteps echoing under the arches of abandoned cloisters make us quake? Why do virgin forests, deserted temples, secluded landscapes affect sensitive souls so delightfully or faint hearts so painfully? If ever we were firmly convinced that we were the one and only living things in some corner of the globe we would be overwhelmed either with joy or with horror, depending on our temperament. And yet has man really cause to rejoice when he has no other company than his own? any reason to dread the absence of a helping hand when the absence of a harmful one is equally assured? What is it that we experience at the sight of sands without footprints, lands without overlords, dwellings without tenants? Do we not perceive everywhere the existence and the presence of unknown beings who have established their empire there and who have the goodness to admit us or the right to exclude us?

I was thinking all this as I leant against the door I had just closed behind me and I couldn't make up my mind to cross the courtyard; for I would have to trample down the long grasses in which I stood knee-deep and from which the sunbeams were beginning to sip the morning dew. What nymph had upturned her basket there and sewn those feathery grasses, those fragile saxifrages rising in their virginal beauty, sheltered from desecration of any sort? 'Forgive me, Sylph,' I said to her, 'or lend lightness to my steps so that I may cross this space without flattening your beloved plants under my feet.' Had anyone seen me, breathless and dusty, leaning mournfully against the door with my suitcase in my hand, they would have taken me for a man in the depths of despair or overwhelmed by remorse; yet never was explorer prouder of his discovery nor did pilgrim more piously greet the Holy Land.

The sylph hadn't disdained to tend the plants the master of the deserted house had entrusted to her. Three lime trees, dividing the yard in two, a bed of larkspurs by the wall, a vine and some tall tree-mallows had attained a fantastic profusion and growth. When I reached the paved section of my little kingdom I was careful to walk on the disjointed paving stones without crushing the greenery that sprang up between the cracks and eventually came to the door, where I was faced with a further problem: long branches of vine were intertwined over the entrance and had grown in leafy screens across the window. I had to lay a sacrilegious hand on them to separate them and lift them up like curtains to clear my passage over this venerable threshold. But it was no sooner crossed than the vine branches slid lithely back, clasping each other firmly as though to forbid my return to the sacred enclosure. I haven't yet disobeyed you, O flexible, accommodating bars of my beloved prison! Each night I sit on the last step of the staircase and gaze up at the moon through your silvery garlands. Every star in the heavens is framed in its turn as it passes behind the translucent network you have hung between us, and sometimes daylight finds me, motionless and silent as the stone on which I sit.

Yes, Franz, I am still in this deserted house, alone, totally alone, never opening the door except to let in a meal, and I can't remember ever having known more soothing, unsullied days. It is a great comfort to me, I assure you, to see that my spirit hasn't grown too old to relish the joys of its lively youth. If inordinate dreams of virtue, if fervent aspirations towards heaven no longer occupy my contemplative hours, I still have, none the less, pleasing thoughts and religious hopes; and moreover I'm not consumed as I was once by the urge to live. The nearer I draw to life's close the more justly and thankfully I savour what good things it has to offer. On the slope of the hill I linger and slow down my descent, casting a loving, admiring glance over the wonders of this place I am going to leave behind, and which I didn't sufficiently appreciate when, on the hilltop, I could have enjoyed it to the full.

You haven't arrived there yet, my child;[4] do not hurry. Don't take the ascent of those sublime summits too much in your stride: once we have come down from them we never climb them again. Your lot is better than mine; get the good of it, don't despise it. As a man you still have in store the riches of your best years; as an artist you serve a more fruitful and attractive muse than mine. You are her well-beloved, whereas mine is beginning to find I am past my prime and restricts me, besides, to melancholy and improving thoughts that would destroy your precious poetry. And so – live all you can! The bright flowers of your garland must have sunshine; the ivy and convolvulus from which mine is woven, emblems of the savage freedom with which the ancient sylvans crowned themselves, grow in shadow and among ruins. I don't complain of my fate and I'm happy that providence has given you a more cheerful one; you deserve it and, were it mine, Franz, I would bestow it on you.

Thus I stayed on at —, initially because I had no alternative, and now for the pleasure of reading and solitude; later, perhaps, I shall continue to stay out of indolence and forgetfulness of myself and the passing hours. But I want to tell you of a bit of good luck that has befallen me in this retreat and has contributed greatly to my affection for it.

You who read widely because you haven't as much respect as I have for books (and with reason since your art can only make you scorn ours), you, I say, who are quick-witted and devour volumes, you don't know how important careful, slow reading is to a lazy mind like mine. I'm not, however, one of those who think that books have a very serious moral or political impact. Philosophy, in particular, strikes me as being the most innocuous of all forms of poetic theorizing and I believe that it is only exceptional people, whether through their strength or their weakness, who can derive from it real solutions or encouragement. Any mind that doesn't seek to be convinced and enlightened by practical experience and lets itself be influenced by fictions is exceptionally constituted. If it is above average it will be fortified and elevated by good books; if below average it will derive great comfort from them and may also be sadly afflicted by what it takes for personal censure. In one case as in the other reading will have played a very minor role in their different developments. Similar results would have been achieved sooner or later even if such people hadn't known how to read. And you know that, for my part, I have the greatest respect for untutored minds. I bow down before great writers and great poets, but there are days when, at the sight of some simple, blessedly ignorant souls, I would willingly burn the library of Alexandria itself.

This said, I may as well confess that, owing to my natural indifference and my inaptitude for any form of social activity, I am one of those for whom getting to know a book can be a truly moral event. The few good books which have really gone home to me in the course of my life have been responsible for the few good qualities I possess. I can't tell what bad works might have done to me; I've never read any, having had the good fortune to be well guided, from childhood onwards. In this respect, therefore, I have only the sweetest and dearest memories. A book has always been a friend to me, an adviser, an eloquent, soothing comforter whose resources I tried to eke out by reserving it for important occasions. Oh, which one of us doesn't recall lovingly the first books he devoured or savoured! Hasn't the cover of a dusty old book, rediscovered on the shelves of some forgotten closet, ever brought back the delightful scenes of your youth? Haven't you thought you saw appear before your eyes the large meadow, bathed in the red glow of evening where you read it for the first time, the ancient elm and the hedge that sheltered you and the ditch whose banks were your couch and your writing-desk while a thrush sang a retreat to its comrades and the cowherd's pipe faded into the distance? Oh how fast night fell on those wonderful pages! How cruelly the twilight blurred the letters on the fading sheet! It's all over! The lambs bleat, the sheep have come back to the fold, the cricket takes possession of the stubble in the plain. The outlines of the trees grow dim in the hazy air, just as the printed letters have before them. It is time to go; the track is stony, the sluice-gate narrow and slippery and the hillside rough. You are bathed in sweat but however much you hurry you'll be late, supper will have begun. It's in vain that the old servant, who loves you, has waited till the very last minute to ring the dinner-bell: you'll have to suffer the humiliation of entering last and your grandmother, unrelenting where manners are concerned even in the depths of her country estate, will upbraid you in a gently reproachful voice, ever so mildly, ever so tenderly, which will go home to you more than would a harsh punishment. But when, at night, she hears your daily confession and you admit, blushing, that you forgot the time, reading in a field, and are ordered to show her the book; when after some hesitation and deeply dreading to see it confiscated before you've finished it, you extract from your pocket . . . what? *Estelle et Némorin*[5] or *Robinson Crusoe*! Oh, then grandmother smiles. Don't worry, your treasure will be returned to you; but you'll have to be in time for supper from now on. What happy times! O my Vallée Noire! O Corinne![6] O Bernardin de Saint-Pierre![7] O the *Iliad*! O Millevoye![8] O Atala![9] O the willows by the river! O my lost youth! O my old dog who never forgot the hour of supper and responded to the distant bell with a pitiful howl of regret and greed!

Goodness! What was I saying? I wanted to talk to you about Lavater,[10] and indeed I shall now do so. As a child I got my hands on a copy of Lavater. Ursula and I used to study the plates with curiosity. We could hardly read. What was the point, we wondered, of this assortment of comic, grotesque, insignificant, hideous or pleasant faces? We searched avidly among the incomprehensible sentences and captions for the main definition of the type; we found *drunken*, *slothful*, *gluttonous*, *irascible*, *political*, *methodical* . . . And then we were completely baffled and returned to the pictures. However, we did notice that the drunkard looked like the coachman, the troublesome scolding woman like the cook, the pedant like our tutor, the men of genius like the effigy of the Emperor on our coins and we were convinced of Lavater's infallibility. Yet all the same this science seemed mysterious and almost magical to us. Later the book was mislaid. In 1829 I met a very distinguished man who had complete faith in Lavater and who made me observe a number of cases to which the science of physiognomy was so obviously relevant that I became very eager to study it. I tried to get hold of the book; it was unobtainable. I forget what preoccupations intervened, but I thought no more about it.

And then, on the day of my arrival, I opened a cupboard full of books and the first thing that I took up was the works of Jean Gaspard de Lavater, minister of the holy gospel at Zurich, published in 1781, three volumes in a French translation, with engraved plates, etchings, etc. Imagine my joy, and let me tell you that I've never read anything pleasanter, more instructive, more salutary. Poetry, wisdom, profound observation, kindness, piety, evangelical charity, true morality, exquisite sensitivity, nobility and simplicity of style, all these I found in Lavater when all I was seeking were physiognomical observations and some conclusions – possibly erroneous, at the least, conjectural and tentative.

Since you ask me for a long letter and since you are always interested in thought processes I shall talk to you about Lavater. In my present surroundings and considering the life I lead, it would be hard for me to provide anything more up to date in literature. I hope with all my heart that you will feel the urge to make the acquaintance of the old inhabitant of this deserted house, the venerable friend I've just discovered here.

Besides it would be nice if you, like all the proud innovators of our century, had always despised Lavater's theories as a tissue of illusions based on a false premise, so that I might have the satisfaction of making you change your mind. Nowadays we think of physiognomy as a tried, condemned and buried science on whose ruins another is rising, phrenology, not yet judged but more worthy of study and attention. I detest the scorn and ingratitude with which our generation overthrows the idols of our fathers and makes much of the disciples, after crucifying the doctors and the masters. To prefer Schiller to Shakespeare, Corneille to the Spanish tragedians, Molière to the Greek and Latin comic writers, La Fontaine to Phaedrus or to Aesop is, I think, not simply a mistake but a crime. In supposing that the imitator who, thanks to skill, time and patience, surpasses his model, has more merit than his master, we are establishing an abominably unjust and wrongheaded practice. However perfect an interpretation or imitation may be, whatever significant or necessary corrections may emerge, however highly finished or improved the work derived from the original, the latter is nevertheless superior, formative, venerable, holy. Indeed ancient Homer can never be equalled even by those who might excel him; for where is the poet who would have any idea of epic poetry were it not for Homer?

Well, I've no doubt that we'll achieve such perfection in the study of the human form that we'll be able to read the abilities and tendencies of our fellow-creatures like an open book. Will Gall,[11] Spurzheim[12] and their successors turn out to have been the masters of this knowledge? No more so than Vespucci[13] was the conqueror of America; yet half the globe is named after him while a small province is at pains to preserve great Christopher's name.

The system of Dr Gall is held in honour, or at least, is still visible today. It is examined and discussed while Lavater is forgotten, gathering dust in libraries; the editions are exhausted and not re-issued. I don't know if you would find it easy to get hold of a copy of one of the finest products of the human understanding. But Gall was a doctor and Lavater a priest. Our positivist, materialistic age has had to prefer a mechanistic explanation to a philosophical discovery. It is none the less a fact that cranioscopy is a feature of physiognomy and that, for Lavater, it is its necessary and fundamental basis. This part of physiognomy is so important according to him that it should be studied on its own. It is for anatomy to discover there the sources of mental change and to deduce, from an exact understanding of the variations in brain structure, a knowledge of man's aptitudes. This learned and patient investigator will emerge some day, adds this citizen of Zurich; he will recall humanity to the truth, or at least to the desire for truth. From discovery to discovery, from experiment to experiment he will overcome prejudice and physiognomy will be acknowledged to be a science, as important, as difficult and as eminent as every other science on which civilized societies are founded and on which they depend.

Full of love, respect and trust in his beloved science the good Lavater modestly relinquishes the honour of being the first discoverer . . . He quotes various precursors: Aristotle, Montaigne, Solomon . . . He quotes the following, taken from the *Book of Proverbs*:

> A haughty eye and a heart puffed with pride.
> Wisdom shows in the face of the wise man, but the fool's eyes range over the whole earth.
> There is a breed of men whose looks are haughty and whose eyes are unblinking.

Lavater also quotes a number of passages from Herder[14] to back his theory: here is a notable one which you have no doubt been lucky enough to read in German, but which I remind you of because it seems

195

to me to illustrate the German aptitude for impressive and felicitous metaphor:

> What hand can grasp that substance located inside man's head and beneath his skull? Can a mere organ of flesh and blood reach this abyss of faculties and internal powers, now in ferment, now in repose? It was a Divine being who took care to conceal this sacred mount, this dwelling-place and workshop of the most arcane operations and concealed it under a forest, symbol of the sacred wood where mysteries were once celebrated. A holy terror overwhelms us at the thought that inside this shady hill are thunderbolts, of which a single one, escaping from chaos, is capable of enlightening, improving or devastating and destroying the earth.
>
> How revealing the forest of this Olympus can be in its natural growth, in the disposition of the locks of hair, the way they fall, divide, intermingle!
>
> The neck on which the head rests shows not what is in man but what he wishes to express. Here its noble, detached attitude denotes the dignity of his situation; there it is bent to signify the martyr's acceptance; and there again it is a pillar, symbol of the strength of Hercules.
>
> The brow is the seat of serenity, joy, chagrin, anguish, stupidity, ignorance and wickedness. It is a brazen tablet on which every emotion is engraved in letters of fire . . . Just where the brow slopes down, judgement seems to mingle with the will. It is here that the mind concentrates and gathers its strength for resistance.
>
> Directly under the brow is its goodly frontier, the eyebrow, a rainbow of peace in its gentler moods, a bow strung with discord in its moments of fury. But in one case or the other it signifies our inclinations.
>
> As a rule the part of the face where the mutual relationships between eyebrows, eyes and nose converge is where the soul – that is, will-power and action – is expressed.
>
> Nature has situated on either side of the head, where it is half hidden from view, the noble, profound and secret sense of hearing. Man was meant to hear for himself; therefore the ear is unadorned. Delicacy, perfection, depth, these are its ornaments.
>
> A delicate, pure mouth is perhaps one of the best testimonials. The beauty of the portal foreshadows the dignity of what will emerge

from it; in this case the voice, interpreter of the heart and of the soul, expression of truth, friendship and the most tender feelings.*

Lavater, after relinquishing the honour of discovering physiognomy to the sages of antiquity, and to modern times that of deducing its poetic content, concentrates on demonstrating how the assiduous and conscientious enquiries that have occupied his whole life have only allowed this difficult science to advance one step further. He invites his successors to correct his errors and to rectify his assumptions. A more humble and gentle man could not be found, especially among scholars; he is truly evangelical in every respect: greeted by nothing but the mockery, contradictions, pedantry and quibblings of his contemporaries, he replies with unfailing composure: Professor Lichtemberg[15] attacks him with more spirit and bitterness than the rest. Lavater, no doubt secretly a little upset (since he admits to feeling nervous and irritable), takes the pamphlet and, restored to his sense of Christian philosophy by his lifelong faith and activity, writes his answer in a spirit of wisdom and charity. He examines the attack with his customary precision and love of order, saying: 'I imagine to myself that, sitting side by side, we are going through this document together and, with the freedom that befits men and the moderation that befits the wise, we are exchanging our respective views on nature and on truth.'

And a little further, struck by a fine peroration of Professor Lichtemberg's, he exclaims innocently: 'This is writing after my own heart! It is under the supervision of a man like this that I would have liked to write my Essays.'

Oh, goodly priest! None the less what is being attacked is the most precious thing which his intelligence has brought forth and which he cherishes most dearly – namely, the morality of his science. His critics (who, as is their wont, are ever humble and tolerant!) find that their modesty and virtue are offended by the sight of this impious innovator inquiring into the mysteries of the understanding. 'What are you about?' they exclaim bitterly. 'You are trying to appropriate what is God's alone, knowledge of the secrets of the human heart. And when you have taught your fellow-beings to analyse themselves and spy upon each other, the wicked will be implacably detested as a result, so that you will have destroyed mercy; the simple-minded will be proudly scorned, so that you will have destroyed charity.' Lavater bows his

* Herder, *Plastik*.

197

head. The objection is a serious one, he says, and comes from a noble mind; but all learning can be fatal in the hands of the wicked, useful and blessed for whoever puts it at the service of good. Does that mean that learning should be abolished because it can be misused? 'But how can you repair or avoid the injustice an error might lead you to commit?' is the reply. 'Or, if we have to accept your own infallibility, will it be true of your disciples? Every day we meet honest men with ignoble features and scoundrels who look frank and loyal.' – Lavater denies this. Any novice who is in a hurry to practise will commit serious mistakes, he thinks; but whoever entrusts the secrets of medicine to schoolboys is taking terrible risks. An enlightened man does more good than an ignorant one does harm; for an ignorant man's reputation won't survive for long whereas that of the true scholar increases from day to day. All learning is a vocation that demands men of experience who are worthy of their mission. As for those allegations of angel-faced scoundrels and vile-looking paragons, he declares that such appearances don't mislead the true physiognomist: 'Often,' he says, 'the symptoms of a generous passion are so similar to those of the same passion when it has degenerated into excess and vice, that an inexperienced eye may be misled. It falls short by a hair's breadth, an imperceptible curve, a dimension which is unnoticeable at first glance. It falls short by so little, we say, but that *little* is *everything*.'

It often happens that the best natures are concealed under the most repulsive appearances. The common eye sees nothing but rack and ruin; it doesn't realize that upbringing and circumstances have obstructed every effort towards improvement. The physiognomist observes, examines and suspends judgement. He hears a thousand voices shouting: 'Look at him! Do you call that a man!' But in the midst of the uproar he distinguishes another voice, a divine voice that also cries: 'See what a man!' He finds cause for veneration where others blame because they cannot and will not understand that this same countenance from which they turn away bears the mark of the Creator's power, wisdom and mercy. He sees cunning in the face of a beggar who comes to his door and it does not repel him; he speaks kindly to him. He looks into the depth of the soul and what does he see? – Alas! vice, confusion, total degradation. But is that all he discovers? What! No good at all? Even if this is the case, he still sees the clay which must not and cannot say to the potter: 'Why did you make me thus?' He sees, he worships in silence and, turning aside, he sheds an eloquent tear, not for men but for Him who created them. Wisdom without goodness is folly. I would not see through your eyes, O Jesus, if you did not give me your heart as well. May justice govern my judgements and charity my actions.

'A clear notion of man's freedom and of the limits that are set to it is needed to make us humble and brave, modest and active. *So far and no further, but so far!* It is the voice of God and truth that addresses you thus; it says to all those who have ears to hear: "Be what you are and become what you can."'

Elsewhere, apropos of physical deformities, the same sense of human tenderness and religious pity recurs as eloquently as ever:

'All that has to do with humanity is a family concern for us. You are a man and all other men are like branches from the same tree, limbs of the same body. O man! Rejoice in the existence of all that has joy in existing, and learn to bear all that God bears. The existence of one man cannot make the life of another superfluous and no man can replace another.'

Such tolerance and such tender understanding in the face of deformity is all the more moving in that no one could be more enraptured by beauty and delicately sensitive to form than Lavater. He goes into ecstasies over the purity of Greek outline, but he perceptively deplores modern imitations of a beauty that is gone. We have cause to believe, he suggests, that in that golden world when everything was godlike, man was godlike also, and that there was in the integrity of line something superhuman about his form which since then has only degenerated and vanished; there are breeds of men that perish. – Yet Lavater might have been less positive in his opinion had he seen many oriental people. I remember meeting on the quays in Venice some Armenians who were almost as beautiful as the gods of Olympus. We can still on rare occasions find even in Western countries features of such nobility that they might have served as models for classical sculpture; and I can't agree with Lavater that nature never produces on earth forms that are totally pure and perfect. None the less I approve of the physiognomist's censure of those *caricatures* of classical art which indifferent painters of his time set up as an ideal. He discriminates between Greek masterpieces and those heads we see on clumsily wrought medallions where the almost non-existent brow, the rigid, abrupt perpendicularity of the nose, the absurdly prominent chin and unnaturally far apart eyes provide only a hideous distortion of beauty.

He deplores the fact that the spirit of careful enquiry and rigorous discrimination has not sufficiently governed even some major artists in their studies of classical art. He feels that Raphael, whom he sets above all other painters, slightly overdoes perfection. 'Everywhere,' he says, 'we perceive in his works a *greatness* which is his main characteristic; but everywhere too we notice a *flaw*; I call *greatness* that which makes a lasting impression and causes ever-renewed pleasure. I describe as a *flaw* that which is contrary to nature and truth.' After a long and scholarly study of the inaccuracies and the sublimities in Raphael's main figures, and after demonstrating that the painter's desire to improve on nature has meant the loss of some of the celestial quality from the face of an angel or Virgin, Lavater ends his analysis with the noble eulogy:

> Raphael is and will always be an apostolic man, that is to say, he is
> for painters what Christ's apostles were for the rest of humanity; and
> in so far as he surpasses, through his works, all the artists of his
> class, so far, too, does his beautiful appearance distinguish him from
> all ordinary beings. Where is there another like him? When I want to
> contemplate to the full the perfection of God's works I have only to
> think of Raphael's form.

Because, according to Lavater, genuine physical beauty is inseparable from the beauty of the soul, this holy passion for beauty is expressed with true artistic simplicity many times in the course of his book. This is what he has to say about a mouth: 'This mouth has a certain sweetness, delicacy, circumspection, kindness and modesty. Such a mouth is made to love and be loved.' Elsewhere, about the expressiveness of hair, he exclaims: 'If it were only for love of your hair, O Algernon Sidney,[16] I salute you!'

I shan't give you a detailed account of Lavater's method. I myself am convinced that his method is valid and that Lavater must have been a practically infallible physiognomist. But I think that a book, however good, can never serve as a complete initiation into the mysteries of a science. It could be wished that Lavater had trained disciples worthy of him and that physiognomy as he himself came to know it could be taught and transmitted in courses and lessons in the same way as phrenology has been. But most likely the store of experience this extraordinary man acquired went down to the grave with him. The fame he enjoyed was a brief and much disputed one.

Thus it would be rash and presumptuous to think of oneself as a physiognomist after reading Lavater's book, even with the utmost care. Nothing can be taught adequately without practice and example. Here the example is a more or less accurately engraved plate. Such engravings are mostly second-rate and, were they better, they would still be incapable of revealing to the most discerning eye all the variations, intricacies and complexities of nature's handiwork. Research should be carried out on human subjects as Gall has done, but also under the supervision of experts; otherwise the most insignificant error of the engraver could lead the adept into an endless sequence of errors with grave consequences. In the future I shall certainly never dare to form an opinion from a physiognomy however straightforward it seems; I shall be infinitely more wary than hitherto of abandoning myself to my instincts or to the rough and ready ideas we all have of physiognomy without having studied it – very bold and wrong ideas for the most part, I assure you.

Suffice to say that Lavater distinguishes two areas of observation: the soft and the firm parts of a face. The firm parts – the forehead, the rigid surfaces, the bridge of the nose, the outline of the chin – denote the *faculties*. The soft parts – skin, flesh, cartilage and membrane – reveal by their deterioration or lack of change, their colour, contour, poise, furrows, tension, excrescence or reduction, the subject's *habits*, his vices and virtues, all that has been *acquired*. The bone structure only indicates what is *given* by nature, so that greatness often is found in the upper part of a face whose lower part denotes a sensuality bordering on brutishness. It must be noted that Lavater looks at things from a spiritual point of view. He believes, like you and me, that man is *free*, that he receives from the hands of providence his fair share in the great inheritance of good and evil left by the first man; and that he is given strength in proportion to his desires, so long as he doesn't spurn the idea of maintaining it by his own struggles with himself. I suppose that materialists, too, acknowledge the influence of education and experience on the constitution and, in explaining human destinies by attributing everything to chance, it is possible to see at a glance all the differences which the mutations of thought and character imprint on our physical appearance. Thus the posture of one body, the shape and position of the limbs, the walk, the gesture, all express the character a man has or would like to be thought to have. The observer's art consists in telling reality from affectation, however skilful and sustained the pose. Here is what Lavater has to say of a man who leans backwards, with his legs wide apart and his hands behind him. 'A sensible, modest man will never adopt such an attitude; this stance necessarily denotes affectation and ostentation, a man who wants to ingratiate himself by showing off, a hare-brained fellow, etc.'

It is true that Lavater would never have applied this observation to Napoleon, and yet it is so apt that it accounts for the contemptuous laughter with which all sensible people greet the actor who, on stage, presents an insolent parody of the man of genius. Only Talma[17] could do it because Talma, in his field, was himself a genius.

On the whole, if after reading Lavater you think of the faces of exceptional men, you will be impressed by the truth of his judgements. These characters are so decisively and boldly stamped by nature that you will recognize them immediately as striking examples. It will not be the same with ordinary subjects. Their little virtues and little vices will be faintly sketched on insignificant features. Their mediocrity derives from a mass of commonplace attributes of which none can be called intelligence, none idiocy. They possess gifts in varying degrees but not one which dominates the others, so that their faces express a number of things without one thing in particular prevailing. How can we draw conclusions from such physiognomies without being exceptionally skilful and patient? Yet the good Lavater, who despises nothing and loves to help and encourage every good instinct however undeveloped, constrains us to decipher the wit, love of order, common sense or memory to be found in these unattractive countenances; when he fails to discover such qualities he manages to praise their candour, gentleness or honesty. One day a beggar holds out his hand; 'How much do you need?' enquires the physiognomist, struck by the honesty he reads on the man's face. 'I could do with nine sous,' replies the fellow. 'Here you are,' says the physiognomist. 'Why didn't you ask for more? I'll give you whatever you ask.' 'I assure you, Sir,' says the beggar, 'you've given me all I need.'

A young man and young girl are brought before Lavater; she begs for bread for the child she has had by the young man; he accuses her of being a loose and deceitful woman; his remarkable self-assurance and appearance of righteous indignation move all who are present; she is confused, does nothing but sob and ask God to make the truth known. Lavater hesitates; he questions them carefully and pronounces in favour of the girl. Soon, after having complied with the law, the youth confesses his guilt. Lavater relates this incident movingly in a manner reminiscent of Kotzebuë's[18] dramas of sensibility.

The great difference between Gall's observation and Lavater's as regards phrenology is that the latter situates the main faculties in the front of the head, while believing that the rest of the skull might 'probably not be without interest' for someone who wanted to make it the object of a special study; whereas the former, dismissing the study of the human face, maps out the site of each faculty and instinct in pencil on the skull. I'm afraid that Gall may have aimed at originality in his systems at the expense of one aspect of the truth in his method. In trying to avoid being the mere disciple of Lavater, in wanting at all costs to create a science, he has given way to dangerous preconceptions. To divide the soul into symmetrical compartments like the squares on a chessboard is, to my mind, so excessively rigorous that it can't escape a touch of charlatanism. I find more nobility, more grandeur and at the same time more probability in Lavater's vast panorama, which includes the whole being and investigates all its activities.

I don't know enough about Gall's system to go into the matter at greater length. Besides, as I said, it isn't by means of a dissertation on physiognomy that I hope to induce you to read Lavater, but by commending this book as an edifying, eloquent work full of interest, earnestness and charm. You will find even in its most systematic sections the same generosity of spirit, the same insistence on tenderness and sympathy; such a deep understanding of the mysteries and inconsistencies in men's souls that this alone would suffice to make it a work of genius. Here is a passage where you will find, at the same time, the quintessence of method, the heat of eloquence, a lofty knowledge of the human heart and the fervour of goodness. It refers to the reciprocal influence of physiognomies on each other:

 The conformity of bone structure in people presupposes also conformity in the responses of nerves and muscles. It is true, however, that difference in upbringing can influence these to the extent that an experienced observer will no longer be able to discern the similarities. But when two such basically similar structures confront each other, they will be mutually attracted; if the impediments that hindered them are then removed nature will soon triumph. They will recognize each other, *as flesh of their flesh* and *bone of their bone*. Moreover, even people with features that are fundamentally at variance may love each other, communicate, attract and resemble each other; and if they are affectionate, sensitive, susceptible natures, the physical resemblance between them that such conformity will achieve will, in time, be even more striking.

....

Conformity of appearance has always seemed to me more striking in cases where, in the absence of external intervention, chance has united a totally communicative nature to a totally receptive one when they have been drawn together by love or necessity. Once the former has exhausted his store and the second received all that is required, their facial resemblance immediately ceases. It has, as it were, reached *saturation point*.

Just one more word for you, over-eager and over-emotional young man! Be cautious in your friendships and don't put yourself blindly at the mercy of an untried friend, for a show of sympathy could mislead you; take care not to surrender to it. Doubtless there is someone whose soul is in harmony with yours. Be patient, he will turn up sooner or later, and when you have found him he will sustain and uplift you, he will give you what you lack and help you to bear your burdens; the fire of his gaze will kindle yours, and his melodious voice will soften the harshness of your own, his thoughtful caution will temper your impetuosity; his affection will leave its imprint on the features of your face and all those who know him will recognize him in you. You will be what he is while still remaining as much yourself as ever. Friendship will enable you to discover in him qualities which an indifferent eye would scarcely have noticed. It is this ability to see and to sense what there is of divine in your friend that will make you look like him.

And here is the portrait of a libertine that seems to me a demonstration of a great talent for prediction:

Sloth, idleness, intemperance have disfigured this countenance. At any rate it is not thus that nature fashioned these features. Those eyes, those lips, those furrows express an impatient, unslakeable thirst. The whole face denotes a man who wants to act and cannot, who feels with equal urgency the need and the inability to satisfy it. In the flesh it is above all the gaze that reveals this ever-thwarted, ever-recurring desire, which is both the consequence and the sign of nonchalance and libertinism.

Young man, see vice of whatever kind in its true guise, and it will be enough to make you flee it forever.

Can you think of anything more beautiful and engaging than this picture of friendship? anything more terrifying than this picture of vice? Lavater quotes in this context a verse from a hymn by Gellert[19] which, in translation, seems to lack neither the power nor the simplicity which ought to be typical of such works:

O you, with aspect dread,
Alas, your charms have fled,
And brilliance of past days.
The furrows on your brow,
Destruction's image, now
Proclaim your erring ways.

Lavater's notes on an engraved plate representing Voltaire's face in more than twenty different poses are no less remarkable for their wisdom and truth:

Here is someone greater and more forceful than ourselves. In his presence we become aware of our weakness but without being ennobled, whereas anyone who is both great and good not only makes us aware of our weakness but, by a secret charm, raises us up above ourselves and communicates some of his greatness to us. We do not simply admire, but love, and far from feeling overwhelmed by the weight of his superiority our exalted hearts expand and blossom with joy. These representations of Voltaire produce nothing of the kind. When we contemplate them, all they suggest is a sardonic streak, a biting witticism. They mortify self-respect and crush mediocrity.

There has never been a reader of Lavater who has failed to leaf expectantly through this portrait gallery in quest of a physical likeness to himself, hoping, by scanning such a physiognomy, to discover the key to his own disposition and his own destiny. Our minds cannot resist dwelling on it with superstitious anxiety. Now I must tell you that a face leaner, more virile and older than that of your best friend, yet bearing a striking resemblance to it, is accompanied by the following analysis. You will be a better judge than I am of the similarities in character. For my part I withhold all comment since your closest friend is the person I have been least able to judge impartially, either in good or bad fortune. – The description is that of an indifferent painter, Henry Fuseli.[20]

We must analyse this physiognomy, and we shall have a great deal to say. The outline of the profile as a whole is in itself most remarkable; it denotes a forceful nature that will not be curbed. The forehead, both in its contours and angle, is that of a poet rather than a philosopher; I see more strength than gentleness in it, a fiery imagination rather than considered rationality. The nose appears to be that of a daring spirit. The mouth suggests a talent for application and precision; and yet this artist finds it hard to put the finishing touches to his canvases. His great vitality prevails over his natural endowment of care and exactness which is still obvious in the details of his works. Indeed there are times when the elaborate finish is in singular contrast to the carelessness of the whole.

One might readily suppose that he is subject to violent impulses. But could one go so far as to say that he is capable of loving tenderly, warmly, excessively? Nothing indeed could be truer although, on the other hand, his affections have to be constantly rekindled by the loved one's presence; if she is absent he forgets her and ceases to worry about her. His beloved can lead him like a child so long as she stays with him. Should she leave him she can expect nothing but indifference. To be driven he requires the whip; he is capable of great deeds, yet minor obligations irk him. His imagination always aims for the sublime and relishes the wonderful. He is not debarred from the Graces' sanctuary but is unwilling to sacrifice to them. In the main figures of his paintings there is a kind of tension which is in truth not commonplace but which he tends to exaggerate beyond the bounds of reason. No one could love more tenderly, his eyes express an affectionate nature; but the shape and bone structure of his face denote a taste for violent scenes, for assertions of authority with a great outlay of energy.

Nature formed him to be a poet, a painter or an actor. But relentless fate does not always give us a will to match our abilities; it often allots a goodly measure of will-power to ordinary beings whose faculties are very limited and sometimes bestows on those who are exceptionally gifted a weak, inadequate will.

I don't know if a biography[21] of Jean-Gaspard Lavater has been written; his life must be as fine and as edifying as his writings. Were I, like you, in Switzerland I would like to go to Zurich for the sole purpose of trying to find out something about the life of this Evangelist. But alas, his name has doubtless faded from the memory of his contemporaries; is there even a gravestone to preserve it? If you have ever been that way, let me know if one exists.

On the other hand one could say that one knows a man's life when one knows his soul, and I can only urge you to read the whole of his description of himself which accompanies the picture representing him. He appears to have a sensitive, subtle, delicate disposition. Without the help of the description you can tell that he has special, I would say almost prophetic, gifts; an untroubled mind adds great gentleness to his mobile features; the serenity of virtue shines through the slight veil of an irritable, impressionable and exceedingly nervous temperament. — Here is a summary of the detailed analysis he gives of his own face and character:

If I didn't know the original I would say with total conviction that it revealed a strong imagination, a lively, spontaneous perceptiveness which doesn't however preserve first impressions for long; a clear mind that seeks to improve itself and is more analytical than profoundly enquiring; there is more judgement than reason; an immense serenity together with great vigour and despatch. This man, I would further say, is not made to serve in the army nor in the routine of an office. A trifle will depress him; let him have freedom of action, he is already sufficiently burdened. His imagination and sensitivity can make a mountain out of a grain of sand; but owing to his natural adaptability a mountain sometimes matters rather less to him than a grain of sand.

He is loving without ever having been in love. Not one of his friends has ever forsaken him. His thoughtful nature helps him to remain faithful to the principles he has set himself and which he has written down in the form of a code of laws:

Be what you are; let nothing be either great or small in your eyes. Be faithful in small matters. Concentrate your attention on whatever you are doing as though you had nothing but that one thing to do. He who has done right at a given moment has performed a good deed for all eternity. Make things easier by either doing, enjoying or suffering. Give your heart to him who governs hearts. Be fair and precise in small matters. Have hope for the future. Learn to wait, learn to enjoy everything and learn to do without everything.

It is interesting to hear him tell how he became involved in physiognomy: 'Until I was twenty-five,' he says, 'I had not yet considered making physiognomic observations. At times, however, on first seeing certain faces, I felt, without knowing why or even thinking of the physiognomy that had provoked it, a kind of shock that persisted for some minutes after the person's departure.'

For my part I have always believed that some constitutions are so exquisite that they are gifted with an almost superhuman perception. Their fleshly envelope is so ethereal, so transparent, so hypersensitive, that the animating spirit within them seems to see through and penetrate the substance which contains or constitutes the material world. Their fibre is so sensitive, so subtle that all those things which are imperceptible to the grosser senses of others make them vibrate, as the gentlest breeze stirs the strings of an Aeolian harp and makes them quiver. You must possess one of these superior, quasi-angelic systems, my dear Franz. Your physiognomy, your disposition, your imagination, your genius denote those faculties which the heavens bestow on their *chosen vessels*. I am of those who sleep by night, who walk and eat by day. I have one of those active, robust, carefree indefatigable constitutions which would take the edge off all delicate perceptions and all mesmeric visions. I have lived too long as a peasant, a bohemian, a soldier. My skin has thickened, the skin on my feet has been hardened by the stones of the highway and I remember with amazement the days of my youth when the slightest worry or the slightest hope made me curl up like a sensitive plant. Why have I turned to stone?

Such has been my fate; but though I have become rough and wild I none the less still venerate superior beings, even to idolatry. The more I feel myself reverting to the state of the common labourer the greater grows my awe and respect for those fragile, nervous creatures who live on electric sensations and seem to read the mysteries of the supernatural world. I'm horribly afraid of fatalists, sorcerers, somnambulists, visionaries, diviners and soothsayers; yet if my fancy is stirred by anything that looks like black magic or the occult I'm so easily impressed by wonders that I'm capable of succumbing to the strange, inexplicable fascination of fear.

Lavater would have had an immense influence on me had I known him, since even from the grave his intellectual power, together with so many virtues and such a profound wisdom, makes such a lively and positive impression on me. Since I've been cloistered in this refuge the memory of all those who are dear to me has appeared to me solely through the magic mirror he has set before my eyes. I bow down before the sight of these cherished phantoms – O my friends, O my masters – before the treasures of greatness or goodness which are in you and which God's finger has revealed in sacred characters on your noble brows! The vast dome of Everard's bald skull, so fine and so huge, so perfect and complete in its contours that one doesn't know which splendid faculty holds sway in him over the others; that nose, that chin and those brows whose forcefulness would make me tremble if the exquisite subtlety of his intellect didn't reside in the nostril, his superhuman kindness in the eyes and his tolerant wisdom in the lips; that head which is both a hero's and a saint's appearing before me in my dreams alongside the terrible and austere countenance of the great Lamennais. Here the forehead is steep – an unbroken wall, a tablet of steel, the site of indomitable vigour and, like Everard's, '*furrowed between the eyebrows by those perpendicular incisions that pertain*,' says Lavater, '*exclusively to persons of very high ability whose minds are sane and noble.*' The firm outline of his profile and the angular narrowness of the face are undoubtedly signs of an inflexible integrity, a monastic austerity, and of the incessant activity of a mind, as brilliant and vast as the heavens. But the smile that unexpectedly humanizes his face turns my awe to confidence, my respect to adoration. Can't you see Everard and Lamennais clasping hands, these two slightly built men who appeared none the less as giants before the amazed Parisians when the defence of a holy cause[22] drew them recently from their retreat and set them up on the hill of Jerusalem to pray and threaten, to bless the people and to make the Pharisees and the Doctors of the Law quake in their synagogue?

They are ever before my eyes as I wander through the big dark rooms of my deserted house at night. Behind them I see Lavater with his clear, limpid gaze, his pointed nose – a sign of subtlety and penetration – his resemblance to a more lofty Erasmus, his fatherly attitude and his merciful, fervent words. I can hear him say: 'Go, follow them and try to be like them; these are your masters and your guides; heed their advice, keep their precepts, repeat the holy words of their prayers. They are acquainted with God and will teach you his ways. Go, my son, so that you recover from your afflictions, so that your soul may be cleansed and clothed in fresh robes and so that the Lord may bless you and count you once more amongst his flock.'

Then I see other, less imposing, phantoms pass, who are none the less full of grace and charm. They are my comrades, they are my brothers. And especially you, my dear Franz; in my mind's eye you are drenched in light, a magic apparition arising in the shadows of my meditative nights. In the candle-light, through the aureole of admiration that crowns and envelops you while your fingers weave new marvels into the marvels of Weber, I love to see your affectionate gaze fall on me and seem to say: 'My brother, do you understand me? It's to your soul that I am speaking' – Yes, my young friend, yes, inspired artist, I understand this divine language and cannot speak it. If only I were at least a painter to perpetuate for ever how you look when the god is upon you, when the celestial gleams set you afire and radiant, when a pale blue flame seems to play in your hair and the most chaste of the muses bends smiling towards you!

But were I to paint that picture I would not like to leave out the charming figure of Puzzi, your beloved pupil. Raphael and his young friend Tebaldeo never appeared before God and before men with more grace than you two, my dear children, as I saw you one evening, in the midst of the hundred-voiced orchestra, when all were stilled to listen to your improvisations; and the youth who was standing behind you, pale, perturbed and motionless as a statue, yet trembling like a flower about to shed its petals, seemed to absorb the harmony through every pore and to open his childish lips to drink the honey you poured out for him. There are some who say that the arts have lost their poetry: in truth, I'm not aware of it. Why! haven't we spent splendid mornings and lovely evenings in my blue-curtained garret, that modest studio which is perhaps a little too close to the snow-laden roofs in winter, a little overheated, like Venetian leads, in summer? But what of it? A few engravings after Raphael, a Spanish rush mat to stretch out on, good pipes to smoke, the funny little cat Trozzi, flowers, a few chosen books, especially poetry (another divine language I understand and cannot speak), isn't that enough for an artist's attic? Read me some poetry, improvise for me on the piano one of those delightful pastorals that make old Everard and me sob because they remind us of our youth, our hills and the goats we led to pasture. While you are doing so let me savour the intoxication of latakia[23] or go into ecstasy in a corner behind a heap of cushions. Haven't we known some happy days? Haven't we been the dutiful children of the God who blesses simple souls? Haven't we seen the hours flit by without ever wishing to speed them on as all our contemporaries do, so as to reach God-knows-what wretchedly ambitious or vainglorious goal? Do you remember Puzzi sitting at the feet of our saint from Brittany[24] who was telling him such beautiful things with apostolic kindness and simplicity? Do you remember Everard, sunk in melancholy rapture while you played, suddenly getting up to say in his deep voice: 'Young man, you are sublime!' and my friend Emmanuel, who concealed me in one of the vast pouches of his greatcoat in order to smuggle me into the House of Peers[25] and who, on returning home, set me down on the piano, saying to you: 'Another time please wrap my dear brother in a paper cone so that his hair doesn't get untidy'? Do you remember the bland Peri[26] with her blue dress, that charming, noble creature who came down from heaven one evening to visit a poet's garret and sat between us two like the wonderful princesses who appear to poor artists in Hoffmann's tales? Do you remember that other visitor, less marvellous but absurd enough to make up for it, with whom we behaved so much like two cheeky schoolboys that I still laugh at the thought of it, alone in the dark night? . . . Hush! The echoes of the deserted house unaccustomed to such impropriety awaken and answer me irritably. The household gods look at each other in surprise, and wonder whether they oughtn't to evict me. – 'I humbly apologize to you, mysterious hosts who tolerate my intrusion here! You know that I respect and fear you; you know that I haven't opened the shutters to let in the sunlight since I came to live here; you know that I haven't drawn aside the curtains to let the neighbours' gaze sully your sacred dwelling-place. I haven't broken the vine branches that cover the walls. I've read Lavater's fine book with care and without disturbing its venerable dust. I've displaced none of the furniture. I haven't plucked the flowers in the yard. I've broken none of your plants. I've walked on tiptoe during the night so as not to disturb the solemnity of your mysteries. Don't banish me, O gods, friends of the pious! Don't send your Larves and Lamiae[27] to trouble my sleep, and if you show yourselves to me let it be as the shades of my friends, with their words of advice and encouragement on your lips!'

It's really very odd that, despite the fact that I'm a terrible coward, I enjoy the life of a recluse so much. It's because I actually relish my fear; it cuts me off from reality, and the sensations it gives me make me realize how much I'm a spiritualist in my beliefs and superstitions. At night when the moon sets behind the Cathedral's Flamboyant spires, sudden gusts of wind passing through the vine branches that festoon my doorway are like convulsive tremors of pain. Then I think of the souls in

211

Purgatory and I pray God to diminish their sufferings and their waiting. At other times, as I sit under the finialled tympanum of the pretty gothic door framed in leaves that reminds me of Faust's and Marguerite's romance, a big black cat suddenly appears at my side without my having heard him come, who mews piteously while offering me his bristling back from which electric sparks fly as soon as I begin to stroke it. He's the neighbour's cat and he comes over the rooftops to deliver me, as a gracious gesture, from insolent rats. Well, despite his good deeds, this Tom looks like a devil; his eyes shine in the dark like live coals and his contortions have something diabolical about them. I wouldn't dare refuse to scratch his ear and stroke his back, for I would be afraid lest he should suddenly resume his true shape and fly off through the air with a wild screech of laughter. Even when there is neither cat nor breeze in the yard there are strange noises which it took me some time to account for. It is an endless trickle of sand, dropping down from the roof tiles onto the branches of vine, awakening a thousand echoes in the leaves they disturb; one would think that a coven of witches with their broomsticks was carrying on in the eaves but it's only the house crumbling away into dust, before it falls into ruin; it is cracking, flaking away and scattering dust on my hair at every moment. What is this – do you want to collapse already, dear deserted house? Will you really last so short a time? Blessed retreat where I've meditated alone and in silence over this sweet page of my life, welcoming threshold which I'll embrace on leaving, sonorous walls where I've slept so peacefully under the wing of my guardian angel; simple, narrow haven, spotlessly clean and tidy inside, delightfully unconstrained and untidy outside, haven't you always been my refuge and my shelter? Have you not belonged to me in some way and didn't I prefer you to the palaces so sought after by men? Oh, you would have satisfied the needs and desires of my entire life. I'd have read the Church Fathers' and the Saints' writings on the solitary life in your monastic precincts! I'd have dreamt here of perfection, dreams which are so easy to summon up far from the world's tumult and the vain chatter of men! I'd have cleansed myself of life's stains; I'd have buried myself as in a spotless marble sepulchre; I'd have interposed your crumbling walls and your curtains of flowering vine between this misguided age and my timorous soul. I'd have ventured outside only to do charitable deeds; I'd have hastened back as soon as my duties had been performed so as to avoid committing sinful deeds. And you want so soon to return to the earth out of which your substance came? Weary of submitting to man's will, you want to break apart and destroy yourself, you who were matter and have been given life by man! So when I come back this way once again all that I shall find, perhaps, in this very place where I bade farewell to your hospitable roof, will be rubble! – But why should I concern myself, fool that I am! I, an insect barely hatched this morning, why should I worry about the crumbling of stones and the impermanence of plaster that has stood for centuries, when this very night I'll have ceased to exist! I weep for these walls that crack, though the furrows on my brow are beyond counting! Before these grasses have withered, my hair will probably have fallen from my skull; before next winter's frost has split these paving-stones my heart will have turned to ice in the grave. What is the life of man, whose every second he numbers, knowing that the last is drawing closer and cannot be avoided? These walls, these festoons of ivy, these lime trees overgrown with hops, these tall gables that rise up as if to rend the skies and are being worn away by the evening dews – do all these contemplate destruction? Do they all listen to the clock's pendulum? Is it for them that its pitiless sound measures out time? Only you in this place, unhappy, ephemeral and fearful man, know what hour it is; you alone understand that mournful voice coming from the clock-tower that divides your life into equal portions without ever stopping or slowing down. Go, take your staff and set out on your journey; you might well return and find the house still standing. Such as it is it will last longer than you; many years will be required to annihilate it; a puff of wind might sweep you away tomorrow.

*   *   *   *   *   *   *   *   *

Last night a violent commotion interrupted my sleep; someone tugged at the bell-rope hard enough to snap it, knocked on the door loud enough to splinter it. Then, just as in a play, he shouted at me through the grating: 'Open in the name of the King!' This time I wasn't afraid; what is there to fear from men when our passport is in order and in our pocket? The gendarmes found nothing amiss with mine; but the ray of light that sometimes filters through the windows of this uninhabited house at night, the frugal meals that pass every day through the wicket gate had been a matter for considerable anxiety and gossip among some of my neighbours. At first my lamp gave them the idea that I was a ghost; but the meals as proof of my physical existence suggested, rather, a conspirator. This morning I had to go and give an account of myself to the magistrates. My innocence was promptly acknowledged; but I learnt during the proceedings that the state of affairs in France had changed while I was in my retreat. The explosion of an *infernal machine*[28] had led to consequences serious enough in themselves, but had also allowed despotism to assume trumped-up rights over the most innocent and peaceful amongst our comrades. Acts of savage repression are expected from that insolent power that calls itself law and order. Well, so be it, Franz! such is life; where there's life, there is suffering and work to do. Will one misfortune more or less dishearten us? Man is free by the will of God. The body can be chained and destroyed; but the mind of man cannot be subdued. It is said that there will be exile and death penalties for our friends; we ourselves are politically insignificant, but we are the offspring of those they would condemn. I know whom you would follow to the scaffold or into exile; you know for whom I would do likewise. And so perhaps we may be meeting again, Franz, no longer as happy travellers, no longer as carefree artists in the pleasant valleys of Switzerland, or in the concert halls, or in our cheerful garret in Paris, but rather on the other side of the ocean or in prison or at the foot of a scaffold;[29] for it's easy to share the fate of those we love when we have made up our mind to it. However weak and insignificant we are we can always persuade a merciful enemy to kill us or chain us up. People will say we want to be martyrs? If that's so – thank God! We've won our cause! Greetings, brother Franz; let's be merry; these are no longer times for lamentation when there is someone to devote our lives to and something to die for. What can they take from us, since we have never asked the world for anything? Do we have any foolish ambition which we have to be cured of? or any devouring thirst to die from? Unhappy are those with possessions; those without are impervious to threats. Can they deprive us of each other? Can they stop us from living for our brothers and dying with them?

While I was out my friend, the owner of the deserted house, returned from the country. He has had the grass in the yard mown, he has had the vines pruned; the windows are open by day and the flies come into the rooms; according to him, the house has been set to rights; according to me, it is devastated. Such mutilations, such vandalism, are they the forerunners of what is about to happen to France? Let's go and see; I'm leaving. Where shall I go? I don't know; somewhere where one of our sort may need someone who has need of nobody, except perhaps God! I have news of you in a letter from Puzzi: you have a mother-of-pearl piano; you play on it by the window that overlooks the lake that overlooks the sublime snows of Mont Blanc. Franz, this is good and beautiful; yours is a noble, pure life; but if our saints are persecuted you'll leave your lake and your glaciers and your mother-of-pearl piano, as I am leaving Lavater and the green branches of vine and the deserted house, and you'll take up your traveller's staff and your pilgrim's bag, as I'm doing now while I embrace you and say: Farewell, brother, and *Au revoir*.

The Prince[1]

'But in the end, what purpose do we serve?' he exclaimed,[2] sinking down onto a stone bench in front of the castle. 'What really good use do we make of our abilities? Who will be any the better for our having lived?'

'We are of use,' I replied, sitting down beside him, 'in so far as we do no harm. Wild birds make no plans for each other. Each one tends his brood. God's hand protects and feeds them.'

'Do be quiet, poet!' he answered. 'I'm sad, not melancholy. I can't trifle with my sorrow, and the tears I shed fall on barren soil. Don't you understand what virtue is? Is it a stagnant pool where the reeds are rotting or is it a rushing stream that flows swiftly and spreads wider on its tireless course to bring new life and moisture to unknown shores? Is it a diamond whose fire must remain conceal   a rock at the centre of the earth or is it a light that erupts like a volca   and spreads its wondrous brightness over the world?'

'Virtue is perhaps none of these things,' I said. 'Neither the buried diamond nor the still waters; but even less an overflowing river or all-consuming lava. I've seen the Rhone's turbulent waters rush madly beneath the Alps. The banks were mutilated by its impatience, no plants had time to grow and flower. Trees were carried away before they were strong enough to resist the onslaught; men and flocks fled to the mountains. The whole countryside was one long desert of sand, stones and pale osier-clumps where cranes, perched on one sticklike leg, dared not sleep the whole night through. But not far from there I saw tiny rivulets silently stealing from a secret cave and trickling peacefully through the meadow grasses whose thirst was slaked by these limpid waters. Scented plants grew in the very centre of the gentle flow; and a wagtail's nest hung over the crystal mirror in which the fledglings saw their own reflection and flapped their wings, thinking it was their mother they saw arriving. Virtue, remember, is concerned with what is good, not with what is exceptional.'

'You're mistaken,' he cried. 'It's to do with both; what is goodness without drive? What is intelligence without strong feelings? You are good and I am an enthusiast; believe me, we are neither of us virtuous.'

'All right! Let's be content,' I said smiling, 'with not being harmful. See this castle; think of those who live in it and tell me if you can't make your peace with yourself.'

'That's a shocking anodyne!' he replied, in a tone that moved me deeply. 'What? Just because there are vipers and jackals we should congratulate ourselves on being tortoises? No, my God, you didn't make me for passivity; and the more that vice creeps and yelps around me, the greater my need to spread my wings and strike those vile creatures with an eagle's beak. What are you insinuating with your peaceful rivulets and secret grottoes? Do you think virtue is like those poisons that become wholesome in small doses? Do you think that twelve worthy men dedicated to obscurity and cloistered within the narrow channels of contemplative life are of more use than a single pious man who goes forth and admonishes? The age of patriarchs is over! Let the disciples arise, let them be seen and heard!'

'Patience, patience!' I said. 'The disciples are on their way; they travel by several routes and in small bands. They are known by diverse names and dress in different colours. The most fervent among them, doubtless because they have been the most sorely tried, are, at this very moment, on the banks of the Red Sea[3] as in the dark caves of the Dauphine mountains, intoning their simple and sublime canticles:

> Lord! your children love you,
> They will be strong and patient!

What if they have had their divisions, their errors, their reverses and their faults? They answer with composure: "We shall perish, we are mortal; but ideas don't die and the one we have cast before the world will survive us. The world treats us as madmen, we are greeted with ridicule and the jeering of the crowds pursues us; stones and insults rain upon us, the most terrible slanders have saddened our hearts; half our brothers have fled in terror; we are consumed by poverty. Every day our little flock is reduced and there will not perhaps be a single one of us left standing to gaze from afar at the borders of the Promised Land. But we have sown in the thinking world a truth that will germinate. We shall die contented and at peace in the desert sands, like the chosen people whose bones strewed the endless plains of Arabia and who left a new young generation to arrive at the green hills of Canaan." Are these the words of madmen? And the priest[4] who, quite alone, one morning crossed his arms on his breast and rising up in the midst of his prayers, his brow and his eyes raised to heaven, cried out in a loud voice: "Christ! Pure love! Holy pride! Patience! Courage! Freedom! Virtue!" – Were these the words of a priest? The walls of his cell were shaken and the angels in the heavens were moved to cry: "Almighty God! A brilliant flame has just shot up over there, from that exhausted world. We have seen it; and behold! the flare has crossed the vastness and come to die at your feet. Do not abandon that world yet, O merciful God! For a ray of light emerges from time to time that could rekindle the sun in its darkened firmament; faint cries, scattered sounds, laments and prayers sometimes pierce the thick mists that encompass it, and those distant voices rising up to us are proof that righteousness has not yet been stifled in the heart of unhappy man." Thus speak the angels, and rest assured, my friend, that none of our good intentions is wasted; God sees them, he hears the humblest prayer and at this very minute as we talk, those stars which are looking down on us and listening are repeating the story of your sufferings to him and telling him of your soul's righteous anguish.'

'O my friend!' he cried, throwing his arms around me. 'Why aren't you always like this? Why so many days of apathy or bitterness? Why so many hours of irony and scorn?'[5]

'Because I suffer from poor health and a weak head,' I replied. 'I'm subject to migraine and spasms. May God forgive me for my unfairness and ingratitude at such times. My invectives against the heavens and my hatred of mankind fall back on my heart like a wave of corrosive bile; it doesn't banish the brightness of the stars and Providence isn't disturbed by it. Exhaustion then brings about the recurrence of resignation and it so happens that, once or twice a month maybe, between rage and imbecility, I find myself well-disposed and calm and able to accept and to pray.'

'Well then, as soon as your soul attains such hours of calm and consolation,' said my friend, 'rush off to your attic, shut yourself in, take up your pen and write! Write with the tears that flow from your eyes, with your heart's blood, and don't write a word the rest of the time. When you are unhappy join us; don't go and walk around over there by damp caves in the moonlight; don't light your lamp at midnight, don't sit with your elbows on your desk and your face in your hands till day dawns. Don't tell us that there are periods of history when worthy men should bind themselves hand and foot so as not to act. Don't tell us that Simon Stylites was a saint, but admit that he was a madman. Don't tell us that virtue is like the chastity of the Vestal Virgins and has to be buried alive to be purified. Don't assume an air of tranquil indifference and wilful inertia that fails to conceal how strong your anguish is. Or if you must say such things, say them only to us and we'll try to contend with them; say them only to me and I'll weep with you and suffer less for not suffering alone.'

I clasped my friend's hand in mine and answered when I had regained my calm: 'Do not believe, however, that it's only idleness that makes me prescribe inactivity for my turbulent friends. When it's in our power to prevent a crime it would be cowardice to wash our hands of it like Pilate; but when, as in our case, we are lost amongst the vulgar masses, then reason and perhaps conscience bid us stay there. Let the man who feels he has been entrusted with a holy mission stand forth from the ranks; God has called him and God will assist him. He will guide his difficult course between the reefs; he will lighten his darkness with the torch of wisdom. But tell me how many Christs you think are born in a century? Aren't you shocked and indignant, like me, at the outrageous number of redeemers and law-givers who lay claim to the throne of our moral world? Rather than seek a guide and lend a willing ear to men who speak from true inspiration, the human race swarms as one man to the pulpit or the rostrum. Everyone wants to teach; everyone believes he speaks better and knows better than his predecessors. That pitiful mumbling which is dominating our age is only an echo of hollow words and resounding pronouncements which our hearts and minds scan in vain for a ray of warmth and light. Truth, unacknowledged and discouraged, lies benumbed or hides in those hearts that are worthy of receiving it. There are no more prophets, there are no more disciples. Those who have gone astray are more eloquent than God's messengers. All our reserves of strength and action straggle in disarray and halt, paralysed by the general turmoil. We'll succeed, you say; but how long will it take? All right! Let us resign ourselves, let us wait! In order to force our way by fire and sword into the midst of this blind, helpless multitude, we would have to burn and massacre indiscriminately. Don't you realize that? How many certain disasters would be required for one doubtful success! How many crimes against society would we have to commit to make it accept one blessing! Such things are not for peasants like us, my friend! And when I see one of my betters open his mouth to speak or stretch out his hand to act I still tremble and look at him searchingly with a hard and suspicious glance that seeks to penetrate to the depths of his conscience. O God! What austere meditations, what sanctifying trials would be required of us before we could presume to play a part on the world's stage! How much one would have had to have learned, how much experienced! It seems to me we'd be better to plant twenty-seven varieties of dahlia in our gardens and to set about trying to fathom the habits of the wood-louse! Let our minds not venture beyond such things, for our conscience hasn't perhaps enough strength within us to control our imagination. Let us be content with leading honest lives within the bounds of a destiny where honesty is possible. Let us be honourable since everything in our family life and under our rustic roofs incites us to be so. Let us not risk our modest cargo of virtue on that stormy sea where so much innocence has perished, where so many principles have foundered. Aren't you seized with an insuperable disgust and a secret horror of the active life at the sight of this château where so many foul plots and well-concealed villainies are forever being engendered and hatched in the silence of the night? Are you not aware that the man who lives there has been manipulating nations and crowns for the past sixty years on the chess-board of the world? Who can tell whether the first time that man sat down at a desk to work, there wasn't perhaps an honest thought in his head, in his heart a noble feeling?'

'Never!' exclaimed my friend. 'Don't profane honesty by such a suggestion; that upper lip, like a cat's, pulled in over that other thick, drooping, satyr's lip – duplicity and lewdness conjoined! and those flabby, rounded features that denote pliability; that disdainful frown on a protruding brow, that arrogant nose and reptilian eye; such contrasts in a human physiognomy reveal a man born for great vices and petty actions.[6] His heart has never felt the warmth of a generous emotion, never has a loyal thought entered that contriving head; he is a freak of nature, so rare a monster that the human race, while despising him, has contemplated him with imbecile admiration. I defy you to sink to the level of what he achieves at his best! Let us pray to the God of worthy men, the God who blesses simple hearts!'

Here my friend stopped with a look on his face of ironic amusements, and after a brief silence continued: 'When I consider the topics on which our minds have dwelt here, practically under the windows of the greatest scoundrel in Christendom — poor children of the wilderness that we are, whose every dream and thought tend towards spreading honesty throughout the world — I feel I could laugh at us! For here we are, tenderly weeping over humanity to whom we are unknown and who would reject us if we attempted to indoctrinate them, while they grovel and bow down before the intellectual power of those who despise them. Just look at the still, pale façade of this old palace! Listen and look: all is dreariness and silence; we might be in a graveyard. At least fifty people inhabit that main building. A few windows are poorly lit; not a sound betrays the master's presence nor that of his friends and attendants. What organization, what respect, what gloom in his little empire! Doors open and shut noiselessly, the servants go about their business, and without their footsteps awaking an echo under those mysterious arches, their work seems to be done by magic. Look at that brighter casement through which the indistinct shadow of a white statue can be glimpsed; that is the drawing-room. That is where huntsmen, artists, dazzling ladies, fashionable men, probably all the cream of French society in elegance and grace forgather. Can a single song, a laugh or a cry be heard coming from that gathering to testify to a living presence? I'll wager they even avoid looking at each other for fear of giving away their thoughts under this roof where all is silence, mystery and secret dread.[7]

'Not a footman who dares to sneeze, not a dog capable of barking. Don't you feel that the air around those Moorish turrets is more sonorous than anywhere else on earth? Has the owner imposed silence on the night breeze and the murmuring waters? Possibly all the walls of his dwelling have ears like those that Dionysius the Elder[8] had installed in his Syracusian stronghold, so that he can overhear every private opinion that is expressed and use his discoveries to further his puerile and shady plots. Listen! I think I can hear the rumble of carriage wheels on the fine gravel of the courtyard. It's the master returning; the castle clock has chimed eleven. There is no more orderly life, no more strictly kept regime, no more carefully pampered existence than that of this octogenarian fox. Go and ask him if he thinks that he is indispensable to the preservation of the human race that he watches so carefully over his own! Go and tell him that twenty times a day you feel like blowing out your brains because you fear that you are not only useless but may remain so, because you are afraid of a life without active goodness; and you will see him smile more scornfully than a prostitute would if a pious virgin confessed to feeling somewhat half-hearted in her prayers, or even slightly bored during holy mass. Enquire what self-sacrifices, what good deeds occupy his days; his servants will tell you that he gets up at eleven o'clock, that his *toilette* takes him four hours (most of which are probably spent trying to put some semblance of life into those marble features which duplicity and soullessness rather than age have petri- fied). At three o'clock they will tell you, the Prince climbs into his carriage and accompanied by no one but his doctor is driven through the lonely avenues of his vast property. At five, the most succulent and recherché dinner to be cooked in France is served up to him. His cook is, in his own line, as unusual, as considerable and as admired a personality as he is. After the meal, each course of which is solemnly heralded with a fanfare by his huntsmen, the Prince consecrates a few minutes to his family and courtiers. Each exquisite word which graciously falls from his lips is received with bowed heads. A canonized saint couldn't inspire more veneration in a congregation of zealots. At nightfall the Prince gets into his carriage once again with his doctor and goes for a second drive. He has just come back and his window has lit up, over there, in that remote wing which is guarded by his lackeys during his absence with such a solemn and absurd air of mystery. Now he will work till five in the morning. Work! . . . O moon, don't rise yet; conceal your timid rays behind the forest's dark horizons! River, hold back your already slow and meagre flow. Leaves, cease to tremble on the treetops; crickets in the fields, lizards in the walls, grass snakes in the bushes don't shake the grass blades, don't disturb the branches of ivy and hart's tongue, don't rustle the dry leaves and brittle stems of nettle and poppy. Let all nature be silent and still as a tombstone: the man's genius is awakening, his power must fill you with terror and awe; one of the ablest and most important princes of the land is about to bend over a desk by the light of a lamp, and, from the depths of his study, like Jupiter from Olympus, he will shake the world with a frown.

'Mere trifles, human vanities! Shows of childish pride, haughty inanities! What else has this remarkable man contributed in sixty years of laborious nights and ceaseless toil? What have the representatives of all the great powers of the earth come to seek in his study? What

222

invaluable services has he rendered to all the sovereigns who have acquired and lost the crown of France during the last half-century? Why has this man's bland gaze always inspired such unspeakable dread? Why has every obstruction been levelled before him? What revolutions has he caused or forestalled? What bloody wars, what public disasters, what scandalous extortions has he prevented? Indeed he must have been truly indispensable, this sensual hypocrite, for all our kings – from the proud conqueror to the narrow-minded bigot – to have imposed the scandal and the shame of his preferment upon us! Napoleon contemptuously characterized him with a cynical and forceful barrack-room epithet; and Charles X, in his days of orthodoxy, was quite right to say of him: '*What is he, after all, but a married priest!*' Did he do anything to stop the tragic downfall of these masters he first flattered and then betrayed? What good has he done? What has he achieved? Nobody knows, nobody can, will or wants to say what title to power and glory this most necessary Statesman has; his most brilliant actions are shrouded in impenetrable mists, his genius resides solely in silence and pretence. What shameless infamy does the pompous cloak of diplomacy conceal? Can you make sense of this way of ruling nations without letting them have a say in the management of their interests or any idea of the future that is being prepared for them? Such are the administrators and stewards we are given and to whom, without consulting us, our fortunes and our lives have been entrusted! We are not allowed to examine their actions or question their intentions. Dark mysteries are in the air, but far further above our heads than the eye can reach. We are used as the stake for unknown wagers in the hands of invisible gamblers – silent ghosts who smile majestically while mapping out our destinies in their memorandum books.'

'And what have you to say,' I exclaimed, 'about the idiocy of a nation that puts up with this disgraceful jobbery and allows sordid agreements of which it is not even informed to be signed in its name, its honour and its blood? Doesn't it make you feel like getting on to the political stage yourself?'

'The more my fellow creatures are debased, the more I want to raise them up again,' he replied. 'I still have hope for them. Allow me to let off steam about this impenetrable man who has moved us around like pawns on his chess-board and has had no desire to devote his powers to our advancement. Let me curse this enemy of the human race who has held sway over the world in order to feather his own nest, indulge his vices and impose on his despoiled dupes a humiliating respect for his iniquitous talents. Humanity's benefactors die in exile or on the cross; and you, you bald and sated old vulture, you will die slowly and reluctantly in your bed! Since death obligingly sets a halo round the heads of all famous men, your vices and infamies will be soon forgotten; only your abilities and your charm will be remembered. Deceiver! scourge whom the master of this world spurned and cast down to earth like the crippled Vulcan, to forge there without respite unknown weapons in the depths of inaccessible caves, you will have nothing to say on the great day of judgement. You won't even be questioned. The Creator who denied you a soul will not ask for an account of your opinions and your passions.'

'For my part,' I broke in, 'I'm convinced that some men's hearts are so puny, sluggish and barren that no affection can grow there. They seem to have more lasting attachments than other people and their relationships are in fact solidly established. Selfishness and self-seeking has fashioned them; habit and necessity maintains them. Since such men rate nothing highly, they never know the disappointments which embitter us poor dreamers who are incapable of loving someone without idealizing him. Often we make mistakes, often we angrily reject what we had cherished. But honour, good faith, scrupulous honesty in others are only, in the eyes of a diplomat, so many levers that can set in motion some mechanism known to himself alone; he is able to manipulate these at the right moment to take advantage of them for the furtherance of unworthy ends hidden to all but himself. In politics this is called *taking a broad view*. If an upright man becomes aware of the diplomat's lack of morality and becomes malleable as he himself grows corrupt, his master's appreciation of him increases apace; because in the diplomatic world what's most useful is most esteemed. Words have a different meaning, principles are viewed from a different angle, emotions have a different significance in that world than in ours. Moreover it's easier than one might think to achieve perfection in that foul art; it's simply a matter of trampling one's conscience underfoot and standing every principle of general morality on its head. True, some may find this impossible in practice; but if we two wanted to act out a comedy to entertain our friends, I bet that, with a little daring and some well-chosen, skilfully expressive, cautiously intelligible words – the sort of blurred-edged words that abound in the French language – we would be able to dress up blatant sophistries very respectably and appear on stage as true statesmen with very little effort or invention. Our friends would understand and laugh; but if some downright ignoramus came to hear us, believe me, he would take us for very great men indeed and go back home shaken, astonished, full of doubts, with his conscience in a poor way and already half-numbed, with all his bad instincts already awakened, trembling with hope at the thought of some permissible theft, some pardonable misdeed and, especially, with his head stuffed with our pretty, courtly phrases which he will repeat to his friends and teach by rote to his children, unaware that these elegant maxims all lead in the end to robbery, rape and murder. Or, if the simpleton is at all enlightened, he'll be seen to rub his hands together, attempt a sardonic smile, a knowing look, let fall in private conversations one or two of our elegant precepts of infamy, and receive as many knowing looks of admiration, as many sardonic smiles of approval as there are kindred spirits in the audience. I don't really resent the inevitable existence of those scoundrels of the élite whom Providence, for some unfathomable purpose of its own, allows to carry out their mission on earth. Fate is directly concerned with remarkable men, for better or for worse. It doesn't have to bother about the common herd. They obey the impulsion of those levers which an invisible hand manipulates. It's this helpless, stupid class, this stagnant sludge that lets itself be turned over and dug, bringing forth everything that is sown in it without asking why, without questioning the value of each poisonous or health-giving root that is thrust into its slimy, motionless mass – it's these forests of thistleheads, which the wind flattens or raises up at will, that I resent – I who would like to stay in the crowd but can't bear its weight, its mutterings, its ineptitude. It's these two-legged sheep that I can't stand, who gaze in stolid stupefaction at their leaders and, surprised to find they have been so unceremoniously shorn, look at each other, saying: "What remarkable men! How well we have been shorn!" Oh you dolts! Even your hogs squeal and don't stand starry-eyed with admiration before the knife that gelds them!'

A window has opened; it is the Prince's. 'Since when have corpses suffered from the heat?' asked my friend, lowering his voice. 'Since when have statues felt the need to breathe the night air? Whose are those two hoary heads leaning out as though to admire the moonlight? Those two old men are the Prince and his . . . what should I call him? For I won't sully the word *friend* which Monsieur de M——[9] appropriates in the presence of servants and underlings – a title he probably wouldn't dare lay claim to in front of their master, who surely scoffs at any term that refers to an emotion. To borrow a term of their trade, I might say that Monsieur de M — is the Prince's attaché, despite the fact that his function consists only in admiring and in noting down in his scrapbook every word those incomparable lips have let fall in forty years. Here is one I'll give you as a sample – one which we'll have to discuss when, if you feel like it, we play our part between two screens at the next Carnival, suitably got up and becomingly solemn, with sticks up our sleeves and boards down our backs to stop us from making any unintentional movements with our bodies or our arms; we shall wear plaster masks and the scene will open with these memorable, historic words: *Let us be wary of first impulses and never give in to them without due consideration, for they are nearly always kindly.* Who would believe that villainy, set out as doctrine for those in good society (a novelty in itself and rather piquant) should have its pedantries and its platitudes? But do you hear that hoarse cry? Which of these two gallow birds of philosophers has just given up the ghost? I'm mistaken, it's the cry of an owl as it flies out of the woods. Good! Screech louder, bird of ill omen, presager of funeral rites . . . Now here, your Excellency, is a voice you can't thrust back down the insolent offender's throat. Do you hear this outspoken graveyard refrain which is no respecter of persons and dares to tell a man like you that all men are mortal – without adding the court preacher's *almost* all?'

'Your indignation is bitter,' I observed, 'and your anger cruel. If that man could hear us this is how I would address him: May God extend your days, unhappy old man! – a meteor soon to fade into eternal night a luminary that destiny displayed to the world, not to lead men towards virtue but to lose them in the endless maze of intrigue and ambition! The heavens, whose purposes are inscrutable, denied you that mysterious spark men call a soul, a pale but pure reflection of Divinity, a light which sometimes shines in the eyes of men and enables us to glimpse immortal hope, a gentle, reassuring warmth which, from time to time, revives our downcast spirits, a vague and sublime love, a sacred emotion which makes us long for righteousness with delightful tears, a religious terror which makes us loathe evil with a quickened pulse. You, whose name I shall not pronounce, were gifted with a vast brain, eager, delicate senses; the absence of that divine and unknown quality which makes the rest of us human made you greater than the first among us, smaller than the last. Infirm, you trampled upon those who were whole and healthy; the most flourishing virtue, the finest constitution was no more than a fragile reed to you; you held sway over nobler beings than yourself; the greatness that they had and you lacked you made your own; and here you are now on the brink of a grave that will be as hollow and chill for you as a viper's. Your breath was frozen like your heart. Beyond the gaping pit there is nothing for you, no hope, perhaps not even the desire for an afterlife. Unhappy man! The horror of that moment will be such that it may perhaps atone for all the sufferings you have caused. To approach you was fatal, it is said; your glance was compelling, like the cold gust on an April morning that withers buds and flowers and scatters them around the bereaved trees. Your words blighted hope and innocence on the brows of those who came into contact with you. You walking riddle! Enigma with a human face! How many fresh blossoms have you scattered? how many blessed hopes and sweet dreams have you trampled under foot? how many cowards have you created, how many consciences perverted or stifled? Well, if the joys of your old age are restricted to the satisfaction of an over-fed vanity, to the infrequent pleasures of a blasé appetite, then eat, old man, eat and breathe in the odour of incense mingled with food. Who would envy your fate and wish you a worse? As for us, who pity you as much for having lived as for having to die, we shall pray that on your deathbed your family's farewells, the tears of some innocent footman, may awaken in you no unfamiliar sensation of tenderness or affection; that no spark may be struck from the flint you call your heart. We shall pray that you may die without ever having been fired by the ray of sunlight which creates love so that your eyes may remain always dry and your pulse steady, that you may never feel the tremor which love, hope, remorse or pain sends through us; so that you may dwell in death's dank bosom without having known above it, on earth, the warmth of vegetation and the stirrings of life; so that, as you merge into eternal nothingness, you do not have to experience the torment of despair at the sight of those souls soaring above you whose existence you scornfully ignored, those immortal spirits which you boasted of having crushed under your supercilious heel and which will rise up to the heavens while yours will vanish like an empty breath: then we shall pray that your last words may not be a reproach to the God in whom you did not believe!'

A faint white shape crossed a corner of the grassy carpet and we saw it climb the exterior staircase of the furthest turret. 'Is that,' said my friend, 'the shade of one of those just men you mentioned come to taunt the heretic by dancing and gambolling in the moonlight?' 'No, that soul, if it be such, inhabits a lovely body.' 'Oh, I see,' he replied. 'It's the Duchess![10] They say that . . .' 'Don't talk about it,' I interrupted. 'Spare my imagination those hideous images and detestable suspicions. That old man may have conceived the notion of such a sacrilege; but that woman is too lovely, it's impossible! If vile debauchery or sordid avarice dwell in such an engaging creature and are concealed under so chaste an exterior I prefer to ignore it, I prefer to deny it. We are men without gall, we are simple rustics. My friend, let us not allow the few pleasant emotions and happy thoughts we still possess to be blighted. Let us not tell our hearts what our minds suspect, but allow them to obey the promptings of our appreciative eyes. Your Grace, you are too charming not to be honest and good.'

'Very well, so be it!' exclaimed my friend, smiling. 'You are as good as you are beautiful, Your Grace. And that's what, this morning, I was only too willing to believe, when I saw you go by. I was lying on the grass in the park under the shade of trees that were aglow with sunshine; through the translucent autumn foliage you appeared to cast golden darts into the moist midday breeze. Clothed in white like a virgin, like one of Diana's nymphs, you sped past, drawn by a fine horse, in a trim, light tilbury. Your hair floated around your guileless brow; and spellbinding gleams shone from your big black eyes (the loveliest in France, it's said); I didn't know at the time that you were a Duchess; I saw nothing but a ravishing woman. I wanted to run after you down the avenue to keep you in sight a little longer. But since then I've been into your chamber and that portrait hanging amongst the draperies of your bed . . .' 'That alone,' I said, 'would stop me from putting the worst interpretation on what are in fact innocent feelings of almost filial gratitude for quite proper kindness and protection. No, no! One can't be corrupt with such bright, gentle eyes, such wonderful youthfulness and beauty, such a proud, frank bearing and melodious voice and those gracious ways. I've seen her tending a sick child; beauty and goodness in a woman attract and sustain each other! I too invoke that God of simple souls you addressed earlier and beg him to preserve me from hearing what I don't want to believe: that there is vice under such an appealing exterior, like a loathsome insect in the heart of a scented flower! No, Paul, let's go back to our village with this lovely vision of the Duchess in our memory; so that, if we ever write some romance of chivalry, we may accurately recall her figure, her hair, her fine teeth, her lovely eyes and the sunshine in the park at noon.'

We left the stone bench and my friend, reverting to his former preoccupations, said: 'Why is it that men – and I amongst them despite myself – are so impressed by intellectual gifts? Why do they alone procure immortality without the aid of any virtue, while the most transparent honesty, the tenderest generosity remain buried in oblivion when they aren't accompanied by genius or talent? Do you realize that this is sad and would convince waverers that virtue is labour wasted here below.' 'If you see virtue as toil,' I replied, 'it's vain indeed. But isn't it rather a pleasing necessity, a condition of life for those who, when young, have really known what it means? Men repay it with ingratitude because men are narrow-minded, credulous, idle, because the appeal of curiosity is stronger than gratitude and the love of truth; but in serving humanity, shouldn't we expect to be rewarded only by God? To work for mankind only in the hope of being carried in triumph is to act according to the promptings of one's own vanity, and such an incentive can only languish and expire at the first disappointment it encounters. We should never expect any personal benefit when we set out on the stony path of dedication. We must try to have enough sensibility to mourn and rejoice in our failures and successes. May our own heart suffice us, may God restore and fortify it when it begins to falter!'

'And yet,' said my friend, who was still unravelling the thread of his earlier musings, 'I admit that I can't help loving Bonaparte, that scourge of the first order, who reduced all lesser scourges to dust and whose shadow is enough henceforth to make them seem absurdly insignificant and inoffensive. He was a great man-killer, but a mighty constructor, an audacious architect of societies; a conqueror, yes, alas, but a law-giver! Doesn't that make up for the ills of destruction? Isn't making laws a greater good than killing men is a great evil? I see him as a powerful agriculturist, a beneficent deity (Bacchus arriving in India or Ceres landing in Sicily) armed with sword and fire, levelling the soil, tunnelling mountains, retrieving wild heathland, burning forests and sowing over all this, on the rubble and the ashes, a new vegetation intended for new men, vineyards and cornfields, endless blessings for endless generations.'

'There is no proof,' I answered, 'that these laws will abide; but even if they do, I can't love the man God used as a bludgeon to beat us into a new shape. Like everybody else I was fascinated in my childhood by the power and energy of this agent of confusion on whom we confer the title of great man as freely as upon Jesus or Moses. Since human speech can't distinguish humanity's benefactors from its scourges, since the epithet *good* is almost a term of scorn and the word *great* can be used for a painter, a law-giver, a military commander, a composer, for a god or an actor, a diplomat or a poet, an emperor or a monk, it's only natural that women, children and ignorant people should have been taken in by him and in 1810 have cried: "Long live Napoleon!" as enthusiastically as today, in Venice, they cry: "Long live the patriarch!" The former made widows and orphans; he was a powerful monarch. The latter feeds widows and orphans; he is a humble priest. What does it matter? Both are great men.'

'Indeed,' said my friend, 'the blind enthusiasm which celebrates genius, charity, courage or talent indiscriminately is more akin to a neurotic excitement than a reasonable feeling. But you must realize that there would be very few great men in the world if such a title were reserved exclusively for good men.'

'I know; but call them what you will, these are the only men I respect, for whom I feel any powerful interest and whom I would inscribe in the annals of human greatness. I would include the humblest and most obscure, from the Abbé de Saint-Pierre with his theory of universal peace to the good Enfantin, despite his absurd get-up and fanciful Utopias; all those in fact who according to their lights combine conscientious enquiry, patient consideration, sacrifices or enterprises for the benefit and happiness of mankind. I would make allowances for their mistakes, for the shortcomings of human nature that are more or less obvious in them; I would forgive them many a sin, as Magdalene was forgiven hers, if I knew for certain that they were capable of great love. But those whose purpose is cold and haughty, those proud men who build for their own glory and not for our happiness, those legislators who bespatter the world with blood and oppress nations in order to have a vaster territory on which to build their huge structures; who care nothing for women's tears, starving old people or the fatal ignorance in which children are brought up; those men who seek only their own aggrandizement and believe that they have made a nation great by making it as active, ambitious and vain as themselves, those I ignore, I strike them off my list: I put our curé's name in the place of Napoleon's.'

'Quite so,' said my friend, who had stopped listening to me. The night was so beautiful that his abstraction communicated itself to me. Sheet-lightning bleached the horizon from time to time and shed pale reflections on the dark rim of the forests that covered the hills. The air was cool and sharp without being cold. This is one of the loveliest spots on earth, and there isn't a king who owns a more spectacular park, trees of a loftier growth, or lawns of a more beautiful green following the curves of a more gracious terrain. This lush, thickly wooded dale is an oasis in the midst of the dreary plains that surround it and give no hint of its presence. One comes unexpectedly upon this ravine bristling with crags and forests, these regal gardens encircling an elegant, romantic Spanish castle mirrored, from its rocky peak, in the waters of an azure river. It's as though one has been transported in a dream to some enchanted land that will vanish as soon as one wakes up; and, indeed, it does vanish after a quarter of an hour, if one simply crosses the valley and follows the road to the south. The endless plains, the yellowish heath and flat horizons reappear. What one has just seen seems to have been a vision.

We took the path that leads to the caves. The poplars by the river stretched out their slender, immoderately long shadows towards us. Deer fled at our approach. We came to the disused quarries which are framed in the richest verdure and whose depths provided a truly theatrical scene. 'Go in under that echoing dome,' said my friend, 'and sing your Gloria. I'll sit over there and listen to the echo.'

I did as he bid me, and when I had finished he came towards me humming the simple words of the hymn:

*Glory to God in the highest and peace on earth to all men of
good will!*

'You'll note,' I said, 'that my hymn doesn't say: Glory on earth to men of learning and intellect. Repose is the most precious gift it is in God's power to bestow; God alone can bear the burden of glory deservedly and simple men who seek to do good are greater in his eyes than great men who do evil.'

Letter Nine

★

To the Malgache

15 May 1836

I've got back home and I find you've left; a letter from you dated from Marseilles reached me almost at the same time. Where are you off to?

> Where we come from there is no knowing,
> And are we sure of where we're going?

I'm writing to you through the *Revue des Deux Mondes*; you'll surely open it in Algiers.

This lawsuit[1] on which my future, my honour, my peace of mind and that of my children depend, I had imagined to be honourably settled. You left me as I was about to return to the family home. Once again I'm evicted from it and all the sworn covenants broken. I must fight back at renewed expense, contest inch by inch a corner of ground, a beloved corner, sacred ground – where the bones of my kindred lie buried beneath flowers sown by my own hand and watered by my tears. So be it! God's will be done! It's not without a feeling of revulsion, almost of dread, that I find myself once again at grips with material problems; but I am resigned and my stoical composure is strictly maintained. The litigant's role is a deplorable one. It's an entirely passive role whose one advantage is that it develops one's patience. To *act* is easy, to *wait* is the hardest thing in the world . . .

Midnight

*　　*　　*　　*　　*　　*　　*　　*　　*　　*

O breath of heaven, spirit of man! O wise, profound and absolute work of the Divinity, glorify the unknown artisan who created you! Spark escaped from the great crucible of life, sublime atom, you are an image of God, for all his attributes, all his elements are in you. You are infinity proceeding from infinity. You are as vast as the universe, and your dearest delight is to inhabit the unknown and travel through it.

*　　*　　*　　*　　*　　*　　*　　*　　*　　*

What has Man, this rickety, peevish creature, to complain of? What does he want? What has he come to? Why is he rolling about on the ground devouring the filth of life? Why, assimilating himself always to the beast, does he clamour for brutish satisfactions, and why all these resentful growls and that stupid whining when such gross pleasures are denied him? Why has he settled for a purely materialistic existence in which what there is of sublime in him has been extinguished?

Ah, that is the cause of all the ills that consume him. Cybele,[2] the beneficent nurse, has had her paps sucked dry by avid lips. Her children, seized with a fever and frenzy, fight over the maternal breasts with monstrous rivalry. There were those who claimed the rights of the first born, of the princes of the earth; and new races have emerged among men, privileged breeds, asserting their divine origin and divine rights while, in fact, God who has seen them appear from the slime of debauchery and the filth of covetousness has disowned them.

And the earth has been divided up like an estate, the earth which has been worshipped as a Goddess. It has become a base commodity, its enemies have overrun it and dismembered it . . . Its true children, simple men who knew how to live naturally, have been gradually confined within narrow bounds and persecuted until poverty has become a crime and a shame, until necessity has turned the oppressed into the enemies of their enemies and the just defence of their life has been called theft and highway robbery; gentleness has been called weakness, innocence ignorance and usurpation called power and wealth. Then falsehood entered man's heart, and his understanding was dimmed so that he forgot that his nature was twofold. His mortal nature found conditions in the bosom of society so hard, tried out so many false ideas, acquired so many unnatural needs, allowed itself to be so troubled and transformed that existence has now no time left in it for a life of the mind. All man's aims, requirements and desires are focused on the satisfaction of his physical appetites, that is, on being rich.

So that, alas, is what we have achieved! Those who are less susceptible to the pleasures of eating, the splendours of apparel or the distractions of society than to meditation and prayer are so rare today that they can be counted. They are despised as madmen, they are banished from communal life, they are known as poets.[3]

O unhappy breed, more and more sparsely scattered on the face of the earth! Remnant of primitive humanity, what have you not to put up with from the great, active, powerful, able and cruel breed that has replaced God's creation in this world! The reign of Japhet's sons is over, the men of today are literally the sons of man. When they perceive on the brow of one of their own offspring some sign of their heavenly origin, they loathe and ill-treat him[4] or at least laugh at him as at a freak and learn nothing from his example; at best they allow him to sing the wonders of the visible creation. As soon as he tries, in the darkness of intellectual life, to grasp some thread through the labyrinth or, disturbing the ashes that centuries of misuse and prejudice have heaped up, to dig under the thick crust of habit in the hope of drawing a faint spark from the extinct volcano, some pale glimmer of divine truth — it is then that he becomes dangerous and is suspected, hindered, discouraged; his intentions are slandered, his methods vilified, he is accused of corruption and sacrilege, his life is blighted, the torch is extinguished in his trembling hand; he is lucky if he is not put in chains as a lunatic.

*   *   *   *   *   *   *   *   *

Yes, the poet is unhappy, deeply unhappy in society. Not that he would want it restructured expressly for him to suit his tastes, as is often mockingly implied; he wants it reformed for itself and according to God's plan. The poet loves righteousness; he is gifted with a particular sense which is the sense of beauty. Those are artists and nothing else in whom this ability to see, to understand and to admire is directed towards external objects only; but when their intelligence goes beyond the sense of the picturesque, when their souls have eyes like their bodies, when they sound the depths of the ideal world, then the conjunction of these two tendencies makes the poet; thus a true poet must be both artist and philosopher.

This constitutes the perfect organic blend for achieving contemplative, solitary bliss; it is the sure and inevitable condition for endless misery in society.

Society, like man, is composed of two elements, a divine and a human: the divine element exists in a more or less pure, a more or less tainted state in our laws. These laws, however imperfect, however ill-expressed, are always superior to the generation they govern. They are the work of the wisest and most intelligent among us.* The human element resides in their abuse, in the prejudices and vices of each generation and, from the time of that perhaps mythical Golden Age from which the poet claims his genealogical descent, each generation has submitted to the promptings of evil more than to those of virtue. Unwritten laws and customs have had more substance than the written laws of duty. Punishment has been of no avail when custom has opposed law. That is why societies forever seeking for good in their institutions have always been invaded by evil. Legislators teach and enforce laws which humanity acknowledges and ignores. Everyone invokes them in his own interests; everyone forgets them when it suits him to do so.

That simultaneously discredited and privileged being we call a poet goes among men with a profound sense of sadness. As soon as he opens his eyes to the light of the sun he looks around for something to admire; he sees nature ever young and beautiful and is overwhelmed with divine ecstasy and inexpressible rapture; but soon inert creation ceases to satisfy him. The true poet is passionately drawn to God and God's works; but it's in himself and in his like that he sees the flame of eternal light burning for him most distinctly and most completely. He wants to find it there unadulterated and to worship God in man as a sacred flame on a spotless altar. His soul yearns, his arms open wide; so great is his need for love he would willingly tear open his breast if it would allow every object of his deep desire and his chaste affection to become part of him; but his clear eye, his searching gaze can't fail to discern human baseness and the work of centuries of corruption. It pierces the outer covering and sees sham souls in magnificent bodies, hearts of clay in marble and gold statues. Then he grieves, rebels, complains and remonstrates. The heavens that granted him this penetrating vision endowed him too with a deep, resounding voice, both for lamentation and for thanksgiving, for prayer and for threats, which imprudently betrays the extent of his anguish. The world's shortcomings draw from him cries of distress; the spectacle of hypocrisy burns his eyes with red-hot irons; the sufferings of the oppressed stimulate his courage, audacious sympathies seethe in his breast. The poet raises up his voice and tells men truths they would rather not hear.

* This obviously refers to lasting laws concerning general morality and not to those that are made and unmade every day in the law-courts and deal with the minor, material interests of a society.

Then the whole foul breed, that shelters behind a feigned respect for the law in order to indulge its vices undisturbed, gathers up stones from the highway with which to pelt the man of truth. The scribes and the Pharisees (that eternally powerful race) get out the scourges, the crown of thorns and the reed, the mocking sceptre which Christ's bleeding hands have bequeathed to all the victims of persecution. The blind and ignorant masses sacrifice martyrs for the sole purpose of contemplating suffering. Jesus on his cross is, for them, no more than a forceful image of a man in the throes of violent agony.

True, from the depth of this abyss of iniquities, a few just men sometimes emerge who dare to draw near to the gallows and bathe the victim's feet with their tears. There are, besides, some weak but honest men, often overcome by the vices of the age but as often penitent, thanks to their pious faith, who come to pour upon his torn feet the balm of expiation. These men bring comfort to the victim; the first prepare the reward. The cloud opens and the angel of death lays his burning finger on the bent brow of the man, soon to awaken an angel himself. Already the celestial harps spread their faint harmonies around him. The dove with the golden feet seems to hover under the sky's incandescent dome . . . Dreams of the spiritual, the futurity of the believer, the ideal of Socrates, the promises of the son of Mary! – all these are the consolations of the poet; the incense and myrrh that he needs for his wounds; the crown of his long martyrdom. That is why the poet must keep them for ever before his eyes when men persecute him; that is why he must live and toil alone without ever, in act or intention, becoming part of this tumultuous world . . .

*   *   *   *   *   *   *   *   *   *

Six o'clock in the morning

I left my room at daybreak to escape from the fatigue that was beginning to weigh down my eyelids. Unusually for me, I've slept poorly for the last couple of nights. I wake with a start from terrible dreams. On principle I never fight anything but avoid it instead; such is the weak man's strength. Thus I've resorted to not sleeping so long as phantoms haunt my bedside. I slung my basket over my arm; I put in it my notebook, my ink bottle, a loaf and some cigarettes and I set off on the road to the *Couperies*.[5] Here I am now at the highest point. It is a delightful morning, the air filled with the scent of young apple trees. The meadows, steeply falling away at my feet, unfold gently over there; they spread across the valley, their carpet still white with frosty morning dew. The trees clustered along the banks of the Indre meander across the meadows in brilliant green curves whose crest the sun is already gilding. I sat down on the last stone of the ascent and, opposite me, on the other side of the ravine, I saluted your white house, your nursery-garden and the mossy roof of your *ajoupa*. Why have you abandoned that happy nest, your little children, your ageing mother,[6] this charming valley and your friend the Bohemian? Swallow on the wing, gone to find in Africa the spring that didn't come quickly enough to please you? Ungrateful man! Isn't it always fine weather where we are loved? What are you up to at this moment? You are probably awake; and you are alone with neither a friend nor a dog. The trees which shelter you were not planted by you; the soil on which you tread isn't indebted to you for the flowers that bedeck it. You are perhaps enduring the heat of a scorching sun while the damp morning chill still numbs the hand that writes to you. You probably have no idea that I'm here watching over your nurseries, your terraced gardens, over all your forsaken treasures. Maybe as you sleep in the doorway to some mosque you see in your dreams those four little white walls within which you spent so much time working, studying, dreaming and growing older. Maybe you are on the top of Mount Atlas . . . Oh, that one word is enough to erase all the beauty of this landscape! The pretty forget-me-nots among which I am seated, the hawthorn hedge that clutches at my hair, the stream murmuring at my feet under its veil of early morning mist, what are these beside Mount Atlas? I scan the horizon, that home of restless spirits, so often scanned and so impossible to possess. All I see is unsurmountable space! . . . O lucky man! You travel through these wild mountains, that powerful range, that formidable backbone of the old world! What snows, what dazzling sunshine, what biblical cedars, what Olympian heights, what palm trees, what unfamiliar flowers are at your disposal! Oh how I envy you them! To think that, a moment ago, I was reproaching you for having left *La Rochaille*![7] – Alas, you are possibly in one of those miserable, exhausted states of mind when what we have doesn't make up for what we would like to have! Poets, poets! A race at once ungrateful, capricious and fretful! But what do you want? What are you seeking? Who gave you all this energy and all this dissatisfaction? What do you make of your vast dreams when you've realized them? Where do you find such superhuman reserves of strength when you are unhappy? And here am I, lost in the delights of the countryside, forgetting that my whole life is in the balance, on endlessly shifting scales; without a thought accepting afflictions which would have driven me to suicide could I have foreseen them two years ago when I wrote to you: 'It's all over with me.'

*   *   *   *   *   *   *   *   *   *

The sluice-gates on the river have just opened. The sound of the waterfall reminds me of the ceaseless harmonies of the Alps, as it rises up in the silence. Bird song from a thousand throats answers it. I hear the nightingale's amorous cadence; over there in the undergrowth the mocking trill of the warbler; high up in the sky the lark's rapturous hymn mounts with the sun. That glorious orb drinks up the mists in the valley and darts its rays into the river dispersing the hazy veil. Now it has caught up with me, with my damp hair, with my paper. It seems to me that I am writing on a sheet of glowing metal . . . Everything is aflame, everything is singing. Cocks are waking each other up and calling to each other from cottage to cottage; the church bells in the town are ringing out the Angelus; a peasant working in his vineyard above me puts down his tools and crosses himself . . . Kneel, Malgache, kneel wheresoever you be! Pray for your brother who is praying for you.

*   *   *   *   *   *   *   *   *   *

It must be eight o'clock, the sun is warm but the air is still chill in the shade. Here I am, behind a rock at the very bottom of the ravine. I'm hidden and protected from the wind as in a niche. The sun is warming my feet which I got soaked in the grass, but which are now bare and resting on a smooth, warm rock, while I have a pythagorean breakfast, with my bread and with water from the pretty stream that flows melodiously under the reeds beside me.

Up there the path is now thick with villagers on their way to church. I'll wait before making my way through the high grasses at the foot of the valley till the kind sun has got rid of the moisture; in an hour I'll pass over dry-shod. In its sleep, the river has left its narrow bed and the path is drowned under a silver sheet. Awake, Nymphs, or the Fauns will take you by surprise and fall in love with you!

*   *   *   *   *   *   *   *   *   *

Ah, God! At this hour my enemies are also awakening! They wake up to hate me. They will rise to harm me. They say a morning prayer, perhaps the only prayer they have ever said, and it is to beg for my undoing. Don't listen to them, good God, protector of poets! I have no material ambitions, no covetousness, no evil desires. You know it, you who look upon me, with the burning eye of heaven. You read the depths of my thoughts, as the sun looks into the depths of the burning-glass which it penetrates with its eager ray and from which it emerges after finding no other flame than that which it has just replenished. Goodness from on high, helper of the helpless, you do not listen to the prayer of the heretic; for every man is a heretic who prays to God for the ruin and the despair of their fellow creatures. You know that I ask you for no man's tears and that I don't want to win so as to become a tyrant but to be free. O my God, put an end to this impious struggle, but don't allow hate and violence to triumph over the innocent. – What have I done, the exiled poet said, to be loathed, banished from my country, hounded from the home of my fathers,[8] slandered, insulted, summoned before the court like a criminal, threatened with humiliating punishments? O Pharisees, you still rule, and what Jesus wrote with his finger in the dust of the courtyard[9] has been erased from the memory of man! . . .

And yet . . . it serves me right! Why, since I was a poet, why, since I had been singled out as one who would belong to nothing and to nobody in order to lead a wandering life, why, since I was destined for melancholy and for freedom, did I accept social bonds? Why did I associate with the human race? That was not my lot. God had given me a silent, uncompromising pride, a deep loathing for injustice, an invincible devotion to the oppressed. I was a wild bird and I let myself be put in a cage; a liana from the tropical forests placed under a cloche in the garden. My senses didn't urge me towards love, my heart didn't know what it was. My mind required nothing but contemplation, my native air, books and music. What need did I have of lifelong chains? . . . O my God! How pleasant these could have been had a heart similar to my own accepted them! . . . No! I was not made to be a poet; I was made to love! It was my misfortune that the hatred of others turned me into a nomad and an artist. What I wanted was to lead a normal human life; I had a heart; it was torn violently from my breast. They left me nothing but a head, a head full of noise and pain, dreadful memories, images of mourning, scenes of outrage . . . And because, while writing stories to earn the bread that was denied me, I recalled my miseries and dared to say that the reason that some people are unhappily married is the meekness imposed on women, the brutality permitted to men, the depravities society hides under a veil and protects under a cloak of abuse – it was because of this, that I was declared immoral, I was treated as an enemy of the human race![10]

. . . Perhaps it is folly and temerity to ask for justice in this world. Can man repair the damage man has done? No! You alone, God, can wash away the bloodstains with which brutal oppression smears the expiatory robes of your Son and of those who suffer in his name! . . . At least you can and wish to do so, since you allow me in spite of everything to be happy at this moment, with no other possession than my inkstand, no other roof than the sky, no other desire than some day to requite good for evil, no other worldly pleasure than that of drying my feet on this sun-baked stone. O my enemies! You don't know God; you don't know that he doesn't grant harmful wishes made in hatred! Try as you may, you'll never be able to rob me of this spring morning!

The sun is beating down on my head; by the riverside, on the fallen tree that serves as a bridge, I have forgotten my troubles. The water ran so clear over its bed of variously shaded blue pebbles; round the boulders of its banks there were so many bright little fins of darting fish; dragonflies hovered in such transparent, variegated myriads that my mind flowed with the insects, the river and its inhabitants. How pretty this little gorge is, with its narrow border of grass and bushes, its rapid, joyful torrent, its mysterious depths and its horizon bounded by the soft lines of cultivated fields! The lane is so winding and alluring! The blackbird silently hopping just ahead of me as I advance is so neat and glossy! I am making my last halt at Rock-Everard. That is the name we gave to the black rock, in whose sharp angle the *pastours*[11] light gorse fires in winter. That's where Everard sat down the other day saying that he asked nothing more of God for his old age than this rock and his own freedom. 'Beauty is small,' he said. 'This enclosed landscape and scanty shelter are more than a man requires for his material needs; the sky is above and the contemplation of the infinite worlds that are in it will suffice, I hope, for his intellectual needs.'

Thus spoke old Everard as he plucked tufts of flowering broom from the rock's dark flanks. It was just how you spoke five years ago, when, two steps away from this rock, you erected your *ajoupa* and planted your poplars. – How is it that you're in Africa? Nothing ever satisfies man in this world; that is his greatness and his misfortune.

*   *   *   *   *   *   *   *

I visited your garden; your poplars are in good health, your river is very full. But that deserted house, those closed shutters, those paths where no children play, that wheelbarrow, which has saved you from so many fits of spleen, now lying broken in a corner, all this is very sad. I went to call on the nanny-goat; she refused all the grass I offered her; she bleated pitifully; I thought for a moment she was asking me what had become of her master.

On going up *La Rochaille* again, I absent-mindedly took the road to Nohant. For a moment I forgot where I was going; I saw before me the road that climbs upwards gradually and, at the top, the white turrets and the warren of our chivalrous neighbour and loyal friend, the lord of the manor of Ars. I could see nothing beyond the hill but I was already aware of my own roof, the familiar walls of my childhood, the nut trees in my garden, the cypress of the cherished dead. I walked fast and effortlessly; I advanced as in a dream, wondering at my long absence, looking forward to my home-coming. Suddenly I realized my mistake; I remembered that hatred had turned the home of my fathers into a fortress I would have to besiege before I could enter it. O Marie![12] O my grandmother with the white hair! When I bade the sacred threshold farewell, I carried off a branch of the tree that keeps watch over your eternal slumber. Is that all that will remain to me of you? You rest beside your beloved son; but on your left, isn't there a place reserved for me? Must I die under an alien sky? Must I drag out a miserable old age far from the inheritance you preserved for me with such love and where I closed your eyes as I hope my children will close mine? O grandmother! Rise up and come to find me! Unwind the shroud in which I buried your worn-out body in its last sleep; may your old bones stand erect again and your withered heart throb in the kindly noonday warmth. Come and help me or comfort me. If I must be banished for ever from your home, follow me to far places. Like the savages of Meschacébé[13] I'll carry your remains on my back and they'll serve me as a pillow in the wilderness. Come with me, don't protect those who don't know you and whom your hands have never blessed . . . But no, grandmother, stay by your son; my children will still come and honour your grave; they know you without ever having seen you. My son looks like that Maurice whom you loved so dearly, whom I, too, resemble so much; my daughter is fair, solemn and already stately like you. Your blood runs in their veins, Marie; may your spirit too be in them; if I'm torn away from them, may your influence watch over them and animate them; may your ashes be their eternal Palladium; during the night may your voice, gentle or stern, comfort or reprove them . . . Oh if you were alive all this wouldn't have happened to me; I would have found a blessed refuge in your bosom and your crippled hand would have regained its strength to intervene, like the hand of fate, between my enemies and me. – 'I am dying too soon for you,' you said on the eve of your last day. Why did you leave me, O you who loved me, whose place has never been filled, who cherished even my faults, who bent my iron will like wax and made this rebellious head bow down with a single glance? – You who, to my eternal regret, to my eternal loneliness, taught me what inexhaustible, absolute, indestructible love means . . . ? Great God, you know she taught me what it was, that passionate love for our young. Do not allow my children to be taken from me! They are too young to bear what I suffered in losing her!

*   *   *   *   *   *   *   *   *   *

Malgache, your mother is old; don't stay away too long. When she is no more, you'll bitterly regret the days you spent far from her and you'll wish in vain you could bring them back.

> *Il tempo passa e non ritorna a noi,*
> *Et non vale il pentirsene di poi.*[14]

242

★ Letter Ten ★

To Herbert[1]

My old friend, I promised to write you a sort of diary of my travels – if travels they can be called – from the Vallée Noire to Chamonix. Here it is, and I beg you to excuse the frivolity of the account. To a man as austere as you only serious matters should be reported, but although I'm quite a bit older[2] than you are, I'm a child, as much in my defective education as in my frail physique. That's why allowances must be made for me, and besides, nothing would suit me worse than a ponderous tone. You've treated me as a spoilt child, all of you whom I love, but especially you, melancholy dreamer, you who are never smiling and lively except when you see me skimming over the quicksands and fantastic clouds of life.

Alas, treacherous and fickle gaiety! like a ray of sunshine between storm clouds, you have so often made me suffer! You've transported me to fairylands of oblivion and you've let mournful spectres penetrate my halls of bliss and sit down silently at my feasts. You've let them ride pillion on my winged horse and tussle with me till they've hurled me down into the world of realities and memories. Never mind! I bless you, spirit of madness, for you are both my good and my bad angel, sometimes ironic and bitter, but more often understanding and generous. Put on your many-coloured veils, beloved fantasy! Spread your rainbow wings; carry me along those well-trodden ways I'm too weak to leave, but where, thanks to you, my feet won't do more than touch the ground, keep alive in me the humble sense of my insignificance, and the capacity to accept philosophically that it is pleasant and convenient to be a nonentity, a state dignified occasionally by a victory won over fruitless aspirations . . . O Gaiety, you, who cannot be true without a clear conscience, or lasting without the habit of fortitude, you were never a companion of my early years and forsook me in those of my prime; but come now like the autumn wind to ruffle my greying hair and to dry the last tears of youth on my cheeks.

And you, my dear old friend, bear with my whimsical prattle and absurd comments. You know that I've no intention of studying the wonders of nature since I'm afraid I don't understand them sufficiently to take much more than a furtive look at them. This time it's only the desire to see cherished friends and the need to be on the move that have led me towards the homeland you've abandoned. You may find it pleasant to hear about it, however briefly and inadequately. There are places whose name alone brings back enchanted scenes, indescribable memories. If only by making you relive them with me I could clear your brow for an instant and relieve the noble burden of care which makes it so pale!

God preserve me from ever speaking ill of wine! The generous blood of the grape, kin to that which runs in the veins of man! What noble impulses you have revived in flagging spirits! What burning flares of youthfulness have you not rekindled in spent hearts! Noble juice of the earth, inexhaustible and patient as the earth and, like the earth, providing a bountiful source of vigour, ever young and glowing – as much for the weak as for the powerful, for the wise man as for the fool! Only those who seek in you a stimulant for gross orgies, an excuse for wild ravings, are your enemies as they are those of Providence. Those who want only to exhaust your beneficent resources, to renounce and scornfully reject the precious rationality God bestowed on man – they only are the desecrators of a celestial gift.

The heavenly origins of the vine are celebrated by all religions. In every nation God intervenes to bestow this priceless gift upon mankind. In our own Bible, Noah's blood was pleasant in the eyes of the Lord, who spared it together with that of the vine[3] as two life-giving streams, eternally blessed on earth.

In the first days of spring I've seen, under those bowers of vine branches which entwine themselves among the fig trees of the Adriatic, women clad in almost Grecian robes lovingly gathering flasks of what they poetically call the *tears of the vine*. This limpid dew escaped drop by drop from the joints of the branches and flowed during the night into jars placed to receive it. I loved the religious care with which these women collected the precious balm in the first light of dawn; I loved the sweet scent of the flowering trellis, the breeze from the Archipelago

244

dying away on the Italian shores, and the sign of the cross they made each time they cut into the sacred boughs. It was a sort of pagan rite preserved and renewed by Christianity. The cult of the young Bacchus seemed to merge with that of the infant Jesus and I couldn't swear that the ancient *Ohé, Evohé!*[4] didn't linger on these old women's lips together with the Christian *Amen*.

I've always seen the cult of rustic gods as the most charming and poetic expression of man's gratitude towards creation. I consider that there are no false gods, that they are all true, beneficial and noble concepts. And as for a religion being infallible, I know that even the best can and must be contaminated like everything that drops from on high into man's estate. But I believe in the wisdom of nations, their gran-deur, their strength, the individuality they derive from the regions they inhabit; and thus I have faith in the pre-eminence of certain ideas related to belief and worship. Eternal truth, forever hidden from mankind, has appeared a little less dimly to those who have sought it in purer atmospheres and under brighter skies. Our own faith is the most beautiful because it is the simplest. It merges well with the austere surroundings that nurtured it, with the great picturesque landscapes and scorching climate in which God revealed himself to man as the one and only God. Polytheism is intoxicating, like the pleasant land where it was born; but I see in it all the conditions of excess and instability that characterize those for whom life has been too easy.

I love the myth of Bacchus, that embryo dormant in a god's thigh and, like Noah, surviving cataclysm; like Noah, saved by a miraculous favour and, like him, bringing to mankind the benefits of a new tree of life. But on the over-bounteous slopes of Greece the vine grows and proliferates with an abundance which man soon abuses and, from the vats where Evohé poured pure libations to his father, there soon emerges the frenetic band of hideous Satyrs and obscene Thyades. Then men demand unrestrained pleasure from what had been given them as a judicious remedy for their weakness and their troubles. Senseless debauchery sullies the steps of the temple; the goat, that stinking sacrifice made to rustic gods, links rites of pleasure to notions of stench and bestiality. Festive chants turn into howls, dances into the gory combats that led to the death of divine Orpheus; the god of wine has become the god of excess and it is austere Christianity with its fasts and its mortifications that has to find a new path along which to lead a drunken, reeling humanity away from its own immoderation.

If I seek the history of vine-growers after the flood in the simpler, more naïve version of old Noah, I find that his descendants make a more religious and sober use of divine fruit. First victim of his own imprudence, he learns at his own expense that the blood of the grape is headier and stronger than his own; he succumbs to it and his pious sons learn abstinence on the very day that they have found a new pleasure. On the scorched hills of Judea the vine multiplies its riches with restraint and man, maintaining a certain respect for the divine aftereffects of the precious plant, inscribes this touching maxim in his book of wisdom:

'Leave wine to those who are overcome with labour and strong drink, to those whose hearts are full of bitterness. Princes shall not partake of wine nor of strong drink. They shall leave them to those who suffer and those who toil in bitterness of heart.'[5]

All honour to those early times! And both affection and regret for the ancient pastors and the world's infancy! Those days were pleasant in the sight of the Lord, when man sought knowledge and no one could guess to what fatal use knowledge would be put; when wisdom was not an empty word but stood in the statutes of the patriarchs for a true and noble need of humanity. Those were days that seem great and almost impossible now when compared to our modern societies. God, Almighty God, you who spoke on the mountain telling me, 'Do thus', and saw your law fulfilled; you whose word descended upon Israel's tabernacles, instructing and guiding your legislators kneeling before you; what feelings can you now have for us in your paternal bosom when you see the land subjected to the ungodly whims and senseless desires of a handful of perverted men? The sacred word *law* is now interpreted as *self-interest*, toil is replaced by cupidity, the holy and sacred rites by inept customs or obscure mysteries, your levites by pontiffs, enemies of the people. Instead of the fear of your wrath or your displeasure, mercenary armies are the only form of restraint our princes know how to use and the masses are willing to acknowledge.

What is there to be said for an age where moral education is totally left to chance, where young people learn neither to regulate their intellectual needs nor to curb their physical appetites, where the texts of the various faiths are explained to them with a smile and advice not to take any of them seriously; or where the only injunction is not to get on the wrong side of the police when they indulge in their first orgy and not to profess too loudly the theory of vices they are free to practise at will?

What are they told about love, the first passion to awaken and the one which, in an adolescent heart, is capable of such noble impulses? Nothing except that they should commit as few follies as possible on account of women, keep their heads with flirts, abstain from rapture, console themselves with prostitutes when they have had no success elsewhere, and always sacrifice the most admirable emotion that can bud in a young heart to self-interest, pleasure or wealth!

What are they told about ambition, that thirst for glory and action which soon stifles the mild yearnings of exclusive affection and often prevents their very existence? Are they advised to channel this generous zeal, to put their acquired talents and natural gifts at the service of mankind? When they were children they read something of the sort in the writings of classical philosophers, but they are now taught to judge these from a purely literary point of view. Then society welcomes them to its frozen heart. 'Give me your insights!' it commands them. 'Give me the fruit of your labours and your midnight toil and I'll give you in exchange enough wealth to satisfy all your vices; for you have vices, I know, and I like them, I protect them, I hide them under my cloak, I secretly screen them with my compliance. Serve me, help me to get rich, give me your talents and your industry, let them help to increase my pleasures, maintain my reign, sanction my turpitudes: and you will have the freedom of the dens of iniquity reserved for my favourites!'

Thus, far from developing and directing the two sources of greatness which young people naturally possess, glory and sensuousness; far from exalting the extent to which they can blend the divine with their ardour and enjoyment of life, present-day society exploits them to degrade man and bind him to a desperately base materialism. It takes pleasure in developing his bestial impulses; it creates and protects dens of corruption and every kind of device to further revive or satisfy his basest needs or even his most perverted fantasies. How can natural pleasures, unrestrained by any moral strictures, by any law, fail to degenerate into excess? How can the love of glory avoid becoming a thirst for riches? How can love and wine not entail debauchery?

All this, I may say, apropos of a patrician orgy in a country inn that I have just witnessed!

I have travelled a great deal in my life; I've stopped at many a village tavern; I've spent the night in many a sordid ale-house between smashed benches, fragments of broken pitchers red with rough, bitter wine; I've risked having my skull beaten in by carters fighting around me; I've heard the obscene language and the ribald songs of villagers on Sunday outings. I've seen starving beggars spend their last penny on spirits; I've seen pretty young women rolling dishevelled in the mud and stage-coach wits exchanging low jests with tavern serving-wenches. Which of us who has travelled on the cheap hasn't seen and heard as much?

Now, I'm not intolerant by nature and although such encounters have often bored, wearied and vexed me I've always taken them with philosophical calm. What right have I to despise the uncouthness and bad taste of men who have been deprived of education? Would I have the face to criticize the pauper for renouncing the dignity of human learning when I and my social equals deny him the use of that knowledge and refuse him work because of it? Why shouldn't those of you whom we have reduced to the state of beasts of burden try to make your fate more bearable by deadening both memory and reason, 'by drinking oblivion of your griefs', as Obermann puts it, with sublime compassion.

What's that you say? – Your daily suffering doesn't strike us as being unbearable; we are deaf to your complaints; we see your unremitting, endless toil without disgust; we harden our hearts to your misery and we find your brief hours of happiness revolting. – Poor wretches! It's quite enough to have your sufferings belittled; your pleasure at least might be allowed to go unhindered. Let the beggars' orgy go ahead! Let them howl outside the houses of the rich; they'll never get in. Let them sleep on the steps of palaces whose delights they can at least dream of throughout a whole night . . . But no! There are police regulations for the poor. The rich man's brothel is open at all hours, while the poor man's tavern closes at night and the watch hauls off to prison those who have neither footman nor carriage to take them home.

Listen to what the rich have to say in favour of such injustice: 'A gentleman's merrymaking is neither noisy nor troublesome; that of the people is worse than that, it is dangerous. The poor don't know the restraint of education.' And the great ones of the world think up all kinds of lofty theories about necessary distinctions, indisputable hierarchies. They recognize that birth is an antiquated notion today and that gold doesn't increase anybody's value. They assert that *education* alone creates a legitimate and sacred superiority. 'Make the common people such as we are,' they say, 'and we'll receive them as social equals.'

There is just one point these men have overlooked, which is that though the common people haven't yet been able to become their equals they themselves have, in the meantime, become equal to the common people where vice and coarseness are concerned.

If I remember right I have seen an aristocratic orgy only on the stage, at the Odéon and Porte-Saint-Martin theatres. I must say that it struck me as being very staid and boring. At any rate it was all very proper. Two or three characters, intent on their own affairs, chatted in asides about matters totally unrelated to the orgy while, seated at a table, a dozen or so splendidly dressed extras raised their cups of gilded wood, rhythmically knocking them together with a dull thud and

> . . . in mournful strain,
> Sadly intoned a Bacchic song.[6]

I was therefore not at all put out by a party of young people dining at a table at the far end of the inn garden. The place was full on account of the fair: not a private room to eat in, not a public room that wasn't chock-full of commercial travellers.

I apologize to a childhood friend of mine who sells me excellent wines and for whom, if it came to it, I'd sell my last pair of boots. May I also apologize to several commercial travellers who wrote me most insulting letters because of some silly joke or other I had made I really don't know where. I beg their pardon, and seriously, I swear it, in remembrance of one whose name lies buried in many grieving hearts. – But after all, I must confess before heaven and earth that I can't stand commercial travellers . . . or at least, I couldn't stand them till this day, which will perhaps help me to make my peace with them.

At any rate, to avoid anecdotal conversations, I accepted the suggestion made by an infernal innkeeper's wife, who looked more poisonous and baleful than anything Gil Blas ever told us about the innkeepers of Spain. I allowed her to set a modest table behind a trellis in a corner of the garden for my children, their nurse and myself. I could have been taken for a village priest, accompanied by his house-keeper and his nephews.

At the other end of the garden there was a big table and a very merry party. 'They are very nice people,' the innkeeper's wife assured me. 'The cream of our local aristocracy. There's Monsieur le Comte, Monsieur le Marquis and Monsieur de —' Thank Heaven, I've no memory for names, Christian or otherwise, but my Señora Léonarda's[7] mouth was full of them and I hoped to see as decorous an orgy as those at the Odéon and the Porte-Saint-Martin. With all due respect for the aristocracy, I've had very little to do with them in my life. I know that they wear gloves, that their chins are well shaven or their beards perfumed; I know that they are pleasant to look at; I would never have supposed they could be so unpleasant to listen to.

You probably expect me to give you an account of the orgy. Well, you are mistaken. First because I was only present at the musical section, the overture as it were; secondly, I was sheltered by the trellis and, thank God, saw absolutely nothing. Finally, my dinner and that of my family was over in ten minutes and I retired more contented than when leaving the Odéon or the Porte-Saint-Martin since at least I'd paid nothing to get in. At the moment I'm very nearly reconciled to Lucrezia Borgia's ways, after seeing how obnoxious drunken noblemen can make themselves to an onlooker.

I was climbing into the coach immediately after the *performance* and I overheard this philosophical remark from a stable-boy to the coachman as the chorus of a song was wafted over the wall: 'If it was *us* they'd say: "The riff-raff's getting riotous!" Since it's *them* they say: "The smart set's having a good time!"' The other proletarian's philosophical reply was as forceful as the circumstances required; were it not for the foolish convention that forbids us to write certain words which were current in the days of Dante and Montaigne I'd have quoted it here, for popular obscenity nearly always bears the mark of genius – it's a savage and terrible appeal to God's justice. That of our betters is nothing but foolish blasphemy – it has no true motivation and therefore no excuse.

O you whom I have misjudged and before whom today I bow my head! O commercial travellers! I still protest that you are very tedious and that witticisms flow – alas, overflow – from your lips; but I swear by Bacchus and by Noah, I swear by all the good and bad wines you sell, that you are more agreeable and polite and have better manners than the young bucks of the local gentry. I testify and will sign it with my blood that you behave a hundred times better in taverns, that your manners are excellent compared to theirs and that it's a thousand times preferable to be in your company and to put up with your table talk than to find oneself even at fifty yards distance from a party of 'very nice people'. – So let peace reign between us and do stop writing me insulting letters – or, at least, please pay the postage!

And as for you, friend of poets from time immemorial, 'generous blood of the grape!' it was you whom the artless Homer and even the melancholy Byron celebrated in some of their most beautiful lines, and you who, through long years, kept Hoffmann's genius alive in his fragile, sickly body. You prolonged Goethe's powerful old age and often gave godlike strength to the greatest artists when their energy had seemed exhausted. Forgive me for having spoken of the perils entailed in your worship! Sacred plant, growing at the foot of Hymettus,[8] you impart your inspiration to the weary poet when, having wandered aimlessly in the plains, he has vain longings to climb once more to the lofty summits. As you course through his veins you give him a magical youth; you restore untroubled slumber to his burning eyelids and bring the whole of Olympus down to meet him in his celestial dreams. Let fools despise you, let the high priests of fashion proscribe you, let the wives of patricians turn away their gaze in pious horror when they see you moisten the lips of the divine Malibran;[9] they do well to forbid their lovers to drink in their presence; the imagination of these men is too contaminated, their memories too full of filth for it to be prudent for them to lay bare all that is going on in their minds. But instead, come, river of life, flow freely into the cups of my friends! They are disciples of the divine Plato, worshippers of the beautiful: they detest the sight as well as the idea of all that is ignoble, they want joy to be unsullied. They believe that a pure woman is no less so when she is in their company at table; that a youth should not profane his lips with a cynic's smile; that an artist should be able to pour out his aspirations without exciting derision. What they want, indeed, and what they *can* and *dare* do, is to reveal all the secrets of their hearts and to have nothing to hide from each other when the grey-blue light of day takes us by surprise around the table in our garret and tenderly, shyly mingles its azure glimmers with the reddening gilt of the guttering candles. Or else outside in the country, when dawn finds us seated in the garden, with flagons and fruit around us and a full moon above; and we laugh because her pale face reminds us of a timorous or absent-minded lady trying too late to withdraw decorously to her abode before the splendour of the sun. What lovely nights of this scorching summer we have just lived through, whose like we may not see for many years to come! dewless dawns; Italian nights; quiet repose on the lawns; melodious and passionate music of the warbler as Venus rose in the sky; such beautiful stars at the hour when day and night struggle for supremacy; twilight scents;

ecstasy and silence followed by gentle words and merry laughter! Return again to enchant our days that are free from ambition and our nights that are free from resentment; and may invigorating madeira and sparkling champagne flow from hour to hour dispelling drowsiness and reviving our wits when my friends are gathered together and I am among them!

From Chalons to Lyon

Stretched full length on the boards of the deck and rolled up in my overcoat, I slept soundly on the steamer till day came and lit up the flat and (whatever the natives may think) far from appealing banks of the Saône. Whose is that open, gentle countenance that seems to watch over my heedless slumber and prevent the sailors from trampling over me as if I were a package? It was indeed a waste of time to study Lavater and Spurzheim if I'm to be so poor a judge of faces! The fact is that yesterday I made a terrible blunder and, taking this pleasant young man for one of the rakes from the inn, I angrily turned down the friendly offer of his carriage. True, on board the steamer we have all become equal and, should this gentleman choose to make fun of me for looking like a student with the manners of a peasant, neither politeness nor gratitude would stop my tongue and I would tell him what I think of him and of his friends . . . But he seems neither ill-disposed nor haughty. We shall wait and see.

Encounter with an old friend – a real godsend on a trip! His comments which are both funny and biting help me to forget that I'm dead tired. He sums up each passenger from head to foot in a single apt word. My heart sank on seeing him for his presence revives whole epochs, strange dreams, a dreadful existence of which he was once the calm and sympathetic witness. But he seems to have sensed that there is a spot in my heart that's too raw to touch and he steers clear of it. He laughs, teases, talks rather as Callot[10] draws. It can be a sign of profound philosophy to be able to see the comic side of life after having drunk its graver aspects to the dregs; in me it's only the result of infinite weakness, I must admit. Never mind! I laugh, I'm happy for an hour; I feel as if I'd been born yesterday.

Paul has an eminently artistic eye and I see all the things the river bank carries away in our wake through his mocking fantasy. The Mâcon church spire makes me burst out laughing; I'd never have believed a church spire could be so funny. Yet Paul never laughs; his solemn

252

merriment, the children's boisterous, noisy good humour, the excellent appearance and tactful good manners of the *legitimist*,[11] the consternation of Ursula, who is convinced that she's on the high seas, my bohemian unceremoniousness – these are enough to make us all the best of friends and to join forces at the inn in Lyon.

'What's our friend called?' whispers Paul, indicating the legitimist.

'I haven't the remotest idea.'

'Let's ask him for his papers,' suggests Paul with dignity.

His passport reveals that he's well-born; we must do our best to forgive him for it. He's wealthy, which isn't of the slightest interest to us; all of which goes to prove that it doesn't help to know a person's name and circumstances. He's pleasant, modest and well-mannered. What more do we need to know? He's going to Geneva; we'll all go together; but no. Paul is leaving us to travel down the Rhone. Fate or fancy are taking him in that direction. Our impromptu friends, my family and I will share a coach and we'll see the lake of Nantua this evening.

Nantua

Unimpressive mountains, diminutive lakes, scant vegetation, a totally unremarkable landscape for anyone who has seen the Alps. And yet here and there a peculiar perspective, a mass of friable rock oddly fretted, bastions and pillars that look as if they had been erected and sculptured by the hand of man, mountains which open out round each bend onto verdant valleys, scenes without grandeur but with plenty of variety following each other in profusion before my absorbed, if not delighted, gaze; that's how le Bugey has struck me on this occasion. Up till now I have found it hideous.[12] – Never read my letters in the hope of finding reliable information about the outside world; I see everything through personal impressions. For me a journey is no more than a lesson in psychology and physiology of which I am the *subject* undergoing all the tests and experiments that appeal to me; I have to put up with all the praise and all the pity, alternately, that we must lavish on ourselves if we are to respond naturally to our passing moods – to the enjoyment or loathing of life, to a hobby-horsical whim, the effects of sleep, the quality of coffee at the inn, etc., etc.

We had set our minds on discovering some fine sights here; for we had been assured, on oath, that this part of the country could boast some outstanding scenery and we trusted our informant implicitly. – So we hire a Swiss car and have ourselves driven to Meriat in pelting rain, accompanied by sudden, unexpected thunder-claps that sound as odd as the shapes of the rocks from which they rebound. The driver loses his way and goes up the mountain instead of down into the ravine. The rain redoubles; no hope now of a picnic on the grass; we eat philosophically in the car. We break open a bottle and toast each other with British composure, when all of a sudden we find ourselves at three paces from the cliff edge. The charioteer, soaking wet and very cross, realizes his mistake. He now wants to turn back but the track is too narrow. The horse objects to breaking its neck; so it's the car that has to suffer for its clumsy construction and rusty springs. Our guide is discouraged by the difficulty of the undertaking. He leaves us stranded with one wheel in the void, a glass in our hand, neither able to get out nor to stay where we are.

Luckily we are in fits of laughter and laughter never killed anyone. We manage to extricate ourselves from the leather box, raise up the car, lead the horse, thrash the driver – and I for my part get my own back for having had a glass of wine, full to overflowing, spilt into the pocket of my smock.

Finally we reach the ravine, not vertically as had seemed all too likely, but by a pretty path covered in wild flowers still sparkling from the rain, and flanked by a stream that is turning into a torrent and swelling from minute to minute. Rain lashes the dishevelled fir trees; clouds race along the sides of the gorge, mist enshrouds the peaks; and, after a thousand bends in the road that snakes its way through the dark forest to its depths, we enter a region which is sublime in its melancholy.

Not a human being, not a chalet roof. Two sheer cliff faces, covered in evergreen trees that appear to grow from each other's crests, hem us in, pressing in close upon us and, with the countless detours, seem to push us onward, shutting us into inextricable solitudes.

I've seen many a more imposing sight, seldom one more austere. The finest veins of the Alps, the Pyrenees or the Apennines don't produce a sturdier or more stately vegetation; nowhere have I seen such beautiful forests of the most gigantic firs, lofty, proud and luxuriant, which seem, in the eminence of the site and in their numbers, to defy destruction and to thrive on the onslaughts of lightning and the axe.

At Meriat all that's left of the Carthusian monastery are a few elegant arcades covered in wallflowers and half buried under landslides from the mountain over which the turf has grown again; the portal still stands and has preserved a monastic air. The torrent rushes noisily behind the monastery, runs alongside it and falls against the corner of an outhouse which it is gradually destroying and will probably carry off altogether at the next storm. What was this building's function at the time of the monks? I fancied that it might have served as a penitentiary and that the waterfall flowed over the roof of a damp cell, filled with terrors. I'm free to imagine what I like since the only guides are two silent, fierce-looking giants, the forest ranger and his daughter, both having much in common with the local fir trees and as proud as ruined Hidalgos,[13] who declare that they are neither innkeepers nor taverners – though this doesn't stop them from plying the rare sightseer who comes this way with all the wares money can buy in a tavern.

In the rain this spot seemed sad, chill and admirably suited to an ever unchanging life and to men dedicated to the cult of a single and absolute ideal. No perspectives, no contrasts; magnificently and uniformly green grassy slopes, depths of forest without issue or the slightest break either for eye or thought; fir trees everywhere, narrow meadows and forests cut into by the invincible bulwark of the mountain and by eternal mists . . . I say eternal although I barely spent an hour there. If they aren't so, if ever a bright sun shines on the monastery of Meriat, if the torrent ever flows limpid and calm, if the dark veils of melancholy are raised for an instant and if such a site attempts a smile, then I declare that it's nothing but a cliché, as they say in painters' studios – that is, worthless, and a failure as far as beauty goes. I renounce my feeling of affinity with it, I erase it from my memory and I consider any traveller who goes there in fine weather to be a vulgarian and a lout.

I was drenched to the skin, which cured me homeopathically of a stubborn cold. In other words I exchanged a bearable cough for a high temperature that compelled me to spend the night in an inn just outside Geneva.

But on waking up I greeted Mont Blanc from my window and saw beneath me all the lovely country of Gex spread out like a vast many-coloured carpet at the foot of the Savoy mountains whose snowy fortress rose on the horizon.

Geneva

'Where do you get off, gentlemen?'
It is the postilion speaking. – Reply:
'At M. Liszt's.'
'Where does he live?'

255

'Exactly what I was going to ask you.'

'What does he do? What's his job?'

'Artist.'

'Is he a Vet.?'[14]

'Why, do you need one?'

'He sells violins,' says a passer-by. 'I'll show you the way.'

We are led up a steep road to the house he's pointed out and the landlady declares that Liszt is in England.

'The woman's crazy,' says another passer-by. 'Monsieur Liszt is a musician at the Opera House; you should go and ask the stage-manager about him.'

'And why not?' says the legitimist. And he sets off in search of the stage-manager. The stage-manager says that Liszt is in Paris. – 'No doubt,' I say indignantly, 'he's got an engagement to play the flute in Musard's[15] band.'

'And why not?' says the stage-manager.

'There's the entrance to the Casino,' says somebody. 'All the young ladies who take music lessons know Monsieur Liszt.'

'I feel like going to speak to that one who's just coming out with a music score under her arm,' says my companion.

'And why not? especially as she's pretty.'

The legitimist bows three times French style, and asks with the utmost courtesy for Liszt's whereabouts. The young person blushes, lowers her eyes and with a stifled sigh replies that Monsieur Liszt is in Italy.

'Let him go to the devil! I'm going to sleep in the first inn I come across. It's his turn to look for me.'

At the inn a letter arrives shortly from his sister.[16]

> We waited for you, but you're late and we're tired of waiting.
> Find us! We've left! *Arabella*
> PS. See the Major[17] and come with him to join us.

'Who's the Major?'

'What does it matter?' says my friend the legitimist.

'What indeed! Waiter, go and find the Major.'

The Major turns up. He looks like Mephistophiles in a customs officer's cloak. He looks me up and down and asks me who I am.

'A badly turned-out traveller, as you can see, and a friend of Arabella's.'

'Right! I'm off to get a passport.'

'Is the man mad?'

'Not at all. Tomorrow we leave for Mont Blanc.'

So here we are in Chamonix; it's raining and night is falling. On the off-chance I make my way to the *Union* – which the natives pronounce *Onion* – but this time I take good care not to ask for the renowned artist by name. I follow the customs of the enlightened nation I have the pleasure of visiting and I describe his person succinctly: skimpy smock, long dishevelled hair, battered straw hat, stringy tie, temporarily lame and permanently humming Dies Irae with an agreeable expression.

'Of course, Sir,' says the innkeeper. 'They've just arrived. Madame is very tired and the young lady in fine spirits. Go upstairs, they're at No. 13.'

'It can't be them,' I say to myself, 'but never mind.' I rush up to No. 13 all set on embracing the first splenetic Englishman I meet. I was sufficiently muddy to make it qualify for a real commercial-traveller's joke!

The first thing I trip over is what the innkeeper calls the 'young lady'. It's Puzzi, astride the carpetbag and so altered, so grown up, his head so heavy with long brown curls, his figure draped in so feminine a smock, that bless me if I know where I am! Thus failing to recognize young Hermann, I doff my cap to him saying: 'Sweet page, tell me where I can find Lara?'[18] At these words Arabella's blonde head emerges from the depths of a hooded English-style cloak; as I turn towards her Franz throws his arms round my neck, Puzzi gives a cry of amazement, we all get into an inextricable tangle of embraces while the innkeeper's daughter – shocked at the sight of a fellow so mud-bespattered, whom up till then she had taken for a tramp, kissing a lovely lady like Arabella – drops the candlestick and rushes off to spread the news that No. 13 has been invaded by a band of strange, unidentifiable beings as hairy as savages and amongst whom it is impossible to tell the men from the women or the servants from the masters. – 'Actors!' declares the head cook dismissively, and here we are stigmatized, singled out, held in abhorrence. The English ladies we meet in the corridors lower their veils over their modest countenances and their imposing husbands discuss the possibility of asking us to give a sample of our talents during dinner in return for a reasonable payment. This seems to be the place to tell you about the most scientific observation I've made in my life.

The islanders of Albion carry around with them a specific fluid which I shall call the British fluid, in the midst of which they travel, as inaccessible to the surrounding atmosphere as a mouse in an insulating apparatus. It's not simply that they owe their unflinching impassivity to the thousand and one precautions they take. It's not because they wear three pairs of breeches one on top of the other that they are always perfectly clean and dry despite the rain and mud; neither is it because they wear woollen wigs that their stiff, metallic curls defy the damp; it's not because each one of them goes around laden with enough ointments, brushes and soaps to beautify a whole regiment of *bas Breton* conscripts that they are always freshly shaven and that their fingernails are impeccable. It's because the outer air has no hold on them; it's because they walk, drink, sleep and eat in this fluid as under a twenty-foot-thick bell jar, through which they stare pityingly at wind-swept riders and walkers with snow-sodden boots. I wondered, while carefully observing the skulls, physiognomies and postures of the fifty or so English of both sexes who recur every night around the dining tables of Switzerland, what could be the point of all those long, dangerous and difficult pilgrimages; and I believe that I've at last discovered it, thanks to the Major whom I persistently consulted on the subject. Here it is: an Englishwoman's sole aim in life is to succeed in crossing the highest and stormiest regions without disturbing a single hair of her head; an Englishman's is to return home after having travelled round the world without having soiled his gloves or worn out his boots. That's why, when they get together in hotels after their wearying excursions, men and women get dressed up and appear, dignified and self-confident in all the impenetrable majesty of their tourist outfits. It's their wardrobes that travel, not themselves, and the individual is no more than an excuse for the suitcase, a medium for the clothes. I wouldn't be surprised to see travel books published in London bearing such titles as: *Rambles of a Hat through the Pontine Marshes; A Coat-Collar's Reminiscences of Switzerland; World Tour of a Mackintosh*. The Italians go to the other extreme. Accustomed as they are to a temperate, mild climate they despise the simplest precautions so that, in our parts, changes in temperature take them so much by surprise that they immediately long for their own beautiful country; they go around with an air of proud disdain and, parading their nostalgia, constantly and vociferously compare Italy with what they have before their eyes. It sounds as if they wanted to raffle Italy like a property and were seeking customers. If there is anything that could dissuade us from crossing the Alps it's having to undergo this sort of peddling of each town or village, whose name alone is enough to move the heart and swell the voice of an Italian whenever he mentions it.

The best tourists and those who make the least fuss are the Germans; they are first-rate walkers, intrepid smokers and usually amateur musicians and botanists as well. They visit the sites slowly and quietly and console themselves for the inconvenience of inns by polishing their shoes, playing the flute and collecting botanic specimens. Solemn as the English, they lack the latters' ostentatiousness and wealth and are as unobtrusive as they are taciturn. They pass unnoticed and disturb no one either with their pleasures or their pastimes.

As to the French, it must be admitted that we know how to travel less than any nation in Europe. We are devoured by impatience, transported by admiration; our senses are lively and perceptive, but we are discouraged at the slightest impediment. Although our home, in general, can hardly be called comfortable, it has a kind of presence that haunts us to the ends of the earth, making us cantankerous, reluctant to put up with hardships or fatigue and filling us with the silliest and most pointless nostalgia. With as little foresight as the Italians, we lack their physical resistance to the ill-consequences of our blunders. We are, on a journey as at war, keen at first and demoralized when routed. Anyone observing a party of French tourists setting off on a steep Swiss ascent may well laugh at all the spontaneous merriment, the foolhardy sprinting on the ravines, the playful haste, all that waste of energy and strength squandered in advance on the wayside, and the attention vainly lavished on the first things they come across. He can be sure that before an hour is up everybody in the party will have exhausted every possible means of tiring themselves out physically and morally, and that towards evening they will arrive straggling, unhappy, harassed, barely managing to crawl to the inn after having bestowed on the sights that were worthy of note nothing but an absent-minded and weary glance.

Now, all this isn't as futile as you may think. A journey, as has often been said, is an epitome of human life. The manner in which individuals of different nationalities travel is a means of knowing both the nation and the individual; the art of travelling is more or less a science of life.

I pride myself in possessing this science of travelling; but how dearly I've paid for it! I wouldn't want anyone to achieve it at such a price, and I can say as much for all that goes to make up my baggage of acquired wisdom and instinctive habits.

But if I know how to travel without getting bored or dissatisfied, I don't pride myself in walking without getting tired, or in being rained upon without getting wet. No Frenchman can get hold of enough of the British fluid to be entirely weatherproof. My friends are in the same state, so that all the way our dress has been the subject of gossip and scorn from the insulated tourists. Yet how rewarding it is to throw oneself down to rest on the moss as soon as one feels like it, to get smoke-blackened in wayside huts, to venture along difficult ways without the assistance of mules or guides, to chase through boggy meadows after a white-winged Apollo with purple markings, to pursue through every thicket one's dreams – that are swifter and lovelier than all the butterflies in the world! – even at the risk of arriving at night in full view of the English guests sunburnt, dishevelled, dusty, muddy and ragged, and being taken for a pedlar!

Apart from that, our stock in Chamonix went up a little because of the Major's appearance in Federal uniform[19] as well as the arrival of the legitimist. Their perfect manners, added to Arabella's dignified beauty, silenced them, even if it did not restore confidence around us. I suspect none the less that the cutlery was counted three times over that night and I, for my part, heard my neighbours, Mrs — and Milady —, two youthful dowagers of fifty and sixty, barricade their bedroom doors as if they expected a Cossack invasion.

'Don't you think,' said the Major, 'that a whole region that has become a guest house for all the other nations cannot preserve its own national identity?'

'Yet mightn't I say the same of your Switzerland?' I replied.

'Alas, who could stop you?' he answered.

'Your Switzerland,' said Franz, 'that puts on such lofty airs but where several thousand English are allowed to indulge their idleness while its doors are closed to refugees! That republic which joins the monarchies in hunting down the martyrs of the republican cause as if they were wild beasts!'

The beating of a drum interrupted us.

'What's that martial noise?' asked Arabella.

'It's the frost setting in and the town crier warning the valley dwellers so that they can light fires near the potatoes.'

The potato is the only source of wealth in this part of the Savoy.

The peasants believe that by establishing a layer of smoke over the middle section of the mountain-side they will intercept the cold air from the upper regions and protect the bottom of the valley from its grip. I don't know if they are right. Were I travelling at the expense of some government, some scientific society or even some journal I'd find that out, and other things too, about which there's a strong chance that I shall never know any more than most of those so-called experts who discuss and pronounce upon such things. What I do know is that this barrier of fires set like signals all along the ravine, provided a magnificent spectacle in the middle of the night. They pierced with crimson stains and columns of black smoke the curtain of silvery mist in which the valley was totally shrouded and lost. Above the fires, above the smoke and the haze, the range of Mont Blanc exhibited one of its last granite strata, black as ink and crowned in snow. This incredible panorama appeared to be floating in the void. Over a few summits, swept clear by the wind, great stars shone in a clear chill sky. These mountain peaks, lifting a dark, compacted horizon up to the skies, made the stars seem brighter. Taurus's blood-shot eye, fierce Aldebaran, rose above a dark spire that looked like the crater of a volcano from which this infernal spark had just shot. A little further Fomalhaut, that pure and melancholy star with its blue tinge, was settling over a white summit like a compassionate, merciful tear falling from the sky on to the poor valley, but about to be seized on its way by the spiteful spirit of the glaciers.

Mightily pleased with myself for having found these two metaphors, I closed the window. But seeking my bed, whose exact location I'd lost in the dark, I bumped my head against a corner of the wall. This put me off making metaphors throughout the following days. My friends were kind enough to say they felt singularly deprived.

The most beautiful thing I saw in Chamonix was my daughter. You can't imagine how self-assured and spirited this eight-year-old belle was, running wild in the mountains. The child Diana must have been like this when, before she was able to hunt the wild boar in fearsome Erymanthus, she played with young fauns on the pleasant slopes of Hybla. Solange's fair complexion defies weather and sun. Her open shirt reveals her sturdy chest whose immaculate whiteness nothing can tarnish. Her long blonde hair floats in loose ringlets down to her strong, supple loins that nothing wearies, neither the short, sharp pace of the mules, nor races up the steep, slippery slopes, nor the rocky gradients we have to climb for hours at a time. Always solemn and fearless, her cheeks blush with pride and vexation if we try to give her a hand. Strong as a mountain cedar and fresh as a flower of the valleys, she seems to guess, though as yet she is unaware of the value of the intellect, that God's finger has marked her brow and that she is fated, one day, to dominate by moral force those whose physical strength now protects her. At the glacier of the Bossons she said to me: 'Don't worry, George dear, when I'm queen I'll give you the whole of Mont Blanc.'

Her brother, though five years older, is less sturdy and less daring. Gentle and mild, he instinctively recognizes and admires her superiority; but he knows, too, that kindness is a gift. 'You'll be proud of *her*,' he often says to me, 'but I'll make you happy.'[20]

Throughout life our children are an eternal worry and eternal joy, tyrannical flatterers, avid for every pleasure and skilled at obtaining them either by persuasion or obstinacy; undisguised egotists, instinctively aware of their legitimate right to independence, they are our masters, however firm we try to be with them. Despite their natural goodness mine are among the most high-spirited and troublesome; and I confess that I can find no way of making them yield to social conventions before they run up against society's marble walls and iron barriers. I rack my brains in vain to find a good reason to give to a soul, fresh from the hand of God and enjoying its unfettered integrity, for accepting such useless and senseless constraints. Without habits which I don't have and a charlatanism I can't and won't adopt I don't see how I could dare to ask my children to acknowledge the so-called need for these absurd trammels. So I've no choice but authority: and I use it when necessary, that is, very rarely; it's something I'd be wary of recommending to anyone who isn't sure of being loved as much as he's feared.

I'm very fond of systems but not of their enforcement. I like the Saint-Simonian faith, I've the utmost respect for Fourier's[21] system; I venerate those who, in this cursed century, have submitted to no pernicious influence and have retreated into a life of contemplation and enquiry to dream up some means of saving mankind. But I believe that we can achieve more with a little positive virtue accompanied by a certain amount of energy than with all the wisdom of nations spun out in books. This comes into my head, not in connection with my children's education, but rather with that of the human race about which Franz was holding forth on the back of his mule, as we were crossing the heights of Tête Noire. And I, on foot, tugging at the bridle of my daughter's mule to coax it down the steep tiers of rock, prattled on at random. I was being taken to task for having shown no inclination for philosophy during our stay at Chamonix. The Major is knowledgeable; Franz is interested in learning; Arabella understands everything in a flash. But I am lazy, careless and as proud of my ignorance as a savage. I was easy prey for the three of them who had all the jargon of German philosophy at their fingertips. I defended myself heatedly and I think none of us understood each other. At first I suspected the Major of trying to catch me out so as to look down on me from the height of his wisdom and pass judgement on the poverty of my intellect. I was in no hurry, as you can imagine, to let him finger all the phrenological bumps and hollows with which nature has endowed me. I only like to talk about myself to people I like and, although I found the Major extremely witty (perhaps even precisely because of that), I felt a secret mistrust of him.

Without a doubt I was quite wrong. In the course of our journey I realized that he was as kind as he was clever; and his mind, which I thought so cold and complacent, is more poetic than mine; I noted this with great shame and great pleasure.

However, considering him to be a bit of a pedant, I was rude to him and mocking for the whole day. In order to be contradictory, I belittled all the fine things he knew and vandalized his metaphysics. He judged me to be more stupid than I am, for which I had cause to rejoice, since from then on he began to feel more friendly towards me and stopped investigating my brain with his microscope in order to discover the satanic revelations which he expected. He saw that I was a pleasant enough fellow, not all that bright and more in the nature of a mayfly than a devil.

Indeed, if he had the better of me in many ways, I maintain that I was not mistaken in what I wanted to demonstrate. My error simply consisted in wanting to combat theories I gratuitously supposed were his, and, in order to refute a show of false, shallow scholarship that I wrongly attributed to him, I made a case against all scholarship, all method and all theory. I believe – may God forgive me for it – that I would have slandered my beloved Jean-Jacques himself had the Major stood up for him. But luckily for me he didn't mention him and I, up to the neck in my dear master's primitivism, held forth, rather less eloquently than he did, against the abuse of learning and the absurdities of an empty philosophy. That's where I was in the right: I loathe philosophies which are profound, arduous, involved and barbarous wherein our minds drown and our hearts wither; those frigid Teutonic metaphysics which analyse the human soul and dissect the mysteries of the Divinity within us, without trying to awaken a generous thought in our hearts or to produce in them a truly religious, truly human emotion. And so I refuted all the eclectic doctors by whom I believed the Major to be infatuated. I clung to facts, to a clear logic and an ardent praxis, to republican principles, to the generosity of French blood, in a word to France – which this Swiss, with his German metaphysics at the ready, seemed to despise. In my endeavour to express all this I talked a lot of nonsense: the wily Major egged me on by calling me a Jacobin; and I, hotheaded child of Paris that I am, was loath to deny my forbears, the sons of our ancestor Rousseau. The discussion was too animated for me to think of making any reservations. It seemed to me that it would have been cowardice not to condone the mistakes, blunders and excesses of 1793 in front of an adversary who feigned to hold our philosophical eighteenth-century France responsible for them; thus as one thing led to another, I got so carried away that I would have been capable of sending to the guillotine the Major, Puzzi, my daughter's doll which rode pillion behind her, and even the mule they were sharing.

Then all of a sudden I realized that the Major, bored or disgusted by my dishonesty, had ceased to listen to me. His head was bent over his book, and in the midst of all this outstanding beauty he had eyes and thought for nothing but a philosophical treatise he'd just taken from his pocket. I did not hesitate to taunt him about it.

'Shut up!' he said. 'You go through life observing the superficial colour, shape and appearance of everything, and you don't know or want to know the cause of anything. You've carefully studied all the mountains from Chamonix to here, haven't you? You've counted the fir trees and you could reproduce in your mind's eye the exact contour of the ranges, just as a map-maker traces from memory the curves of the Saône on a sheet of paper. During that time I've been seeking for the principle of the universe.'

'And you've found it, Major? Please let us share in it.'

'You're an impudent fellow,' he said. 'I've found nothing at all; but

I've thought about the universal principle and, as a subject for meditation, it's worth more than the act of staring up at the sky without thinking about anything.'

Then, spurring on his mule he left us behind, still squinting down at his book and muttering under his breath a sentence he'd just read and which was apparently not quite clear to him: *The absolute is identical with itself.*[22]

'By the time we reach Martigny at eleven o'clock this evening,' I ventured to suggest, 'he'll probably have discovered twenty-three thousand ways of interpreting those six words. Obviously nobody could be cheerful with such problems to solve.'

'You are both equally at fault to jeer at each other,' said the sage Arabella. 'Anyone who indulges his own fancies without worrying about other people's opinion is a wise man. There's one thing more stupid than the indifference of ordinary people to the beauties of nature; that's forced enthusiasm, endless exclamations. If the Major isn't in an artistic frame of mind this morning, he shows more good sense and wisdom by letting himself be totally absorbed than by trying in vain to revive his dormant enthusiasm.'

'Besides,' Franz added, 'I don't know what right we have to despise his indifference to the landscape; for we've done nothing but wrangle since we set out. As for Doctor Puzzi, he's solemnly catching grasshoppers along the hedgerows, which isn't much more poetic.'

Towards the end of the day we found ourselves on the highest pass of the mountain and assaulted by an icy wind that blew the sleet in our faces. Bent double over our mules we buried our noses in our cloaks. The Major was impassive and engrossed in his absolute. Ten minutes and a quarter of a league lower down we entered a temperate zone and the gorges of the Valais opened out at our feet, crowned with violet summits and divided by the Rhone as by a silver ribbon. Night was upon us before we had crossed at a gallop the belt of grassy meadows intersected by innumerable streams that leads to Martigny. A large hole in my boot compelled me to get onto the Major's mule and ride pillion behind him and his absolute. He didn't miss the chance of teaching me a lesson.

'Systems,' he said, 'are not quite as despicable as people would have us believe who are incapable of following the simplest argument for a quarter of an hour and of understanding the most lucid theories. Habits of the mind that enable us to take in at a glance every aspect of an idea are excellent; and when we have succeeded in grasping without effort and comparing clearly and soberly all the moral and philosophical data current in the intellectual world, I consider that we are at least as able to judge our times as when we cross our arms saying: All that is obscure is unintelligible, all that is difficult is unattainable.'

'Well said, Major! Down with obscurantists!' cried the company in one voice.

I wasn't happy, especially since the mule's pace was uneven and the infernal Major dug in his spurs at each sentence, which shook me up violently. I was heartily tempted to push him into the first ditch and to carry on without him; but I was afraid he might retaliate with some more subtle mischief; and since I have the misfortune to be very heavy-handed with my jokes, I accepted my lot while awaiting a better chance. Kind-hearted Arabella, noticing my discomfiture, generously stood up for me.

'If all you have found in learning is the satisfaction and pleasure of being able to judge your times,' she told the Major, 'that's not much help for the rest of us. It's not only intelligence men need, but love and action. That's probably what Piffoël[23] has been trying to prove in his ravings during the last three hours; and that's what the Major pretends not to understand, though he's as well aware of it as we are.'

'No, no!' I exclaimed crossly. 'He's only aware of the contrary. Since the Major is learned, what does he care about the sufferings and humiliations of simple ignorant folk? If the Major has affinities with people of lofty character all the better for him and for them but the world gets no comfort from it and common mortals no relief. Find if you can a means of expressing your knowledge in a clear, terse text! And when you have founded a nation on this you'll be free to write thirty volumes of statutes for it. Till then you are no more than Brahmins, you hide the truth at the bottom of a well, and your mysteries are so complex, your premises so smothered in hieroglyphics that even your oldest disciples can barely expound them. Unless you take the bull by the horns and expose all the risk and suffering that a great expiatory crisis involves, your riddles can only provoke laughter, and on many counts you amply deserve the accusations of hypocrisy that are levelled at you. That's why all your learned baggage does nobody any good; that's why we know nothing or, when we presume to examine and interpret it, we become utterly confused.'

'And yet,' said Franz, 'you can be sure that the world's future is to be found in everything. All the different elements of renewal will unite some day to constitute an impressive whole. Oh no! So many scattered endeavours can't return to darkness; so many noble aspirations, so many generous impulses can't be stifled by the implacable indifference of fate. What do the errors, the flaws and the dissensions of the champions of truth really matter? Today they struggle separately and are afflicted despite themselves by the chaos and the intolerant vanity of this century. They can't rise above the contaminated atmosphere. Lost in a wild confusion they fail to recognize each other; they flee from or attack each other instead of gathering under one flag and acknowledging the leadership of the strongest and purest among them. They waste their strength in partial actions, in negligible skirmishes. This exhausted generation must pass away and disappear like a winter torrent. It must carry with it our prophetic lamentations, our indignation and our tears. In its wake fresh and better disciplined troops, wise from our reverses, will pick up our arms, scattered over the battlefield, and discover the magic virtue of the arrows of Hercules.'

'My dear Franz, let us embrace, and may God hear you!' I cried, jumping down from my mule. 'For a musician you talk and reason tolerably well!'

The Major concealed a smile, looking at us with a paternal eye. His heart warmed to our outburst of hope, and I began to see him as less diabolical than it had been my fancy to suppose him.

At that point, a grumpy maidservant opened the doors of the Hôtel Grande Maison at Martigny.

'There's no reason to pull a face,' Franz, who was in a lively, bellicose mood, told her point blank.

She very nearly threw her candlestick at him. Ursula began to sob. 'What's the matter?' I asked her. 'Alas!' she replied, 'I knew you would take me to the other end of the world! Here we are in Martinique! We'll have to cross the sea to get back home; they were right when they told me you wouldn't stop at Switzerland!' 'My dear woman,' I said. 'Set your mind at rest and pat yourself on the back. The first because you are in Martigny, Switzerland and not in Martinique. The second because you are as good at geography as Shakespeare was.'

She seemed flattered by this last remark. Franz gave orders to the servants that the party should be wakened at six in the morning. We threw ourselves on our beds, utterly worn out. I'd done most of the trip on foot, about eight leagues. The Major was well aware of this and he had a surprise in store for me. He shut himself up with his treatise on the absolute and with Puzzi whom he cuffed to stop him from snoring; and all through the night he sought the true meaning of that terrible sentence: *The absolute is identical with itself*.

By four o'clock in the morning, having found none to his total satisfaction, his satanic bad temper flared up and he came and made a tremendous din outside my door. I woke up, got dressed in all haste, packed my bags and began to rush around the house, bustling, rubbing my eyes, fighting against exhaustion and afraid of being late. Profound silence reigned everywhere; I was just thinking that the party must have left without me when the Major emerged from his room in his night-cap, yawning:

'What's wrong with you?' he asked with a ferocious smile. 'Why are you up so early? You make a very trying travelling companion. Do keep quiet, we still have an hour to sleep.'

'*Damned* Major!' I shouted angrily.

And the epithet[24] stuck – though it's much too expressive for me to allow my pen to trace it here. It's a synonym for anointed; and, since speech is eminently logical, when it's placed after the noun it denotes sublimity.

Fribourg

We entered the church of Saint-Nicholas to hear the finest organ that has ever been built. Arabella, who is accustomed to sublime achievements, and whose soul is lofty, exacting and imperious[25] towards God and man, seated herself haughtily on the edge of the balustrade and, letting her gravely contemplative gaze wander across the lower nave, waited, and waited in vain for the heavenly voices that echo in her heart but whose resonances no mortal voice, no instrument made by mortal hands can ever convey to her ears. Her heavy golden locks uncurled by the rain fell over her white hand; and her eyes, in which the blue of the sky mirrored its fairest shade, questioned human capability at each note that emerged from the huge instrument. 'It's not what I'd expected,' she stated simply, without realizing the implications of her words. – 'You're hard to please!' I retorted. 'The glacier wasn't white enough for your taste the other day in the mountains! Its great summit that might have been hewn from the flanks of Paros, its sharp needles, beside which we look like pygmies, you didn't find worthy of your proud gaze. The voice of torrents, according to you, is dull and monotonous; you marvel no more at the height of fir trees than at that of the reeds by the river bank. You measure the heavens and the earth. You require the palm trees of sweet Araby on the top of Mont Blanc and the crocodiles of the Nile in the Reichenbach's[26] foam. You'd like to see Cleopatra's fleet on the motionless waves of the Mer de Glace. So what planet have you come from, you who despise the world we live in? And now you won't be content till that sullen old man who is staring at you in amazement has discovered some power under his wig rather greater than God's to satisfy you!'

For Mooser,[27] the aged instrument-maker who had built the great organ, a man as mysterious, mournful and surly as Hoffmann's man with the black dog and the macaroons,[28] was standing at the far end of the gallery and looking at us gloomily and suspiciously. A peculiar man if ever there was one, resolutely Swiss, who didn't appear to find at all to his taste the simple, sublime tune our great musician was attempting on the organ. To tell the truth, he wasn't making the most of the mechanism. He was simply in quest of the purest possible sounds and omitted to entertain us with even the smallest thunder-clap. Also the cathedral organist (a plump, rosy-cheeked young man, a colleague of our friend, well-known to him and slightly patronizing) kept pushing him gently aside and, finally, taking his place unceremoniously, tried to demonstrate by sheer muscle-power, the admittedly impressive potential of musical charlatanism. He toiled so hard with his hands and his feet, his elbows, wrists and, I believe, knees (remaining perfectly phlegmatic and gentle the while) that we enjoyed a complete storm, rain, wind, hail, distant shouts, dogs in distress, travellers' prayers, calamity in the cottage, wailing of terrified children, tinkling of stray cow-bells, crash of thunder, creaking of fir trees, and *finale*: total destruction of the potato crops!

As for me, simple peasant that I am, artist or rather unskilled labourer, enraptured by the harmonious din and recognizing in this slapdash canvas scenes from my rustic life, I went up to the Fribourg maestro and exclaimed effusively:

'Monsieur, that was magnificent. Please let me hear that thunder-clap again! But I do believe that if you were to sit down abruptly on the keyboard you'd produce an even more all-embracing impression!'

The Maestro looked at me in surprise; he didn't know a word of French and to my great regret, my friends refused to translate my request into German on the pretext that it was improper. So once again in my life I had to resign myself to having my desires unfulfilled!

But old Mooser had remained impassive throughout the storm. Upright in a corner like some stiff, angular, medieval sculpture, scarcely even at the very climax of the tempest did an imperceptible smile of satisfaction flit across his lips. True, apart from myself, the whole party had been brutally insensitive to rain, thunder, cow-bells, stray cows, etc . . . I even thought that such a lack of appreciation concerning the pulmonary powers of his instrument had wounded him deeply; but the verger soon revealed the real cause of his preoccupation. Mooser is dissatisfied with his creation – and I swear this is unjustified, since even if he hasn't yet achieved perfection, at least he's made something which, of its kind, is the closest there is to perfection. But like every great expert the good man has his foibles. Thunderstorms, it would seem, constitute his ideal. A sublime hobby-horse indeed and worthy of Ossian himself! But not easy to tame, and always ready to escape through some loophole just as the patient artist thinks he's curbed it. Just think! The voices of the winds in all their auditory forms have been captured by the organ's mechanisms as Eolus and his numerous descendants were entrapped in Ulysses' water-skins;[29] only the lightning, the rebellious, unrealizable lightning, the lightning which is neither sound nor noise and which Mooser, none the less, wants to express in some sound or noise, is absent from Mooser's thunderstorm. Here then is a man who will die without having realized the impossible and who will not enjoy his fame for the lack of a flash of lightning in music. I think you ought to have pitied him, Arabella, rather than mocked him; this man's madness is not unrelated to the holy malady that devours you.

After having explained Mooser's dream to us very solemnly and without the slightest doubt as to its realization (for he even tried to make us hear, by a sort of whistle, the sound of *light*) the verger took us inside the flanks of the huge instrument. All those human voices, those trumpets, that orchestra of imaginary musicians imprisoned in tin tubes, made us think of those Genii of Arabian tales, condemned by superior powers to moan and groan in sealed metal chests.

We had been told that Mooser had been summoned to Paris to build the organ at the Madeleine; but the verger informed us that the project had come to nothing. The French government, less generous than a Swiss canton, was probably scared at the thought of having to pay a suitable price for a first-rate job. Yet obviously Mooser is the only person capable of filling the vast nave of the Madeleine with the great clamour of prayer set to music and only there could he ever display all the resources of his knowledge. Thus the monument and the artisan call out for each other.

It was only when Franz let his hands run freely over the keyboard and played us a fragment of Mozart's Dies Irae that we realized the extent to which the Fribourg organ surpasses anything we know of the kind. Already the previous day we had heard the organ of the little township of Bulle, which is also the work of Mooser, and had been enchanted by the quality of the sound; but the improvements in that of Fribourg are notable, especially the effects of the human voice which, piercing through the bass chords, completely deceived our children. We could have told them some fine tales about this invisible choir of maidens; but we were all engrossed by the Dies Irae's austere notes. Never had Franz's Florentine profile appeared more pale and pure, in a darker cloud of mystical terrors and religious sadness. There was a certain harmonic combination that kept recurring under his fingers and whose every note was expressed in my mind by the harsh words of the funeral hymn:

> *Quantus tremor est futurus*
> *Quando judex est venturus*, etc . . .[30]

I don't know whether these words corresponded, in the mind of the master, with the notes I assigned to them, but no human power could remove from my ears those terrible syllables, *quantus tremor* . . .

And all at once, instead of depressing me, this threat of judgement seemed to me like a promise that made my heart beat faster with an unknown bliss. A confidence, an infinite serenity assured me that eternal justice would not destroy me; that I would, together with all those who are oppressed, pass unnoticed, perhaps forgiven, under the great harrow of the Last Judgement; that only the powerful and the mighty of this world would be ground to dust before the countless victims of their assumed rights. The *Lex Talionis*, the law of retaliation, reserved for God alone by the apostles of Christian charity and solemnized by so grave and sweeping a hymn, didn't seem to me to be too frivolous an activity for celestial power when I remembered that the crimes thus punished were the degradation and servitude of the human race. Oh yes! I said to myself while the divine anger rumbled above my head in thunderous notes, fear will be the portion of those who didn't fear God and offended him in the noblest of his handiworks! of those who violated the sanctuary of our consciences, of those who put their brothers' hands in irons, who darkened their eyes with clouds of ignorance! of those who declared that the slavery of nations is of divine institution and that an angel brought down from heaven the poison which marks the brow of monarchs with madness or folly; of those who traffic in human beings and sell their flesh to the dragon of the Apocalypse – of all those, the portion will be dread, and to them the reign of terror will come.

I was in the thrall of one of those fits of vitality such as fine music or a good wine can induce, a state of inner excitement where the long benumbed soul seems to grow like a torrent about to burst its sheath of winter ice, when turning, I noticed on the face of Arabella an angelic expression of compassion and piety; no doubt she had been moved by strains more suited to her temperament. In a work of art the different combinations of sounds, lines or colours set secret codes within us vibrating and reveal mysterious connections between each individual and the outside world. Where I had evoked a war-like God's vengeance, she had gently bowed her head, well aware that the Angel of Revenge would leave her unscathed, and she has been moved by a sweeter, more touching passage, perhaps by something like:

Recordare Jesu pie . . .[31]

During this time clouds were covering the sky and the rain beating against the window-panes; then the sun reappeared, pale and slanting, to be extinguished a few minutes later by another shower. These sudden shifts of light made the neat white cathedral of Fribourg seem even brighter than usual, and the figure of King David, painted in the costume of a character from a play by Pradon,[32] with a black wig and red Morocco-leather ankle boots, appeared to smile and to be about to dance once again before the Ark. And in the meantime the organ thundered like the voice of mighty God and the composer's inspiration caused the whole of Dante's Inferno and Purgatory to soar upwards under the narrow arches, with their ribs painted pink and grey.

The children, stretched out on the floor like puppies, were dropping off to sleep and dreaming of fairies on the gallery steps; Mooser was sulking and the verger was asking the Major for our names and qualifications. At each of our mischievous guide's ambiguous replies the worthy and magisterial inquisitor glanced at us, now in disbelief, now in wonder.

'My word!' he said, detecting from afar Arabella's lovely, distinctive brow. 'So that's a Parisian lady? And what next . . . ?'

'What next?' retorted the Major, pointing at me. 'That fellow in a soaking wet smock and muddy gaiters, with two kids at his feet? Well he's . . . they are three of the pianist's pupils.'

'Indeed? And he takes them around with him?'

'It's one of his foibles to drag his school around with him. He teaches his theories very seriously from cliff-tops and on the back of a mule.'

'It's true,' said the discerning magistrate of the city of Fribourg, 'that they all wear their hair long and falling about their shoulders as he does; but,' he added, fixing his enquiring gaze on the equivocal person of Puzzi, 'what's that?'

'A famous Italian prima donna who follows him incognito.'

'Oh ho!' cried the simple fellow, with a truly cunning smile. 'I knew at once that one was a woman! . . .'

Then all at once the great organ's lungs were gasping for breath, its voice faded away and it gave a last sigh under Franz's hands. The first stroke of Vespers had just chimed and the spirit of Mozart himself might have pleaded in vain with the organ blower that he put off for a single minute his snuffling singsong recital. I felt like going and giving him a good beating and I thought of you, gentle Theodor, playful Kreissler, Hoffmann[33] – bitter and charming Hoffmann! Ironic and tender poet, the spoilt child of all the Muses, romancer, painter and musician, botanist, entomologist, mechanist, chemist and something of a wizard! It was in the midst of the fleeting scenes of your artist's life, when you were prey to the cruel and comical struggles into which you were drawn by your love of beauty and faith in a sublime ideal, and when you were at odds with the callousness or bad taste of the bourgeoisie, it was then (while you worshipped the one and cursed the other) that life came home to you as being sometimes deliciously happy, sometimes ravaged with cares, but most often farcical; – a conclusion which owed much to your courage, to your philosophy, and, I'm afraid, to your intemperance.

But, farewell, my dear old friend; that's digression enough to last a fortnight. I leave you to set out for Geneva.

My tender love and hearty handshakes to our Parisian friends.

★

Letter Eleven

★

To Giacomo Meyerbeer[1]

Geneva, September 1836

Carissimo Maestro,

You gave me leave to write to you from Geneva, and I venture to avail myself of this permission since I am well aware that you will never be accused of *camaraderie*[2] with a poor poet like me. That's why I'll fly in the face of convention and tell you how much I admire you, without fear of offending your modesty. I'm no dispenser of fame; where art is concerned I am an insignificant novice whose enthusiasm masters can accept with a smile.

Therefore I'll tell you about a day in my travels, a day that began in a church where I thought of no one but you and ended in a theatre where I spoke of no one but you. To avoid boring you with personal details I'll give you a summary of my musings and of my encounters.

I went into the Protestant church and listened to the canticles, the noble anthems, the simple and valiant hymns, half-martial and half-mystical, sacred relics from the heroic days of a faith already as old and as waning as our own.

Were I to judge the Protestant faith by the sermon I heard and Protestants by the unremarkable people who barely filled one corner of the church, I would be entitled to heap arrogant scorn on this religious concept, its rites and its followers; but since this is the trend nowadays I shall forbear to do so, being ever wary of things that are in fashion and of fashionable literature in particular. This miserable generation is so shortsighted that in thought as in vision it dwells constantly on the present; it judges men of all times by the ailing men of today; it has an answer for every problem, considers servitude to be our natural human condition, indifference to be our permanent disposition, weakness and selfishness our inevitable characteristics, our inescapable shortcomings. It no longer believes in great men or great matters, and the reason for this is obvious.

Those who have arranged their lives so as to avoid the solemn trivialities and pedantic vexations which are the main intellectual fare of the times are still able to admire the past and are therefore more lenient towards the present; since they know what yesterday was like they can tell what tomorrow could be; neither the immediate present nor the age in which they live offer any absolute truth about the progress or regression of mankind.

Contemporary men (as they are now called) who see Calvinist and Catholic churches equally empty and Protestants making as light of their faith as we do, infer that the Reformation was, from the start, the dullest thing in the world and the religious form this concept adopted, the meanest and dryest of all. Owing to a very odd reaction, which the quirks of fashion alone can explain (since from the relatively recent days of Benjamin Constant there was nothing but praise on all sides for the Reformation and distaste or blame for Catholicism) the entire *writing* and *ranting* generation has espoused a latter-day orthodoxy, curiously blended with an inveterate atheism and a magnificent disdain for Christian observance. Even some of the mildest men of letters who were appalled by the savage reprisals of '93 have, I am told, casually composed (between a visit to the Comic Opera and an ice at Tortoni's) such innocent declarations as this one: 'The massacre of Saint Bartholomew's Day was quite simply a great and wise measure of *high diplomacy* without which the throne and the altar would have become the prey of factions.' So long as things are seen from *above* there are neither murderers nor victims in the massacre of the Huguenots, but a war of legitimate defence, provoked by dangerous conspiracies against the security of the State, etc., etc.

The words *factions* and *security of the State* have been admirably exploited for as long as oppressors and oppressed have existed. Every time the possibility of salvation has dared to enter the minds of the latter the former have set themselves up as defenders of their own rights and privileges under the pompous name of governmental inviolability and public security. Whenever a power is threatened it remembers the shopkeepers whose riot broke a few windows, and it sends the liberators of human intelligence to the scaffold lest they disturb the sleep of the City's venerable burghers.

Our generation, which was once sufficiently strong and proud to

276

get rid of the Jesuits in the person of Charles X, isn't very consistent in my view when it scorns every brave attempt at reform and insults Luther's great name in his religious successors. Which of us was not touched by *faction* in 1830? Didn't the dynasty of Charles X stand for the *security of the State* also? Wasn't it necessary – in order to achieve, to a certain extent and in a certain sense, the rehabilitation of an entire nation, in order to shake off the yoke of unspeakable privileges and hasten imperceptibly the slow but inevitable institution of popular justice – wasn't it necessary, I repeat, to break a great many windows and disturb a great many slumbers? I hope, furthermore, that all the slogans at the service of monarchic charlatanism have lost any significance they may once have possessed, and that those who use them cannot look each other in the face without smiling.

I might acknowledge the rationality and wisdom of our new-born Catholics when they assert, as they do, that they ostracize all bad priests and dissolute monks and ascribe to them all the discredit into which their beloved orthodoxy has fallen, if only they didn't heap ever harsher curses and deadlier scorn on those who purify the gospel. But their logic is at fault when they attack Luther's reform with such violence and then claim to be the new reformers, the perfect Christians.

If convents and benefices were reinstated they would be the first to protest and to play Luther and Calvin all over again, without bothering to notice that the idea wasn't a new one and that the way towards a just reform has already been trodden by nobler and surer steps than theirs. I'd very much like to know whether these stalwart supporters of the Catholic faith condemn the measures taken by the National Assembly concerning church property. On the contrary, I suspect that they find them very much to their liking and would be none too happy to see abbeys and monasteries re-consecrated at the expense of the farm-steads their parents established, forty years ago, on the ruins of these properties which were so easily acquired and so lucratively exploited – so nice to snatch, in a word, and so nice to hold on to. If they despise Luther and Calvin for having waged war against wealthy ecclesiastics in the interests of Christian perfection and not for the benefit of a new clergy, I would advise them to refrain from boasting about it and to keep their own national properties, without slandering the memory of those who were the first to dare to preach the poverty, chastity and humility of their divine master to the followers of Jesus, and who paved the way for what has already befallen the Catholic clergy in France and is now happening in Spain. The overt hypocrisy of those who attack them would be horrifying if their puerility, their infatuation with the first paradox that occurs to them, their apish dispositions, their total absence of reasoning power didn't make them ridiculous.

Having taken up my stance on these fundamental questions, I had no hesitation in entering the Geneva church and listening with great indulgence to a sermon delivered by a gentleman of very fine appearance whose name I am sincerely thankful, for that very reason, to have forgotten. He informed us that if industry is flourishing in Switzerland it's because Geneva is Protestant (leaving us freedom to believe that if industry is flourishing in France, it's because we're Catholic). He told us further that God invariably sends wealth to pious men, which I found neither wholly convincing nor entirely consistent with the spirit of the Gospels; then, further, that if the congregation lacked fervour the price of goods might well drop, commerce go to the dogs and the burghers be forced to drink inferior wines and smoke stale tobacco. I believe he may even have added that the mountains and the beautiful lake which Providence has bestowed on the Protestants of Geneva might be destroyed by a divine decree if they didn't attend the holy service more assiduously. The congregation withdrew well satisfied after singing the canticles, and I was left alone in the church.

When the nave had been cleared of those impassive individuals on whose brow Lavater might have inscribed the one word *correctitude*, when the snuffling preacher had ceased to deliver his paternally prosaic remonstrances, then the Reformation, that unadorned, powerful concept which has neither veils nor mysterious ornaments, presented itself to me in all its grandeur and nakedness. This church without side chapels or sanctum, its clear windows lit up by brilliant sunshine, its wooden pews where equality reigns (at least during prayers), its cold bare walls, all that aspect of orderliness which seemed to have settled overnight on the wreck of a Catholic church like the chill aftermath of an entirely military take-over, overwhelmed me with respect and sadness. Here and there some faces of a pelican or a chimera, relics of the former cult, twined apologetic and captive around the capital of the columns. The great arches were neither Papist nor Huguenot. High and deep, they seemed to have been built to receive every form of aspiration towards heaven, to respond to all the rhythms of prayer and religious invocation. From stone floors that no Protestant knee ever warms, solemn voices seemed to resound, the tones of a calm, secure triumph and the expiring sighs and murmurings of a tranquil end, resigned, confident, without death-rattle or lamentation. It was the voice of Calvinist martyrdom, a martyrdom without ecstasy or delirium, a torment where suffering is stifled by austere pride and august certainty.

These imaginary hymns naturally assumed in my mind the form of that fine canticle in your opera, *The Huguenots*; and, while I dreamt I heard the cries of Catholic indignation and a sharp volley of musketry outside, a tall figure passed before my eyes, one of the noblest dramatic figures, one of the loveliest personifications of the idea of faith that art has ever produced in our time: Meyerbeer's Marcel.[3]

And I saw that bronze statue standing clothed in buffalo hide, quickened by the divine fire the composer had brought down upon him. I saw him, Maestro, forgive me my presumption, just as he must have appeared to you when you sought him at the uncompromising and steadfast hour of noon under the glowing arches of some Protestant church, vast and luminous as this one. Though you are a musician, you are more a poet than any of us! In what secret recess of your soul, in what hidden treasury of your mind did you find those clear, pure features, that concept, simple as antiquity, true as history, lucid as conscience, strong as faith? It was not long ago that you were on your knees in the sensuous darkness of Saint Mark's, constructing your Sicilian cathedral[4] on a still vaster scale, smothering yourself in Catholic incense at that dark hour when tapers are lit, making the gold and marble walls sparkle until you were overcome and bowed down by the tender and terrible ecstasies of that holy place. How then was it, when you entered the church of Luther, that you were able to evoke its austere poetry, revive its heroic dead? — We thought your soul was unquiet and timid like Dante's when, drawn by his own genius into hell and paradise, he was horrified or moved to compassion at each step. It was as if you had fathomed the secret of the invisible choirs when, at the elevation of the Host, the angels in the mosaic of Titian move their great black wings against the golden background of the Byzantine dome and float above the kneeling congregation. You had pierced the impenetrable silence of the tombs and, beneath the vibrating paving stones of cathedrals, you had heard the bitter lamentation of the damned and the threats of the angels of darkness. You had grasped the hidden significance and sublime sorrow of all those strange and sombre allegories. Between the angel and the devil, between the fantastic heaven and hell of the Middle Ages, you had seen man divided against himself, torn between the flesh and the spirit, drawn towards the shadows of bestiality, yet protected by his quickening intellect and saved by divine hope. You had depicted these struggles, these fears and torments, these promises and raptures in solemn, touching strokes while leaving them cloaked in their poetic symbols and you had known how to touch and disturb us with chimerical characters and improbable situations. That is because a man's heart beats within the artist's, bearing the burning imprint of real life; it is because true art never creates anything insignificant and because the sanest philosophies and the sweetest human affections always preside over genius's most brilliant fancies.

But after that Catholic masterpiece, *Robert*, weren't we entitled to believe that all the inspiration and all the power of your German mind (that is to say, your conscientious and learned mind) had been awakened under the sky of Naples and Palermo? Aren't you a grave, profound Northerner set on fire by a Southern climate? All the charm of your music, all the pungency of your style, were reflected for me in your touchingly modest manner, in your conversation, so full of grace and shy animation, and in the kind of battle that your artistic fervour seems to wage against the somewhat apprehensive pride of a man of the world. Yet apart from the sublimity of that lofty inner *self*, concealed by convention and by a justifiable reticence, I wondered if you could long continue to treat science and poetry, Germany and Italy, Catholic pomp and Protestant solemnity at one and the same time; for there was already a certain amount of Protestantism in Bertram's[5] sombre, rebellious spirit which sometimes interrupts his cries of pain and rage to mock and scorn the credulous faith and the empty ceremonies that surround him. That fine contrast of audacious doubt and desperate courage with a mystical longing, an enraptured yearning for saints and angels, already denoted a combination of conflicting forces, a lively understanding of the fascination which religious thought and attitudes can exert on a man. Talking of *The Huguenots*, critics have said that there is no such thing as a Protestant music any more than there is a Catholic music; which amounts to saying that Lutheran hymns sung in Germany are no different in nature from the Gregorian chants of the Sistine chapel; as if music were only a skilful arrangement of sounds more or less successfully combined to appeal to the ear, and as if by simply adapting rhythm to the dramatic circumstance, the emotion and passion of lyrical drama can be adequately expressed! I confess that I don't understand, and I wonder if the main beauty of *William Tell*[6] doesn't reside in its Swiss pastoral character so admirably understood and so nobly interpreted.

But there's many another paradox published concerning you that I'd rack my brains in vain to comprehend. Until such mysteries are resolved I remain convinced that the most perfect of all arts has the ability to depict every shade of feeling and every phase of emotion. Apart from metaphysical disputations (which for my part I don't mind doing without) music can express everything. For describing natural scenes it possesses a range of abstract colours and forms that may not be precise or detailed but are thus all the more vaguely and delightfully poetic. More exquisite and vast than the most splendid of paintings, doesn't Beethoven's Pastoral Symphony open up enchanting perspectives to our imagination, an entire Engadine or Misnie valley, a whole earthly paradise where the spirit soars upwards leaving behind and discovering new limitless horizons; scenes where storms rage, where birds sing, where tempests arise, break and abate, where the sun drinks up the rain from the leaves, where the lark shakes the dew from its wings, where a bruised spirit expands, where a heavy heart is unburdened, where mind and body are revived and, merging with nature, relax in delight and repose?

When, in *Pré-aux-clercs*,[7] confused sounds fade into the distance and the curfew's melancholy strain is heard, listless as the time of day, fading like the light, is there any need of the Opera's red-painted curtain and a skilful sleight of hand with six lamps for the imagination to evoke the gradually dimming glow of the horizon, the clamour of the town gradually dying away, slumber spreading its grey wings in the twilight, the murmur of the Seine becoming increasingly audible as human songs and cries recede and grow fainter? – At this point in the performance I like to shut my eyes and see a much warmer sky, a city painted in truer colours (*pace* Monsieur Duphonchel)[8] than his splendid stage designs and skilful effects of waning light. How often have I cursed the inevitable sunrise that accompanies the last chorus of the second act of *William Tell*! O canvas, cardboard, tinsel and stage effects! what have you to do with that wonderful prayer in which all the rays of the sun unfold majestically, lengthen and flare, in which the King of Day appears in all his glory and seems to burst through snowy peaks and emerge from the horizon with the sacred hymn's last note! But music has yet another greater power in this respect. There doesn't have to be a whole melody; a few modulations are enough to bring black clouds across the face of Helios and to eclipse the azure of the sky, to make volcanoes erupt and the Cyclops roar in the bowels of the earth, to revive the humid wind and make it sweep over terror-stricken trees. Alice[9] appears, the day is calm, nature sings its untamed, primitive chants. Suddenly witches are weaving circles in their wild saraband at her feet. The foundations are shaken, the grass withers, subterranean fire flows from every pore of the groaning earth, the atmosphere darkens and ominous gleams light up the rocks. – But the midnight revels vanish into inaccessible caverns, nature reawakens, the sky clears, the air freshens, the stream, stopped short in its course by terror, runs once more; Alice kneels and prays.

By the way I must, despite the length of this digression, tell you, dear Maestro, of an insignificant and wholly personal affair for which I've always wanted to thank you. Two years ago, in mid-winter, I spent two of the saddest months of my life in the country.[10] I was suffering from spleen and was at times on the very brink of insanity. All the furies, all the demons, all the serpents, all the broken, trailing chains of your witches' sabbath ran riot in my breast. When, according to the usual course of all diseases, these fits began to pass, I had an infallible means of speeding up the transition and of recovering my composure in a few minutes. This consisted of installing at the piano my nephew,[11] a good-looking, rosy-cheeked, curly-haired youth, full of tender, monk-ish dignity and gifted with an impassive brow and unfailing health. At an agreed signal from me he played the melody I so much love – which accompanies Alice at the foot of the cross – a perfect and delightful replica of the state of my soul, of the passing of a storm and the revival of hope. What poetic and religious comfort fell like blessed dew from those smooth and penetrating notes! Even the finch in my white lilac bush forgot the cold of winter and, dreaming of springtime and love, began to warble as in the month of May. The day-lily on the mantelpiece opened and, unfolding its silken petals, breathed over my head, at the last chord, its virginal perfume. Then the aloe pod in my Turkish pipe would come alight, the fire would flare up in a great white blaze and my nephew, as patient as a steam-engine, as devoted as a son, would repeat the adorable passage twenty times over until he saw his dear uncle discard the twelve ells of flannel in which he was wrapped and venture a few graceful capers in the middle of the room while hurling his cap to the ceiling and sneezing for twenty minutes. How could I not bless you, my dear Maestro, who have cured me so many times, and so much better than any physician, since it was quite painless and entirely free of charge? And how could I ever believe that music is an art intended merely for pleasure and for simple observation when I recall having been more moved by its effects and more convinced by its eloquence than by all my philosophical readings?

But to return to the production of *The Huguenots*; I must confess that I never expected such an intelligent and powerful work and would have been content with less. I hadn't foreseen all that you could, and indeed had to, make of the subject – that is of the idea of the subject, since what subject would have come amiss to you after the apocalyptic poem of *Robert*? However, I'd so much enjoyed *Robert* that I couldn't hope to enjoy your new work any better and went to see *The Huguenots* with a sort of sadness and apprehension, not on your account but on my own. I knew that your knowledge of instrumentation and your skill would be such that, whatever the words and the subject, you would find ingenious resources and ways to captivate your audience. You would know how to overpower the unwilling, and to still the critical Cerberuses by giving them plenty of gilt on their gingerbread in the form of all your great orchestral effects and all your inexhaustible wealth of harmony.

I wasn't worried about your success; I knew that men like you impose whatever they want and that when inspiration eludes them learning makes up for it. But it's not so easy to hoodwink poets, those underdeveloped, sickly beings who know nothing, study few subjects, yet perceive and guess almost everything, and who get no warmth from the altar that hasn't been visited by a sacred fire. How happy I was when I found that I was moved and touched by that enthralling tale, by those real, unallegorical characters, as much as I'd been troubled and disturbed by the symbolic conflicts of *Robert*! – I'd had neither the leisure nor the composure to peruse the libretto. I was rather amused by the style when I read it afterwards; but I understand the difficulty of writing lines that have to be sung, and otherwise I'm most grateful to Monsieur Scribe (unless it was you who provided the plot and the main situations) for having thrust you abruptly into a new arena, a different period, a different country and especially a different religion. You had already given proof of your remarkable talent for expressing religious emotions; it was an excellent idea of his (always assuming it wasn't you who gave it to him) to provide you with another form of religion which enabled you to tap new resources.

But I'd like to know how, with thirty or so insignificant little verses, you were able to create such individual characters, to make leading roles where the librettist had only given you minor parts. The rough, intolerant old servant, faithful to his friends as to his God, ruthless in battle, suspicious, anxious and fanatical in cold blood but sublimely serene and joyful at the moment of martyrdom, is indeed Lutheran in the truly poetic sense, in all the ideal and artistic acceptance of the word which implies the *possibility* of perfection. That tall, beautiful, dark girl, brave, enterprising, elevated, contemptuous of the care of her honour as of her life and passing from Catholic fanaticism to the serenity of a Protestant martyr, is a generous, forceful character too and worthy of taking her place beside Marcel. You managed to give Nevers, the handsome youth in white satin (who has, if I'm not mistaken, four words to say in the libretto), a pleasant, elegant, chivalrous appearance, an attractive nature despite his impertinence when he describes with endearing melancholy the distress his marriage will provoke among all the ladies at court.

Except in the last two acts Raoul's part – despite all your skill – does not overcome the blundering stupidity with which Monsieur Scribe has invested it. Nourrit's lively sensitivity and rare intelligence struggle in vain with the sentimental mayfly he has to enact – a true victim of circumstance, as they say in novels. But how he recovers in the third act! How he carries off a scene[12] which has been rather too hastily condemned by a puritanism otherwise estimable; a scene which I, who see no harm either in fainting fits or day-beds on stage, find very moving, very sombre, very frightening and by no means anachronistic. What a duet! What dialogue! Maestro, how well you know how to sob, pray, tremble and vanquish in Monsieur Scribe's stead! O Maestro, you are a great dramatic poet and a great novelist! I abandon your little pageboy to the critics; he can't rise above the thanklessness of his state; but I defend against all comers the last trio, which is an unparalleled scene only broken off and interrupted because the situation requires it, because you have some concern for dramatic veracity. You refuse to admit the possibility that there is a *musician's music* and a *writer's music*; for you there is only one music, that of true emotion and convincing action, where the charm of the melody doesn't contradict the situation by giving the hero a conventional cavatina with coda and an inevitable virtuoso passage, as he falls on the battlefield riddled with shots.

284

I think it's high time art was subjected to the rule of common sense and the innocent spectator was no longer obliged to ask himself: 'How can those people sing when they are in such distress?' Singing should here be a true lament and art should be sufficiently liberated from hackneyed conventions to move the simplest people and make them feel more than a decorous response. You have proved that this can be done, and when Rossini wanted he could prove it too.

However, allow me to ask you something. It's very impertinent of me, and I detest impertinence in all its forms and with all its pretensions. So please don't imagine that I'm giving you advice. But occasionally, you know, an ignorant person may have a good idea which can be of use to an artist, in the same way as he can get his most daring insights from the least sophisticated and most unexpected impressions: the splendour of churches from the wild sweep of a forest, a complex and skilful melody from rustic sounds, from some momentary breeze, some murmuring stream. Here then is what bothers me: are all those conventional forms necessary – the coda, that sort of uniform heavy framework? Or the virtuoso passages that recall the perilous pirouettes of ballet-dancers? Why should the voice be made to modulate from the highest to the lowest notes of the register at the end of every piece? Why do the effects of the loveliest phrases have to be ruined by hackneyed, unvaried modes? Don't you think a day will come when the public will have had enough of it and will realize that the action (which, whatever one says, is inseparable from the lyrical movement) is continually interrupted by such inevitable repetition; that all elegance, innocence and freshness is marred or effaced by inflexible rules, by unintelligent and trivial formulas which nobody dares to contravene? Liszt compares this formula to the words with which we end all our official letters: 'I have the honour of being your very humble and obedient servant . . .', without asking ourselves if their implications are false and absurd or correct and heartfelt. It appears that the general public still cherishes such antiquated customs and refuses to believe that a scene is ended if there aren't a few trite measures of undistinguished singsong, neither melodious nor harmonious, neither aria nor recitative? In such absurd situations our interest is in abeyance; the actors, compelled to be exaggeratedly theatrical, shout themselves hoarse and grow frantic while reiterating words of insincere rapture, unsustained by the slightest melody. The overwhelming effect of passion or emotion awakened by all that preceded is lost and annihilated by such formulas, as it would be if, in the midst of a tragic scene, the dramatis personae suddenly animated by the state of affairs started taking their bow over and over again.

You haven't yet entirely freed yourself in this respect from an uncouth public's ignorance or from the demands of unenlightened singers. It was impossible for you to break free, I'm sure. Perhaps, indeed, it was only by means of all this padding, imposed by convention, that you got your finest ideas accepted. But couldn't you now influence your audience, impose your wishes, compel it to do without leading-strings and introduce it to a purity of taste of which it is unaware and which no one has yet been able to proclaim freely? This vast success, the resounding victories you have won over the public, give you certain rights and perhaps certain responsibilities as well, for above popular favour and human glory there is the cult of art and the faith of the artist. You are the man of the present, Maestro; become the man of the future as well . . . And if my idea is foolish and my request unseemly let us forget about it.

While I am still dreaming, let me say that I dream of a poem for you which would transport you to the very heart of paganism: *The Eumenides*, that frightening opera of Aeschylus,[13] ready-made for you; or the death of Orpheus, so dramatic, so easy to adapt in association with someone like you who can turn a canvas of gauze into a veil of gold or precious stones. Were I capable of stitching two rhythms together, Maestro, I'd come and beg you to dictate each scene to me, and I'd rejoice in seeing you tackle Greek melodies that might be more abundant and satisfying and perhaps require less accompaniment than your former subjects. I'd watch you achieve what the public seems to defy you to do, and, like all great artists, respond to menaces, by victory. But such joy cannot be mine: how could I write verse when I don't know how to write prose? – As for my Greek subject, you know better than I what you must do; but I'm ready to wager that it will tempt you some day.

Maestro, I'm no scholar, I sing out of tune and can play no instrument. Forgive me if I don't speak the technical jargon of the critics. Were I even an enlightened dilettante I wouldn't sift through your masterpieces in the hope of finding some imperceptible flaw that would enable me to air my scraps of knowledge; I'll not endeavour to discover whether your inspiration comes from your mind or from your heart, an odd distinction that means absolutely nothing, the eternal reproach that critics address to artists: as if the same blood didn't flow in the breast and the brow; as if, even supposing that there were two distinct parts of our bodies where the sacred fire could be kindled, the warmth that ascended from the heart to the brain and the warmth that descended from the brain to the heart didn't affect our artistic production in the same way! If they said you were *bilioso-nerveux*[14] and that your work was produced more slowly, with less haste perhaps but also with greater perfection than that of more sanguine, full-blooded natures, I might grasp, more or less, what was involved, and I'd find it quite natural that you wouldn't have every temperament at the same time; but what do I care if you place on your piano a pitcher of pure, crystal-clear water rather than a flask of fiery Cyprus wine and correspondingly, if you can get more inspiration from the one than most people can get from the other? What pedagogical fervour makes these poor literary arbiters always doubt their instincts and rack their brains with questions such as whether the Venus de Milo was made left-handed or right-handed. Considering the pains taken by men of real worth to solve the mysteries of the workshop and uncover the secrets of an artist's vigils and day-dreams, one is filled with distress and sorrow at such a waste of no doubt fertile intellects, such a squandering of potential in order to arrive at what they like to call *insight* and *impartiality*.

No doubt it's right and necessary for men of taste to show ordinary mortals the way and educate them. But we shouldn't forget that our reactions are quickly deadened when we practise even the most admirable trade unremittingly; surgeons become inured to suffering, to risk and to death; while judges easily get into a rut and, abandoning wise induction, end up by placing too much confidence in their suspicions and in drawing arbitrary conclusions that distort the truth. And the critic proceeds in much the same way: conscientious at first, he gradually adopts a meticulous casuistry and eventually, by dint of rationalizing everything, can no longer feel anything. When feeling is absent arguments become specious and the estimation of a work more and more unrewarding, difficult and perhaps even impossible. At the end of a meal where the guests have grossly overeaten, the finest dishes lose their flavour, and the surfeited palate ceases to distinguish between the freshness of fruit and the heat of spices. Those who want to savour and experience all the pleasures life has to offer may end up one day refusing to sleep on a soft bed, convinced that a primitive bed of mosses is warmer and more luxurious. A deplorable error of artistic judgement but an inevitable condition of human nature! We were shown the early endeavours of a budding talent and judged them perhaps more indulgently and sympathetically than they deserved; we were young ourselves. But as critics of others' creations we tend to age more quickly than when we create. When we see life as an endless show in which we either don't condescend or don't dare to participate, we soon grow tired of those who are involved, because we are tired of ourselves. We follow the artist's progress, but without realizing we have lost through inaction all the sacred fire he has, unknown to himself, acquired from the gods by hard work; and the day he produces his masterpiece we are incapable of appreciating it. We look back with nostalgia to the first time that we were thrilled by his work; a time that is lost and buried for ever in the richness of the past, a sweet and precious emotion for which we weep, never to find it again. The artist has become Prometheus; but the man of clay has petrified and remains lifeless under the sacred breath. We declare that the artist has degenerated and we believe we are telling the truth!

Such is the story of the public's reactions to art and that of each generation's reaction to politics; but it's a story which is alarmingly summed up in the brief intellectual existence of the unlucky man who decides to be a critic. He lives through a century in the space of a few years; his beard has hardly started to grow and already his brow is furrowed with boredom, weariness and disgust. He might have had a respectable or even a brilliant career in the midst of productive artists; but he hasn't the energy any more, he has no faith in anything, least of all in himself.

When, in a moment of unusual courage and thirst for knowledge, we glance at some of the thirty or forty literary judgements which appear in print the day after some flash-in-the-pan novel has been published, we are amazed at all the witticisms, learned arguments, ingenious parallels, subtle dissertations written, as a rule, in a rich, ornate, scintillating style; and we are sorry to see such treasures – which at other times might have provided a year's reading-matter – cast pell-mell at the feet of careless readers who barely notice them – and with justice; since even supposing they got at the truth in this kaleidoscope of conflicting ideas and opinions, it would be so futile, so hackneyed, so easy to condense into three lines, that they would have wasted their time in pruning an oak to obtain a matchstick. Thus a sensible person will himself examine the subject under discussion, judge it according to his natural instinct and pay no heed to the amount of space the critics think it deserves.

Not that I despise criticism as such; I honour and respect its aim and its possible and desirable effects so much that I'm sorry to see it deviate from its course and do more harm than good to artists, while giving more entertainment than instruction to the idle, indifferent and scornful public. I'd like to believe that those who practise it are full of integrity and motivated by no other passion than the love of beauty and truth. For this reason I deplore the fact that this useful and respectable body should be so badly constituted that its influence has become unacceptable, not to say disastrous and that its stock declines each day in the face of the jokes and surmises of an ignorant crowd. This then would be my Utopia if I had to seek a remedy for so much error and confusion:

First I would want the number of those who write reviews to be much greater while the number of reviews published would be far more restricted. I would want criticism to cease to be a career and reviews stop coming out every day and on every subject. Since the public requires its newspapers and since the columns of newspapers are the chairs of eloquence assigned to certain professors of aesthetics, I'd want each paper to have its jury, which would elect competent men according to the paper's origin and spirit, who would be required to write on works of some significance. I suggest that a bunch of youngsters without education, taste or experience shouldn't be allowed to judge their elders, to make or break growing reputations on no other recommendation than an easy style, copious and fluent composition and an ingenious and pleasant wit. I feel that no one should presume to take up criticism as a profession, but that every man of ability and knowledge should fulfil the serious and noble function as a duty, and out of love of literature, in the certainty of getting an honest living from it if need be, since even the priest is allowed to live off his religion.[15]

I am not one of those who believe that artists alone ought to judge artists. I think on the contrary that it's usually a bad thing, and that, in the hands of rivals of the same profession, journals would soon become an undisciplined and undignified battleground in which, as passion would be uppermost, truth would be further away than ever. The role of critic demands, certainly, special knowledge, and in addition, a calm and disinterested judgement and it is very difficult to find such calm and disinterestedness in anyone who feels his destiny is in the hands of the public. So without excluding certain artists, whose experience, established position or exceptional character would give sufficient guarantees, I would grant few means of influencing public opinion to those who are themselves dependent upon it.

And if the hordes of youthful wits who live off reviewing complain of no longer having a means of advertising their skills or of exercising them, then I would answer: 'Be thankful for measures that compel you to work and create. You were doing the work of eunuchs and slaves; you were condemned to bathe the children of the rich, dress and undress them and take them out for walks. Become fathers in your own right. Whether your children are handsome or misshapen, healthy or sickly you'll love them because they are yours. Your life of hatred and contempt will be turned into an existence of love and hope. You will not all be great men but at least you'll be men, which you are not at present.'

And if, in order to become more thoughtful and judicious, critical judgements become less numerous (which is inevitable), if the proprietors of the journals complain of empty columns and the public about the lack of reviews, why shouldn't these unfilled pages – so sought after and, alas, so hard to come by – be available to those unknown, humble young men of talent who are reluctant to write criticism without the required experience, and who vainly seek a means of emerging from the obscurity where they wilt, for lack of an editor to discover them and allow them the use of his paper and print gratis? Why shouldn't all those young reviewers who are obliged to be at the ready, like firemen or police officers, for every new production, and to write solemnly through the night about the most trivial lampoons produced in every little theatre of the realm (when they are sure to make a whale out of a minnow), why shouldn't they, I ask, be called upon to publish from day to day those poems and novels which they have in manuscript or dormant in their brains, at present stifled by the demands of a stupefying trade?* Poor young people! Art's young levites, your talents nipped in the bud by the shocking exigencies of the press, you who might joyfully and willingly have been the disciples of the great masters and have got satisfaction, and above all, profit from it; don't be afraid that I

* When I wrote this it seemed probable that my idea would remain at the stage of Utopianism. Its practice has become quite common and the novel by instalments has contributed considerably to literary production.

condemn you without pity and that I underestimate what there was, what there perhaps still is, of greatness and integrity in you. I can guess your secrets, I know your disappointments, I've drunk from your cup of sorrows! I know that more than one among you, seated at night in your cold, miserable garret, is obliged to have ready for the next day a tidy suit and new gloves (the contemporary equivalent of the crust of bread for yesterday's artists) – and you have bent your tear-stained face over the pages of some fine new book which hatred or envy has directed you to condemn, and for which your fellow-feeling is so strong that you have to fling the book to the other end of the room so that you can damn the artist without a hearing. I pity you who have been made to blush for yourselves! And woe betide those who have become incapable of blushing!

But why, Maestro, have I entertained you for so long on the subject of French critics? You occupy too lofty a position for such things to worry you,[16] and you probably aren't even aware that they tried to dispute the honours which the European public has everywhere bestowed on you. Far be it from me to wish to console you for some injustice you doubtless accepted with the smiling benevolence of a conqueror, if indeed it ever even reached your ears. I don't know whether men like you are as modest as their gracious welcome and exquisite courtesy lead us to suppose; but I know that an awareness of their own strength makes them wise. They dwell with the gods and not among mortals; they are good because they are great.

Do you remember, Maestro, that one night I had the pleasure of meeting you at a concert given by Berlioz? We had the worst seats possible, since Berlioz is anything but considerate in the distribution of tickets; but for me it was a stroke of fortune to be where, thanks to the crowds and to chance, I happened to be. They were playing the *Marche au supplice*. I shall never forget your understanding handshake nor the unrestrained sensibility with which you, with all your laurels, applauded the great underrated artist who struggles so heroically against an ungenerous public and a harsh fate. You would gladly have shared your trophies with him, and I left with tears in my eyes, though I couldn't have said why, for is it surprising that you should be like this?

Letter Twelve

To Monsieur Nisard[1]

Sir,

There are very few critics whose praise is worth acknowledging or whose errors are worth challenging. If I accept your compliments with gratitude and try to defend myself against your strictures it is because your article suggests, not only talent and intelligence, but a great deal of tolerance and honesty into the bargain.

Were it only a question of satisfied vanity I would have nothing but my thanks to offer you; for you commend the imaginative quality in my stories more highly than it deserves. But it's precisely because your approval delights me that I find it hard to accept your blame in other respects, and it's in the hope of clearing myself that (reluctantly and uncharacteristically) I take the liberty of talking about myself to somebody whom I haven't had the pleasure of meeting.

You assert, Sir, that the purpose of all my books is to discredit marriage. Allow me to exempt four or five[2] – and *Lélia* amongst them – which you quote as attacks on this social institution, but where so far as I know it's never mentioned. *Lélia* indeed, more than any of my other works, might serve as an answer to your reproach that I am attempting to reinstate the 'egoism of the senses' and to preach a 'metaphysics of matter'. Nor when I was writing it did *Indiana* seem to me to be a defence of adultery. I believe that in this novel (where, if I remember rightly, no one commits adultery) the *lover* (*that king of my books* as you wittily call him) cuts a poor figure compared to the husband. *Le Secrétaire Intime* is (if I'm not entirely mistaken as to my intentions) about the joys of conjugal bliss. *André* is neither *against* marriage nor *for* adultery. *Simon* ends with a marriage just like a fairy-tale by Perrault or Madame d'Aulnoy;[3] and as for *Valentine* whose conclusion, I admit, is neither original nor skilful, the expected calamity intervenes

292

to stop the adulterous wife from enjoying in a second marriage a happiness for which she has failed to wait. In *Leoni* the marriage problem is no more at issue than in *Manon Lescaut*, of which I attempted, from a purely aesthetic point of view, to make it a sort of counterpart. Indeed, desperate love for an unworthy object and the subjection imposed by the strength of a corrupt being on another blinded by its own weakness – these are not presented in their outcome in any more prepossessing a light than in the Abbé Prevost's incomparable novel. There remains, then, *Jacques*, the only one of my novels which, I believe, has been fortunate enough to receive some attention from you – and that is certainly more than any work of mine deserves from any serious person.

It's quite possible that *Jacques* really does confirm all the hostility you found in it to domestic order. It is also true that people have drawn from it quite opposite conclusions and may well have been equally justified. When a book, however trivial, fails to prove clearly, unequivocally, incontestably and irrefutably what it set out to prove, that's the book's fault but not always the author's. He has grossly sinned as an artist; his inexpert, uncontrolled hand has played his thoughts false; but as a man he had no intention of misleading his readers or tampering with the principles of eternal truth.

In Florence and Milan many tales, true or false, are told about the immortal Benvenuto Cellini. I've heard that he frequently undertook the execution of a vase and carefully outlined its shape and proportions; but that when he came to the point of making it he sometimes got so exceedingly engrossed by a given figure or garland that he would enlarge the one to make it more poetical, or distort the other to give it a more graceful curve. Thus, carried away by his preoccupation with a detail, he forgot the whole for some accessory and, realizing too late that he couldn't recapture the original design, he would produce, instead of the bowl he had set out to make, a trivet; instead of the ewer, a lamp; instead of a crucifix, a sword-hilt. Thus, pleasing himself, he displeased clients who had commissioned a specific work.

While Cellini was at the peak of his career these transports of his only enhanced his talent – each of his works was perfect and faultless of its kind; but when persecution, a disorderly life, imprisonment, travels and poverty began to tell, a less steady hand and less ready inspiration made him produce works that, though wonderfully finished in every detail, were incredibly unskilled as a whole. Bowls, tripods, ewers and sword-hilts converged in his mind, clashed with each other, reunited and finally jumbled together in shapeless, useless structures that lacked all logic and unity. What happened to the great Benvenuto in his decline is what happens all the time to lesser artists who haven't yet reached their prime and perhaps never will. That's what happened to me when I wrote *Jacques*; and it may well be that all my other works reflect the impatience of the enthusiastic, clumsy craftsman who indulges his passing fancies and bungles the end because he gets carried away by the means.

Thus it isn't to you as the reader who judged me so favourably and so harshly that I appeal against his own verdict; but to you as an artist whose talent has undoubtedly known its youthful season and its hours of temptation. The latter ought to be extremely cautious in his assessments since he knows that the hardest thing on earth, what might be called the supreme triumph of the will, is to say what we want to say and do what we want to do.

So it's the *workmanship* rather than the intention you ought to blame for what you find unpalatable in my books. And maybe you shouldn't have accused me so relentlessly of anti-social aims; but neither should you have thought I was so skilful, clever and resolute in my means of execution. In short my talent is probably much inferior and my conscience much superior to what you imagined. Most artists spend their lives producing the fragmentary parts of a whole that will always remain buried in the sanctuary of their minds.

What I do accept as entirely correct is your verdict that:

'The downfall of husbands, or at least their unpopularity, such was the aim of George Sand's work.'

Yes, Sir, the downfall of *husbands* would indeed have been the object of my ambition had I felt that I had the power to become a *reformer*; but if I've not been entirely successful in making myself clear, that's because I didn't have that power and because I'm more a poet by nature than a legislator. You will, I hope, acknowledge this humble claim.

But all the same I believe that the novel, like the drama, is a school of morals where the *abuses, follies, prejudices* and *vices* of an age are subjected to a censure that can take any form it pleases. I've often written the words *social laws* in the place of the terms italicized above and never once did I think there was any risk in doing so. Could anyone suppose that I wished to change the laws of the land? In fact I was

294

amazed when some Saint-Simonians, conscientious philanthropists, worthy and earnest seekers after truth, asked me what I would put in the place of *husbands*. I replied in all innocence that it would be *marriage*, just as I believe that religion should be substituted for those priests who have given it such a bad name.

It's true that I may have grievously sinned against language when, speaking of the abuses, follies, prejudices and vices of society I spoke collectively and said 'society'. And also I frequently made the mistake of saying marriage rather than married people. No one who knows me even superficially could be at all misled, since he would know that I have never considered reforming the constitutional Charter. I thought the public would take so little notice of me that it would never enter anybody's head to question my use of words or to subject a miserable poet hidden away in his garret to a sort of inquisition, force him to account for all his actions, thoughts and beliefs and to define the precise meaning of more or less vague expressions which were generally used, however, in a self-explanatory way. It's possible that the public played no great part in all this and that the male readers, pretending to be shocked, indulged in a little puerile gossip on a subject that wasn't really worthy of such a melancholy honour. But one thing is certain and that is that I'm to blame for not being perfectly clear, precise, logical and exact. Alas, Sir, I reproach myself every day with a heinous sin, which is that I'm neither Bossuet nor Montesquieu;[4] but I haven't, I confess, much hope of amending this fault.

You direct a further serious reproof at me, namely: 'It might perhaps be nobler, if luck has not been with you, to refrain from scandalizing the world at large with your misfortunes and turning a private matter into a social problem . . .' etc.

The whole paragraph is elevated in thought and in style, I find no cause to quarrel with the sentiment you express in it. I set patience and selflessness above all else and I've nothing to say in so far as the reproof concerns me personally. Were I writing to a priest, perhaps my general confession would earn me an absolution, accompanied by a reprimand and penitence. But to date only Jean-Jacques has been entitled to a public confession. Therefore I shall reply in general terms.

It seems to me that people make a great affectation of patience and selflessness. It seems to me (I may be wrong) that we do not live in an age of independence and unlimited pride; I don't think that men of today have a very lively sense of their dignity or that they should be encouraged to prostrate themselves even more than they do already before conventions and interests that have no connection with religion, morality, order or virtue. In the same way, I don't think that the wives of such men bear comparison with Spartan mothers for their courage or with Roman matrons for their national pride.

In short, my vision may be blurred but it seems to me that we have greatly abused *silence* by making it a means of avoiding *violent crises of marriage* and the *inconveniences* (it would be better to say *calamities*) of *separation*. In the days of faith, the days when Christ was worshipped, selflessness and patience were the virtues which above all had to be instilled into women who had but lately left behind the Druidic altars, the bloodstained camps and war-councils in which their husbands had let them meddle a little too enthusiastically, perhaps; but today when our customs haven't, as far as I am aware, much in common with the forests of Germany, especially since the Regency and the Directoire have taught women how to get on tolerably well with their husbands, I'd have thought that, since frivolous stories have to have some kind of moral, one might do well to adopt this one: 'Women's misconduct is *very often* the result of men's savagery and infamy.' Or this: 'Lying is not virtue: cowardice is not abnegation.' Or again, even this: 'A husband who light-heartedly neglects his responsibilities to indulge in blasphemy, merriment and drink *is sometimes* less excusable than the woman who betrays hers in tears, suffering and propitiation.'

To put an end to my total agreement with your judgements, I shall tell you that this love which I 'extol' and enthrone on the ruins of 'infamy' is my Utopia, my dream, my poetry. This love is great, noble, beautiful, voluntary and eternal; but this love is marriage as Jesus meant it, as St Paul explained it, even as, if you like, the Civil Code represents it when, in Chapter VI of Part V, it defines reciprocal duties.[5] Such a marriage is what I require of society as an innovation, or as an institution that has been lost in the mists of time and which we would be well advised to revive, to extract from the dust of ages and the mire of habit, if we wish to see true conjugal fidelity, true peace and the true sanctity of the family take over from the sort of shameful contract and senseless despotism which has been brought about by the world's squalid decrepitude.

But you, Sir, who contemplate this social problem from such a lofty height, you, tolerant philosopher, strong and sensible moralist who do not believe in the danger of so-called *immoral* books, why, when writing apropos of me these three or four fine pages on public morality, did you miss this unique occasion to chide the cupidity and the dissolute, violent behaviour of men which so often authorizes or provokes the criminal acts of women? Wouldn't you have fulfilled more thoroughly your self-imposed duty to society if you had come out strongly in favour of that age-old Christian ethic which prescribes gentleness and charity to the head of the family? I'm not concerned here with exceptional cases, *ill-assorted matches*. Every kind of marriage will be intolerable so long as custom persists in showing unlimited indulgence to the errors of one sex while the austere and salutary rigour of past ages is retained solely to judge those of the other. I am much aware that it requires some courage to declare openly to a whole generation that it is unjust and corrupt. I know that by writing what we think we make a great number of enemies among those who find some profit in the vices of our time, and that when we have acted thus frankly we must expect to experience for the rest of our lives a persecution that invades even our privacy; but I also know that since some women have shown such courage, it wouldn't be unworthy of a man, and especially of a conscientious, gifted man, to forgive what is lacking in their efforts and to assist and protect whatever honesty and sincerity may be found in them.

Had you lived in the days when *Tartuffe* was condemned as an ungodly work, you would have been among those who, far from setting themselves up as the champions of hypocrisy, resisted with all the strength of their convictions and with all the integrity of their hearts the damaging interpretations of criticism: you would, then as now, have made a declaration, signed with your own blood,[6] that the mind which produced *Tartuffe* was an eminently pious and honest mind, that God can't be slandered in the person of a hypocrite, that a family's dignity and peace aren't endangered when ungrateful villains are evicted from its midst. Admittedly *Tartuffe* is a masterpiece and worthy of every support from eminent minds, both as to subject and achievement.

But if some writers' pens are silenced for ever, if the lively hues of the great ages have faded, if instead of Aristophanes, Terence and Molière we have only George Sand and Co., perennial human frailty is none the less still there before the critical philosopher's eyes, still bleeding and leprous, worthy of honour and compassion. *Justice*, the eternal dream of simple souls, is still erect as ever (at a distance, it's true), but radiant, necessary, claiming our every effort and our every desire. Gentlemen, since all you have to judge are pale compositions, wouldn't this be a further reason for you to get to the heart of the matter, and to spare the apostle in order to encourage the principle? In this way you might compensate for the inadequacy of our means and restore to our age what it lacks in strength and genius.

It remains for me to thank you, Sir, for the advice you were good enough to give me. Once again I plead guilty, since if you have sometimes failed to understand me, that is my fault and not yours. He who observes a battle from the hilltop is in a better position to assess the army's mistakes and losses than the man who marches in the dust and in all the excitement of the conflict. Thus the uninvolved critic knows more about the hotheaded artist and his work than the artist himself. Socrates often had occasion to say to his disciples: 'You were going to define knowledge for me and you've given me a definition of music and dance; that's not what I asked for and neither is it what you meant to answer.'

★ Acknowledgements ★

Everyone who writes about George Sand must be a beneficiary of the impeccable scholarship of M. Georges Lubin. His notes to his admirable edition of *Lettres d'un Voyageur* have been indispensable, especially when he is drawing on his unequalled knowledge of those friends and acquaintances in the George Sand circle who have not made their way into the reference books. The needs of English readers are, of course, different from those of the scholars and researchers who benefit from his comments, but inevitably there has been a certain overlapping of my notes with his. Where, however, I have used any of M. Lubin's entries verbatim, I have acknowledged the borrowing with his initials, thus: (G L).

As *Lettres d'un Voyageur* deals so much with George Sand's own history I have often felt it necessary to include some biographical background in the notes. For those readers who want to supplement their knowledge of George Sand and her life, I would recommend the lively and excellent biography by Curtis Cate (Boston, 1975). That, along with one or two of Henry James's discriminating essays on his 'dear old George', should be enough to enlighten new Sandists.

Notes

★

The few footnotes were written by George Sand. The Introduction is annotated very lightly because most of the people in it to whom I refer are mentioned again in the Letters and are then dealt with fully in the notes.

The following abbreviations have been used: *G S*, George Sand; *LV*, *Lettres d'un Voyageur*; *HV*, *Histoire de ma vie*, George Sand's autobiography, as published in *O A*, *Œuvres autobiographiques*, two volumes, edited and annotated by Georges Lubin (Gallimard, Pleiade, 1970–71); *Corr*, *Correspondance de George Sand*, twenty volumes, texts collected, annotated and edited by Georges Lubin (Garnier, 1964–87); *RDM*, *Revue des Deux Mondes*.

Introduction

1. The year after G S's death, Matthew Arnold compiled a brief list of the works which would give an idea of her essential quality to someone who had never read her. *Lettres d'un Voyageur* was one of the four books that he selected out of about sixty. He considered the characteristic features of her writing to be 'the cry of agony and revolt, the trust in beauty and nature, the aspiration towards a purged and renewed society'.

2. Baudelaire: '*Le style coulant si cher aux bourgeois.*'

3. In 'Sketches and Hints' (*OA* II, pp. 589–90), the young Aurore wrote some touching lines for her grandmother's album. They were written as a consolation to her grandmother for the death of her son, Maurice (Aurore's father): '*Ne te désespère donc pas, ma bonne mère. Tous deux voyageurs dans la vie tu a pris la route la plus longue, moi la plus courte . . . Nous avions un rendez-vous pour ne plus nous quitter . . .*' (So, my dear mother, do not despair. We are both travellers through life, only you have taken the longest road and I the shortest . . . We had agreed to meet and never more to part . . .)

4. François Buloz (1803–77), editor from 1831 onwards of the *RDM* which he turned into the most influential periodical of the century and to which he attracted all the great writers of the age.

5. Prosper Mérimée (1803–70), French novelist, master of the short novel form. (His very short and disastrous affair with G S took place in 1834.)

6. Casimir Dudevant (1795–1871), son of Colonel Dudevant, a Baron of the Empire. His marriage to G S took place in 1822 when she was just eighteen. It was one of impulse and doomed from the start, for in temperament, intellect and interests they were totally opposed. Casimir would have been content with his life at Nohant as a country squire, hunting, drinking and occasionally wenching, but his idealistic and lonely young wife yearned for love and congenial companionship.

Preface to the Second Edition

1. . . . *preserved my epistles*: Some of the Letters were indeed genuine extracts from correspondence with friends, or at least based on them, e.g., Letters Four and Nine (see *Corr* III, pp. 349, 392). On the other hand, a considerable amount of artistry went into 'filling in the gaps'.

2. *gouty old uncle*: The character of the uncle is discussed in the notes to Letter Five.

3. *I am no different . . . reader*: '*Je suis votre semblable, hommes de mauvaise foi!*' Cf. G S's address to the reader and Baudelaire's final line in his poem, 'Au Lecteur' (1855): '*Hypocrite lecteur, mon semblable, mon frère.*' In his early years, Baudelaire was an admirer of G S's work; it was later that he turned against 'the woman Sand' (see Léon Cellier's article, 'Baudelaire and George Sand', *Revue d'histoire littéraire de la France*, Vol. 67, pp. 239–59, for parallels in their writings and an account of how their interests converged in the 1840s).

4. *The second volume*: Letters Seven to Twelve.

Letter One

1. *Letter One*: This Letter was subtitled 'To a Poet' when G S sent it to Musset before publication. Alfred de Musset (1810–57), French poet, playwright and novelist, was already an established poet when, in 1833, he met G S as a fellow contributor to the *R D M*. Her influence can be seen, especially in *On ne badine pas avec l'amour* and his play, *Lorenzaccio*.

2. Basta: Enough.

3. *the man*: Musset.

4. Ciao, egregio dottore: So long, eminent doctor. *Schiavo suo*: Your humble servant.

5. *Kreissler*: Johannes Kreissler, an autobiographical character in E. T. A. Hoffmann's unfinished novel, *Kater Murr*. Hoffmann (1776–1822) was

famed for his tales of the grotesque and fantastic, and was a considerable influence on other Romantics.

6. spleen: G S's use of the term 'spleen' was that which was current among writers in the 1830s and later. It signified oppressive dejection, annihilating hopelessness, whereas in the eighteenth century (e.g., in Pope's *Rape of the Lock*) 'spleen' was a fashionable ailment of the upper classes, much nearer to 'the vapours'. See also Baudelaire's poems under the heading of 'Spleen et Idéal'.

7. *a whole poem*: This brief encounter on a coach is reminiscent, in its sensibility, of Laurence Sterne's *A Sentimental Journey* (1768). Sterne (1713–68) had long been a favourite of G S.

8. *Brod and . . . Urhan*: Henri Brod (1779–1849), first oboist and Chrétien Urhan (1790–1839), first violinist – two virtuosi. (G L)

9. *Habeneck*: François-Étienne Habeneck (1781–1849), violinist and conductor. He was the founder and director of the Société des Concerts du Conservatoire.

10. *nailed to a cross*: Cf. some of Musset's poetry written about this time, especially 'La Nuit de Mai' (1835), in which the poet is the martyr, crucified by life, whose despair puts him beyond the reach of his Muse's reproaches for his idleness. In their exhortations, at least, the Muse and G S can be equated: *'Prends ton lyre, O paresseux enfant.'*

11. *Linger . . . skies*: From Musset's poem, 'Le Saule', the last two lines of Canto Two. (Lubin has pointed out that G S is here quoting from Musset's slightly different MS version.)

12. *overturned*: The description which follows is of Musset's grave illness and delirium in Venice. (See *Corr* XI, p. 552.)

13. *You too . . . faith in that*: This extract is a preview of a passage in Letter Eighty-seven of *Jacques*, an epistolary novel written by G S in Venice, and not published till September 1834. The stoical and world-weary hero, Jacques, eventually commits suicide on a glacier, for the sake of his young wife and her lover. Balzac commented: 'Mme Dudevant's latest novel is a word of advice to husbands who are in their wives' way, to kill themselves and so leave their partners free.'

14. *turmoil*: It was a metaphor she had obviously been working on. It appears in Chapter Twenty and again in Chapter Twenty-four of *Jacques* as 'the grain of sand' (i.e., mistrust) which had dropped into the calm lake of the husband's content and made it turbulent.

15. *a man*: i.e., Pagello. The conversation bears the mark of having been written for Musset's benefit – as does the final scene of the Letter.

16. *Milo of Croton*: A famous athlete who accomplished remarkable feats of strength.

17. L'Auberge des Adrets: The play in which Frederick Lemaître, the noted French comic actor, made his reputation as Robert Macaire.

18. forestière: Foreigner.

19. *marble temple*: The temple built by Antonio Canova (1757–1822) to house his sculptures and paintings. It is still a striking landmark, with a disappointing interior.

20. *Princess Borghese*: The Bonaparte family were patrons of Canova, and Napoleon's sister, the Princess Borghese, posed for him as Venus.

21. morbidezza: Softness.

22. *Psyche*: Canova's *Cupid and Psyche* is in the Louvre.

23. *rich uncle . . . doctor*: I am indebted to Dr Norma Perry for her helpful elucidation of this passage.

24. *Constantinople*: A genuine, though unfulfilled, project of G S.

Letter Two

1. *the living*: Liszt so admired this dream sequence that he thought of translating it into music. (See *Corr* IV, p. 449.)

2. *with my dreams*: See *HV* V, Chapter Three for GS's account of her return to Venice after seeing Musset off at Mestre – when she was so fatigued by her long ordeal that she saw everything upside-down. In this passage, however, she is in full control of her vision and her imagination.

3. *Bianca Cappello's house*: The house at the far end of the Rio Sant' Aponal from which Bianca Cappello (1548–87) fled in 1563 with her lover, a banker's clerk. She was later the mistress, and from 1579 the wife, of Francesco de' Medici, Duke of Florence.

4. a casa: At home.

5. *scapular*: A short cape.

6. Con lei . . . amor: With her, on peaceful waters / I strayed on the laguna. / She, with steadfast look / Gazed up at you, O moon! / What was she thinking then? / Was it a dying heart-throb? / Was it a love new-born?

7. Foresto: A foreigner.

8. Erba: Grass.

9. farniente: Idleness.

10. benedetta: Blessed one.

11. Coi pensieri . . . come ti: With melancholy thoughts / Cease to torment your heart. / Come, let us take a gondola / And go far out to sea.

We'll pass the ports and islands / That hem the city round; / The sun sinks in a cloudless sky / And the moon will soon appear.

. . . .

Then, spreading her pale light / Over the silvery waves, / She postures and cajoles / Just like a love-sick maid.

This breeze that's sporting with / The ringlets of your hair, / Is free of all the dust / From horses and coach wheels.

This little oar which rocks us / Does not assault our ears / As does the crack of whip-lash / As do the shouts of men.

. . . .

You are lovely, you are young / You are fresh as any flower; / The time for tears draws near for all, / Make merry now and love.

. . . .

The Greeks of old imagined / Venus, within a shell; / Within a gondola, perhaps, / They'd seen charms such as yours.

12. *the man in Shakespeare*: Hamlet.

13. *oil paintings*: These were the paintings, no doubt, which Pagello took with him to pay his way in Paris. G S, in the end, pretended she had sold them and paid him for them.

14. amorosa: Lovingly.

15. *The woman*: A former mistress of Pagello, who did utter threats against G S. (See *Corr* II, pp. 690, 697, 806 and notes.)

16. coltellata: A dagger thrust.

17. traghetti: (Normally) crossings, ferries, passages.

18. facchini: Street-porters.

19. *Bucentaur*: The state barge which the Doge used on Ascension Day for the ceremony of the wedding of the sea.

20. Bianco, biondo e grassotto: White, fair and fat.

21. *Robert*: Léopold Robert (1794–1835), a French painter who had been a pupil of David.

22. barcaroles: Gondoliers.

23. corpo di Bacco: By the body of Bacchus. *sangue di Diana*: By the blood of Diana.

24. Ma la fama: But what about fame. *Ma la fame*: But what about hunger. Count Charles Gozzi (1718–1801) was an Italian dramatist whose gay and brilliant plays had been rediscovered by the Romantics.

25. pescaor: Fisherman. *Aqua fresca e tenera*: Fresh, soft water.

26. Oberon *or* William Tell: These were recent operas – Weber's *Oberon* (1826) and Rossini's *William Tell* (1829).

27. vechio: Old man; *lustrissimo*: Your Honour; *E gnente, semo Nicoloti*: It's nothing, I am a Nicoloto.

28. mio fio: My son.

29. le oneste piume: The honourable plumage.

30. Mi son Nicoloti, paron: I am a Nicoloto, Master.

31. In preson! . . . lustrissimo: To prison! Me! Why, Your Honour?

32. sbirri: Italian police officers.

33. su protezion: Your protection.

34. Gnente, lustrissimo . . . fato un Nicoloto: Nothing, Master, unless it's just that we made a Nicoloto.

35. vechio birbo: You quibbling old rascal.

36. E nù . . . cristiani: Neither do we; we are Christians.

37. Sior . . . Gambierazi: Yes, Signor, my friend Gambierazi.

38. Ancà mio fio: My son, also.

Letter Three

1. Addio, caro: Goodbye, my friend.

2. *the Abbé de Lamennais*: Félicité Robert de Lamennais (1782–1854), a French writer, philosopher and priest, whose radical doctrines in religion and politics led to frequent censure. His outspoken attack on the reactionary nature of the Vatican, *Les Paroles d'un croyant*, had recently been published.

3. *a Carlist*: The legitimist party in France in 1834 supported the claims of Don Carlos (the first of the Carlists) to the Spanish throne.

4. *his Holiness*: The encyclical against *Les Paroles d'un croyant* had just been issued.

5. *the Emperor Francis*: Francis I, Emperor of Austria (1768–1835).

6. *Lord Byron*: Byron (1788–1824) visited the convent of San Lazzaro frequently throughout his three years in Venice, collaborated in an Anglo-Armenian Grammar which was published at his own expense, and translated into English from Armenian two epistles from St Paul to the Corinthians. (G L)

7. *M. de Marcellus*: The Comte de Marcellus (1776–1841), a royalist deputy until 1830.

8. Elle marche . . . l'admirer: She walks, she flies, she metes out glory; / One is tempted to adore her. / And *even* seeing this *noble* Victory, / After seeing Rome, *we* must admire her.

9. *Japhet's last descendants*: A reference to the third son of Noah, founder of the Aryan race to which the Armenians belong.

10. *Cadi*: A Turkish judge.

11. *Capellari*: Mauro Capellari, Pope Gregory XVI, was Pope in 1831.

12. *Cydalise*: Probably Cidalise. See *La Nuit et le moment ou Les Matines de Cythère* (1755) by Crébillon (*fils*), in which a sophisticated dialogue between Cidalise and her wooer, Clitandre, takes place in her boudoir and, eventually, in bed. The reputation of the novelist, Claude-Prosper Jolyot de Crébillon (1707–77), for his elegant and witty amorality, was still considerable in the nineteenth century. (I am very grateful to Dr Angus Ross for his scholarship in tracking down the source of Cidalise.)

13. sagra: Consecration.

14. frittole: Literally, the place in which food is fried.

15. *Punchinello . . . Pantaloon*: All characters in the *commedia dell'arte*.

16. *Manin*: Ludovico Manin, 1726–1803.

17. semata: A speciality of the Café Chioggia, a cooling drink made from almonds, orange-flower water and melon pips. (GL)

18. *Erminia*: The principal female character in Tasso's *Jerusalem Delivered* (a work which GS devoured at the age of eleven and found far too short).

19. *hideous in design*: GS's unsparing condemnation of the Byzantine mosaics of Torcello is tempered somewhat by the Abbé's case for them.

20. *the brothers Zuccati*: GS's short novel, *Les Maîtres mosaistes* (1838), in which the Zuccati brothers figure, is an imaginative reconstruction of fifteenth-century Venetian life.

21. *Vallée Noire*: The name first given by GS to the country of her Berrichon novels.

Letter Four

1. *To Jules Néraud*: This Letter, though based on fragments of letters written to her friends in 1834, was not published till 1836 in the *RDM*, at the time of her lawsuit. Jules Néraud (1795–1855) was a friend and neighbour of long standing. A lawyer and botanist, he was given the nickname of Malgache by GS, because of his frequent botanizing trips to Madagascar. See Letter Six for her full account of him.

2. *circumstances have not changed*: In other words, Madame Néraud had not ceased to be jealous of the relationship of her husband and his young neighbour. (GL)

3. *an insect*: Twenty-five years later, in *Valvèdre* (1861), GS's mature hero recommends a close study of the natural world as a defence against romantic introspection and intellectual self-analysis. (It was a novel which appealed very much to Matthew Arnold in his middle age.)

307

4. *ajoupa*: A wooden summer house in Néraud's garden, constructed in the style of the ones he had seen in Madagascar.

5. *the parting's tree*: i.e., 'the tree of partings'.

6. *Les Natchez*: A novel written in 1826 by Vicomte François-René de Chateaubriand (1768–1848).

7. *Rollinat*: François Rollinat (1805–67), a lawyer, was the wise friend and counsellor of G S. He represented Indre in the National Assembly of 1848.

8. *prevail*: This passage, with its excess of self-justification and self-praise, is very clearly an 1836 addition to the earlier letters, written by G S with an eye upon her public image and impending separation suit.

9. *Show us . . . Jacques*: The assumption is that her children will, by then, be well-enough read in her novels to allude to the suicide scenes in *Indiana* (1832), *Lélia* (1833) and *Jacques* (1834).

10. *some day*: Next day, in fact.

11. *the just man*: This passage is discussed in the Introduction, in the commentary on Letter Nine.

12. *the ivory track*: *La route d'ivoire*. Possibly an oblique reference to the Ivory Gate – in classical mythology, the gate of sleep, through which false dreams were sent from the lower world, i.e., G S has not been totally deceived by her mirages and phantoms and has kept to the straight and narrow path of rectitude.

13. *The Eucharist . . . Alfieri*: The Abbé Gerbet (1798–1864) was an enthusiastic disciple of Lamennais; he wrote *The Eucharist* in 1825. Madame de Staël (Anne-Louise-Germaine Necker), the celebrated French novelist and writer (1766–1817), was, with Chateaubriand, one of the chief forerunners of the Romantics in France. Two of her best-known works are *Corinne* (1807) and *De l'Allemagne* (1810). Her *Reflections on Suicide* came out in 1813. Vittorio Alfieri (1749–1803) was a poet and dramatist and Italy's leading pre-Romantic writer.

14. *Nothing . . . rhetoric*: 'Rien ne soulage comme la rhétorique' – an observation which was remembered, years later, by Jane Carlyle as 'a shrewd remark' of G S, when justifying her own eloquent and despairing outpourings.

15. *Cleopatra*: Alfieri's first play (1775) was entitled *Cleopatra*.

16. *Linnaeus*: Charles Linnaeus (1707–78), eminent Swedish botanist and naturalist.

17. *Trenmor*: The ex-convict in *Lélia*, who represented age, wisdom and calm stoicism, as well as reason.

18. *a naked, bleeding heart: Un cœur tout saignant mis à nu*: Lubin comments that if Baudelaire had not said that he borrowed his title *Mon cœur mis a nu* from Edgar Allan Poe, his source might well be thought to be *LV*.

19. *Abbé Prevost*: *Manon Lescaut* (1731), a novel by the Abbé Prévost (1696–1763). GS's *Leone Leoni* (1834) was a reversal of Prévost's theme; in her short novel it is the heroine who feels passion for the unworthy lover.

20. *Julie . . . Saint-Preux*: Rousseau's ill-fated lovers in *La Nouvelle Héloïse* (1761).

Letter Five

1. *To François Rollinat*: This Letter was published in the *RDM* in January 1835, under the title *Lettres d'un oncle*.

2. *Pylades*: The faithful friend and confidant of the doomed Orestes.

3. *friendship*: For some time after her return to Nohant from Italy, GS kept open house for many of her loyal neighbourhood friends and their lively young wives – a distraction which at times intensified her own sense of remoteness from their youth and their interests.

4. *Toby*: A long paragraph from the original Letter as published in the *RDM* has been omitted. It is a passage which makes more understandable, though not more credible, the intermittent presence of the aged uncle as the narrator. Apart from the reference to him as Toby, there is no indication in the revised text of any connection between this persona and that of Uncle Toby in Sterne's *Tristram Shandy*. In the original, GS presents him as both a comic and pathetic figure, with his gout, his humours and his legs wrapped in yards of flannel – but it is, above all, the sensibility of the old soldier upon which she concentrates: 'You don't know, children, what incurable wounds are bleeding, deep in his heart, under his armour of unconcern and cheerfulness. You make fun of his campaigns in Flanders, you call him Uncle Toby, and you ask him what news there is of the siege of Maestricht, and you are unaware, you infants, what your uncle's campaigns are . . . Tell me, have you ever heard of the shores of Despair and the fields of Desolation?' . . . Tristram would scarcely have recognized this character as 'my Uncle Toby', innocent and trustful, but it is quite clear that Sterne was GS's starting-point.

5. *twelve children*: Rollinat was unmarried. GS means his eleven brothers and sisters and his youthful old father, who had gambled away the family fortune; Rollinat bore the whole responsibility for the family. (See *HV* IV, Chapter Thirteen for GS's account.) (GL)

6. *Et moi . . . la tête*: Georges Lubin points out that the fragments from Pascal's *Pensées* were not published until 1844, and suggests that GS may have become acquainted with them through Sainte-Beuve. The literal translation of '*Moi aussi, j'aurai mes pensées de derrière la tête*' is: 'I, too, shall have my thoughts from the back of my head,' i.e., contradictory afterthoughts.

7. *Dutheil*: Alexis Dutheil was one of the most jovial and witty of G S's friends, for long a drinking companion of her husband, who none the less took her part in the separation troubles.

8. *Monsieur de Bièvre*: The Marquis de Bièvre (1747–89) was well-known for his punning and word-play. The verse and G S's comments were quoted appreciatively by George Eliot in a letter of 1848.

9. Cur valle . . . operosiores: 'Why should I exchange my Sabine valley for the burden of wealth?' G S's is a much romanticized version of the liaison – and the poverty. Watelet bore the burden of wealth without any difficulty. The 'maisonette Moulin-Joli' was situated on an isle in the middle of the Seine, a 'so-called "English" garden', as Horace Walpole coldly described it, 'in which indulgence has been granted to every nettle, thistle and bramble'. None the less, a costly show-piece.

10. *a portrait*: Possibly a picture of Benjamin Franklin, whom G S greatly admired. In *Corr* II, p. 861, she mentions that his picture hangs close to her bed.

11. *Erebus*: The primeval darkness, the underworld.

Letter Six

1. *To Everard*: i.e., Louis Chrysostome Michel (1797–1853), known as Michel de Bourges. The son of a republican slain by loyalists, he had worked his way up to being a lawyer of great renown and the recognized leader of the republican party in Bourges and much further afield.

2. *swineherd-Apollo . . . Admetus*: Apollo, when banished from Olympus after slaying the Cyclops, spent nine years as Admetus's serf. (A recurrent theme in this Letter is G S's sense of the superiority of the egalitarian lawyer to his 'brothers'.)

3. *Fleury . . . Planet*: Alphonse Fleury and Gabriel Planet, both lawyers and Berrichon friends of G S, were also ardent republicans; they had just introduced her to Michel de Bourges.

4. *Midas*: Michel de Bourges's imperfections as a 'king' may not have been as obvious as the ass's ears of Midas, but the comparison is scarcely flattering.

5. *Marius*: Caius Marius (155–86 BC) was a great Roman general who came from a plebeian family and whose rivalry with Sulla, the dictator, caused the first civil war, in 88 BC.

6. *crowned blockhead*: i.e., Louis Philippe, the ruler at the time, described earlier, with heavy sarcasm, as 'one of that splendid breed of legitimate rulers'.

7. *Franklin*: Benjamin Franklin had been a hero for G S since her youth.

8. *Marius . . . Minturnus*: Following his defeat, Marius narrowly escaped death in the marshes of Minturnae.

9. *of any kind*: Georges Lubin suggests that Michel de Bourges may not have been as austere and as uninterested in wealth as G S believes.

10. *Egypt*: i.e., she is no longer worshipping 'false gods'. (Exodus XXXII)

11. panporcini: Cyclamen (or sowbread).

12. *Tyrol*: See Letter One for the lingering scent of a sage-bush.

13. *Cape Sunium*: A high rocky promontory in Attica, on which the temple of Athene was built – but here obviously a favourite site in the neighbourhood. G S was certainly familiar with the best-known reference to Sunium – by Byron in *Don Juan*, Canto III: 'Place me on Sunium's marbled steep, / Where nothing, save the waves and I, / May hear our mutual murmurs sweep'. A following line, 'A land of slaves shall ne'er be mine', seems apt for her new hero, Everard, as well as for Byron.

14. *Spartacus*: Spartacus headed an insurrection by slaves in 73 BC.

15. *Jacob's angel*: Genesis XXXII: 24–9.

16. *Carbonaro*: The Carbonari were members of a republican secret society formed in Naples (1808–15) to free their country from French domination; the society became an organization opposed to all reactionary governments. By about 1820 it had spread to France, and played an important part in French politics until the revolution of 1830.

17. *Cuvier*: Baron Georges Cuvier (1769–1832), the French naturalist and anatomist.

18. *Monsieur de Jussieu*: Antoine Laurent de Jussian (1748–1836), a noted botanist.

19. *Lallemand*: Lallemant was a student shot by a soldier of the royal guard in 1820 for shouting *'Vive la Charte'*. There was a large assembly at his funeral, and Michel de Bourges delivered a seditious address at the graveside. (GL)

20. *Rhea* (or Cybele): The Great Mother Goddess. (On a Roman altar relief she is shown with a naked torso.)

21. *oenotheras*: Fragrant evening primroses.

22. *Obermann*: (1804), A novel by Étienne Pivert de Sénancour (1770–1846). *Obermann*, written in letter form, in which the hero contemplates Nature and his own doubt and melancholy, was much influenced by Rousseau and *Werther* – and, in turn, when revived by Sainte-Beuve in the 1830s, greatly influenced, among others, G S and Matthew Arnold.

23. *A lady of our neighbourhood*: Not hard to identify as G S. It should, however, be said that genuine friendship was very important to her and that

friends played a large part in her life. Her involvement with Néraud seems indeed to have been one of affection, not passion.

24. *Cardenio*: A character in *Don Quixote*; an intellectual madman, crazed by disappointed love.

25. Centaureum erythrea: A plant of the gentian family.

26. *his Virginie*: *Paul et Virginie* (1787), a novel by J.-H. Bernardin de Saint-Pierre (1737–1814).

27. *natural shyness*: G S's tendency to fall silent in unfamiliar company is well authenticated.

28. I shall go: i.e., join up, become a volunteer in the revolutionary army.

29. *one true apostle*: Presumably the Abbé Lamennais.

30. *Saint-Simon*: One of the aims of the Saint-Simonists was to bring about a community of property.

31. *Taglioni*: Marie Taglioni (1804–84), the celebrated ballet-dancer.

32. *ancient Babylon*: Babylon stands for art, the new Rome for revolution and reform.

33. *fantastic symphony*: La Symphonie Fantastique by Hector Berlioz (1803–69) was played for the first time on 24 November 1833; G S was present at the concert.

34. *Lycurgus*: The legendary reformer and legislator of Sparta.

35. *Sicambre*: The Sicambri were a powerful German tribe whose revolt was first mentioned by Caesar.

36. *Chatterton*: The play by Alfred de Vigny had its début on 12 February 1835.

37. *the Petites-Maisons*: A lunatic asylum in Paris.

Letter Seven

1. *To Franz Liszt*: Liszt was in Switzerland with Marie d'Agoult, who had left her aristocratic husband and children to live with the young composer.

2. *Monsieur* —: i.e., the *Revue des Deux Mondes*.

3. *Puzzi*: Hermann Cohen (1820–71), an infant prodigy and favourite pupil of Liszt, his nickname from German *putzig*, droll. (G L)

4. *my child*: Liszt was then aged twenty-four and G S thirty-one.

5. Estelle et Némorin: (1688), A novel by the Chevalier de Florian.

6. Corinne: *Corinne or Italy*, a novel by Madame de Staël (1807). (Cf. Arnold: 'George Sand speaks somewhere of "her days of *Corinne*". Days of *Valentine*, many of us may in like manner say, – days of *Valentine*, days of *Lélia*, days never to return! . . .')

7. *Bernardin de Saint-Pierre*: The author of *Paul et Virginie*. See Letter Six, note 26.

8. *Millevoye*: Charles Hubert Millevoye (1782–1816), a minor French poet whose poems were published in 1801.

9. *Atala*: A romance by Chateaubriand which first appeared in *Le Mercure de France* in 1801.

10. *Lavater*: Johann Kaspar Lavater (1741–1801), a Swiss theologian and poet, chiefly remembered for his work on physiognomy.

11. *Gall*: Franz Joseph Gall (1758–1828), a German physician, the founder of phrenology.

12. *Spurzheim*: Kaspar Spurzheim (1776–1832), a disciple of Gall.

13. *Vespucci*: Amerigo Vespucci (1451–1512), an Italian explorer, the supposed discoverer of America.

14. *Herder*: GS ascribes the passages briefly, in her footnote, to 'Herder, *Plastik*'. Lubin annotates them: Herder, *Complete Works*, Vol. VII.

15. *Professor Lichtemberg*: Georg Christoph Lichtenberg (1742–99), a German physicist and satirist.

16. *Algernon Sidney*: (1622–83), An English politician and patriot.

17. *Talma*: François Joseph Talma (1763–1826), a famous French tragic actor.

18. *Kotzebuë*: August von Kotzebue (1761–1819), prolific, very popular German dramatist.

19. *Gellert*: Christian Furchtegott Gellert (1715–69), poet and novelist of the German Enlightenment.

20. *Fuseli*: Johann Heinrich Füssli, 1741–1825 (Henry Fuseli RA). In England a more influential painter and lecturer than GS implies. He was not only a childhood friend of Lavater but later a friend of William Blake, whom he introduced to Lavater's mystical speculations.

21. *a biography*: Lavater's son-in-law, G. Gessner, wrote a *Life* of Lavater, on which the *Memoirs* of Lavater, in Thomas Holcroft's translation of the essays, is based.

22. *a holy cause*: Following a strike of Lyon silk-workers, a ban on trades unions had been imposed. The subsequent revolts led to savage street-fighting and, initially, two thousand arrests. Michel de Bourges was one of the leading defence lawyers and GS, for the first time, experienced the excitement of political involvement.

23. *latakia*: A fine kind of Turkish tobacco, produced near and shipped from Latakia (the ancient Laodicia).

24. *our saint from Brittany*: Lamennais came to Paris to support the republican cause.

25. *House of Peers*: G S attended one of the sessions of the trial, dressed as a man. (A full account is given in *H V* V, Chapter Eight.) The good friend who was supposed to have smuggled her in was Emmanuel Arago, lawyer and part-time vaudeville writer, later a distinguished politician.

26. *Peri*: i.e., Marie d'Agoult. *Peri* (from Persian mythology) meant, by then, a genii endowed with grace and beauty. It became a fashionable term in the nineteenth century – Charlotte Brontë uses it frequently.

27. *Larves and Lamiae*: Larves were the opposite of *lares* in Roman mythology, i.e., mischievous spirits of dead members of the household, who spread terror and destruction. *Lamiae* were wolves or vampires.

28. infernal machine: In July 1835, a Corsican named Fieschi attempted to blow up the carriage of Louis Philippe. (G L)

29. *a scaffold*: G S is somewhat previous in sounding the alarm, though, because of her alliance with republicans, she did come under surveillance. In 1848, several of her friends were indeed exiled.

Letter Eight

1. *The Prince*: Charles Maurice de Talleyrand-Périgord, Prince de Benevent (1754–1838), a famous French diplomat and statesman.

2. *he exclaimed*: G S and some of her liberal Berrichon friends visited Valençay in September 1834. The conversation is with François Rollinat.

3. *the Red Sea*: In 1833 a group of Saint-Simonians, led by Prosper Enfantin, made a journey to Egypt in connection with a scheme for making a canal across the isthmus of Suez.

4. *the priest*: i.e., Lamennais.

5. *irony and scorn*: This Letter was written at the same time of despair as Letters Four and Five.

6. *petty actions*: G S's savage invective against Talleyrand here, and throughout the Letter, would no doubt be actionable today. She later admitted that, when she heard how her 'sally' had upset Talleyrand, she wished she had not written it – or had at least concentrated less on him as a personality.

7. *secret dread*: Lubin has pointed out that G S is here letting her imagination run wild. Certainly it has the mystery and the trappings of a Gothic tale.

8. *Dionysius the Elder*: (430–367 BC), the Tyrant of Syracuse. The analogy with Talleyrand is given extra brutal force by the fact that Dionysius was regarded by the ancients as the worst kind of despot – cruel, suspicious and vindictive.

9. *Monsieur de M—*: Casimir, Comte de Montrond (1769–1843), was Talleyrand's confidant and political agent, and assisted him in his intrigues.

10. *the Duchess*: Dorothée de Courlande, Duchesse de Dino (1792–1862), Talleyrand's niece by marriage. When the Duchess had been alerted by her friends to the presence of the notorious novelist in the château, she showed the party round some of the private apartments – and chronicled her impression of 'the heroine of the group' as 'insignificant in appearance', lacking in grace but having 'fine eyes' . . . 'She has a dry, trenchant tone and her judgements on the arts are definite. Her speech is recherché.'

Letter Nine

1. *This lawsuit*: GS had applied for a legal separation from her husband, Casimir Dudevant. The separation which had been hanging fire for a year was granted in February, contested, confirmed again in May and once more appealed against by Casimir for the last time.

2. *Cybele*: The Phrygian goddess, the Great Mother of all life in Nature.

3. *known as poets*: 'Poet' is used very freely throughout by GS, as indeed by other Romantics and Victorians, to denote the rare being who is unmaterialistic, loves beauty and goodness and speaks the truth about the abuses of civilization. In other words, a poet does not have to write poetry. GS's description of herself as a poet accords with the references to her by critics such as Lewes and Arnold – but it must certainly have increased Baudelaire's animosity to her, in view of the stringency of his demands for poetic discipline: 'Without form and concentration there is no poetry.'

4. Anyone who reads early GS and Baudelaire consecutively will be aware not only of their shared heritage but of her influence on some of his poems, e.g., Letter Nine, 'The Albatross' and 'Benediction'; Letter Two, 'Harmonie du Soir'. (See the comments of Antoine Adam, in the Classiques Garnier edition of *Les Fleurs du mal*.)

5. *the* Couperies: GS describes the *Couperies* as 'a modest but charming walk from La Châtre, a shady track between the hillside and the slow-moving Indre'.

6. *ageing mother*: Lubin points out that there is no mention of Néraud's wife as she had died the previous year.

7. La Rochaille: The district in which Néraud's house was situated.

8. *home of my fathers*: Until the lawsuit was settled, GS was denied access to the château of Nohant.

9. *the courtyard*: 'Let those among you who are without sin, cast the first stone,' St John VIII: 6–9.

10. *Why, since I was a poet . . . human race*: This passage was quoted in full by Matthew Arnold in his obituary article on GS in 1877.

11. *pastours*: Shepherds.

12. *Marie*: The grandmother of GS, Marie-Aurore de Saxe, Madame Dupin de Francueil.

13. *Meschacébé*: A reference to *Atala*, a novel by Chateaubriand.

14. *Il tempo . . . di poi*: Time passes never to return to us / And sorrow is then of no avail.

Letter Ten

1. *To Herbert*: When this Letter appeared in the *RDM* and, later, in the first edition of *LV*, it was dedicated to Charles Didier, a Swiss writer, whom GS had met two years before but who had recently become enamoured of her. Estrangement followed and, in the second edition of *LV*, the dedication was changed to what Didier angrily called 'the fantasy name' of Herbert.

2. *a bit older*: GS was one year older than Didier.

3. *the vine*: Genesis X:20.

4. Ohé, Evohé: A joyful cry associated with the name of Bacchus.

5. *Leave wine . . . heart*: A version of Proverbs XXXI:4–7.

6. *in mournful . . . song*: Boileau, Satire III, 141–2. (GL)

7. *Señora Léonarda*: An innkeeper in Alain-René Lesage's novel, *Gil Blas* (1715–35): 'Dame Leonarda . . . this fair angel of darkness . . . with lips fallen in, a huge aquiline nose that hung over her mouth, and eyes that flamed in purple . . .' (translated by Tobias Smollett).

8. *Hymettus*: A mountain overlooking Athens, famous for its delicious honey and its grey-blue marble.

9. *Malibran*: Maria Felicita Garcia Malibran (1808–36), a celebrated opera-singer.

10. *Callot*: Jacques Callot (1592–1635), the French engraver and painter.

11. *the* legitimist: GS refers from now on to the 'pleasant young man', whose overtures she had earlier snubbed, as 'the legitimist' (i.e., a supporter of the elder Bourbon line, a conservative).

12. *hideous*: Cf. GS's vision of France before she left Italy, at the end of Letter Three.

13. *Hidalgos*: (Spanish) A member of the lesser nobility.

14. *a Vet.*: *Artiste veterinaire* was an obsolete pleasantry for veterinary surgeon.

15. *Musard*: The orchestra at the Musard concert hall, rue Vivienne in Paris. (GL)

16. *his sister*: Liszt's 'sister', Arabella, was his mistress, the Countess d'Agoult.

17. *the Major*: Adolphe Pictet (1799–1875), a Swiss artillery major and philological scholar. He published, two years later, his version of the excursion, under the title, *Une Course à Chamonix, conte fantastique*. (G L)

18. *Lara*: G S, in comparing Liszt with Lara, is paying him tribute as a typical arresting Byronic hero, '. . . careless of praise / A high demeanour and a glance that took / Their thoughts from others by a single look'.

19. *Federal uniform*: The pact of 1815 which had recognized the sovereign rights of all the twenty-two cantons of Switzerland had made provision for a Federal army.

20. *I'll make you happy*: The second part of Maurice's forecast, at least, was to come true.

21. *Fourier*: Charles Fourier (1772–1837), French social reformer, who advocated a system of social reorganization based on cooperation in capital, labour and talent, involving communities or *phalanges* of members. His influence, like that of Saint-Simon, made itself felt in England, especially in the 1830s and 1840s. (Even Lady Waldemar, in Elizabeth Barrett Browning's *Aurora Leigh* (1856), in an effort to keep up with the trend, read 'half-Fourier through'.)

22. identical with itself: The caricature by G S of the participants in this argument is reproduced in Georges Lubin's *Album Sand* (Editions Gallimard, 1973), p. 136.

23. *Piffoël*: G S's nickname, from *pif*: nose. In her caricatures of herself her nose is always much exaggerated.

24. *the epithet*: i.e., 'sacré' rather than 'damné'.

25. *imperious*: G S's presentation of the fastidious and hard-to-please Comtesse d'Agoult has a certain asperity about it.

26. *the Reichenbach*: A tributary of the Aar, in Bern, celebrated for the beauty of its cascades.

27. *Mooser*: Aloys Mooser, a native of Fribourg, built the famous organ between 1824 and 1834. It has 7,800 pipes and is played daily in summer for the delight of tourists.

28. *Hoffmann's . . . macaroons*: In Hoffmann's tale, 'La Maison Deserte'.

29. *Ulysses' water-skins*: *Odyssey*, Book X.

30. Quantus . . . venturus: What terror is in store for us / When the judge returns . . .

31. Recordare . . . pie: Remember, holy Jesus.

32. *Pradon*: Nicolas Pradon (1632–98), undistinguished dramatist, caught

up in literary quarrels and much ridiculed. Racine was temperate: 'The only difference between M. Pradon and me is that I know how to write.'

33. *Hoffmann*: Different names taken by Hoffmann in his tales.

Letter Eleven

1. *To Giacomo Meyerbeer*: Giacomo Meyerbeer (1791–1864), German composer of opera, who wrote for the Paris stage and was later Royal Director of Opera at Berlin. He had great success with his operas, which were highly coloured and spectacular.

2. camaraderie: In italics because it was then still a neologism (introduced by a friend of GS, Henri de Latouche). (GL)

3. *Marcel*: The hero of *The Huguenots*, which was first staged in Paris in 1836.

4. *Sicilian cathedral*: *Robert the Devil* (1831) has a Sicilian setting.

5. *Bertram*: A character in *Robert the Devil*.

6. William Tell: Rossini's opera, *William Tell*, was first staged in Paris in 1829.

7. Pré-aux-clercs: An Opéra-Comique produced by L. J. F. Hérold in Paris in 1832.

8. *Monsieur Duphonchel*: Edmond Duponchel (1795–1868), a director at the Opéra in Paris.

9. *Alice*: A character in *Robert the Devil*.

10. *in the country*: See Letters Four and Five.

11. *my nephew*: The 'nephew' was François Rollinat's younger brother, Charles.

12. *a scene*: The reviewer whom GS is attacking, Blaze de Bury, wrote of this scene that it was 'scandalous. Here the music plays the role of an infamous procuress.' *RDM*, 15 March 1836, pp. 703–704.

13. *Aeschylus*: A suggestion taken up by Meyerbeer later, when he wrote choruses for the Eumenides. (GL)

14. bilioso-nerveux: i.e., nervous and choleric in temperament.

15. *religion*: GS is indebted to Liszt for some of her ideas on criticism. (GL)

16. *worry you*: Flattery – or idealizing – came very readily to GS's pen and, in the case of Meyerbeer, it was patently untrue that he was above caring about criticism.

Letter Twelve

1. *To Monsieur Nisard*: Désiré Nisard (1806–88), literary critic and author of an article on GS in the *Revue de Paris*, 15 May 1836.

2. *four or five*: The dates of publication of the novels cited were as follows: *Lélia*, 1833; *Indiana*, 1832; *Le Secrétaire intime*, 1834; *André*, 1835; *Simon*, 1836; *Valentine*, 1832; *Leone Leoni*, 1834 and *Jacques*, 1834.

3. *Madame d'Aulnoy*: The Comtesse d'Aulnoy (1650–1705) was, like Charles Perrault (1628–1703), best known for her fairy-tales.

4. *Bossuet nor Montesquieu*: Jacques Bénigne Bossuet (1627–1704), French orator; Charles-Louis de Secondat, Baron de Montesquieu (1689–1755), French social and political thinker and satirist.

5. *reciprocal duties*: The Civil Code, Chapter VI, deals with the respective duties and rights of husband and wife, e.g., Article 212: 'The spouses owe each other mutual fidelity, help and assistance.' (G L)

6. *your own blood*: Lubin comments appositely that this is perhaps doing rather too much honour to M. Nisard, who was 'always very respectful to the Establishment'.